LEONARDO DA VINCI

LEONARDO DA VINCI:

Psychoanalytic Notes on The Enigma

by

K. R. EISSLER

International Universities Press, Inc., New York

Manufactured in the United States of America
by Hallmark Press, New York

To the memory of
Ernst Kris

Table of Contents

List of Illustrations

Facing page 170

· ix ·

Acknowledgments

I am deeply indebted to Dr. Renato J. Almansi for the invaluable assistance he gave me in gaining a grasp of some of the source material that has not been translated from the Italian. His help required a sacrifice of time that was unusually great and beyond what I had expected when I turned to him. Without his unstinting assistance the text would show still greater shortcomings than are unavoidable when an author has the temerity to write about Leonardo without a knowledge of Leonardo's language.

My debt to Mr. Seymour A. Copstein is likewise great. Without his linguistic tact and his generosity in time, to say nothing of the many suggestions he made regarding questions of content and his frequent help in avoiding inconsistencies and errors of detail, my manuscript would have been much the worse. Yet, responsibility for eventual defects in its present state is wholly mine.

Mrs. Kate T. Steinitz magnanimously rendered irreplaceable service by advice, literature, and photographic materials. Her knowledge, resources, and experience as Librarian of The Elmer Belt Library of Vinciana at Los Angeles combined with her own enthusiasm have become legendary and her help is indispensable to anyone who is interested in research on Leonardo.

I am further indebted to:

Dr. Robert C. Bak, for lending me important books from his library;

Professor Eugenio Battisti, for having sent me a transcript from Lomazzo's important manuscript at the British Museum (Add. Mss. 12196) and for having given me permission to publish part of it;

Mme. S. Béguin, Assistante aux Peintures, Musée du Louvre, for information regarding some paintings at the Louvre;

Dr. Elmer Belt, for many reprints and other publications he put at my disposal;

Dr. Bernard B. Berglas, for interpreting some of Leonardo's anatomical drawings;

Mrs. Julie Braun-Vogelstein, for reading the manuscript and making valuable suggestions;

Dottoressa Cecilia Calabresi, for reading an Italian source book;

Professor Renzo Cianchi, for numerous communications containing important information regarding Leonardo's family, in particular the birth date of Leonardo's youngest brother.

Sir Kenneth Clark, Prof. Erwin Panofsky, and Prof. Jakob Rosenberg for their gracious replies to letters of inquiry;

Signor Elio Conti for helping me to gain at least a modicum of understanding of the Quattrocento Florentine tax system;

Mr. Bern Dibner and Mrs. Adele Matthysse of the Burndy Library of Norwalk for their kind cooperation;

Dottoressa Giuseppina Fumagalli for having answered most graciously letters of inquiry;

Mr. A. S. B. Glover, for his painstaking work in preparing the Index and for calling my attention to some of the shortcomings in the manuscript;

Dr. E. H. Gombrich for patiently listening to some of my arguments and for reading part of the manuscript and advising me on many points;

Miss Rosalie B. Green for the important information she gave from the Index of Christian Art at Princeton University;

Prof. Moses Hadas for his translation of a Latin text;

Dr. Otto Isakower for valuable suggestions and lending me literature;

Dr. A. S. Kagan for the careful supervision of this publication;

Prof. Friedrich Kessler, Dr. Anton Hermann-Chroust, and Dr. Stephen Kuttner for their opinions on a question of law;

Miss Inge Klimpt for generous bibliographic assistance;

Dr. Richard Kuhns for his suggestions after reading the first part of the manuscript.

Dr. George C. Leiner for his help in evaluating a statement Leonardo made about a problem in pathophysiology;

Miss Mary McCarthy for her gracious answer to an inquiry;

Mrs. Eva Meyer, Librarian at The New York Psychoanalytic Institute, for her unfailing cooperation in providing access to reference materials;

Mrs. Lottie Maury Newman for many suggestions, corrections, and the particular care with which she read the manuscript;

Mr. T. D. Nicholson, astronomer at the Hayden Planetarium, for helping solve a problem in chronology;

Dr. Bernard L. Pacella for permission to quote from a Freud letter in his possession;

Mr. Carlo Pedretti, whose recent arrival to our shores is most heartily welcomed by all researchers interested in Leonardo, for invaluable help and advice;

The Rare Book Division of the Academy of Medicine of New York for reference and photographic materials;

Professor Raymond de Roover, for answering an inquiry;

Miss A. H. Scott-Elliott, Keeper of Prints and Drawings at Windsor Castle, for her invaluable assistance in obtaining the beautiful reproductions from the Royal Library;

Mr. Charles Seymour, Jr., for information regarding Cennino Cennini's Handbook;

Dr. Raymond Stites for his letters of reply and the suggestion of literature;

Dr. Owsei Temkin for calling to my attention a decisive passage in the pseudo-Aristotle *Problemata*.

I am further indebted to the following for helping me obtain or giving me permission to use the reproductions included in this volume:

Academy of Art, Siena;

Accademia dell'Arte, Venice;

Archives Photographiques de la Caisse Nationale des Monuments Historiques, Paris;

Bildarchiv Foto Marburg, Marburg;

The British Museum, London;

Christ Church (Archives), Oxford;

Fratelli Alinari, photographers, Florence;

Galleria Borghese, Rome;

Galleria Nazionale d'Arte Antica, Rome;

Giraudon, photographer, Paris;

Istituto Poligrafico dello Stato, Rome;

Kunstverlag Wolfrum, Vienna;

Emmanuel Mas, photographer, Paris;

Metropolitan Museum of Art, New York;

Musée du Louvre, Paris;

Museo Archeologico, Venice;

Museo Civico, Pisa;

Museo del Prado, Madrid;

Museum Boymans-van Beuningen, Rotterdam;

The National Gallery, London;

William G. Niederland, M.D.;

The late Reginald Herbert, 15th Earl of Pembroke, Salisbury;

Pinacoteca dell'Ambrosiana, Milan;

Umberto Rossi, photographer, Venice;

The Royal Academy of Arts, London;

The Royal Library, Windsor Castle, Berkshire;

Miss Ilse Rumpler, photographer, New York;

Sammlung des Regierenden Fürsten von Liechtenstein, Vaduz;

Soprintendenza alle Gallerie, Florence;

George Spearman, photographer, Windsor Castle;

Vatican Museums and Galleries, Rome;

Victoria and Albert Museum, London.

But most of all I have reason to feel grateful to my wife, Dr. Ruth S. Eissler. It would not be possible for me to say which of the ideas in this book are genuinely mine and which I owe to her.

K.R.E.

New York
April, 1960

LEONARDO DA VINCI

Introduction

When I started out seriously to occupy myself with the life of
Leonardo da Vinci I had no other intention but to inquire into the
validity of Professor Meyer Schapiro's criticism of Freud's study
Leonardo da Vinci and a Memory of His Childhood (1910). In the
course of this inquiry I had to deal also with questions of methodology
and therefore it seemed appropriate to put the result of my endeavor
as a concluding appendix to my book on Goethe. It should thus have
served indirectly as a justification of the attempt I had made to apply,
as best I could, the method whose basic pattern was set once for all
by Freud's first major essay in the field of historical biography.
However, the Goethe manuscript, too bulky as it was to be likely to
achieve early publication, could ill bear this additional weight.

The purely polemic nature of the original essay is fully preserved in
Part I. Although my original intent was exclusively critical and comparative, I did derive inferences from the detailed study I became
involved in. Consequently it appeared appropriate to set forth my
own ideas about selected problems of Leonardo's life. This I have
done in Part II, which should not be considered as more than an
aggregate of ideas as they came to me in the original critical pursuit.
There was no intention of attempting anything like a biography of
Leonardo or of arriving at final conclusions regarding the many problems encountered. That Part is, therefore, a presentation of disconnected suggestions (for convenience often set forth dogmatically)
that may or may not prove valuable to the future biographer of one

of the most enigmatic personalities that has so far appeared in Western culture.

My original polemic intention has, as the reader will notice, given color at times also to the second Part, and both Parts of this study will perhaps be looked upon as a kind of apologia for the biographical method that is derived from Freud's writings. Anyone who has followed the psychoanalytic literature on art will be bound to agree that it needs no apologia for its quality. From Freud's Leonardo study in 1910 to Kris's volume of *Psychoanalytic Explorations in Art* (1952), the first attempt at a systematized presentation of the subject matter, there is a steady development of deepened understanding, broadening of investigated areas, and clinical validation.

Nevertheless the validity of the method Freud used, and the conclusions he reached in his Leonardo study, have been questioned recently from three sides. I want to say a few general words about these types of criticism.

1. *Criticism by psychoanalysts.* In this group belongs the paper by Wohl and Trosman (1955), one of whom may be regarded as a psychoanalyst. Their contribution has little merit except for one interpretation. It is a good example of that type of literature that is notable for its misapplication of pseudo sociology to psychological problems. I will have only few occasions to refer to it.

2. A noteworthy paper by Neumann (1954), who is a scholar of the Jungian school, has recently been translated into English. Its subject is Leonardo's relation to the Mother Archetype, but its substance goes beyond this and includes Leonardo's genius and a critique of Freud's Leonardo study. Neumann's essay offers a propaedeutic opportunity for an exposition of the differences that separate a scientific psychology—or at least one that endeavors to be as scientific as one today can be—from one that is characterized by a strange melange of correct observations and a fixation to mythical thinking. Tempting as it was to set forth these differences here, on the occasion of a practical example, and to let the reader decide for himself which set of theories harmonizes with the data of experience, I did not do so. A discussion of the concept of the archetype alone would require an extensive treatise.[1]

[1] For a detailed critical discussion of Jungian psychology from the psychoanalytic viewpoint, see Glover (1948-49).

The chief point to be made about Neumann's criticism of Freud's Leonardo study is that it is not relevant. It is not a matter of the actual errors the author commits, such as insisting on interpreting Leonardo's childhood memory as if Leonardo had written about a vulture (pp. 10, 25) although he actually referred to a kite, or asserting that Leonardo's father disinherited him (p. 25) (the father died intestate), or that Freud published his Leonardo study anonymously (p. 11),[2] or erroneous interpretations of some of Leonardo's philosophical statements.

The author could correct all these mistakes without changing his main theories one iota since these do not grow out of the study of the factual material. Leonardo is in Neumann's treatise a puppet of archetype. Jung's transpersonal approach dispenses with the study of a person's life history, and a direct connection is established between contents of works of art or philosophical statements and archetypes. In my estimation Neumann's article does not partake of psychology, or of any science for that matter. He may be right or wrong. What he says is outside the realm of validation but depends on the accident of intuition or inspiration. I cannot think of any historical find that might confirm or disprove any one of his claims. A psychoanalytic apologia does not need to take his criticism into account.

3. When we turn to the group of art historians that have subjected Freud's Leonardo study to critical analysis the situation is, of course, quite different. Even if it turns out that the psychoanalyst disagrees with every argument of the historian, still a weighing of his arguments should prove profitable for both disciplines since their claims remain, or at least should remain, within the scope of the validatable. Professor Schapiro's paper (1956)—though, as the reader will see, I can only rarely agree with his inferences—seems particularly suitable in this respect. It is erudite, clearly written, and encompasses a broad area of problems. Moreover, it concerns itself with the content of Freud's reconstruction as well as his methods and therefore serves excellently as an illustration of what distinguishes the two disciplines.

Only after finishing my manuscript did I become familiar with Raymond Stites's article "A Criticism of Freud's Leonardo" (1948a), which, though it contains good points, is marred by some errors that

---

[2] The author evidently confuses Freud's Leonardo study with his paper on Michelangelo's *Moses* (Freud, 1914c).

are difficult to understand. Quite rightly the author says that pleasant and unpleasant childhood impressions are stimulated by frustrations the artist is exposed to in adult years and that elements of both may become *leitmotifs* in his creations until appeased by works of art (p. 259). Yet one does not see in what way "Freud closed the door to the above discovery," as the author claims (p. 259), and Fraiberg (1956, p. 83) quite rightly traces the essence of this proposition back to the beginnings of psychoanalysis when Breuer (1895) wrote:

> Goethe did not feel he had dealt with an experience till he had discharged it in creative artistic activity. This was in his case the preformed reflex belonging to affect, and so long as it had not been carried out the distressing increase in his excitation persisted [p. 207].

It is noteworthy that this thought, which was to assume such an important function in the psychoanalytic theories of art, was casually stated as early as the baptism of psychoanalysis. Stites has evidently studied Freud's text, yet he criticizes him for allegedly having claimed that Leonardo painted all women with the Mona Lisa smile (Stites, p. 265).[3] Now one of Freud's principal theses hinges on his assumption that Leonardo started to endow women (and young men, for that matter) with that smile only *after*, as a mature artist, he had met Mona Lisa.

It is easy to see how a misunderstanding can come about as the result of mistranslation. It is different with Freud's theory of sublimation. Even some psychoanalysts encounter great difficulty in grasping the clinical and genetic validity of this mechanism, as a paper by Harry B. Lee (1939) shows, and therefore the historian, who has not had the benefit of clinical observation, cannot be blamed for misinterpreting the meaning of sublimation.[4] (Cf. also Johnson, 1949.)

Yet, by and large, comparing the more recent critical literature on Freud's Leonardo study with that of earlier years (for example, Hemmeter, 1924), progress is undeniable. The argument about

[3] The author kindly informs me that this statement was based on Brill's translation of Freud's book on Leonardo. See Brill (1947, p. 75), where it is evident that Freud's "seiner weiblichen Figuren" has been so translated as to convey the idea that Freud meant *all female figures,* whereas the context shows clearly that he did not. Cf. Freud: *"From that date* [that is Leonardo's meeting Mona Lisa] the captivating smile reappears in all his pictures and in those of his pupils" (Freud, 1910, p. 109; italics added).

[4] See Sterba (1940) for a summary of clinical problems that must be understood in order to penetrate into Freud's theories of art.

whether an element is libidinal or not, which filled so much of earlier unconstructive debate, seems to recede; crude manifestations of the Victorian spirit, such as recurred recently in a violent attack against another of Freud's historic papers, have become rare and solitary.[5]

It is the rise in the level of debates between psychoanalysis and some of the nonanalytic disciplines that is one of the most encouraging signs at a time when the most rampant distortions and falsifications of psychoanalysis occur in pseudopsychoanalytic groups that maintain an official standing by juggling a psychoanalytic terminology that has been emptied of its original meaning.[6]

4. An additional consideration of considerable moment to me arises from the fact, of which I have recently become aware, that Professor Schapiro's essay has been proving persuasive among some of the students in the Freudian institutes themselves. Many of them, moved by his presentation, have been inclined to conclude that Freud's Leonardo study has been refuted and is no longer a valid object of study. My own presentation here, even if it falls short of that rigorousness I aim at, may help these students of psychoanalysis

[5] Macalpine and Hunter (1956) reproduced for the first time the paintings of the devil on which Freud's paper on a demonological neurosis (1923) was based, and claimed that on none of them did the male genitalia find representation (p. 103f.). Niederland (1958) in his excellent review of Macalpine and Hunter shows that, aside from the traditional phallic symbols which also abound in these representations of the devil, one plate depicts realistically a huge phallus (p. 110).

[6] The ink was barely dry on these hopeful words when I came across a paragraph that contains as many confusions as words and provides a specimen, coming from across the ocean, of what we may have to expect from the future, for some time at least. Richard Wollheim (1959), reviewing the result of Adrian Stokes's recent wedding with Kleinian psychology, comments as follows about "criticism inspired by orthodox theory": "In the first place, Kleinian criticism does not demand material about the artist's mind and experience on the same extravagant and impossible scale as Freudian criticism. For Freudian criticism is essentially interpretation in terms of instinctual impulse: after a few cursory references to sublimation, the Freudian critic settles down to discover the latent content of art, as of a dream (and Freudian art-criticism is closely modelled on Freudian dream-interpretation), one needs to know a great deal about the associations and circumstances of its creator. Kleinian criticism, on the other hand, by relating the work of art not to the variable impulses of the artist's id but to the invariable processes of the artist's ego, can dispense with voluminous biographical material. In other words, the change from a predominantly id- to a predominantly ego-interpretation has obvious economic advantages" (p. 43).

Without wanting to say anything about Mrs. Klein's psychology in general or approach to art specifically, or Mr. Stokes's views on the ego, how is one to explain the reviewer's abysmal confusion about the variable id and the invariable ego? How can anyone who has the slightest perceptiveness about art, about the delicacy and difficulty of art psychology, feel opposed to "voluminous biographical material" and indulge in the pejorative "extravagant and impossible" regarding the labor of the genetically and historically minded researcher? It sounds like a nightmare.

to evaluate this book of Freud's more thoughtfully than otherwise they would, and to apply to Professor Schapiro's study a test no less strict than he calls on them to apply to Freud's. If they do so, with the expected result of learning anew that promulgations even from sources of expert authority should not be accepted without checking, they will be better able to see how useful indeed Freud's Leonardo study still is.

And if my labors have no more effect than that, I shall still feel greatly gratified.

I
POLEMICS

1

Introductory Remarks

Freud's essay on a childhood recollection of Leonardo da Vinci, published in 1910, still holds a position more ambiguous than almost any other of his writings. Many analysts regard it as one of the dearest to them of Freud's writings because of its depth of insight, boldness of reconstruction, and literary beauty. Yet a scholar of the eminence of George Sarton even went so far as to say of it, a few years ago, that he knew of no scientific book more arbitrary, and that Freud's fame had given it undeserved prestige (1953, p. 11).[1]

This sweeping rejection, well-nigh condemnation, of Freud's book is surprising from this scholar, in view of his expressed attitude toward biography: "It is the historian's main duty to revive the personalities, rather than to enumerate their scientific excrescences. Discoveries may be important, but personalities are infinitely more so" (Sarton, 1948, p. 20).

One might have expected approval, if for no other reason than Freud's enlargement of the biographical area and his forging a tool that

[1] "Je ne connais pas de livre scientifique plus arbitraire que ce livre de Freud auquel sa gloire a donné un prestige tout à fait immérité." See also Sarton (1957, p. 220).

helps in penetrating into what would otherwise remain unknown.[2]

To Freud himself, as Jones reports, the study remained one of his favorite works, and nine years after its publication in a letter to Ferenczi he called it "the only pretty thing" he had ever written (Jones, Vol. II, p. 347).

The precipitating occasion for writing the study, we are told (Jones, Vol. II, p. 346), was observations Freud made in a patient who struck him as having the same constitution as Leonardo's but lacked his genius, as he wrote to C. G. Jung on October 17, 1909.[3] But Freud's interest in Leonardo dates further back. In a letter to Fliess in 1898 he made a remark about Leonardo's left-handedness and the reported absence of any love affair in his life. In 1907 he also mentioned Merezhkovsky's novel *The Romance of Leonardo da Vinci*, which he read in the German translation, among the ten books he enjoyed most (Freud, 1907).[4]

The point has also been made that Freud's interest in Leonardo was based on his personal affinity to that genius whose unquenchable thirst for knowledge and devotion to discovery are indeed comparable to his own (Jones, Vol. II, pp. 346, 423f.). When Freud, writing in his "History of the Psychoanalytic Movement" of the inner and outer tribulations of his early lonely years, notes that at that time he thought he would be ignored during his life and only much later would someone else rediscover his findings and thus belatedly bring him honor (Freud, 1914b, p. 22), he is setting forth what was the fate of Leonardo, the scientist, whose discoveries, written down in a barely legible handwriting, slumbered for centuries in recondite places before becoming generally known in the course of the nineteenth and twentieth centuries (Belt and Steinitz, 1948, pp. 192-197; Richter, Vol. II, pp. 393-399). Thus one may surmise that Freud's anticipation of the fate of his scientific work indicates an early identification with Leonardo.

---

[2] It is of interest to examine what a man like Sarton, who has done so much for our knowledge of the history of science, has contributed to our understanding of the scientist's personality. His biographical sketches, and even a longer treatise on an eminent man like Galen (Sarton, 1954), never go beyond common-sense psychology, and I do not recall a psychological observation of his that might not have been forthcoming from a run-of-the-mill biographer of our times. See, for example, his biographical essay on Évariste Galois, one of the most fascinating personalities a historian could turn to (Sarton, 1948, pp. 83-100).

[3] Implicit in this statement is a basic observation of Freud's that is also asserted in the study (Freud, 1910, p. 136) but that possibly was overlooked or not sufficiently acknowledged by some of his critics. This is the observation that psychoanalysis is, by its nature, not a method equipped to explain geniushood.

[4] Mr. James Strachey (1957, p. 59f.) has gathered the pertinent biographical material.

It is also worthy of remark that this study was not only the first but also the last venture of Freud's into the field of historical biography as Mr. Strachey (1957, p. 60) has pointed out.[5]

In the fifty years that have elapsed since Freud wrote the biographical study not only has there been change within the realm of psychoanalytic concepts and theories, but historical research into Leonardo's life has likewise progressed. It may be of interest to the psychoanalyst to know in what light Freud's early attempt at psychological reconstruction of a historical personage appears in view of what is known today about Leonardo.

A welcome opportunity to carry out such an intention, at least in part, is offered by Professor Meyer Schapiro's paper on "Leonardo and Freud," in which the historian of art musters all the historical arguments that can be arrayed against the validity of Freud's reconstruction.

A critical weighing of the author's argumentation will provide a useful short cut toward taking stock of the extent to which Freud's findings and conclusions were justified at the time they were written and still hold up or have to be altered in the light of knowledge accumulated since 1910.

The biographical method as such was not new to Freud, for every extensive psychoanalytic case history is biographical. His first major clinical psychoanalytic publication, *Studies on Hysteria*, published with Breuer in 1895, amply demonstrates his great gift for building a coherent life history out of such facts as a psychoanalytic inquiry brings to light.

With his Leonardo study, Freud went a step further and applied his method to a historical personality. The challenge obviously was to demonstrate the superiority of the psychoanalytic method by applying it to the only childhood recollection that Leonardo had recorded in his writings—an item that had been left untouched by his biographers. This childhood memory became the pivot of Freud's study and he took it as the base of a daring reconstruction of some aspects of Leonardo's development and personality.

Freud used for this purpose a variety of methods. First, the meaning of the childhood recollection had to be established. In order to decipher

[5] This, however, may need some revision depending on whether or not Freud's psychoanalytic study of Woodrow Wilson, which he wrote in collaboration with William C. Bullitt (see Jones, Vol. III, p. 150f.), had the character of an essay in historical biography.

it Freud made use of the vast clinical experience he had accumulated during his twenty-odd years of analytic work, which had laid the ground for an insight into childhood memories in general and into the early phases of childhood development to which they ordinarily refer in particular. Once he had established the meaning of the recollection, he brought it into genetic connection with some known facts of Leonardo's later life, or, where biographers had suggested alternatives, used it as a means of choosing among them.

Conversely, by bringing to bear upon certain undisputed facts of Leonardo's adult years—facts partly of events, partly of attitude—the light of his interpretation of this childhood memory, Freud drew some conclusions as to Leonardo's childhood development. In turn, he hypothetically reconstructed certain events of Leonardo's childhood and adult life that appeared to be necessary links between the recollection (and what the interpretation revealed it stood for) and known facts. Known facts, reconstructions, interpretations, and postulated childhood development were then synthesized into a presentation of some general developmental trends in Leonardo's life and of a certain character structure. Despite the obvious intention to limit the biographical endeavor, Freud, by drawing into his investigation so many facts and aspects, laid the cornerstone of a far more sweeping study, namely, a comprehensive analysis of Leonardo's personality. Yet evidently Freud had never intended to set forth what could be called a psychoanalysis of Leonardo da Vinci. The focus of his endeavor lies, as the title says, in the childhood recollection and the conclusions that can be drawn therefrom.[6]

Thus Schapiro's critical investigation quite rightly sets in at this point.

---

[6] Yet for a biographical reminiscence concerning Freud that would strongly militate against this view, see Stites (1948a, p. 261).

2

The Childhood Recollection

The childhood memory upon which Freud based his reconstruction and interpretation was jotted down by Leonardo on the verso of a page of text devoted to observations on the flight of various birds, mainly of the kite. Leonardo wrote:

> To write thus clearly of the kite would seem to be my destiny, because in the earliest recollections of my infancy it seemed to me when I was in the cradle that a kite came and opened my mouth with its tail, and struck me within upon the lips with its tail many times. [MacCurdy, 1956, p. 1122; C.A. 66 v. b].[1]

On the basis of a large number of observations regarding equivalent information received from his patients, Freud drew the conclusion that this recollection must refer to the infant's early oral phase and that the bird's tail was a substitute for the mother's breast. It also seemed of con-

[1] Dr. Renato Almansi informs me that the literal translation of the last part is: ". . . and struck me with such a tail inside of the lips many times." Cf. Mr. Strachey's comment on Freud (1910, p. 82, n. 1). The literal translation may be important inasmuch as Dr. Almansi tends toward connecting Leonardo's account with a type of oral fondling that is a customary caress of infants in some parts of Italy. Dr. Almansi also calls my attention to the translation of *parea* as "it seemed." The Italian word is much stronger than that and is close to *apparire,* from which it is derived and which means "to become visible."

sequence to Freud to explain why Leonardo selected this particular species of bird. Here, however, an element entered that is rare in Freud's writings and that had fateful consequences. In the German translation of Leonardo's *Notebooks* the Italian word *nibbio*, meaning "kite," was translated as "vulture."[2] It was, accordingly, the vulture whose possible significance to Leonardo Freud sought to trace, citing ancient sources and attempting to reconstruct how the vulture had been looked upon historically.

It is, of course, unfortunate that Freud was misinformed, and one cannot but be grateful to those scholars who detected and pointed out the error. But pains must also be taken not to wipe out Freud's whole contribution while correcting the translation error by which he was misled.[3]

In the first place, it should be noted that Freud's thesis, like any other scientific statement that goes beyond mere description, is contingent, and must be understood as containing a tacit hypothesis. In this case it might be formulated thus: "If Leonardo recorded the vulture fantasy as an early childhood recollection, and if the vulture had such and such a meaning, then I draw the conclusion that a certain event took place in Leonardo's infancy." Now, to show that Leonardo never recorded a fantasy about a vulture is to invalidate one of the premises and hence to disprove Freud's conclusion, at least in the form in which he asserted it. In the same way, a paleontologist's reconstruction of an extinct animal would be faulty if it rested on inferences derived from a bone that did not belong to the skeleton in question and that someone had handed him by mistake. But the paleontologist's method of reconstruction would not thus be shown to be wrong, and neither is Freud's method of attempting to reconstruct Leonardo's childhood. Schapiro (1956) himself understands this principle perfectly well, and it seems at this point that his objection is not to the kind of conclusion that Freud drew but only to the particular premise on which the conclusion rested (p. 178). That premise was at fault so far as the avian species was concerned. In so far as Freud's interpretation does not refer specifically to the kind of bird, it may be expected to be correct.

2 See Maclagan (1923), Stites (1948a, p. 266), Neumann (1954, p. 7), Jones (1953-57, Vol. II, p. 348), Wohl and Trosman (1955, p. 33), Schapiro (1956, p. 151), Strachey (1957, p. 60f.).

3 Mr. Strachey (1957) has expressed an identical view (p. 61f.).

But here the criticism of the historian and philologist goes a step further. Schapiro reminds us that the recording of incidents of the kind that Leonardo reported regarding his own infancy was "an established literary pattern" (p. 152) and occurs often in mythology. He cites Cicero's text *On Divination* and traces the source from which Leonardo might easily have known about typical incidents that in antiquity and later were attributed to the infancy of heroes and outstanding personages as omens of future greatness. Some of these incidents refer both to animals and to the infant's mouth, and are actually of the structure of the childhood recollection reported by Leonardo.[4]

With the introduction of historical prototypes at this point Schapiro opens a discussion that refers to a principal issue: When he formed the recollection, was Leonardo a medium of the historical past or was he revealing something personal and intimate? We shall have to cope with this type of problem from time to time as we proceed. The historian's hypothesis would reduce the self's spontaneous participation to zero. The main motive would then be that of imitation.

However, from a psychoanalytic viewpoint, behind the apparent tendency to imitate the ancients suggested by the historian, a potent narcissistic motive may be surmised, since in this instance imitation would have led to a community with some of the greatest minds of the past.

The impulse to form the asserted childhood recollection would then have stemmed from Leonardo's ambition, from his conviction that he was a genius—or perhaps from some doubt as to his genius, as the case may be. He would have wanted to make sure or was sure that he would hold a place of greatness in history, and therefore claimed to have had in his own infancy an experience which by tradition was a propitious sign in the lives of those who later ascended to great fame. Why this ambition should have found such a devious mode of expression would still remain unexplained. But the historian perhaps regards the desire to imitate as a sufficient motive.

Notwithstanding the presence of marked ambition and consequent conflicts, clinical experience shows that narcissistic motives of this type

---

[4] Of course, one wonders why, then, there are not more instances of such childhood recollections being recorded by other outstanding Renaissance artists. Or, at least, one should expect from the historian some explanation that would make it comprehensible why it occurred in Leonardo's instance and not in others.

do not suffice to form a dream or a cover memory. Particularly in the case of Leonardo, who gave free expression to his ambition (see, for example, MacCurdy, 1956, p. 57f.; C.A. 119 v. a), the motive for a disguised presentation is wanting.

In order to explain the presence of the kite in the recollection Schapiro points out that on the obverse of the page on which it is reported Leonardo discussed the flight of the kite. Traditional tale and reality pursuit would thus explain the essential manifest meaning of the recollection. Although the analyst feels unable to put much stock in the former—how much Leonardo actually read is still a highly disputed matter (de Santillana, 1953)—he will agree with the historian's claim regarding the latter. Since it was not a vulture that Leonardo recalled as having settled down on his mouth when he was an infant, Freud's remarks purporting to explain Leonardo's selection of a vulture among the numerous possible choices are also untenable.[5]

Since evidently the childhood recollection of the kite came to Leonardo's mind while he was doing his research on the flight of the kite, there is no objection to listing his scientific interest as a precipitating factor. Quite independently of what species of bird was involved, Freud was fully aware that one might try to explain the recollection by exactly the motives Schapiro cites. "One might," Freud (1910) writes, "be satisfied with explaining it [the recollection] on the basis of his inclination, of which he makes no secret, to regard his preoccupation with the flight of birds as pre-ordained by destiny" (p. 84). Freud appraised such an explanation as an "underrating" of the recollection (p. 84).[6] Indeed, the explanatory value of this factor is particularly meager. It amounts to saying that Leonardo formed a childhood recollection about a kite because he was preoccupied with kites, and the utmost we could learn from Leonardo's report would be

[5] They referred to Egyptian mythology and doctrines of patristic writers. An Egyptian Mother Goddess was represented with a vulture head; furthermore, the belief that there were no male vultures led to the explanation that vultures are impregnated by the wind, which, in turn, was cited in defense of the Virgin Birth (Freud, 1910, pp. 88-90; cf. also Hárnik, 1920).

[6] In 1919 Freud added a footnote (Freud, 1910, p. 82) in which he elaborated upon a suggestion Havelock Ellis (1910) had made in his review of Freud's essay. According to Ellis, Leonardo's account might have been based on reality. The bird need not have been a vulture. Freud agreed with Ellis upon the possible reality of the event and added that the mother might have observed the bird's visit to the child and taken it as an omen. Such stories coming from parents are often integrated as genuine recollections. Freud considered it a general rule that adult fantasies about childhood are attached to trivial but real childhood events. This factor, Freud thought, would not speak against his interpretation.

that he was ambitious and interested in the flight of kites, all of which would easily be determined from other sources. In other words, after the analysis of the recollection we would know no more about Leonardo than before we set out.

And yet repeated clinical experience demonstrates that cover memories contain the subtlest contents of repressed memories. This clinical observation, to be sure, should not encourage a neglect of precipitating factors, which hold a real, if secondary, place in the web of links that finally lead to a cover memory or a dream. Freud himself spent much acumen on unraveling precipitating factors that led to one of his own cover memories (Freud, 1899; Bernfeld, 1946; Jones, Vol. I, p. 11), and in his comprehensive book on dreams he gave due account of day residues, which are the equivalents of recent precipitating factors in the case of cover memories. Precipitating factors are often the most important clues that lead the analyst to the unconscious meaning of a content that is to be explained. But if the precipitating secondary factor is taken as a static stimulus, it will not assist in the deciphering of a recollection. The secondary factor is closer to the conscious than to the unconscious, and refers to the subject's present. It is, therefore, relatively easy to discover its meaning, which in turn, adumbrates the unconscious meaning of a dream content or of a symptom.

Applied to Leonardo's recollection this means that we would have to know why Leonardo was so eager to discover the art of human flying, and so preoccupied with the flight of birds, particularly of kites. About the latter Schapiro tells us only that Pliny held a view identical with Leonardo's about one aspect of the kite's flight (p. 152), thus making Leonardo again a medium of tradition. The observation per se, correct as it may be, that Leonardo's childhood recollection came to his mind while he was making his research on the flight of the kite, does not warrant Schapiro's claim that "Leonardo's choice of the kite as the bird of his destiny has apparently more to do with his scientific problem than Freud supposed" (p. 152).[7] One is rather inclined to say that Leonardo's association of an infantile recollection with a scientific pursuit may shed some light on the latter.

Here is the place to make a general statement about the difference

[7] Thus Schapiro's erudite reasoning leads back precisely to a factor of which Freud was well aware, and which he had been compelled to reject as the principal causative agent in view of contradictory clinical observations (Freud, 1910, p. 84).

between the philological research of the historian and that of the psychoanalyst. The two examples I have given of the former show that the historian tries to find the *type* of motive, whereas the analyst tries to discover its *specific content*. Schapiro tells us that the recollection was born out of Leonardo's imitation of the ancients or his ambition to vie with them and out of his interest in a research topic. Freud, however, knew from the analyses of his patients that the bird in this recollection was a maternal symbol. Freud's philological research was devoted to the effort to discover what kind of mother was represented in Leonardo's recollection, and that research led him to believe that it was the image of a friendly, pleasure-giving mother.

If it were possible that the motive per se could be unearthed by philological research, as Schapiro sought to do in connecting Leonardo's recollection with preceding similar instances, then unavoidably the image that must emerge will be that of a lame, almost passive, mind that can only grasp what is offered by an outside source.

When Freud interpreted the vulture which he believed to be a part of the recollection, he did not claim that Leonardo formed his recollection in imitation of some literary source. Freud wrote: "He [Leonardo] once happened to read . . . and at that point a memory sprang to his mind, which was transformed into the phantasy . . ." (1910, p. 90). Although present psychoanalytic theory would assume that a subject's unconscious is quite capable of forming symbols or fantasies of this kind without specific stimulus, Freud's assumption may still serve as an adequate model of the relation between precipitating factor and unconscious content that are amalgamated into a new unit.

We notice that the precipitating stimulus becomes productive because the repressed, ever ready to intrude into the system of consciousness, can use it for this very purpose. The precipitating stimulus is not a force that on its own account produces a reaction of such kind in the person. The precipitating stimulus is seen here by Freud in connection with the live mind that is in a state of conflict; its very capacity to elicit a process in Leonardo's mind is revelatory of the existence in that mind of a personality factor significant for him.

If Leonardo's preoccupation with the flight of the kite was one of the factors that precipitated the recollection—and offhand there seems to be no reason to dispute this assumption—then one has to form a new hypothesis about what endowed this preoccupation with the capacity of contributing to the formation of the recollection.

The basic principle of psychoanalysis is the law of overdetermination, which says that all psychic phenomena are multifunctional and determined by a series or plurality of forces. Consequently, even if it could be proved that ancient tradition had its say in Leonardo's childhood recollection, this fact alone would not have any bearing on Freud's theory unless it could also be proved that Leonardo's mind was working on an imitative level exhausting its potential in mere copying.

At the same time we have, of course, to acknowledge that a factor of peripheral value in one science may be of central value in another. That Leonardo used an ancient model at all—a hypothesis I personally doubt—may be an important finding for the historian who is studying Leonardo's relation to antiquity and its bearing on the artist's procedures.

Schapiro himself does not seem satisfied with his explanation; he appears to take notice of Leonardo's internal conflict, and, after he has rejected Freud's assumption that the bird stood for a good, pleasure-giving mother, he searches for an appropriate substitute. Wohl and Trosman (p. 36) had noted that Freud might have been warned against the image of a friendly mother by the hostile quality of the verb *percuotere* ("to strike," "to beat"), which Leonardo used in describing the bird's action.[8] Had he known that the fateful bird was a kite, he would, of course, also have done what Wohl and Trosman (p. 36), and after them Schapiro (p. 156f.), presumably did, namely, check the index of Leonardo's *Notebooks* and read all the passages that refer to the kite. And like them he would, of course, have come across the fable Leonardo recorded under the title of Envy (see MacCurdy, 1956, p. 1074; H 5 v.) in which the kite is pictured as a mother animal that, out of envy, deprives its children of food when it sees them too fat.[9]

[8] In order to explain this element, Freud introduced an additional hypothesis (Freud, 1910, p. 107) that stands today in contradiction to theories he evolved later.

[9] However, it is surprising to hear Schapiro suggest that Freud would not have used the fable of the kite for the interpretation of the childhood recollection because "the father of psychoanalysis dismissed this part of Leonardo's writings as 'allegorical natural history, animal fables, jokes and prophecies, trivialities unworthy of so great a genius'" (p. 157). What Freud—who like no one else before him applied the hermeneutic method to jokes and folklore—actually did was to *characterize* these sections of the *Notebooks* "as scarcely

Schapiro quite rightly suggests that in the light of this fable one may assume that "Leonardo did not forgive [his mother] Caterina his illegitimacy and her willingness to abandon him to a step-mother" (p. 157). By suggesting that Leonardo's childhood recollection affords the interpretation of a hostile mother,[10] he draws a psychological conclusion with which psychoanalysts will generally agree, in contrast to the pastiche psychology he is prone to apply on other occasions.

The matter is not so simple in the case of Schapiro's contention that only the vulture meaning of the bird was usable for Freud's theory of homosexuality (p. 155f.). Here the psychoanalyst is actually in an awkward position. Freud interpreted the bird (which, according to his source, was a vulture) as a symbolic representative of the nourishing, love- and pleasure-giving mother. According to his reconstruction, the illegitimate Leonardo spent blissful years of early childhood with his mother, Caterina. Freud thought that the abundance of maternal gratifications in early years, followed by an abrupt separation when he had to join his father after the latter's wife proved barren, contributed greatly to Leonardo's later homosexuality. Now when it turns out that the bird in question was a kite, and that the kite probably was a symbol of a hostile mother, the analyst again claims that it fits into a constellation consistent with a homosexual end result. The psychoanalyst thus exposes himself to the reproach that he interprets data according to his prejudices, whatever these data may be. However, what appears to be prejudice actually reflects the content of the unconscious, which harbors opposites in close proximity, as can be demonstrated with particular obviousness in the case of psychological peculiarities of homosexuals. Clinically one finds in them an intense fixation to the mother (the attachment of homosexuals to men is, as Freud said, the expression of their faithfulness to the mother [1910, p. 100]); yet they also intensely hate their mothers, and their

---

worthy of so great a mind" (1910, p. 70), thus referring to the problem constantly encountered in research on Leonardo, namely, the bearing which medieval philosophy or superstitions have had on Leonardo's writings (cf. Duhem, 1909-13; de Santillana, 1953). It is not clear where Schapiro gets the notion that Freud would ever have rejected such material as a potential biographical source. Cf. also Freud's warning, made in the same essay, against the careless rejection of "the body of legends, traditions and interpretations found in a nation's early history" (1910, p. 84).

[10] Wohl and Trosman (1955, pp. 36, 38) made this interpretation of the childhood recollection. The claim to priority that Schapiro (p. 178) raises seems unwarranted. Bergler (p. 81) had as early as 1945 made a general remark about the hostile aspects of Leonardo's relationship to his mother, as Wohl and Trosman point out in their survey.

faithfulness to the male sex is also meant to demonstrate the contemptibility of women (mother). Which part of this complicated relationship to the mother will show up in a cover memory cannot be predicted. Therefore the evaluation of a particular symbol (bird) depends, in an instance where the subject's associations are unavailable, on philological research, and this is an area where even the most experienced analyst needs the research results of another discipline. The analytic insight into a particular situation may in turn have its bearing on the historical research, not only by raising new types of problems, but also by increasing or decreasing the probability of particular alternatives left undecided by the historical evidence at hand. It is the potential value of psychoanalysis as an instrument of reconstruction of historical events that Schapiro rejects. He criticizes Freud for having drawn, from his theory of the infantile origins of homosexuality, conclusions regarding "the specific relationships and events," whereas, according to Schapiro, he was entitled to "infer only that Leonardo had a fixation upon his mother" (p. 156).

We are here in the middle of an important argument. Freud actually thought he was capable of drawing conclusions regarding specific circumstances of Leonardo's external childhood environment, whereas the historian wants to grant psychoanalysis only the right to set forth the data of the internal milieu. As a matter of fact, Freud was here using the psychoanalytic method for seemingly unusual purposes. In his clinical work the analyst usually receives the information about external circumstances from the patient himself, and the therapeutic struggle rages about the existence of unconscious processes—including the unconscious meaning that reality events and reality factors had for the patient. However, not infrequently a patient has completely repressed the memory of a person or a place that had a leading bearing on him, and the analyst makes far-reaching reconstructions regarding the external milieu. (See, for example, Bonaparte, 1945.) Of course, this part of the psychoanalytic reconstruction is, for obvious reasons, discussed far less often than the reconstruction of the internal milieu.

In its application to history the potential of psychoanalysis as a tool of reconstructing external reality is destined to play a major role.[11]

___

[11] In the recently published third volume of his Freud biography, Jones reproduces Hans Kelsen's report of a brilliant instance of Freud's capacity to divine external reality factors from the content of a dream (Jones, Vol. III, p. 80). I was familiar with this example

When Schapiro holds that Freud committed an error of principle in extending his interpretation in this direction, he exhibits unawareness that all relevant psychological material carries the earmarks of both sectors, of not only the internal but the external milieu. To be sure, very often we are not in a position to separate them out, and only the meaning in terms of the internal milieu is realized. Yet, depending on the respective contents of the recollection, dream, fantasy, or what not, and the extent of our knowledge of the adult subject, we may be able to draw far-reaching conclusions regarding a vast number of details of external environment and of what may summarily be called the subject's external vicissitude.[12] Whether Freud's reconstruction was correct or not, Leonardo's childhood recollection, the illegitimacy of his birth, and his latent homosexuality as an adult are three facts that rightly can be taken as the cornerstone of a reconstruction of the childhood milieu. Since one of the factors, the childhood recollection, was partly misrepresented to Freud, his reconstruction was bound to go partly astray. The extent to which this happened I will discuss briefly later, but I wished first to set right the question of principle.

That done, it appears to me that Schapiro begs the question when he says that Freud "ignored" other possibilities of external circumstances "because of his certitude about the vulture and its legend" (p. 156). Freud had no reason to doubt the correctness of the account he had received of the childhood recollection. The meaning he attributed to the vulture can be well attested, and if Leonardo had actually written of a vulture, I do not see from what quarter Freud's theory could be justly attacked. The alleged vulture recollection confirmed observations Freud had made up to then in homosexuals, and his conclusions were legitimate and in accordance with scientific requirements. The fact that Leonardo actually did not write of a vulture but of a kite gives occasion to demonstrate how sensitive an instrument psychoanalysis really is. It would have called psychoanalysis seriously into question as a reliable method if further historical research had

---

before it was published and had submitted the dream to several analysts, requesting their opinion. There was none who showed Freud's acumen. I conclude that Freud possessed a superior power of inferring from fantasies or their derivatives not only unconscious processes but likewise external reality factors that a person wished to conceal.

[12] For recent endeavors to apply the psychoanalytic technique for such purposes in a historical setting, see Greenacre (1955, p. 107f., et passim).

confirmed conclusions that Freud deduced from premises later proved wrong.

There is also a point of methodology here that distinguishes Freud's method from the Jungian. Neumann (1954), while acknowledging the error of taking the bird as a vulture (p. 6, et passim), still proceeds as if Leonardo had written of a vulture. He writes:

> . . . the bird of Leonardo's childhood fantasy, considered in its creative-uroboric unity of breast-mother and phallus-father, is symbolically a "vulture" even if Leonardo called it a "nibbio" [p. 13].

Although it is proved that the word *nibbio* was translated as vulture in the text used by Freud, Neumann does not hesitate even to claim that Freud's error was due to an activation of "the archetypal image of the Great Mother within him" (p. 11). Such ratiocination is irreconcilable with the kind of scientific method that has proved efficient. It amounts to asserting that whatever creative minds produce will bear the earmarks of the archetype of the Great Mother. The historical detail that is the cornerstone of any historicopsychological research is rejected in favor of mythology.

Freud's law of overdetermination which can be proved by an abundance of observations states that all mental processes, as far as they are observable, are correlated with a plurality of forces that can be ordered in accordance with three agencies, the provinces of the personality: ego, superego, and id, and also carry the imprint of external reality, since the ego as mediator also molds the stimuli that originate from that source. Even if not all phenomena show equal traces of all dimensions and even if there are a few that are representative of only one or two, we may rest assured that a solitary childhood recollection, recorded by an adult, is a rather complicated configuration, to say the least, and is a compound derived from the major part of the psychic spectrum. It indicates a one-sided approach to the variety of aspects of human life, or a grievous reduction of the multidimensionality of human existence when one seriously denies the many-facedness of such a memory. First we saw the historian, who will scarcely acknowledge in the childhood recollection more than the bearing of the ego, its ambitions, its reality pursuits. Now the Jungian psychologist tries to reduce it to not even a manifestation of the individual child's love for his individual mother but merely to the symbolic representation of the Archetypal Feminine (Neumann, p. 10). I do not intend to enter here into a discussion of the concept of the archetype but only stress Neumann's general aversion to Freud's "personalistic view and interpretation" (p. 11), as if it really were a subordinate or accessory matter whether a child is separated from his mother immediately following his birth, during the oedipal crisis, during latency, or whether he has the privilege of her affection until he reaches the fringe of maturity. This nebulous "Archetypal Feminine" seems to respond quite differently to each of these eventualities, as those who care to observe minutely the unending stream of details of human existence can confirm.

3

The Mona Lisa *Problem*

The interpretation of Leonardo's enigmatic childhood recollection was, however, only one of Freud's biographical aims. He also attempted to demonstrate in Leonardo's works of art the effects that can be traced back to the recollection and what it stands for. After all, there was another enigma in Leonardo's work that had aroused the curiosity of almost every historian who had devoted himself to his life and work: the smile of the *Mona Lisa* (Plate 1).

Leonardo painted the *Mona Lisa* probably between 1503 and 1507. Even among the artist's contemporaries the portrait had already made the deepest impression and Leonardo was never able to wrest himself from it. It never reached the one who had commissioned it, but was taken by Leonardo to France, where it may have remained with him until he died.[1] Whatever Leonardo's explanation of his unwillingness to relinquish it—such as the alleged necessity of carrying it to its final completion—there seems to have been established an indissoluble

[1] The story that he sold it to the king of France is not proved and seems a legend. Hildebrandt (1927) takes it for certain that the *Mona Lisa* got into royal possession only after Leonardo's death, and he finds it significant that Leonardo did not part with the portrait during his lifetime (p. 174).

bond between the artist painter and the image. Furthermore—and this seems to be a point (one of the few) on which most historians agree in the many controversial issues presently to be reported—this smile did not appear in Leonardo's work prior to his painting the *Mona Lisa* but appeared in one form or another thereafter in most of his paintings of the human face that have reached posterity. To be sure, his biographer Vasari reported that in Leonardo's early years, when he was still a tyro in his teacher Verrocchio's studio, he sculptured smiling faces of women. Some have even thought—but this is not probable—that it was these sculptures that stimulated the teacher to represent the smile that can be found in his own work. It is more probable that Leonardo's interest was called forth by his teacher. Be this as it may, in no portrait or Madonna painting prior to the *Mona Lisa* is this smile found, nor has it been claimed for those that have been lost.

As is bound to be the case with a phenomenon as elusive as a smile, and a painted one at that, no precise description can be given of the characteristics that make this smile in Leonardo's work unique. Freud seems to have been most impressed by those descriptions that referred to the smile of the *Mona Lisa* as containing a double nature, a certain ambiguity of love and sinisterness. Recently the ambiguity has been remarked again; this time in the observation that the viewer is aware of the inner life of the person portrayed, but she holds herself aloof from him and does not reveal her secret (de Tolnay, 1952, p. 25).

Freud's conclusion was that (1) the smile as painted by Leonardo was a real quality of the woman whom he was depicting, and (2) this smile evoked in Leonardo the recollection of his mother's smile.

Vasari's report that "While Leonardo was drawing her [Mona Lisa's] portrait he engaged people to play and sing, and jesters to keep her merry, and remove that melancholy which painting usually gives to portraits" (p. 11) can be cited in favor of the first conclusion; yet this might have been arranged by Leonardo not necessarily for the purpose of depicting realistically the model's smile. Max Dvořák believes that the motive as recorded by Vasari was the correct one, namely, to relieve the lifelessness of the reproduction of a model (1918-19, p. 191).[2] Yet Freud's first conclusion does not appear to me to be germane to the second conclusion, which is the really decisive one.

[2] De Tolnay expressly says that the face is not a naturalistic study but a generalization of traits (1952, p. 24).

Whatever the relationship may have been between the actual appearance of the subject and the final artistic form Leonardo found in portraying the woman, the most relevant external factor is whether or not the model smiled in a way that moved the artist. The assumption of such a factor is not contradicted by Vasari's report and may even be favored by it.[3]

The second conclusion, as so often in psychoanalysis, is not capable of being supported by direct proof. It can be judged only in terms of degrees of probability. There is the pathognomic argument, raised by Freud, of the two seemingly mutually exclusive emotions that appear in the facial expression. Leonardo, as an adult, succumbed to the homoerotic tendency, and, since this tendency develops in connection with certain experiences of the little boy with his mother, the mother was the source of tenderness and affection as well as the source of ill luck.[4] Thus Freud was able to explain genetically a prominent feature of the portrait that had puzzled a good many historians by referring to the adult's specific attitude toward a person who played the most important role in his life. We would say today that man's ambivalent attitude toward the woman (mother) is reflected in the smile of the *Mona Lisa.* Freud, though familiar with the facts of ambivalence in 1910, had not yet recognized ambivalence as a general law of emotional life.[5] Pathognomic arguments appear in Freud's work at crucial points, the most prominent one being his using the infant's physiognomic expression following satiation at the mother's breast "as a prototype of the expression of sexual satisfaction in later life" (Freud, 1905a, p. 182).

[3] It is not clear whether Max Dvořák when he wrote his historical remarks on the *Mona Lisa* (1918-19, pp. 190-194) was thinking of Freud's study. Some of his polemic remarks sound as if, without mentioning Freud, they had also been directed against him (see particularly p. 190). Dvořák believes it to be a prime misunderstanding when "psychological viewpoints whose subtlety stems from the nineteenth century are injected into this portrait [*in dieses Porträt psychologische Gesichtspunkte hineinzutragen, die in ihrer Subtilität erst dem XIX. Jahrhundert angehören*]" (p. 191). Nevertheless, by and large Dvořák's art-historical analysis, except for his assumption of a genetic nexus with previous portraits by Leonardo, seems to me to be compatible with Freud's postulated psychological history.

[4] I have been able to observe this accusatory attitude toward the mother in a homosexual patient. It started as soon as he discovered the extent of his affection for his mother. The accusation also served the purpose of a defense against his own wishes, which he claimed had been aroused by the mother's seductive behavior. This patient, however, had not been abruptly separated from his mother, as happened to Leonardo, but entertained an intense affection for her until late adolescence.

[5] The term was coined by Bleuler in the same year in which the Leonardo study was published (1910).

The value of pathognomic arguments is debatable. In the instance of the infant's instinctual life they have been replaced by a number of other techniques and observations. For the genetic interpretation of an artistic element these techniques are of no avail. In general, it seems to me that contemporary experimental psychology does not esteem pathognomic arguments,[6] but I will present later an instance drawn from another genius's life that is comparable to the one under discussion and that led to a documented explanation similar to that Freud suggested in the case of the *Mona Lisa* portrait. Thus comparative psychopathology may serve here as a technique of verification.

If it is proven that an artistic element that occupied an artist in his youth (in the sculptures of smiling, female heads)[7] then disappears from his work to reappear lightninglike in the portrait of a mature woman when the artist is over fifty years old, never to leave him again but to occur in the pictures of other women and young men, then today too one would feel inclined to assert with a high degree of probability that all facts are genetically interconnected and are referable to a conflict in the artist related in one way or another to his mother. Clinical observation confirms the assumption that an infantile, probably repressed, memory established the tie between the artist and this model, which evidently was stronger than that with other women whose portraits he had painted. Indeed, clinical data gathered since 1910 have overwhelmingly demonstrated the rule that the child-mother relationship has a fateful bearing on the adult's vicissitudes, and there seems to be no reason why the genius should be exempted from the operation of this rule, which is basic to the development of the members of the human species.

I am properly convinced that the structure of the genius personality, particularly of the genius who is creative in the field of art, is in essential respects different from that of other human beings. Freud was most careful in his essay not to draw any inferences regarding the specific character of Leonardo's genius from analogies with his every-

[6] For an exposition of problems inherent in the doctrines of pathognomy, see Bühler (1933).

[7] Schapiro, however, suggests that Vasari erroneously ascribed to the youthful Leonardo plaster sculptures of smiling women that had been made by Verrocchio (p. 165). In view of clinical experience accumulated since 1910, Freud's reconstruction would, in my estimation, gain in probability if it turned out that the depiction of smiles did not hold too prominent a place, or did not occur at all, in Leonardo's work prior to the painting of the *Mona Lisa*.

day clinical observations. But in a question that concerns not the structure but the contents of human life, we regularly observe that the genius wrestles with contents that are identical with those that the rest of mankind must cope with (Freud, 1913b, p. 187): how else could the genius have an effect, be understood, and admired?

At this point I wish to adduce an extrinsic factor that may have had a bearing on Leonardo's relationship to Mona Lisa. It is a doubtful clue and I present it for what it may be worth. I derive it from a detail of Mona Lisa's life. Lisa di Antonio Maria di Noldo Gherardini was born in Florence in 1479 and was married to Francesco di Bartolommeo di Lanobi del Giocondo (1460-1528) in 1495. Both came from prominent Florentine families of high rank, the husband holding several public offices. The only other detail of her life usually mentioned is the death of a daughter who was buried in Santa Maria Novella in 1499. It may be observed that Seidlitz (1909b) does not accept it as certain that the child was Lisa's, since, the husband having been married twice before, she could have been the offspring of one of his previous marriages (p. 266). But in principle one may accept the opinion of most historians that it was her child.[8] Now, most historians, in view of Vasari's report that Leonardo took four years to paint the portrait, date the beginning of Leonardo's work as in 1503, shortly after he returned from his service to Cesare Borgia which had interrupted his second Florentine stay (1500-1506). Of course, Vasari's secondhand information is not binding, and historians like Douglas have felt free to assume that Leonardo started a portrait of Mona Lisa shortly after his arrival in Florence in 1500.[9] He needs this early inception in order to prove his very engaging theory that Leonardo first painted a cartoon of the lady in which he presented her quite differently from the way we know her today, namely, mourning for the loss of her child.[10] The work was then interrupted by Leonardo's departure for the Romagna and—still according to Douglas (1944, pp. 99-101)—when he returned the subject had changed and this new appearance made Leonardo drop his erstwhile intention to replace it

[8] I have not found any reference to later progeny in the literature.

[9] The literature Douglas (1944) cites in conjunction with his hypothesis was not accessible to me.

[10] For a reproduction of the cartoon in question, see Douglas (1944, Plate XLIX). The editors of the catalogue of the Leonardo da Vinci Loan Exhibition consider that the cartoon may be authentic (Los Angeles County Museum, 1949, p. 115, No. 92). For a contrary view, see Pedretti (1959b, p. 34, n. 1).

with the vision he laid down in the final product. Although the historical evidence on which Douglas based his deduction will be rejected by most historians, by his reference to the death of the daughter he brought up what I still think is a detail that deserves attention.[11]

Whether Leonardo started the portrait in 1500 or in 1503 would not be decisive. But if she had had only one child and that child had died, the conclusion that her disposition would have been mourning or melancholic makes sense, particularly in view of the social background of the persons involved. This possibility admitted, or even taken as probable, Leonardo would have faced a situation quite close to what may have been his central conflict. His favored feminine subject had, in accordance with the times, been the Madonna, the mother devoting herself fully to her son. In Mona Lisa he faced the type of mother who has lost her infant but cannot forget it, has not replaced it, and remains faithful to its memory. This may suggest two reactions in the artist: resentment, elicited by the memory that his own mother had given him up as a child—that is, forgotten him; and jealousy that this woman could not wrest her thoughts from the child and turn toward him who had lost a mother in early childhood. If he by chance observed a fleeting smile in her face, he would have been fascinated for it meant that this mother too was capable of forgetting the child and evolving an interest in the person facing her. In such circumstances too Leonardo might have had a personal interest in seeing the subject's smile return and stay on her countenance as long as possible for it contained consolation for a past loss, and even restitution. Yet pursuing the clue suggested by Douglas has not taken us far afield from Freud's reconstruction.[12]

I am aware how easily my proposition may be rejected and do not expect that it will convince anyone who has so far felt opposed to Freud's reconstruction.

[11] The theory that the woman in the portrait is wearing a widow's veil has been refuted by Douglas (p. 118).

[12] Douglas's hypothesis of a diphasic history of the Mona Lisa portrait was recently revived by Pedretti's assertion regarding the authenticity of a Mona Lisa cartoon showing the subject at the age of twenty or twenty-two (Pedretti, 1959b). However, if Pedretti's identification of the subject as Giuliano de' Medici's mistress is correct (1959b, p. 24), this would disprove Freud's conclusions.

4

The Anna Metterza *Problem*

Freud's next step, the reconstruction of the subjective background of Leonardo's *Anna Metterza* (Plate 2), is rather difficult to discuss for several issues are involved, some of them unconnected with the psychoanalytic area.

Once the genetic background of the discrete element of the smile in the Mona Lisa portrait was established to his satisfaction, Freud examined whether the appearance of this element in other works of Leonardo spoke for or against his reconstruction. Interestingly enough the painting closest to the *Mona Lisa* in time is one whose subject alone seemed to confirm his interpretation and which contained a significant variant of this element. This is the *Anna Metterza*, which depicts Saint Anne, the grandmother of Jesus, Mary, the mother, and the child Jesus, a combination of personages that holds a place of its own in iconography. The facial expression of the two women shows the famous Leonardesque smile, this time without the sinister admixture. Here Freud's reconstruction of Leonardo's childhood is to be recalled. He assumed that the boy spent his early years with Caterina, his natural mother, and was taken between the ages of three and five into his father's home. There he lived with his paternal grandmother

and his father's first wife, whom the father had married the year
Leonardo was born and who had remained childless. Thus, according
to Freud, Anne and Mary would represent on the one hand stepmother-
grandmother and on the other natural mother-stepmother. The latter
was, Freud thought, strongly suggested by the representation of the
two women as almost coetaneous. The *Anna Metterza* would then be,
in terms of the artist's unconscious, a representation of a fundamental
aspect of his childhood situation. To what extent fulfillment of the
boy's wishes which had remained unfulfilled in reality, or denial of
the tragic and its replacement by the desirable, contributed to the end
result encountered in the Louvre painting, is not to be discussed at this
point.

The problem is solely: Is it reasonable to assume a relevant connection between the events in Leonardo's childhood as reconstructed by
Freud and Leonardo's having painted the subject of the *Anna Metterza*,
particularly in view of certain details such as the smiles and the
coetaneity of the two women? Under what conditions would we regard
this connection as proved, or at least probable? It is safe to suppose that
Freud's assumption would encounter less or no opposition if, since
1910, certain new documentary evidence had been found—let us say,
an entry by Leonardo in a notebook remarking that he often thought
of his mother and grandmother, or a sentence in which Anne and
Mary and these two members of his family were brought together in
one way or another. Such an entry would have suggested a conscious
interconnection between the elements in question and Freud's intuition
would have been confirmed. Oddly enough, such a find might
have diminished the value of Freud's reconstruction in the eyes of the
analyst, since it would have proved a conscious motive in Leonardo
and thrown a doubt on the unconscious motivation. To be sure, many
a genius in the field of art achieves at certain periods of his life a
greater insight into his own unconscious than the ordinary man commonly does, but in view of the high degree of distortion encountered
in Leonardo's childhood recollection and the paucity of references
to his childhood in his notes such a remark would rather raise new
problems than solve those that exist. In speculating about conscious
processes that might have paralleled the unconscious ones as reconstructed by Freud, we should not assume more than occasional flashes
perhaps referring to vague childhood recollections and disappearing

as soon as they have intruded.[1] Consequently Freud's reconstruction cannot be confirmed or disproved directly by any documentary evidence. The basis on which the psychoanalytic technique, when clinically applied, is prone to verify reconstructions, the subject's dreams, associations, etc., is forever gone.

Thus one cannot help asking whether such problems can be solved at all, or whether it is impossible that meaningful, potentially verifiable answers to such questions should be found. It is not surprising if the historian tends to reject any kind of psychological explanation as mere speculation. If he does, then since the analyst evidently will not abide by this stringency of method, the two disciplines are to remain apart and the cross-fertilization which one might anticipate would lead to new insights is made impossible.[2]

Notwithstanding the absence of direct proof, in relevant applications of psychoanalysis to history the degree of external and internal probability is to be considered. The external probability refers to factors that can be established only from objective evidence such as documentary proof and the whole apparatus at the historian's command; the inner probability rests on knowledge of and insight into the laws of the human mind. However, this is the proper place to cite Freud's warning that "the probable need not necessarily be the truth and the truth not always probable" (1937-39, p. 30).

I wish to weigh first the inner probability that the *Anna Metterza* painting was genetically connected with Leonardo's childhood. If the first step of Freud's reconstruction regarding the smile of the *Mona Lisa* is accepted, then I do not see any particular difficulty in also taking the second. The smile reappears, as in subsequent paintings, also in the one that was painted simultaneously with the *Mona Lisa,* and therefore allows the assumption that it refers genetically to the mother. Furthermore, whether Freud's particular reconstruction of Leonardo's childhood is correct or not, it is certain that he was of illegitimate birth—and we shall see later that this factor played a larger role in his life than some historians wish to admit. Thus a painting that

[1] The wealth of emotions that might have been present is another unknown factor that is to be disregarded in this context.

[2] Waelder (1960) discusses anew the question of validation in psychoanalytic research. His viewpoint can fruitfully be applied to areas outside of psychoanalysis proper such as that under discussion here.

stresses the sequence of generations and their harmonious interconnection prepared by providence is almost bound, in a man whose mother was unwed and from whom he was separated early, to touch upon a conflict directly connected with his own mother. The illegitimate child that grows up in his father's house away from his mother has to deal in his fantasy with the natural mother and the woman who is the head of the household in which he grows up. One could set forth numerous associations between the subject of the *Anna Metterza* and Leonardo's childhood, but all of them are speculative and will have no greater evidential weight than the main argument set forth by Freud. I think that today, when the supreme bearing of the child-mother relation and of the specific constellation of the oedipus triangle has been established and demonstrated in such a large number of instances, one can postulate that an accomplishment such as the *Anna Metterza*— on which Leonardo, the nonconformist, the unbeliever, the giant who struggled so hard for his integrity and mental independence, spent years of effort—must have been, aside from the usual participation of the unconscious in the creation of great art, connected with deep layers of the repressed.

To be sure, there have been phases in the history of art when the individuality of the artist was overruled by an extraneous demand and the practicing artist had to obey a strict code of performance; there have also been artists who by individual bent were conformists and without external pressure made themselves pliable instruments of social demands, and surrendered their individuality. Under such conditions it may be impossible to consider the work of art as a biographical clue. Both conditions are absent in the case of Leonardo. I make no doubt the *Last Supper* contains biographical clues too, although they are less conspicuous than in the *Anna Metterza*.[3] Here the personal possibly disappears behind the subject depicted, but that does not mean that the personal is absent; it only means that we cannot yet make this personal factor visible.

The *Anna Metterza* lends itself to an extraction of the biographical factor, and it seems to be more than coincidence that a prominent situa-

---

[3] The anecdote claims that the representation of Judas was used for personal revenge, but this is not probable and would not contribute to the psychological understanding of the painting.

tion in Leonardo's childhood can be put into so many associative connections with the topic of the painting.

There are more arguments in favor of Freud's thesis which a discussion of the historian's objections may give the occasion to set forth. At one point Schapiro (1956) tries to show that Freud raised a point that disproves his own theory. The *Anna Metterza* exists in two forms: the cartoon, now in the Royal Academy at London (Plate 3), and the Louvre painting.[3a] There is no doubt that the latter was painted after Leonardo had met Mona Lisa, but there are two opinions about the dating of the former. Most historians believe that it was done before 1500 and only few date it later, that is to say, after his meeting the Gioconda.[4]

In a footnote Freud declared himself in favor of the earlier dating and thought this "would fit in excellently with our arguments" (1910, p. 115, n.). Schapiro believes Freud forgot this early dating of the cartoon when he presented his main thesis, namely that Mona Lisa inspired Leonardo to paint the *Anna Metterza* (p. 164f.). However, the footnote was added by Freud much later in 1923, and if Schapiro's interpretation of Freud's thesis were correct, the footnote would mean rather that Freud had "forgotten" his main thesis—which is hardly believable.

An exact reading of Freud's text of 1910 will show that Freud's thesis does not exclude Leonardo's preoccupation with the Anna Metterza subject prior to his meeting Mona Lisa but only requires that the element of the Leonardesque smile did not appear before that time in the representation of Anna Metterza (or any other painting for that matter).[5]

[3a] A third version, the so-called Servite cartoon, was done by Leonardo in 1501. It has been lost. There is a presumed copy of this cartoon probably painted by Andrea del Brescianino (formerly in the Kaiser Friedrich Museum) (Bodmer, Plate 61 and Suida, p. 77, Plate 131). This copy shows the faces of the two saints unsmiling, and St. Anne is depicted considerably older than St. Mary.

[4] Hildebrandt (1927), on not quite convincing grounds, gives 1491 as the latest date for the cartoon in the Academy.

[5] The passage in Freud's essay that probably gave rise to Schapiro's misinterpretation is the following: "It would best agree with our expectations if it was the intensity of Leonardo's preoccupation with the features of Mona Lisa *which stimulated him to create the composition of St. Anne out of his phantasy*" (1910, p. 111, italics added). The following, however, suggests that this sentence referred to the smiles with which he endowed the two saints. "For if," Freud continues, "the Gioconda's smile called up in his mind the memory of his mother, it is easy to understand how it drove him at once to create a glorification of motherhood, and to give back to his mother the smile he had found in the noble lady" (p. 111f.).

The footnote of 1923 shows clearly what Freud had in mind.[6] The reality experience (the perception of the smile of the Mona Lisa) had the effect of structuring a childhood recollection. Whereas in the early London cartoon the two female bodies are almost a unit and look like one body with two heads, in the Louvre painting they are differentiated (though at some points still difficult to keep apart). The two representations can be compared to the two (or more) forms in which a memory may appear in a patient's mind in varying degrees of clarity in the course of an analysis. According to Freud, the accretion of clarity of the two female bodies (though still not completely achieved in the later version) was caused by the accidental confrontation of the adult with a perception that coincided with a repressed image.

This conscious impression brought upon Leonardo by reality increased the forcefulness of the repressed image which now became strong enough to intrude at least temporarily into consciousness and thus helped to differentiate the more primitive image in which two women of importance to the infant had been fused. The smile of the Mona Lisa had become the point of crystallization around which the primitively fused could separate out its parts. This remark of Freud's accords well with innumerable clinical observations. In Leonardo's instance all the precursors of the final version of the *Anna Metterza* show the artist's struggle with a problem that seems to come to rest when Anne and Mary are at last endowed with the smile and lovingly watch the playing infant.

Schapiro's objection which I have just discussed holds only a subordinate position. Of the principal arguments with which he assails Freud's thesis one refers to historical data that are susceptible of verification and which allow us to dispense for a while with speculation. The questions involved are how often the subject of Anna Metterza had occurred in Italian painting prior to Leonardo and whether Leonardo was original in representing St. Anne as almost coetaneous with St. Mary. Schapiro claims that neither the subject nor this aspect of

6 However, Freud's construct regarding the effect of Leonardo's meeting with Mona Lisa on the final outcome of the *Anna Metterza* would have to be dropped if it were proved that the Leonardesque smile already appeared in the cartoon in 1500. If I understand Schapiro correctly, he does not claim that the smile appears in Leonardo's work prior to Leonardo's meeting with Mona Lisa, but rather that Leonardo's interest in the subject of Anna Metterza predates that meeting. As stated above, this claim alone does not contradict Freud's construct.

the treatment was original with Leonardo, but both were traditional and therefore do not justify inferences regarding Leonardo's individual problems or his individuality.

As I will explain later, I do not think these two questions to be germane to Freud's thesis, but no doubt the kind of answer they found in 1910 made Freud's thesis appear more or less probable then, when much of what is taken for granted now was still a matter of novelty and doubt. Schapiro unwarrantably lectures Freud on the ground that such questions are not to be decided by the psychoanalyst but by the historian of art; the uninitiated reader would never divine from his criticism that Freud, of course, made no claim regarding the history of art on his own authority but based himself on Richard Muther, whom he cites profusely and who, though he now holds only a minor place as a historian, was still an expert famous in his times.[7]

Freud was being quite cautious when he wrote that "St. Anne with her daughter and her grandchild is a subject that is rarely handled in Italian painting" (1910, p. 112), for Muther's statement might easily have been taken as meaning that the theme of Anna Metterza had not occurred in Italian painting prior to Leonardo, although Muther did not spell this out in explicit words (1909, p. 309f.).[8]

About the coetaneity of the two women and Leonardo's particular arrangement of the composition Muther did not leave any doubt as to all this being original with Leonardo (1907, p. 23; and 1909, p. 309). Therefore the most Schapiro would have been entitled to claim—if indeed, as we shall presently see, criticism on this score is correct at all—is that present views do not support the opinions of those historians on whose judgment Freud relied, and that to this extent doubt must be cast on his conclusions.

[7] It is regrettable that even now discussions of Freud's work are not conducted *sine ira et studio* and a paper otherwise meritorious such as that under discussion is marred by the evidence of prejudice that I will have to expose at another place too.

[8] Dvořák, who knew Italian Renaissance like no one else, says of the Anna Metterza theme: "The strange motive that was in Italy rather rare . . . [*Das merkwürdige Motiv, das in Italien ziemlich selten war . . .*]" (1918-19, p. 189). Heydenreich says of Leonardo's painting, "iconographically it is a genuinely new creation" (1954, Vol. I, p. 42). D'Ancona writes as follows: "This image of Mary in the arms of Anne was especially favored in Italy during the thirteenth and fourteenth centuries. To the original two-figured group, the figure of the Christ Child was added and this three-figured group gained great popularity in the fifteenth century" (1957, p. 39). But the author adduces as examples only the Masaccio and Leonardo paintings. In a footnote she continues: "The representation of the Virgin Mary with St. Anne, with or without the Child, is very frequent" (n. 96). I have, of course, considered only representations of the three generations united in the iconographically typical way that is meant by the term *Anna Metterza*.

This is a difficulty that confronts most instances of applied psychoanalysis. Progress in the fields to which psychoanalysis has been applied may invalidate the premises on which the psychoanalyst rested his deductions. It should not surprise us very much if, in the last five decades, historical research unearthed new facts that contradict one or another of Freud's conclusions. In this instance it would not even be as consequential as Schapiro thinks, since the issue involved is only of secondary importance.

Yet, whatever the consequences, it is surprising to discover that a perusal of the literature cited by Schapiro does not seem to confirm his claim, and, oddly enough, Muther, though he deserves the small esteem in which his many works on the history of painting are held, appears to have been quite correct in the two points under scrutiny. Thus all the existing Anna Metterza paintings specifically recorded in Kleinschmidt's standard work (1930) as having been painted by Italian masters earlier than 1500 number only fifteen, few enough to warrant the Muther-Freud statement of rarity in view of the enormous wealth of religious painting in Italy.[9]

An even greater surprise is experienced when the frequency of coetaneity in the Anna Metterza paintings of the Italian schools is checked. Schapiro's reasoning is quite strange on this point. He proves that St. Anne was frequently depicted as young. Yet the majority of instances he cites concern scenes of the life of St. Anne where Mary does not appear at all, or where St. Anne is a bystander taking a subordinate position in the total painting. The question of St. Anne's age, of course, takes prominence only in the Anna Metterza paintings, where the *succession of generations* is the central theme of the whole composition. Of this kind Schapiro adduces only one single example where St. Anne and St. Mary are represented as coetaneous. This is Luca di Tommè's *Anna Metterza* of 1367 (Plate 4) where St. Anne "is simply an enlarged replica of her daughter" (Schapiro, 1956, p. 164). Yet just this factor undoes the purpose for which the author

[9] To be sure, the figure fifteen is certainly too low, for Kleinschmidt mentions other paintings of Anna Metterza without enumerating them separately. Some of them may have been painted before, others after, 1500. At any rate, it is evident that this iconographic theme was by no means a frequent subject of the Italian masters, at least prior to Leonardo. See also Kaftal (1952), where only two paintings are recorded as representing St. Anne. Miss Inge Klimpt was kind enough to go through van Marle's history of the Italian schools of painting (1923-38) for me and found only fourteen recorded instances of Anna Metterzas.

wishes to use it. The difference in the succession of generations is overemphasized by the difference in size and the faces are left identical because they are ageless. Here I need only to quote what Schapiro says about "the hieratic note in the scale and rigidity" of medieval representation: "The relative ages and the order of generations, corresponding to the order of authority in the family, are symbolized by the varying size and level of the figures" (1956, p. 163). Why does he then claim Luca di Tommè's painting as an instance of mother's and daughter's coetaneity?[10]

As far as I can gather, then, in this point also Muther (and Freud following him) were right; Leonardo seems to have been the first, at least in Italian painting, to represent the two saints as almost coetaneous in an Anna Metterza.

Yet the main argument Schapiro raises against Freud's thesis is a type of argument we have encountered earlier, namely, the historical argument: "He [Freud] does not ask, for example, what was thought of Saint Anne during that period . . ." (p. 158). Schapiro thereupon proceeds to give a summary of the cult of St. Anne in the fifteenth century. R. Langton Douglas had already wondered why writers on Leonardo had not dealt with this question of hagiography, and Schapiro follows essentially what Douglas had presented less at large twelve years earlier (1944, p. 26). Schapiro reminds us of the great adoration that was bestowed upon her during Leonardo's lifetime, the reasons for this upsurge, its theological background, and the theological arguments involved in it.

The point Schapiro has in mind is evidently the suggestion that Freud overvalued the personal meaning of Leonardo's choice in painting the *Anna Metterza*. How can we correlate the depiction of a current theological topic with the uniqueness of a, so to speak, accidental combination of unconscious factors in the artist's repressed, the author seems to ask. And, indeed, if Vasari was right in his 1568 account

[10] I owe thanks to Miss R. B. Green, Director of Christian Art, Department of Art and Archaeology, Princeton University, who informed me of twelve Anna Metterza representations in Italy prior to 1400. When I raised the question of the coetaneity of Anne and Mary in these paintings she answered: "Of these, the Boston panel shows Anne and Mary as the same size, but we cannot say whether they are about the same age because the group is so small. Elsewhere there is usually a distinct difference in size and therefore an assumed difference in age. The two are perhaps most nearly alike in facial features in the polyptych in Siena [our Plate 4], but here too the small size of Mary implies that she is much the younger of the two." I feel, of course, particularly pleased by the last sentence since this confirmed a view I had formed myself.

that the painting of the picture came about because Leonardo returned to Florence just at a time when "the Servite friars had allotted to Filippino the picture of the high altar of the Annunziata,"[11] one may easily think that the choice of subject was imposed upon Leonardo by those who commissioned it and therefore is devoid of any connection with the artist's repressed conflicts. Even if this were the correct history of the painting's origin, the conclusion would not be rigorous; we would have to recall what Freud said about *Macbeth*, which "was written as an occasional drama on the accession of the King who first united in his person the crowns of the three kingdoms. But does this historical occasion cover the whole content of the drama, or explain its grandeur and its mystery?" (1916-17, p. 86). One has to repeat this argument *mutatis mutandis* in dealing with Schapiro's historical objections.

Whether or not Freud was adequately informed about the doctrine of the history of the Immaculate Conception is of no concern here, because that history, interesting as it is, cannot provide the information necessary to answer the question at issue, namely: What meaning did the *Anna Metterza* have for Leonardo's unconscious?

First the historian conjured up a Leonardo who imitates the ancients when he forms a childhood recollection, who follows Pliny when he is interested in the kite; now we are to assume a Leonardo who copies the paintings of his predecessors, follows their example in detail, and is swayed by the theological disputations of the day. Indeed, at one point our author, when discussing a drawing of Leonardo's in which St. Anne is pictured as an old woman, even goes so far as to write:

> Leonardo's vacillation between the young and the old Anne recalls the uncertainty of the doctrine of the Immaculate Conception during this time. Supported and opposed by various groups, the doctrine won a momentary tolerance by the papacy, only to lose it in the following years [Schapiro, 1956, p. 165].

Here a Leonardo is implied who keeps his ears glued to what the theologians say about St. Anne and, depending on the theological fashion of the day, replaces a young St. Anne with an old one or vice

[11] The correctness of Vasari's claim has been doubted (Douglas, p. 25, and others). It also should not be forgotten that Leonardo occupied his mind with the Anna Metterza subject already in Milan prior to any time when as far as is known he could have been commissioned to paint a picture of that kind.

versa: indeed a most incredible picture of Leonardo. Again we encounter the question of the day residue (a matter of little concern to
Freud at this point), and this time we may be certain that the historian
made a wrong guess. A man whose ear was so subtly attuned to the
ups and downs of theological disputations might, one suspects, have
left a record different from what one finds in his *Notebooks,* which are
strikingly devoid of speculations about hagiography or hagiologic inferences, and one is inclined to look upon correlations such as the author
here suggests as psychological monstrosities.

Apparently Leonardo was preoccupied with the subject of the
Anna Metterza over many years. He was groping for a solution. The
question of whether St. Anne should show signs of old age or be
close in age to her daughter remained unsettled for quite a while. It is
highly probable that it was through the contact with Mona Lisa that
he found a solution. Thus the general scheme Freud had suggested
regarding the emergence of literary works and which Schapiro (p.
164f.) tries to refute seems to hold true also for the one element in a
work of the visual arts. Freud wrote:

> A strong experience in the present awakens in the creative writer a memory
> of an earlier experience (usually belonging to his childhood) from which
> there now proceeds a wish which finds its fulfilment in the creative work.
> The work itself exhibits elements of the recent provoking occasion as well
> as of the old memory [1908a, p. 151].[12]

Schapiro—and this is perhaps characteristic of the historical approach
when applied to a purely psychological problem—proceeds in general
in a static way. For example, in the case of the *Anna Metterza* he does
not raise the question of whether Freud's theory stands or falls depending on whether Leonardo was truly original in representing the two
saints as of approximately the same age. If it could be proved that
Leonardo was actually original in this, it would, of course, increase
the probability of Freud's thesis. But even if it should turn out that
Leonardo had in this conception Italian predecessors (or predecessors

---

[12] Again I wish to state that the psychoanalytic point of view does not mean overlooking
or neglecting the historical precipitating stimulus, the day residue. If contemporary interest
had not turned at all toward the question of the Immaculate Conception, Leonardo might
not have found this subject, so appropriate for the expression of a specific deep-seated
conflict; it is, of course, also conceivable that a specific historic situation may stimulate a
pattern of conflicts in the repressed which without such external stimulation might have
remained dormant forever. See Freud (1900, p. 560f.) for a similar relationship between
dream, unconscious wish, and day residue.

from wherever else whose work he might have been acquainted with), the question would still remain to be answered why Leonardo followed them and not those who depicted St. Anne as an old woman.[13] Strangely enough, Schapiro takes it for granted that Leonardo was imitating those who assertedly had painted young St. Annes. I think the very raising of this question shows how little psychological bearing the mere enumeration of *predecessors* really has.

Even if the artist is reduced by the historian to an automaton-medium of his predecessors, Western cultural reality has been alive enough to expose every member of the elite—particularly in Leonardo's times—to a variety of influences. Thus the automaton-medium must be left at least a minimum of activity,[14] since in order to act at all he must, we have to assume, make choices within the trends created by the activity of his predecessors.[15]

Schapiro disregards an important fact of psychological historical research. The historian is interested in manifest, objective forces. He can study them in the concrete evidences that have survived. For him, the interpretative factor is reduced to the possible minimum, or,

[13] Muther thought that Leonardo had an aversion against depicting old age (1907, p. 27). Put in this way Muther's statement requires qualification. Leonardo certainly had no aversion against intellectual occupation with the problem of old age, which was included in his topics of research (see Belt, 1952, 1954, 1956), and, no doubt, the depiction of old men was not alien to him either in paintings or drawings. But old women seem to show up rather rarely in his drawings, except in the so-called caricatures, in which aggression is given free rein. From his paintings, the theme of the old woman seems to be banished. In this context the following quotation from Leonardo will be of particular interest: "Old women should be represented with eager, swift, and furious gestures like infernal furies; but the action should be more violent in their arms and head than in their legs" (Richter, Vol. I, p. 341; No. 583; Ash. I 17 v.). Cf. the advice with Leonardo's instruction on the same folio about the manner in which old men should be depicted.

[14] The area of individual creativity left Leonardo by Schapiro will be discussed presently.

[15] Cf. Hildebrandt (1927) for a strong repudiation of the time-honored method used by the historian of art of searching for antecedents. "The genius poses to everyone who dares approach him the cardinal demand to be measured exclusively by his own yardstick. References to borrowings [*Entlehnungen*] are utterly worthless if they are not looked at from the viewpoint of reorganization [*Umgestaltung*]. What the force creating the new has made out of the old motif is what is essential, not the empty fact that such a borrowing occurs" (p. 31). Hildebrandt calls the viewing of the genius as dependent on "influences" "nearsighted philology" (p. 30). In all this Hildebrandt is wrong in principle. As long as the historian is aware of the limited area that is covered by his findings there is no argument between the historical and other methods. Only when he extends that area and sets forth conclusions that cannot possibly be derived from the study of antecedents alone does Hildebrandt's criticism become relevant. It is, by the way, noteworthy that despite the many valuable contributions he made, he failed to accomplish his goal of deriving Leonardo's work from his personality. For the whole range of problems that—to borrow Croce's vocabulary (1901)—may be characterized as the difference between the artist as an *empirical* and an *aesthetic* person, see Kris's exemplary study of Franz Xaver Messerschmidt (Kris, 1933).

at any rate, applies to a level different from the psychological. In principle, the result of his research could be validated if he could be made a contemporary of the time period into which he is inquiring. The analyst, on the other hand, is trying to unearth a factor that—since it is presumed to be unconscious—would be denied by the object of his investigation. If we could interview Leonardo himself, we probably would not get those answers that might decide whether Freud was right or wrong as to most of his conclusions, whereas most of the problems raised by Schapiro fall within the area in which the subject is in principle capable of deciding what the correct answer is. Even this, of course, is true only to a limited extent, since the genius is often unaware also of the specific historical influence to which he was reacting. Further, the difficulty that Freud would have encountered in a suppositious interview with Leonardo is the very difficulty that he had to face when he sought to convince the reader of 1910.

Much that today will be taken as self-evident because it has been set before us in so many instances still had to have its probability demonstrated in 1910, partly because it is in the very nature of unconscious factors that they cannot be exhibited concretely, and partly because some time must pass for the demonstration to sink in. When Freud read in Muther that the coetaneity of the two saints was original with Leonardo (which probably is correct, as I have tried to prove), it was a welcome additional confirmation of his hypothesis. Would he have dropped his theory if Muther had held Schapiro's opinion, that that element was traditional? I doubt that he would. I rather suppose that he would have drawn the same conclusion from the fact of Leonardo's choosing to follow the one tradition as against the other. I am aware that when the analyst reasons in such a way he risks being considered obstinate, dogmatic, and prejudiced. When the vulture turned out to be a kite we insisted that it did not disprove the genetic connection of the recollection with homosexuality, and now when there is called into question the originality of an element in the *Anna Metterza* upon which Freud based his conclusion we still maintain that Freud's reconstruction may be correct or, at least, is not touched upon essentially by a vastly different historical opinion.

I have now to qualify my earlier criticism that the historian's image of the genius Leonardo amounts to that of an automaton-medium. Schapiro finds Leonardo's *Anna Metterza* original in two respects:

first in an iconographic detail, and second in matters of style (which will be taken up in the next section).

The iconographic detail referred to is the replacement of the infant St. John, who still figures in the London cartoon, with the lamb in the Servite cartoon and in the Louvre painting. Schapiro cites Pietro da Novellara's letter (Goldscheider, 1944, p. 19, No. xi) to prove that this element had its due effect upon Leonardo's contemporaries.[16] Schapiro asks whether, "in this image of the fatherless Holy Family, Leonardo does not project (and conceal) a narcissistic and homosexual wish in replacing the figure of Christ's playmate John—an ascetic and the victim of an incestuous woman—by the lamb which stands for both John and himself" (1956, p. 170). It is not quite clear how the author wants this interpretation to be understood. In order to obtain a psychological understanding of this element in terms of psychoanalysis, one would, in my opinion, have to view it in a broader context than Schapiro does. One would have to recall the *Virgin of the Rocks* (Plate 5), painted earlier than *Anna Metterza* (between 1483 and 1490), where the St. John child is embraced by the Virgin, and the Christ child, blessing his little relative, sits at some distance from his mother. It was unusual to arrange the children in such a way.[17]

Thus the following sequence is encountered. In the *Virgin of the Rocks* the St. John is quite close to Mary; in the London cartoon, the Christ child is between his mother and John; and in the final *Metterza* John has disappeared, but the Christ child strives away from the mother and turns toward the lamb. Such a sequence can be brought into a meaningful connection with the problems that grow out of a child's conflicts and fantasies about his position in the family, his acceptance or rejection, in short, the range of problems that Freud made the center of his inquiry.

This longitudinal view sounds like the biographical record of a child that gradually loses his mother, when one follows up John; it sounds like the gradual gain of a mother when the record is viewed from the position of the Christ child. Depending on how broad an area one tries to include in the interpretation, such as the possibility

---

[16] However, from this reaction alone no reliable conclusions can be drawn regarding the artist's motives or intentions.

[17] For the iconography of St. John, see Lavin (1955). It is not clear from the article whether the closeness of St. John, rather than of the Christ child, to Mary appeared for the first time in the Leonardo painting.

that St. Anne is adumbrated in the earlier painting of the *Virgin of the Rocks* in the figure of the angel, other far-reaching perspectives are opened. Be this as it may, Schapiro's interpretative suggestion which I have recorded above gives occasion for an instructive observation. For in this instance it is he who risks the frowns of the historian, who may reproach him for not having studied Renaissance iconography sufficiently. The historian might point out that Leonardo left Florence in 1482 and therefore missed a stage in the development of the meaning of St. John that culminated in the view that he shared with Christ the foreknowledge of the Passion. When he returned to Florence in 1500 and became acquainted with this development an abrupt change took place in his drawings and a lamb was substituted for the saint.[18] Here again we see the historian apparently bringing to naught a psychological insight, this time one suggested by a historian.

It also strikes me that Schapiro's implied interpretation of the lamb and Freud's interpretation of the two mothers are not so very much apart. Schapiro's reasoning sounds like saying Freud was wrong or unjustified in drawing certain conclusions from certain elements, but the same conclusions can be reached by use of a different element. Thus Freud was, after all, correct in connecting the painting with Leonardo's homosexuality, that is to say, with a well-circumscribed attitude toward the mother and other males, and one wonders why the author had to make this detour and criticize Freud before suggesting by a different series of conclusions the same point he first objected to.

[18] For this iconographic remark, see Lavin (1955, p. 99).

5

Problems of Form and Style

When one points to features of style and form as a second area in which Leonardo was original one may easily anticipate that here at last an area of agreement has been reached between the psychologist and the historian. For surely it is a matter of general agreement that Leonardo was one of the greatest painters and this implicitly assures him a place as an originator of style and form.

If I nevertheless discuss here questions of style and form, I do so because of a general issue involved. For in this area also Schapiro has drawn conclusions that purport to militate against Freud's reconstruction and in addition makes an unwarranted attack against the late Dr. Ernst Kris.

I wish to start with the latter point.

Kris, uniting an outstanding psychoanalytic career and a no less outstanding reputation as a historian of art, was in a unique position to add a comment upon Freud's *Leonardo* study. He wrote:

> The child [Leonardo] raised by two mothers—the peasant mother and the wife of his father, in whose house he grew up—was stimulated to unite almost for the first time in Italian painting the Virgin and St. Anne with the infant Christ. Unity between the three was established not only by gestures; they seem to merge into each other since they are inscribed into a pyramidal configuration [Kris, 1952, p. 19].

Whether one agrees with Kris's suggestion or not, one has to reason in a truly astonishing way, as I shall presently show, in order to call it "a lapse in historical and aesthetic understanding" (Schapiro, 1956, p. 171).

One may take issue with Kris as to whether Leonardo united "almost for the first time in Italian painting" the three holy personages, depending on what numerical value one feels entitled to attach to the word "almost."[1] Be this as it may, Schapiro's criticism of a lapse in understanding is not directed at this point but at Kris's allegedly claiming that Leonardo invented "the pyramidal form as such" (p. 171). As we shall presently see, this would not have been Kris's claim particularly, since representative scholars of Renaissance art, whose opinions Schapiro ignores, agree upon Leonardo's contribution to Occidental painting by introducing the pyramidal form.

Kris was in this context primarily interested in the psychological nexus. I think this becomes clear also from a subsequent statement of his regarding the quest for a psychoanalysis of style when, returning to Leonardo's St. Anne painting, he is in search of a childhood experience in which "the construction of a pyramidal unit into which the figures are made to fit" (Kris, 1952, p. 20) might have been rooted. He was, of course, all the more justified in raising this question on this particular occasion since Leonardo achieved here one of his greatest original artistic contributions. Schapiro contests this—without justification, as I subsequently demonstrate. Sir Kenneth Clark (1939) writes: "He [Leonardo] has *discovered* the secret of that pyramidal composition which became an academic dogma of the high Renaissance" (p. 22; italics added). And Heydenreich (1954) warns against "overlooking the actual principle of composition here promulgated *for the first time:* . . . the group built up in an entirely new way, three-dimensional, plastic and spatial" (Vol. I, p. 43; italics added). Popp (1928), when comparing Leonardo's art with Michelangelo's, praises the former for having been the first who found the means of unifying groups by subsuming several figures into the geometrical figure of the pyramid, as documented in the *Anna Metterza* (p. 24). Also, what Max Dvořák said in his lectures on the history of Italian Renaissance art leaves no doubt that he regarded Leonardo as the inventor of the pyramidal form in Italian painting (1918-19, p. 189). Dvořák even

[1] See my previous reference to Dvořák and Heydenreich.

went further and asserted that Leonardo introduced the triangular composition. Thus he wrote that in Leonardo's *Adoration of the Kings*, the Madonna and the three kings form a triangle "the *first* [italics added] somewhat loose example of triangle composition that later changes into the pyramid composition [*Das erste noch etwas lockere Beispiel der Dreieckkomposition, die sich später in die Pyramiden- komposition verwandelt*]" (p. 150).[2] Thus Kris would have been amply justified in regarding Leonardo as the originator of the pyramidal com- position in Renaissance painting.

In order to prove his point, Schapiro contends that the pyramidal configuration was traditional in Italian painting, and he cites the *Anna Metterza* of Masaccio (1401-1428) in the Uffizi Gallery (Plate 6). However, as anyone who looks at a reproduction of that painting will agree, the group is composed in the shape of a vertical, oblong rectangle ending in a triangle. It is all the more remarkable that Schapiro should attribute a pyramidal composition to Masaccio for the author he cites expressly states that Leonardo was original in that respect in his *Anna Metterza*. Heydenreich, in a special study (1933), described the Masaccio type of *Anna Metterza* as "un groupe de person- nages étagés l'un derrière l'autre" [a group of persons stepwise one behind the other] (p. 216). The other traditional type of *Anna Metterza* Heydenreich finds well presented in Gozzoli's *Anna Metterza* (Plate 7) which, as he says, shows "des personnages alignés" [persons lined up]. He expressly says that Leonardo created "un type inédit" [a new type]. Evidently Heydenreich too, in this special study, regards the pyramidal configuration as new in Italian Anna Metterza paintings, for he criticizes Wölfflin, with whom he otherwise agrees, for describ- ing Leonardo's composition only as a triangle (Wölfflin, 1899, p. 33). Thus Schapiro could construe a lapse in Kris's remark only by arbi- trarily describing a rectangular arrangement of the personages as pyramidal.[3] Indeed one is hardly able to find a disagreement between Kris and representative historians of art, aside from Schapiro, so far as the formal aspects of Leonardo's painting are concerned.[4]

[2] However, Dvořák finds the pyramid composition already in the *Virgin of the Rocks* (p. 176) and sees in the *Anna Metterza* only its further development to a firmer structure (p. 189).

[3] Is this the root of the author's slip in writing that Masaccio's *Anna Metterza* is in Santa Maria Novella instead of the Uffizi Gallery?

[4] As a concluding remark I wish to point to a characteristic of the humanities, namely, the margin of ambiguity that is inherent in the basic concepts they use, in contrast to the

To return to the former of the two points cited earlier, Schapiro seems to hold it against Freud that he "ignored" (p. 167) the factor of form and style. Schapiro finds the true original feature of Leonardo's *Anna Metterza* in the way movement is represented: movement of the single personage in the relationship of limb to body, and movement that flows and counterflows throughout the whole group. As far as I can see, Schapiro in this proposition is approximately following Wölfflin's text (1899, p. 33f.), which was available and well known in 1910 when Freud published the *Leonardo* study. Accordingly I believe the author is mistaken when he writes that Freud "ignored" these features. No doubt they are not included in Freud's study although they must have been well known to him. The reason for this omission is self-evident: these features were not and still are not accessible to psychological analysis. It is not evident why the author was surprised at their absence from Freud's essay.

The stylistic question raised by Schapiro attains importance in view of his endeavor to take the *Anna Metterza* out of the context of Leonardo's previous representations of the Holy Family. He regards the *Anna Metterza* as an attempt on Leonardo's part to go a step beyond what was accomplished in the *Last Supper* (Plate 8). He does this by finding a similarity between one of the apostle groups in the *Last Supper* and the *Anna Metterza* group. Dvořák, on the other hand, clearly draws a genetic line from the *Adoration of the Kings* through the *Virgin of the Rocks* to *Anna Metterza* without neglecting the *Cenacolo* (1918-19, p. 189). To be sure, if a correlation does exist between stylistic development and choice of maternal themes, it may be made the basis of an argument for or against Freud's thesis. I personally believe that such correlations are not decisive. Even if Schapiro were right in his linking of "a work which has nothing to do with a maternal theme" (p. 172) with *Anna Metterza*, this would not necessarily have any bearing on the reconstruction of the painting's psychological meaning.

We are at this point in the midst of a discussion of the psychology of artistic forms. If Schapiro were right that the stylistic closeness of

---

natural sciences, whose basic concepts, though also vague at the beginning, become precisely defined as those sciences advance. Thus, I can imagine that a scholar may one day "detect," so to speak, a pyramid in Masaccio's *Anna Metterza*, but then he would have to coin a term to characterize the new compositional pattern introduced by Leonardo.

Anna Metterza to the *Last Supper* speaks against the assumption that the maternal meaning of the former also has psychological relevance, then we would have to assume a parallelism between form and psychological function. It may turn out that this parallelism actually exists in some or all instances, and if it does it will facilitate immensely research in the field of the psychology of art. Such a correlation, however, has not yet been proved, and, as I have said, I doubt it will. Is the merging of a family in a pyramid form a reliable sign of a corresponding psychological unity in the artist, as Kris might have felt inclined to assume?[5] Does the articulation of contrasts through which conflicting impulses were represented within a compact group demonstrate a corresponding psychological content, the members of the family being at variance but still held together by the traditional family form as Schapiro suggests (p. 172)? Freud himself perhaps came close to applying the same method when he interpreted the relations between the two female bodies in the London cartoon and in the Louvre painting, but his remarks can still perhaps be considered as referring to content, or, at least, to an element of perception that is measurable and simpler than the elusive element of style. Freud correlated only degrees of clarity of perceptual contents with states of fusion or diffusion of imagery.

In a psychological analysis of style, it must also be considered that experts differ vastly on questions of style; in many instances the forms of personal renderings resist even description. These difficulties may be overcome by the evolvement of techniques more subtle than the current ones. Yet even if agreement on points of form and style should be achieved, will this facilitate psychological research? The psychologist can only proceed in a point-by-point fashion, take a formal point out of the ensemble, and deductively correlate it with a psychological trait. The key by means of which he can establish these correlations remains always the similarity of terminology: what is unity or disparity here is supposed to coincide with what we call unity or disparity there. This is a questionable procedure. In some instances the identity of terms may coincide with identity of the referents, in others not. In other words, I do not yet see the possibility of obtaining evidence as to the correctness of the key by means of which we are to convert properties of form and style into psychological data.

[5] For Kris's attitude toward the problem of psychology of style, see later.

Kris put this problem into precise terms. He was fully aware that "the psychology of artistic style is unwritten," and anticipated the tremendous ingenuity and labor that would be necessary if the task was ever to be accomplished. The method of choice would be to break with the traditional division of form and content and establish their interrelation, following the pattern Freud set in transforming formal characteristics of the dream into latent dream thoughts. Kris suggested such an example but withdrew it because of the absence of specific evidence (1952, p. 22). He suggested that possibly Leonardo's inserting figures into a superimposed geometrical body, as in the *Anna Metterza*, may be meaningfully connected with his interest in procreation and pregnancy. Now, it is striking that Raymond Stites (1948b) claims to have discovered below St. Anne's right foot the depiction of at least one and possibly several fetuses in various stages of development. I have not been able personally to confirm this discovery, and of course one feels overcautious after Pfister's claim to have discovered the "vulture" of Leonardo's cover memory in the shape of a puzzle picture in the clothing of St. Mary (1913, pp. 145-151). But I wonder whether, if Stites's discovery should be confirmed, this would be the specific evidence Kris was searching for and whether we may here at last behold a well-documented instance of a psychoanalytic explanation of a formal quality by the use of content. It is far from my mind to think here of a conscious nexus. The theme of *Anna Metterza* per se would supply enough reason to tempt an artist to slip in unnoticed the trace of an embryo, since the general subject matter is the succession of generations, that awe-inspiring providential law of nature which makes mankind capable of spanning what impresses the individual as eternity—a law in which the embryo plays no minor role. It would be well in keeping with Leonardo's distrust in the detail of Christian dogma if he set his knowledge of the biology of nature in contrast to the providential aspect that fills the ostensible content of the painting.

Withal, we see how much alive the problems still are that Freud raised half a century ago in trying to explain the psychological background of Leonardo's *Anna Metterza*, and one is impressed by the broad realm of originality (formal as well as substantial) that is contained in that painting but which the historian of art tried unduly to retrench.

As said before, even if the painting were, in this degree, not original, it would by no means disprove Freud's construct, but the actual broadness found and attested to by eminent scholars increases the degree of its probability.

If we examine this problem in a broader context, we may venture to say the following: the historian of art will try to explain the novel content of a painting as being correlated to the specific phase of the painter's artistic development. Of course, in the development of all great painters (and most of the less than great ones) the more or less gradual or abrupt evolvement and solution of purely artistic problems can be traced. I think there is no area of disagreement here. Although we do not know what Leonardo was consciously thinking of when he worked on his various *Metterza* versions, we may rest assured he did not plan to elaborate on his various childhood mothers, but was probably intensely absorbed in problems of light and shade, movement, spatial presentation, and allied matters. Does this exclude the bearing of childhood conflicts on the painting? I believe the historian overlooks the interplay of the personal and the artistic spheres. One artistic phase may facilitate the expression of one group of conflicts and the subsequent one may activate a quite different group. Since the axis of Freud's study was the follow-up of one specific childhood recollection, he did not have to deal with this type of problem.

We encounter here a score of unresolved problems. Does the personal conflict steer the artistic problem or vice versa?[6] Can the purely artistic problem be so intense that it overrules any influence of the personal conflict? Does the artistic factor have the power to activate a suitable personal one? It would be folly to try to speculate upon such questions without a careful clinical examination, but this much may tentatively be said: in the genius, the two are probably blended (cf. Bychowski, 1951), and if anyone has supposed that Leonardo as an artist was nothing but the medium of a series of artistic problems, he has misunderstood. The creation of art is, after all, a live process and therefore *must* be nourished from the unconscious. The unconscious itself—the id and the repressed to be more exact—however, are not yet tinged by aesthetics but deal with contents and archaic impulses.

Be this as it may, Schapiro raises in this context two problems that I will elaborate upon. In a footnote added in 1919, Freud stated that

[6] Kris (1933) in his study of Franz Xaver Messerschmidt (1736-1783) made a valuable contribution to this problem.

the expert may feel disinclined to follow his thesis about the bearing of the artist's subjective background upon the smile of *Mona Lisa,* in view of a similar smile in archaic Greek sculptures or in figures painted by Leonardo's teacher Verrocchio (Freud, 1910, p. 107).[7] Schapiro takes this footnote as an indication that Freud "was aware of the weakness of his reasoning" (p. 165).

It would, however, have been unusual for Freud to have written this footnote on such a basis, for he was always quite candid when time had made him insecure about a past conviction. I rather think the footnote asserts the strength of Freud's conviction regarding the correctness of his reconstruction, which he apparently continued to maintain despite the objection he anticipated or had actually met. Indeed, Freud cannot have meant to assert the depiction of *smile* in general has the function he attributed to it in the instance of the *Mona Lisa;* he says clearly that he is concerned with the *Leonardesque* smile (1910, p. 107). Thus I think Freud had in mind exactly what Schapiro seems to miss when he writes: "Only his [Leonardo's] personal rendering of the inherited smile, its singular qualities which depend on the artist's style . . . may be referred to Leonardo's character" (p. 166).[8]

When Clark (1935) writes: "A style is like a smell and can only be described in terms of itself. The visible acts are without the technical vocabulary of music or the symbols of mathematics, and their effects can only be conveyed by cumbersome analogies" (p. 24), he clearly states the reasons why Freud could not, in describing the *Mona Lisa* smile, go beyond "the terms of itself."

Yet Freud in his attempt to explain why a smile appears in the *Mona Lisa* portrait and to trace the genesis of this element has not really explained a point of style. The smile *and* the way it was painted by

[7] Christensen (1944) discusses outside influences without questioning Freud's basic assumptions. However, he thinks "of the delicately blissful expression of the Madonna of French Gothic sculpture, coming to Leonardo through its reflection in the Pisano tradition" (p. 158).

[8] Schapiro's stress on the historical antecedents of the Leonardesque smile loses even more of its ostensible relevance in view of Dvořák's setting forth the difference in meaning of the Greek-archaic and early Gothic smile from the Leonardesque (1918-19, p. 192). I believe that such differentiation is also possible regarding the smile found in Verrocchio's *œuvre.* At least, one is entitled to say that the smile in the teacher's work is not identical with the one found in Leonardo's work from the *Mona Lisa* on. Moreover, in paintings of the young Leonardo that are preserved, a smile appears in the countenance of Madonnas, but there also a distinctive difference from the later rendering is observed. For a discussion of the various types of smiles in art, see Kris (1939).

Leonardo are an inseparable unit. The psychoanalytic interpretation aims in this instance at a unit which includes Leonardo's personal rendering of the smile, which is covered by the term *Leonardesque*. As far as form and style are concerned, the smile could, in principle, have been painted in several different ways. The actual style in which Leonardo painted it grew out of what cursorily may be called his genius, his personal talent that made him capable of rendering the smile in a way that made it part of the most famous portrait in the world. We thus have the *impulse* or the personal necessity to paint a certain smile and the *medium* through which the impulse, the intention, the wish, will be realized. In the end product the content and the medium form an entity, both still accessible to separation by logical analysis. The psychoanalytic interpretation refers to the total configuration, smile, as rendered at certain points of Leonardo's artistic development, but it cannot say what the specific causes were of Leonardo's specific selection of medium through which he concretized the specific image, beyond the bearing of a specific event in his life history.

The second point to be discussed here is a clinical one. Schapiro writes:

> This complex quality of the whole [the smile] may well depend on structures of Leonardo's character disclosed by Freud. It may be, too, that the artist adopted and developed the existing theme of the smile with a special ardor because of the fixation upon his mother. But Freud's theory provides no bridge from the infantile experience and the mechanisms of psychic development to the style of Leonardo's art. In Freud's book the original elements of the work of art are simply representations of childhood memories and wishes; . . . in writing of the smile, Freud does not hesitate to infer an exact accord of the painting and the infantile impression underneath all the modalities of the smile in different pictures [p. 166f.].

The author misses in Freud's study, so to speak, the internal psychic metabolism, that is to say, the series of psychic processes that link the early impression with its later effect or effects as manifested in the work of art.

Indeed, just the section in which Freud discusses the *Mona Lisa* problem is introduced by a general statement on "the profound transformations through which an impression in an artist's life has to pass before it is allowed to make its contribution to a work of art" (1910, p. 107), a transformation that is not discussed or hypostasized by Freud in the case of the smile. To be sure, the smile of the Gioconda and the smile of the mother are set into direct correlation in Freud's study. Whether Freud thought the two were identical or whether he thought the one stimulated the memory of the other and both were then fused, or that the various modalities of the smile as they appear in Leonardo's paintings were approximations toward the original childhood memories—or that any other possible connections may have existed—cannot be decided. I think that Freud was mainly concerned at that time to demonstrate that a connection existed between the two at all, and I do not know what facets of the problem would have been made the center of his study had he written it twenty years later, or what he thought about the question when his interests centered in ego psychology.

However, Schapiro's question is a clinical one: do childhood impressions find direct representation in works of art? We shall not be able to find an answer regarding the smile of *Mona Lisa*, but I wish to adduce a comparable instance that appears well documented.

In reading and rereading Goethe's *Werther* I have been struck each time by a certain sentence that impressed me as the peak of the whole novel. This is a sentence in the letter in which for the first time the tragic lover lets Lotte, the married woman with whom he is hopelessly in love, know that he is going to commit suicide.

> When you climb up the hill on a fine summer evening, then remember me as I so often came up the valley, and then throw a glance over there to the churchyard to my grave, how the wind rocks the high grass now this way, now that, in the glow of the sinking sun [*Wenn du hinauf steigst auf den Berg, an einem schönen Sommerabende, dann erinnere dich meiner, wie ich so oft das Thal herauf kam, und dann blicke nach dem Kirchhofe hinüber nach meinem Grabe, wie der Wind das hohe Gras im Scheine der sinkenden Sonne hin- und herwiegt*] [Goethe, 1774, p. 160].

The sentence is of an incredible tragic power. The vividness is compelling. The finality of Werther's existence, the despair of the youth about the necessity of having to leave life without the consummation of its bliss, the anticipation of the beloved woman's beholding his grave, all this is joined together in the simplest language possible and creates in the reader a feeling of almost unbearable sadness. When subjected to the effect of this passage it never dawned upon me that the infantile root of this overpowering element could ever be discovered.

In the first book of his autobiographical novel, *Dichtung und Wahrheit*, Goethe reports that as a child he learned by heart, before he understood the words, the aria *Solitario bosco ombroso* ["Solitary, shaded grove"]. In most editions of Goethe's works this aria is wrongly attributed to Metastasio. Therefore I was unable to find it and establish its content until Professor Levarie luckily solved the problem.[9] It takes us with surprising directness to the sentence quoted from Goethe's *Werther*. It is the song of an unhappy lover who takes refuge in a grove. Nothing pleases him, he has lost his peace of mind, he hates himself. Is Phyllis perhaps here? He looks for her everywhere, etc. He hears a noise and thinks for a moment it could be Phyllis.

> Ah, it is the sound of the river that shatters
> Among these stones its cool liquid,
> And does not murmur, but weeps,
> Out of pity for my sorrow.
> But if she returns in vain and belated
> Will the return be and the pity;
> How piteously her sweet regard
> Will weep over my ashes [literal translation by Seymour A. Copstein].

I do not hesitate to infer a direct connection between this aria heard by Goethe in early childhood and the sentence in the novel of the adult. Since it was Goethe's mother that he heard sing the aria and she seemed to do so only reluctantly in order to comply with his father, who was trying to develop her talents, the oedipal background of the sentence under discussion can be reconstructed with fair accuracy. The two contents are surprisingly similar and the internal psychic metabolism almost nil. It seems that in this masterpiece just the leading element from which the strongest effect issues is directly connected with a highly charged infantile experience. Surprisingly enough the impression was obtained by the child at a time when ego functions were still poorly developed—the child allegedly did not understand the meaning of the words—which possibly increases the similarity with Freud's thesis regarding the smile of the *Mona Lisa*. But again the psychoanalyst is at a loss to explain the form in which the childhood recollection found its expression by the adult writer. The sentence

[9] It is a canzonetta by Paolo Rolli (1687-1765). See Levarie (1957).

does not sound very impressive in its English translation, but the German original is superb, as I said before. Despite its simplicity of structure an incredibly large number of images is condensed into it. There is particular richness of spatial directions and time dimensions. Although this example has no bearing on the visual arts in general and on the smile of the *Mona Lisa* in particular, it may still serve as a warning against the rejection of Freud's claim that an artistic element may be the direct representative of an early childhood impression.[10]

As correct as Schapiro is in raising the question of form, that is, of the formal qualities that endow the painting of a smile with such an incredible effect, the question that the psychologist raises regarding the fact that it has this effect is just as valid. It seems that—at least with the wane of medieval times—art that elicits in the beholder a profound agitation has to grow from deep, if not from the deepest, layers of the artist himself. To be sure, not all that comes from the bottom of the repressed has this effect—something, the formal excellence, has to be added; it will take a long time before, if ever, this aspect as well finds its psychological explanation. But it appears to me that Freud may in 1910 have intuitively grasped what future research will perhaps confirm in incidents more opportune for documented proof than the smile of the *Mona Lisa*: that just those elements in a work of art—whether visual, literary, or musical—that have an overwhelming effect are direct, that is, scarcely transformed, representatives of crucial, early childhood impressions.[11]

---

[10] We are also accustomed to find sometimes in a neurotic symptom an almost undisguised repetition of an early childhood experience. Freud (1920b) recorded a childhood experience of his own that was transposed almost directly into one of his greatest scientific discoveries. He was even able to trace a scientific term that he considered original with him to something he had read at the age of fourteen.

[11] Here the difference of perspectives of the historical and psychological disciplines may come out with particular sharpness: the historian, and probably rightly so, will emphasize the difference between the last two strophes of a more or less lame canzonetta that the ardent fantasy of the boy filled with his personal imagery, and the superbly styled sentence of the adult, whereas the psychoanalyst will emphasize *the almost identical* contents.

6

The Historian's vs. the Psychoanalyst's Conception of Man

Of greater interest perhaps than the difference of opinion about the recondite problem inherent in Leonardo's *Anna Metterza* will be an examination of the psychoanalytic conception of man, as far as that can be discerned in the Leonardo study, and how this conception deviates from the historian's. A glimpse of the difference was afforded earlier. In the final section of his essay Freud gives a summary picture of some trends in Leonardo's psychosexual development. It is a genetic synthesis of the many inquiries into biographical details and character traits he had gathered in previous sections. The historian rejects not only Freud's explanations of the biographical detail but also most if not all of Freud's analysis of character traits (cf. also for what follows Hartmann, Kris, and Loewenstein, 1951).

For Freud, man is a system in conflict. The principal question is: what is the origin and nature of the conflicting forces and what is the outcome? He uncovers in Leonardo the conflict about massive sadistic (aggressive) impulses. These were partly absorbed in strong reaction formations, such as pity and orderliness. In many instances of Leonardo's type the reaction formations do not absorb the total aggression, or are not constantly effective. Thus Freud was able to show in

Leonardo manifestations of both—of reaction formations as well as of the sadistic-aggressive drive. As an example of the former Freud cited among others Leonardo's vegetarianism and the enjoyment he derived from returning birds he bought on the market to liberty; as examples of the latter, he cited Leonardo's accompanying condemned criminals to the place of execution in order to study their facial expressions, his devising the cruelest weapons of attack, and his participation in Cesare Borgia's brutal military campaigns.[1]

At this point the fundamental issue between history of art and psychoanalysis shows up with impressive clarity. Schapiro seems to doubt that Leonardo's kindness to animals is a sign of repressed sadistic feelings. He reports a superstition prevalent in Paris where people of all walks bought birds on the market and freed them, "a magic sacrifice that promised success, whether in love or business or examinations." Leonardo's abstention from animal flesh Schapiro proposes to explain "as a medical belief, sustained by philosophical conviction"; it was inspired perhaps by ancient authors in vogue among the Florentine Neoplatonists: "He might have read in Porphyry's treatise *De Abstinentia ab Esu Animalium* (IV, 16) that the wisest of the Persian magi abstained from meat" (Schapiro, 1956, p. 175).

Thus, as earlier, the motives given are, on the one hand, participation in a group superstition, and, on the other, imitation of an ancient philosopher! Here we notice the total failure to perceive man in his conflicts but the reduction of man to the mirror of custom and tradition. Is it really conceivable that Leonardo after reading Porphyry's treatise closes the book and decides not to eat meat from now on because the philosopher has so advised? This is a papier-mâché Leonardo, a puppet of his book-learning devoid of individual life.

It seems his contemporaries took Leonardo's behavior as quite remarkable and unusual. There is a letter preserved written from India in 1515 by Andrea Corsali to Giuliano de' Medici. He wrote:

[1] The historian also reproached Freud for "ignoring" many of Leonardo's paintings and drawings. An inquiry into Leonardo's total artistic work was, of course, beyond Freud's intention. His principal aim, inasmuch as it referred to Leonardo's artistic work, was to pursue the psychological history of one element. It is not evident whether the historian believes that the corresponding history of other works would have disproved Freud's main thesis. In one point which Freud could easily have fulfilled Schapiro is correct: Freud might have included in his study Leonardo's relationship to his teacher Verrocchio. As far as I can see such an analysis would have complemented and supported Freud's analysis of Leonardo's relationship to his father and to Lodovico il Moro, his patron.

Certain infidels called Guzzarati do not feed upon anything that contains blood, nor do they permit among them that any injury be done to any living thing, like our Leonardo da Vinci [*Alcuni gentili chiamati Guzzarati non si cibano di cosa alcuna che tenga sangue, nè fra essi loro consentono che si noccia ad alcuna cosa animata, come il nostro Leonardo da Vinci*] [Richter, Vol. II, p. 103f., n. to No. 844].

Thus Leonardo's contemporary thousands of miles away from Florence was struck by a resemblance between Leonardo and a people that appeared quite strange to him because of its particular abstemiousness from aggressive behavior.[2]

Oddly enough, a document is preserved that confirms Freud's suggestion that in some of Leonardo's attitudes we may see the reaction formation against strong sadistic impulses. Among Leonardo's *Notes* the following address to Man is found:

King of animals—as thou hast described him—I should rather say King of the beasts, thou being the greatest—because thou dost only help them, in order that they may give thee their children for the benefit of the gullet, of which thou hast attempted to make a sepulchre for all animals [Richter, Vol. II, p. 103f. No. 844].

However much preceding literary sources may have contributed to such a gruesome entry, the man who wrote it, unless a mere copyist, was involved in a severe oral-sadistic conflict. When the mouth becomes "the sepulchre for all animals" a depression is present or is to be warded off.

The gulf that separates the two disciplines is broad and clear cut, in the enumerated instances. In turning to the problem of Leonardo's sexuality we are bound to encounter new ones. There is in the first line Freud's contention that Leonardo felt an aversion against the physically sexual, a conclusion he based on known facts of Leonardo's life (the absence of any evidence of an amorous attachment to a female), a direct statement of Leonardo's regarding the disgust aroused in him by the act of procreation, and the absence of the erotic and obscene in his *Notebooks*.[3]

2 This letter also demonstrates that Freud's concept of the Renaissance for which he is castigated by Schapiro was after all not wrong. Cf. Freud (1910, p. 68f.) and Schapiro (1956, p. 158). Cf. also Burckhardt (1860, p. 279), where a view similar to Freud's is expressed.
3 I will later adduce still other evidence that confirms Freud's statement.

Here the historian falls into captious remarks inasmuch as he attributes to Freud the "statement that Leonardo betrays an extreme repression in his total avoidance of erotic subjects" (Schapiro, p. 175), a claim Freud never made since he limited his remark to Leonardo's *Notebooks,* I presume on the tacit assumption that in these papers "free association" had the best chance to manifest itself.

At any rate, the historian points to Leonardo's *Leda* and *Saint Jerome* paintings as erotic subjects and thus raises the interesting problem of what in art is erotic. Although the Leda subject may be called erotic inasmuch as its traditional representation depicts a nude female body, it is only necessary to compare Leonardo's drawings and the copy of his painting with depictions of the same subject by other painters (such as that attributed to Michelangelo [Plate 26] or the corresponding painting by Correggio) to assert a certain reduction of the directly erotic element in Leonardo's painting. Of course, the point is debatable in the absence of an objective frame of reference.[4]

On the other hand, as Freud pointed out, the *Mona Lisa* may be regarded as one of the greatest Occidental achievements of erotic art. It would be a mechanical approach to equate the nude and the erotic. From this point of view one feels inclined, of course, to find in Leonardo's *Saint Jerome* strong erotic elements, although it definitely is not an erotic subject. Indeed, the inseparableness of sexual excitement, repentance, and, to a certain extent, disgust which, according to my way of seeing the painting, is encountered in the depiction of St. Jerome's face is incomparable (Plate 9). Yet ought it not be of general significance that Leonardo here is the master in representing sexualized defenses? Freud's interests did not run to such subtleties in 1910. Leonardo's *Notebooks* are an intimate record of what attracted his interest and moved his mind. The erotic is unquestionably absent there and that alone is a relevant datum to demonstrate Leonardo's pervasive aversion against sexual aspects.

In a footnote (n. 101, p. 175) Schapiro reminds us of an ancient report referring to Leonardo's lascivious compositions. If this should be confirmed later I do not think it would necessarily refute Freud's thesis. Notwithstanding the greatest aversion against the directly sexual and the formation of strong defenses the instinctual factor may temporarily overpower even the strongest dams. Freud never looked upon

[4] About the *Leda* painting I will have more to say later.

Leonardo as a man lacking in strong drives. He emphasized the necessity of assuming that already as a child he had to deal with particularly unruly passions. The evidence so far available proves the aversion. Whether there were moments when, despite the aversion, Leonardo's sublime art submitted to the lewd, no one can assert or deny at present. In view of observations in a type of genius related in many ways to Leonardo, namely Goethe, I feel inclined to assume that Leonardo was not spared such moments either. Goethe unquestionably had an aversion against sexuality and his "official" work is pervaded by a high degree of chastity even when he is dealing with erotic subjects. Yet his private papers contained some very "lewd" productions.[5] In Goethe's instance, the flow of biographical data being extensive enough, the conditions can be approximately determined under which, despite an unmistakable aversion against the sexual aspect of life, crudity penetrated into his production.

In his study Freud approached a problem that still waits for definite clarification: the quality of instinctual gratification that is optimal for creativity. Two years prior to his *Leonardo* study, Freud had published a definite view on this point. After asserting the individual variability of "the relation between possible sublimation and indispensable sexual activity" he continues:

> An abstinent artist is hardly conceivable; but an abstinent young *savant* is certainly no rarity. The latter can, by his self-restraint, liberate forces for his studies; while the former probably finds his artistic achievements power-fully stimulated by his sexual experience [Freud, 1908b, p. 197].

I do not know whether this view would still be upheld. Yet even if it should turn out to be statistically correct that creative intellectuals tend more toward abstinence than creative artists, this would not necessarily hold true for the genius. What is correct for the talent is not necessarily valid of the genius, since in my estimation the genius is not to be looked upon as a quantitatively enhanced talent but as one different in quality—a view that does not deny that in the talent or in a patient some observations can be made that are valid also of the genius.

---

[5] I omit here a discussion of Goethe's early *Sturm und Drang* period, possibly the equivalent of that phase in Leonardo's life when he was tried for alleged homosexual activities.

Freud links up Leonardo's relative inhibition of artistic creativity (the small number of finished paintings, the increasing and absorbing interest in scientific research) with a state of abstinence in Leonardo, believing that optimal sexual discharge would have favored artistic creation. Yet in view of the perfection of the few creations that have reached us from Leonardo one could also speculate on the possibility that without abstinence the quality of the few paintings would not have been so high. Moderate gratification of the instinctual demand might have resulted in increased production in quantitative terms, so it may be argued, but militated against the supreme quality Leonardo achieved. Only the genius totally deprived of the possibility of physical discharge because of an insuperable inner barrier could throw his total energy into the creative act. To be sure, one may continue to reason, the price to pay may be the qualms and hesitations that beset the artist Leonardo, but this price is not too high in view of the excellence of the result. Schapiro (1956) seems to have something of this kind in mind when he refers to a letter by van Gogh as "a strong statement of a view contrary to Freud's" (p. 176, n. 104). This is a letter van Gogh wrote at the beginning of August, 1888, to his friend Emile Bernard in which he discusses his own sex life and that of other famous painters:

> Personally, I feel that continence is good for me, that it is enough for our weak, impressionable artists' brains to give their essence to the creation of our pictures. For when we reflect, calculate, exhaust ourselves, we spend cerebral energy.
> Why exert ourselves to pour out all creative sap where the well-fed professional pimps and ordinary fools do better in the matter of satisfying the genital organs of the whore, who is in this case more submissive than we ourselves? [Vincent van Gogh, Vol. III, p. 509f.].

So far van Gogh; no doubt, he could not have expressed himself in terms more contradictory to what Freud suggested. Interestingly enough, this was written by van Gogh two years almost to the day prior to his suicide. Yet, in order to evaluate this passage properly problems such as van Gogh's sex life, its bearing on his creativity, and the structure of his psychosis would first have to be cleared away.

Van Gogh knew that his view was not paradigmatic. He added a postscript: "Cézanne is a respectable married man just like the old

Dutchmen; if there is plenty of male potency in his work it is because he does not let it evaporate in merrymaking."

"Not to let it evaporate in merrymaking" seems to be the problem, and van Gogh possibly belonged to a type of artist who, if he indulged in merrymaking, would "let it evaporate" totally and not retain the vigor necessary for virile creations.[6]

Goethe, in whom, as in Leonardo, there was a conflict about the distribution and harmonizing of artistic and scientific strivings, was fortunate inasmuch as he succeeded in obtaining that minimal sexual release[7] which was necessary to avert a catastrophe.

It may seem strange, however, in view of Freud's opinion of 1908 on the effect of abstinence on scientist and artist, that just during a short period of relative sexual liberty Goethe contemplated the possibility of relinquishing the career of writer and poet and becoming, so to speak, a full-time scientist. This apparent contradiction to Freud's hypothesis is resolved by the consideration that abstaining from a gratification and indulging in it may result in similar consequences impropitious for the creation of art, for this requires intense conflicts and either choice may preclude that optimal level of conflict which is conducive to the creation of great art. The problem is more complicated than can be set forth here. Apparently when the index of libidinal tension sinks too low the momentum toward artistic creation is in danger of fading. The problem imposed upon the artistic genius by the sexual drives is really a terrible one if maximum creativity is to be maintained in terms of quantity and quality. The opinions of artists on this topic are, as can well be imagined, divided. An early reference is found in Cennini's *Handbook* (written sometime before 1437 and probably sometime after 1400[8]):

> There is another cause which, if you indulge it, can make your hand so unsteady that it will waver more and flutter far more, than leaves do in the wind, and this is indulging too much in the company of women [p. 16].

Dürer (1471-1528) advises that a student of art should not be allowed to live in the quarters of women, should not see a woman

---

[6] In the letter to Emile Bernard the central question deals with the circumstances that lead to virile artistic creations.

[7] Possibly he had to pay even for this minimal release the price of a partial psychosis.

[8] I owe thanks to Mr. Charles Seymour, Jr., Curator, Renaissance Art, Department of the History of Art, Yale University, for this information.

naked or touch her, since nothing weakens understanding more than impurity (Holt, 1957, p. 309).

An expression of a contrary view can be found in a letter Goethe wrote in 1784 to one of his ducal friends who had unfavorably criticized a painting Goethe had sent him. Goethe confidentially informed the duke that the artist, Johann H. W. Tischbein (1751-1829), had not yet had intercourse.

Had he enjoyed the delights of the female body with body and soul . . . certainly his paintings would breathe more life and lust, and he would not produce puzzling hybrids. [*Hätte er die Reize des weiblichen Körpers mit Leib und Seele genossen, . . . gewiss seine Gemälde würden mehr Leben und Wollust athmen, und er würde keinen räthselhaften Zwitter producieren*].

And a strong expression in favor of the fair sex can be found in Whistler's (1834-1903) literary work (Goldwater and Treves, 1945, p. 350).

I have selected samples at random. A vote might easily show a fifty to fifty division of artists' opinions as to the advisability of genital gratification. Therefore, an enumeration of opinions does not clarify the point and the problem requires a study of the individual instance and an understanding of the structure of the creative personality and its typology.

A comparative study of sex life of geniuses, however, may well confirm one day Freud's view that Leonardo's libidinal economy, though geared to the demands of the highest sublimation, still was weakened in its primary purpose by subjecting the psychic apparatus to a strain that went beyond his capacity to endure. I will have more to add about Leonardo's sexuality in Part II.[9]

There is a view—to be discussed later in detail—that may be adduced as a final argument against Freud's basic concept of Leonardo. The idea seems well founded that for Leonardo knowing an object and depicting it were two aspects of the same thing. How then could one

[9] Freud's views on Leonardo's sexuality have also been questioned by Wohl and Trosman (1955). A large part of their paper is taken up in expounding how wrong Freud's views were on homosexuality. For this purpose they quote many psychoanalytic papers on homosexuality that were published after 1910 without one single reference to Freud's work on homosexuality since that time, thus glossing over the fact that most of the cited views on homosexuality were evolved under the guidance of the progress Freud had made in his general research as well as in that on homosexuality.

construe Leonardo's prevailing turn toward knowledge as a deficit resulting from a defect in instinctual economy, as Freud did? Indeed, for Leonardo perfect knowledge and perfect depiction seem to have been identical, inasmuch as an object can be perfectly depicted only when it is perfectly known, and it is perfectly known only after it has been perfectly represented.[10]

Yet that which in the objective world of human values may be identical may subjectively be quite different. Knowing and depicting may have identical meanings for the subject, but in order to know and to depict quite different subjective functions have to be activated. The distribution of cathexes, after all, has to be different if each of these activities is to lead to equally great achievements.

But the one activity which in addition to the other would, as it seems, only have fulfilled the demand Leonardo imposed on himself stepped back more and more. What should be geared harmoniously together became separated.[11] To have viewed Leonardo's gigantic attempt at synthesizing two disparate functions in correlation with two developmental trends, the instinctual conflict behind and in the complex whole, was no minor achievement of Freud's, and takes the whole conflict out of comparison with the situation of van Gogh. It strikes me as possibly highly characteristic of the historian that he considers the psychologist's scientific conclusions on the same plane with the artist's personal expression of his subjective mood. Schapiro proceeds here as if, independently of the circumstances of their origin, texts are to be treated as equivalent objects to which textual analysis and criticism must be applied; thus the result of research and the artist's subjective account became interchangeable data.[12]

I wish to draw from a different field a striking example of how a historian may block the understanding of important records. Almost all the letters have been preserved that Goethe wrote to Charlotte von Stein, with whom he maintained an intense relationship for about a decade. Since the whole relationship of the poet to this woman seven years his senior is enigmatic for many reasons (the genius underwent

[10] This can be best demonstrated in Leonardo's anatomical drawings (see Esche, 1954). More will have to be said later about the problem of knowing and depicting in Leonardo.

[11] Esche (1954, p. 61) also admits indirectly the disparateness of Leonardo the artist and the scientist, despite the opposite view she takes at the outset.

[12] Though Schapiro's remark is contained in a footnote and does not refer to the subject matter of his article it still may indicate the distance that separates some aspects of the discipline of the history of art and of psychology as represented by psychoanalysis.

a surprising personality reorganization, during that decade), it can easily be imagined that this unique record is a true treasure trove for the psychologist. Yet Wilhelm Bode (1907), who in his time was an authority on Goethe research, when writing about this record takes as his point of departure the language typical of that time—the period of intense enthusiasm, exuberant and sentimental outbursts of emotion. That language was picturesque, expressive, emotional, and certainly exaggerated if measured by the yardstick of the present. Therefore he warns against taking these letters at face value.[13] Although Goethe writes in them intensely and extensively of his love for Charlotte, one should consider, Bode thinks, that this was true also of Goethe's letters to Auguste von Stolberg, a woman whom he had never met and to whom his letters were addressed at a time when he had a beautiful bride, with whom he was passionately in love. Therefore, the reasoning goes, despite his protestations he could not have been in love with Auguste and therefore the letters to Charlotte do not prove that he felt love for Charlotte. Here we find the *Zeitgeist* used to reduce the potential value of an exceedingly important psychological record almost to zero.

When Schapiro (1956) writes: "But although Freud, in his ethnological papers, was deeply aware of the collective patterns in culture and referred them to some universal psychic process or mechanism, in writing on Leonardo he ignored the social and historical where they are most pertinent to his task" (p. 158), he comes quite close to Bode's implied *Zeitgeist* theory. To be sure, in *Totem and Taboo,* Freud (1913a) demonstrated the impact of a group situation on cultural development and thus showed his capacity for dealing sensitively with historical forces. There is no objection to writing a history of the Renaissance in which Leonardo would be the medium of his times and his individuality would be reduced to the small area of formal, aesthetic and iconographic innovations. However, from such a study the man Leonardo could not be known. In like manner, to read Goethe's letters to Charlotte von Stein as a document of the *Schwärmerzeit* means to bypass a major psychological problem. Indeed—what the historian may consider as highly improbable—the poet may be in love

---

[13] Cf. Brown (1920): "In interpreting [Goethe's letters to Frau von Stein] we have doubtless to remember the effusiveness of the times" (Vol. I, p. 233), and at another place he warns that Goethe's correspondence was in large degree forced and artificial in accordance with the convention of the day.

with a fantasy sweetheart to whom he writes with greater passion than he may feel for the beautiful bride he embraces—although as an old man the fantasy sweetheart may be almost forgotten and the real bride of the past may be heralded as the only one that was ever truly loved (Eckermann, p. 574; March 5, 1830). Of course, like all documents Goethe's letters to Charlotte von Stein also have to be examined as to the truth or hypocrisy—as the case may be—that they contain. In the *Schwärmerzeit* people lied and pretended too, as they have done in all times, but the seemingly exaggerated, sentimental language was more often than not the messenger of a psychological truth. If in that era terms of kinship were used for relations of friendship (Bode, 1907, p. 283), I see in it the sign of deep psychological wisdom. Then in a letter of the Marchioness Maria Branconi, in her time heralded as Germany's most beautiful woman, to the chaste Lavater, we read of the handkerchief and the lock which she had from him, and of her garters which he had from her (Bode, 1907, p. 289). We may know that Lavater's wife was wrong when she became suspicious and destroyed her late husband's correspondence with the charming marchioness, for the odds are high in favor of their relationship's having been honorable in terms of a behavioristic psychology; but, however much the *Zeitgeist* may have contributed to their strange exchange of fetishistic objects, we still feel entitled to assert that the sublimation of their instincts did not completely succeed.

The *Zeitgeist* is the same for all members of a society or class or group, and whatever man does it can be correlated to social historical forces, whether he commits a crime or whether he makes a sublime contribution to the culture of the world. To be sure, in each single event we shall grasp another band of the spectrum, but no study of history will convey to us knowledge of why the one enlarged mankind's criminal record and the other its cultural.[14] Here psychology enters in its own right. When Freud discovered in Leonardo's ambivalence toward his own creations the artist's identification with his own father, that is to say, that an irrational force compelled the artist to treat his paintings as miserably as the father had treated him as a child, the historian may be right that the psychologist "will convince few readers"

14 Of course I do not mean to deny the bearing of the *Zeitgeist* on everything that is created within any specific culture. For an analysis of the concept of the *Zeitgeist* see Boring (1955).

(Schapiro, p. 176), but the psychologist may still be right and have discovered here one of the primary incentives that render men apt to make cultural contributions of greater originality than those of women (cf. Rank, 1907, p. 70; 1924 passim).

Does this now mean the psychoanalyst can dispense with the study of history when he applies psychoanalysis to an event that took place in a past historical period? By no means. As the naturalist in his inquiry into the life of animals studies their natural habitat, the psychologist has to know the cultural habitat of the object of his inquiry. The fundamental point of disagreement appears to be—assuming Schapiro's study is typical—that the historians stop at an analysis of that habitat and adhere to a crude stimulus-reaction relation which, though it used to be accepted, has long since been outgrown by the biological sciences. Man is not the medium of his culture. The area of individuality—even if it were no more than man's selection among the innumerable cultural stimuli that surround him—is larger than the historian assigns to him.[15]

Schapiro thinks that works by psychoanalysts in general suffer from their habit "of building explanations of complex phenomena on a single datum and the too little attention given to history and the social situation" (p. 177). This accusation that psychoanalysts "build on a single datum" seems to me, in the present instance at least, misleading, to put it mildly. Does the physicist "build on a single datum" when he considers what revisions in Newtonian physics may be necessitated by repeated observations of the red shift? Or would it be fairer to say that he tries sedulously to bring an unintegrated item of information into systematic relation with the whole body of available data, and remains willing to revise his notion of the system underlying those data if the new item will not fit into the old system? Leonardo's childhood recollection was precisely such a "single datum." Its significance had not been explicated; it had not been fitted into any attempt at a serious systematic account of Leonardo's personality and career—least of all by Leonardo's own "explanation." It was, accordingly, a legitimate

[15] I have critically discussed a variety of Schapiro's propositions and fear lest I may have left the impression that he intends to attack psychoanalysis or objects to its method. The opposite is true. He stresses that his criticism of Freud's *Leonardo* does not question the truth of psychoanalysis. But, aside from Freud's having posed new and important questions unsuspected by earlier writers, Schapiro does not seem to find anything of merit in Freud's study. He admits that no better answers than those which Freud found have been given (p. 177f.).

point from which to grapple with the arcana of his personality; indeed, to the alert biographer it challenged investigation. It is hard not to suppose that what Schapiro is objecting to is not that the datum is single, but that it is singular. To deny to psychology a valid occasion for pursuing, even to explosive consequences, research into singular items of data is to force it back into the kraal of academicism out of which Freud so brilliantly led it. In general Schapiro disregards essential differences in methodology, aims, and fundamental concepts between his science and psychoanalysis. I wish to refer to his own suggestion as to how, by the use of the psychoanalytic method, the disappearance of St. John from Leonardo's *Metterza* painting may be explained, and to point out how easily by playing the role of *advocatus diaboli* I could dismiss his proposition by referring to recent icono graphic research.

It appears to me that, by and large, for every new theme in a master's work, and for the vast majority of formal elements and details, the philologist, iconographic expert, and historian are able to find causative factors outside of the psychological area. Schapiro seems to believe that as long as such factors can be shown to have been relevant the psychological explanation is out of place, superfluous, or downright wrong, a reasoning that necessarily leads to the conclusion that the psychological explanation may properly begin only where the historical and iconographic inquiry does not find an answer. This strikes me as if in the interpretation of dreams reference to the dreamer's personality were permitted only in regard to those elements that are not connected with the day residue. I wish to liken the vast knowledge that is obtained from iconographic and historical research to the day residue.[16] It is extremely important to know the day residues when interpreting dreams. They are a reliable compass in leading us through the ambiguous and deceptive contents of the unconscious which are always characterized by manifold meanings. In the same way, in every work of art a large number of, so to speak, day residues will be discovered. Yet the long history of precedent cases and the historical constellation at the time a work of art was created, important as they are for the understanding of its aesthetic, philosophical, and religious

16 Beres's recent paper (1959), which reached me too late to be sufficiently cited, contains a similar, if not quite so broad statement (cf. p. 34).

meaning, or its *Geistigkeit*, still do not tell us the secrets of its creator, and every work of art requires, if its total history is to be understood, psychological insight.[17] Summarily one may therefore say: every work of art is also a psychological problem. This multiplicity of meaningful contexts into which every work of art fits is illustrative of a basic law of the human mind that Freud (1900, passim) described as the law of overdetermination and Robert Waelder (1936) as the principle of multiple function. The law says that every psychic phenomenon is determined by multifarious forces, that is to say, by several forces that originate from each province of the personality and from external reality. This law can be easily applied to every objective achievement of the human mind, such as a work of art, a science, or a religion. Each such achievement is the carrier of multiple meanings, and it is a violation against the live cultural process, of which man is the center, to alienate the products of the human mind from that very mind and to treat them as if they were products of the antecedent members of their class or any other force outside of it.

We observe precisely in some of the greatest, such as Shakespeare, the most individual and self-willed, a tendency to fit themselves into traditional patterns, in so far, for example, as one finds that Shakespeare chose as subjects of his own plays an astounding number of themes that have historical antecedents. Does the study of this ancestry really tell us much about the meaning of what Shakespeare created? Does not the choice of topic alone—in view of the innumerable alternatives offered by the cultural past and present—contain the elements of individual conflicts?

The multiplicity of forces that are active until a work of art is finally created seems confusing; so, too, do the functions it fulfills and the meanings it has. I wonder if psychology can contribute a central concept that could function as a kind of common denominator to the manifoldness of phenomena compounded into a cultural element such as a work of art. It looks to me as if one of the leading objective functions of all great artistic achievements, particularly in

[17] Panofsky (1939) acknowledged this fully in his work on Piero di Cosimo. After having set forth the literary roots of some of Piero's paintings and having thus given the general background from which they evolved, he concludes that the artist's special attitude "can only be explained on psychological grounds" (p. 65), and in dealing with Michelangelo's sculptures for the Tomb of Julius II he discusses the very personal meaning they had for him (p. 218).

the visual arts, is, not only to give pleasure of a certain kind, but to stimulate the differentiation of the personalities of the beholders. Cultural change is correlated to ego changes. One of the ways in which the group member's ego is to acquire the adaptation that has become necessary in the course of imperceptible historical changes— or one of the ways by which it is prepared for that adaptation—may be discovered in the compelling effect the artist exerts upon the beholder inasmuch as he forces him to identify or empathize with the artist's productions.[18] Such identifications, endowed with degrees of inner participation varying from cool empathy to passionate submergence, take hold of the beholder by means of artistic enjoyment.[19]

I think this viewpoint can nowhere be better studied than in the unending series of paintings representing St. Mary with the infant Christ. Here a mother-child relationship, quite alien and probably even offensive to the man of antiquity, was over and over again presented to the beholder, and art functioned as a guiding rope along which the egos of group members were proffered the integration of a new differentiation. In order for it to be able to function in this way, the creative artist's personality had to differentiate a new image of that relationship. Thus by the exact description of the new ego differentiation that is contained in each masterwork, a keystone may be found upon which all the meaningful contexts rest: the artist's own conflict, the aesthetic antecedents, the historical forces active at the time of creation, and the effect of art upon the successive generations of beholders.

In the last paragraph of his paper Schapiro states that he does "not mean to oppose historical or sociological explanations to psychological ones" and he adds that the former "are in part psychological" (p. 177). It is gratifying to see that at least in theory there seems to be less disagreement than might be expected in view of the controversy regarding the correct interpretation of the data of Leonardo's life. Yet it is my impression that this agreement in theory is more apparent than real, for the author continues: "But if all historical explanations depended on psychology, we could not correctly apply the psychological con-

18 For the audience's reaction to the artistic product, see Kris (1952, pp. 56-59, 61-63).
19 This does not mean to say that identification is the only mechanism through which a work of art affects the beholder.

cepts . . . , unless we knew the state of the individual and his human environment—data that cannot be supplied without historical study" (p. 177f.). Here, I think, the synthesis implicit in the initial statement is negated and a substantive dichotomy between history and psychology is adumbrated. To get to the bottom of this issue, we would have to investigate the use Schapiro makes here of such terms as "explanation" and "study."

Suffice it to say summarily that Freud selected, for his biographical purpose, items in which his subject's behavior deviated sufficiently from the average of his times so that one could be sure the *personal* was relevant, and other items in which the historical ingredient does not seem to be of the kind Schapiro refers to.

There can, of course, be no doubt that the psychoanalyst has to know the results of historical and iconographic research; but what he does with that knowledge in order to reach psychological conclusions will more frequently than not strike the historian as far-fetched and inconclusive. Schapiro dismisses us with the admonition that the analyst should inform himself better about Leonardo's life and art and the culture of his time before applying his science to the psychological study of that life (p. 178). Wohl and Trosman (1955), with their little understanding of the subtleness of the genius, believe that the problem could have been solved if Freud had "allowed his manuscript to be scrutinized" by an expert in history (p. 39). These writers bypass the essential question that is at issue between the historical sciences and psychoanalysis and that cannot be resolved as long as the historian and philologist do not acquire full insight into psychoanalysis and are restrained by the bias of our time from obtaining maximum knowledge of the structure of the human mind by consistent and longlasting clinical work. Once this organizational barrier has been removed a generation of historians may arise that will appreciate Freud's essay more than is currently done. When we read that the historian of art, at least in 1952, still used "common-sense psychology . . . , to account for the change of style" (Schapiro, 1953, p. 287) it may become self-evident that the two disciplines cannot come to terms at present.[20]

[20] In the light of a paper like Gombrich's study (1957) on Lessing, it is to be admitted that selected minds may be capable of balancing and synthesizing the two disciplines in an almost ideal fashion even prior to the reorganization of the training of the cultural scientist suggested above.

The discussion with the historian has gone more and more into the field of methodology and I will now return again to the biographical detail, setting forth some of my own views as they developed in the course of the foregoing critical analysis. Of course, there will also be occasion to supplement the discussion with the historian.

II
HISTORICAL NOTES

7

Selected Problems of Leonardo's Childhood

The document most frequently cited to disprove Freud's basic construct is the last page found in a notary protocol of Leonardo's great-grandfather. There, Ser Antonio, Leonardo's paternal grandfather, recorded among the births and baptisms of his progeny also the exact hour and date of Leonardo's birth, the name of the priest who baptized the infant, and of the witnesses thereof, who were close neighbors and prominent citizens. Möller (1939), who found and published the document, is certain it proves that Leonardo was born in his grandfather's house,[1] that the unwed mother was welcomed by the family, and Leonardo spent his whole childhood with his father's family.[2]

This would put an end to Freud's basic construction of the infant's having spent his first three to five years with his mother away from the father and then, having been forced to separate from her, joining the father, whose first wife had remained childless.

As can well be imagined, critics of Freud's essay seized on this find

[1] See for an opposite view Cianchi (1952b).
[2] The author hardly justifies his reasoning; the results of his archival inquiries, which he announces in his article, have, I believe, never been published.

and concluded, like Möller, without any further deliberation that here at last the conclusive proof has been unearthed that Leonardo spent the years from birth to his departure to Florence in his father's house. However, it strikes me that the researchers who applied so much ingenuity and subtlety to weighing the pros and cons of Freud's inferences—usually with the result that they proved them to be wrong—did not raise the question of the alternative conclusions implied by this important document.

After all, documents require a critical analysis. They may contain, for example, a lie. In this instance, to be sure, there is no reason to suspect deception. We can be reasonably certain that the facts really took place as reported by Ser Antonio. But the factual content of this document is rather poor. Documents acquire their full importance only when we put the facts reported into the middle of live processes of happenings, and this can usually be done only by going beyond the narrow limits of the bare facts which they record.

Actually, the family record assures us only of three facts: (a) Leonardo's illegitimate birth, (b) the exact date of his birth, (c) the place and circumstances of his baptism.

Anything more is based only on inferences and contains all the possibilities of error that loom when the secure harbor of evidence is left. There is no word said about where the infant spent the following few years, and the next document, possibly of less reliability than the family record, as we shall see, that gives evidence of Leonardo's whereabouts is Ser Antonio's tax record of 1457, in which Leonardo is listed as a *bocca* (mouth)—which means here a tax-deductible dependent who shares the grandfather's household.

The question will rightly be raised why the conclusions all authors have drawn since the family record was found should be doubted. Even if the record does not say anything about the whereabouts of Leonardo during the next few years, the probability that an infant baptized in his grandfather's house and found living there five years later should have spent the intervening years at another domicile is so low that any other conclusion seems far-fetched and highly improbable. Though I am not a historian of the Renaissance, I can cite at least one historical example that repeats the premises on which Möller based his conclusions and still resulted in an outcome vastly different from the one he presumes. Benvenuto Cellini had a daughter by a fifteen-year-old girl whom he had taken into his house as a model. His best friend, the Royal Physician, held her at baptism. French custom did not permit more than one godfather. The two godmothers—one of noble birth—were wives of outstanding men, one a nobleman and the other a wealthy merchant. Cellini gave his mistress a dowry and sent her to a relative. He lost all track of his child.[3]

We have here, at least, one well-documented instance of an illegitimate Renaissance child whose baptismal start in life was even more promising than that of Leonardo and who lost all further contact with the father. Perhaps Cellini's procedure was atypical of his time, but Ser Antonio, the grandfather—we shall take up the father's history presently—in turn was apparently not quite what would be called a conformist.

The family originated in Vinci but gravitated toward Florence in the course of the fourteenth century. With Ser Piero, Leonardo's great-grandfather, the family became well established in Florence. He was notary of the Signoria, resided and died in Florence (1417). He married a Florentine woman, who stayed in Florence after her husband's death. Ser Antonio, Leonardo's grandfather (1372-1464), however, retired to Vinci and lived the life of a country squire. Pierpaccini (1952, p. 10) even says that he did not obtain a degree, which would mean that he never was a notary although he married into a notary's family, and Smiraglia (1900, p. 5) reports that he had no particular profession. It is strange that this man discontinued the family tradition, separated from his mother, and gave up city life for life in a small provincial place. His son, Leonardo's father (1426-1504), was the very opposite as far as can be concluded from a biographical outline: energetic, ambitious, active, and successful, he restored the old family tradition and became the most sought-after notary in Florence, where he started out in 1448. In 1449, he was nominated guardian (*mondualdo*) of a Caterina di Stefano in Pisa and was on that occasion called a Florentine notary public and regular judge. The tax rolls of 1451 do not mention him as living in Vinci. This is also the year from when on all acts except a few were notarized by him in Florence (Smiraglia, p. 7). Consequently, from that time on he was almost

---

[3] Von Oettingen reports that the certificate of baptism with the names of the godparents is preserved. He is surprised that a daughter who must have been so welcome to the father should have later been treated with neglect (p. 305, n.).

exclusively in Florence. In 1452, he married Albiera di Giovanni Amadori (1436-1464), a wealthy Florentine girl. As Cianchi (1952a, p. 49) says, one must assume, contrary to earlier views, that Ser Piero, Leonardo's father, lived more in Florence than in Vinci after his marriage, and that he probably had his own house there. This is made almost certain when we hear that his wife died in Florence in the course of a childbirth on June 15, 1464.

It is worth while to consider these facts because they are suggestive of a possible antagonism or rivalry between Ser Antonio and Ser Piero, the son doing brilliantly all that his father should have done had he continued the family tradition. If only we had a hint what Ser Antonio's motive was in retiring from Florence where his mother lived and where his father had spent most of his life!

I conclude that the grandfather, Ser Antonio, particularly celebrated the early arrival of progeny since he had been fifty-four years old when his first child was born.[4] But was he ready to shoulder the financial responsibility for the newcomer? Did the father, who got married in the same year, have great interest in the infant? One receives the impression that these Florentine citizens were hard-boiled, money-minded, niggardly fellows who thought twice before accepting responsibilities that would increase regular expenses.

This observation, whether it is correct or not, does not, of course, prove anything. It is brought up only for the purpose of demonstrating that the environmental conditions of Leonardo's early years have not been reliably ascertained as the majority of contemporary Leonardo biographers are prone to make us think. Furthermore, there is a very intriguing issue involved in the next document in which Leonardo's name shows up: the grandfather's tax return of 1457, from which we learn that the name of Leonardo's mother was Caterina and that she was at that time married to Accattabriga di Piero del Vacca. This man, Antonio, was a lime burner who lived in Vinci from March, 1449, to August, 1453 (Cianchi, 1952a, p. 37). His kiln was a few kilometers from Vinci on the road to Empoli.[5]

This tax declaration, innocent as it may look, contains a very intriguing point. This rests on the fact that, according to Pierpaccini

---

[4] Oddly enough, despite Ser Piero's promising beginning he repeated his father's pattern inasmuch as he had to wait until 1476, when he was fifty years old, before his first legitimate child was born.

[5] It may be noteworthy that Leonardo's father rented the same kiln in September, 1469.

(1952), whereas in the Italy of the Renaissance a man would not feel compelled to conceal illegitimate progeny, the identity of the mother was customarily kept secret. I have found no way of confirming Pierpaccini's claim, but it makes sense to me and I am ready to accept it here.[6] It is indeed a problem why Ser Antonio did not record the mother's name in the family chronicle, but revealed it, seemingly without necessity, in a public record. Pierpaccini's answer that Ser Antonio wanted to conceal the true identity of Leonardo's mother and therefore deliberately substituted the name of Leonardo's wet nurse as a red herring has not been accepted. Although it could be correct, it does not sound probable.

Be this as it may, the question Pierpaccini raised impresses me as crucial. It has not been considered by any other writer on Leonardo as far as I know. In my estimation, the first step toward a constructive discussion of this problem would be to get a clear understanding of the Florentine tax system. Then only would one be in a position to speculate with some reliability about the way Ser Antonio handled the tax return of 1457.[7]

Apparently, the only source available at present is Canestrini's book (1862), and I presume that further research will be necessary before all pertinent data and facts will be known.

As far as I have been able to find out, the Florentine government determined, in accordance with the economic necessities, when the citizens had to submit a tax declaration; the regular annual tax return of our economic system was not known in Quattrocento Florence. In these declarations a report had to be given of all taxable items and claimed deductions, such as the number of dependents. It must be considered, however, that tax declarations were probably quite generally as unreliable at that time as our present income-tax returns. Man's desire to pay as little taxes as possible is almost certainly perennial and one of the invariable human motives that need no further historical inquiry. Actually, many of Leonardo's biographers do not rely on them. For example, a historian as exact and conscientious as Sarton (1957) puts Leonardo's entrance into Verrocchio's studio in the year 1466

[6] This is the only meritorious point in Pierpaccini's paper as far as I can see. The many unwarranted claims and theories he sets forth otherwise may be a reason to hold the paper in general in low esteem.

[7] I owe thanks to Signor Elio Conti for the help he gave me in my endeavors to reach an understanding of the pertinent tax returns.

(adding that it may have been a little later) (p. 234), although Leonardo's grandmother reported in her tax record of 1469 that her grandson was among those who were living at her house in Vinci (Douglas, 1944, p. 5); Valentiner (1949a, p. 46), as some others, calls it improbable that Leonardo moved to Florence before 1469.[8] Now 1457 was the first year after Leonardo's birth in which a tax declaration was due, that is to say, if I understand the situation correctly, the first opportunity to obtain a tax reduction by declaring the child as a dependent. Until then apparently the child would have been a liability without providing any tax advantage.

If the boy had until then been staying with his mother, and if Ser Antonio, faced with the prospect of a financial gain, now became more inclined than before to have his grandchild in his household, then it may have become necessary to take measures that would allay suspicions that might arise in the tax agency. My question would be: are there known instances of people who took children in their households and claimed parentage in order to gain tax advantages?

The picture I draw here of Ser Antonio may appear unwarrantedly cold and calculating. It is not meant to be. Ser Antonio might have been interested in the boy, who lived not too far away from him, and still the final decision to make him part of his household may have been taken under the additional impact of an expected tax saving. My suggestion, however, would explain in a simple way why Ser Antonio thought it necessary to let the tax agency know before being asked what the boy's exact relationship to his family was. If the boy had been living with his parental family since his birth, there would have been no necessity to utter a single word about his origin. If, however, he had been recently taken in, this may have necessitated naming the only material witness that could confirm Ser Antonio's claim to an additional dependent.

Thus, it may one day turn out that Freud was right in presuming that the boy joined his parental family around the age of four. The motive he suggested, Albiera's barrenness, does not seem likely. It is almost certain that Leonardo's father and stepmother lived in Florence and therefore had little contact with the child.

I have gone into these details not because—as I will presently show

[8] For the variety of dates suggested as probable for Leonardo's departure to Florence, see Valentiner (1930, p. 47).

—they are any longer germane to Freud's construct, but because there are historical data that (*accidentally,* I am inclined to say) may confirm Freud's construction of 1910.

In view of the clinical experiences accumulated since 1910, it is to be said that the trauma Freud postulated as having injured the boy between the ages of three and five may have the same effect—and, for that matter, even a much stronger one—if it occurs when the child is considerably younger.

The choice of the unmaternal kite as symbol in the childhood recollection also suggests that the separation from the mother may have occurred much earlier. If there were not the strange incident with the tax declaration of 1457, I would not hesitate to suggest that Leonardo probably spent only the first few months, at most the first year and a half, with his mother and then was taken to his grandfather's house. Möller's claim that Caterina was an accepted member of the father's or grandfather's household is quite unjustified. If we consider the physical difficulty of raising infants, I do not see any particular objection to assuming that the infant was left with his mother until he had reached some degree of independence, so that his nurture in the new household would be less burdensome. For the father who was energetically pursuing his career in Florence at that time, it was probably quite immaterial where the boy spent the first few years of his life.

Since Caterina's husband lived in Vinci only until August, 1453, this would be another date to consider for the infant's change of environment.

The fact of Caterina's early marriage is, I believe, a proof that Leonardo, even if he was not welcome in his grandfather's house, did not spend a long time in the sole possession of his mother. We find here evidence that is to be correlated with Freud's erroneous assumption that a bird friendly to the offspring figured in the childhood recollection. Indeed, the adult had plenty of reasons to use a symbol signifying a bad mother, particularly if we assume that, if indeed he did stay with his mother for a few years, he may have witnessed one or more pregnancies and observed the mother's nursing of infants (cf. Schapiro, 1956, p. 156). If this is correct, the bird's striking with his tail inside the infant's mouth may well symbolize a fantasy, the content of which was wished upon the suckling stepsibling. The aggres-

sive component of the cover memory would then contain wish fulfillment as well as self-punishment in one.

In view of the corrected content of the childhood memory, one may
have, indeed, to assume a shorter period than Freud did for Leonardo's
stay with his mother. Yet, as I stated before, there is no external
evidence that would necessitate doubt that Leonardo the infant spent
a significant period of time with his mother. I have pointed out above
that in the three paintings the *Virgin of the Rocks,* the London cartoon,
and the Louvre *Anna Metterza,* the history of two children is presented:
the Christ child moving from a distance ever closer to his mother
and finally displacing St. John, whereas St. John is moved away from
his original closeness to St. Mary and is finally driven away. I wonder
whether these two sequences are the derivatives of Leonardo's relations
to one and the other family. Do I misuse the application of psychoanalysis when I look upon Leonardo's first major independent painting, the *Adoration of the Kings* (Plate 10), as being connected with
an earlier developmental phase before the dichotomy of these two
movements, as presented by the subsequent paintings, brought conflict
into the child's life?

At any rate, we would like to know what the child's position was in
the Accattabriga family. Did he receive privileges in view of his descent
from a social group superior to that of his mother and stepfather? Did
the family have a monetary interest in his living with them, since they
might have received compensation for his upkeep? And how did the
mother feel when she compared husband and former lover? The latter,
after all, seems to have been a dashing, successful young man, who,
in view of the number of his subsequent wives and children, would
strike one as rather passionate. If the infant boy was a memento of a
single ecstatic night, she may have responded to his presence with
renewed recalls of the past and felt closer to her past lover than to the
possibly less attractive laborer she had married. But even if the infant
was soon brought into his grandfather's house, he may have met his
mother from time to time.[9]

The situation must have been unusually confusing for the boy,
for it is not probable that a family situation as complex as the one this

[9] The reader will have noticed that the various reality situations I suggest are partly
contradictory to each other. Yet they have a common denominator: an early attachment
to the mother that subsequently resulted in a deep frustration and concomitant ill feelings.

child had to face was less puzzling to him than it would be to a child of today. Here was a mother of lower status than the family with which he was to live permanently. Her husband had the same first name as the boy's grandfather (Antonio), and Leonardo's father had the same first name as the stepfather's father (Piero). The high status of the grandfather's family and the ensuing amenities were over against the maternal affection that he may have felt when he was with the Accattabrigas, and the inferior conditions in which she lived. The trauma of separation that Freud telescoped[10] into one event that presumably took place between the ages of three and five may have occurred repeatedly whenever the child had contact with the mother and had to return to the grandfather's house. From this repeatedly being sent away from an affectionate mother to a grandfather who quite possibly was stern and demanding, the hostile character of Leonardo's early childhood recollection may have been intensified. Further, the conflict aroused by the attachment to two households may have generated a feeling of doubt in the child as to where he really belonged and be genetically connected with the frightful feeling of isolation that has struck many biographers.

Also, in view of the period which, according to the record, Accattabriga spent near Vinci, there is the possibility that not only the father but also the mother got married in 1452. Thus, the exceptional thing may have happened that the father and the mother of this child got married to other spouses the very year their first son was born.[11]

When we find among Leonardo's *Profetie* the riddle: "Fathers and mothers shall be seen to bestow much more attention upon their stepchildren than upon their own children" (MacCurdy, 1956, p. 1120; B.M. 212 v.) we may find in it, though the answer given is "Of trees which give sap to grafted shoots" (ibid.), the primary plea of a child that had had occasion to feel abandoned, deserted, and forsaken.

[10] See Anna Freud (1951) for the "telescoping of events": "An action which we see the infant repeat a hundred times may in later life be represented as one traumatic happening" (p. 26).

[11] Hildebrandt (1927) without giving any reference states that both parents married the year Leonardo was born (p. 29).

8

The Caterina Problem

But despite all the good reasons, conscious and unconscious, that Leonardo may have had for feeling deeply hurt by his mother, his attachment to her must have been an excessive one.

In his *Notebooks* the name Caterina appears four times: (1) a random note: Caterina came on the sixteenth day of July, 1493 (MacCurdy, 1956, p. 1156; Forster III 88 r.); (2) an expense account of January, 1494, regarding two payments to Caterina (MacCurdy, p. 1157; H 64 [16] v.); (3) a list of expenses for the burial of Caterina (MacCurdy, p. 1129; Forster II 64 v.), who very probably was the same as mentioned under (1) and (2); (4) the following fragment: "tell, tell me how things are passing yonder and whether Caterina wishes to make . . ." (MacCurdy, p. 62, n. 1; C.A. 71 r. a). This last will occupy us some more later and we may be able to derive from it a clue to an understanding of that Caterina who suddenly appeared in the life of the adult Leonardo.

Disagreement has developed among biographers whether Leonardo was referring in these contexts to a Caterina who was employed in his house as a servant or to Caterina his mother, who may have joined him in Milan and stayed with him until she died. Freud, following

Merezhkovsky, believed the latter;[1] many historians, but by no means all, have assumed the former.

Wohl and Trosman (1955), though they rightly say that the historical evidence per se is not clear regarding this Caterina's status, castigate Freud for his conviction. Whether he was right or wrong on this point—its irrelevance to Freud's main thesis will be shown presently—it would have been fair to let the reader know that among those who favor the view that Caterina was Leonardo's mother we find some of the most sober of his biographers. Luca Beltrami (1921a), one of the best informed scholars of Leonardo documents, devoted a special study to this question and he seems convinced of the maternal relation. Valentiner (1949a) writes:

> A somewhat fantastic yet not wholly improbable theory has connected her [the mother] with a housekeeper of the same name employed by Leonardo at Milan forty years later [p. 45].

It may be also noteworthy that a more recent writer again asserts the probability of the Milanese Caterina's being Leonardo's mother (Fumagalli, 1952, p. 30).

Caterina is, to be sure, not the only female name that appears in Leonardo's writings, but it is astounding how few female names do appear at all in his *Notes* and how rarely Leonardo refers to particular women. A tendency to avoid mental contact with women in the free interplay of his thoughts may well be postulated. If all passages referring to women are placed side by side, Leonardo's (probably unconscious) misogyny becomes quite apparent. Among the thirteen

---

[1] Freud (1910, p. 104, n.) cites Merezhkovsky for a fifth reference to Caterina. This is erroneous since it does not refer to Caterina but to the Santa Caterina hospital. It may throw light on the spirit and accuracy of the critical paper by Wohl and Trosman (1955) that the authors hold Freud responsible for this error. Any objective reader of Freud's paper will agree that the authors' accusing Freud of "garbling of the original text" or "errors persistently indulged in" (p. 36) is based on arbitrary misquotations where Freud did not do anything but quote from Merezhkovsky (1902, p. 403f.). The authors' preposterous comment is all the more out of place since this particular entry was not decisive for either the novelist or Freud, and other historians, as we shall presently see, shared Merezhkovsky's assumption although they knew of the error he had committed in this one instance. I have not been able to trace the history of Merezhkovsky's mistake. In his case too it would be out of place to speak of a garbling of the original since the whole question is simply whether a passage should be read as *asca* or *a Scā* (Merezhkovsky, p. 404; Richter, Vol. II, p. 352, No. 1404; Forster II part 1, 3 r.). Whoever knows how difficult it is to decipher Leonardo's manuscripts will respect such differences of opinion. Freud must have felt reassured regarding this alleged reference of Leonardo's since Merezhkovsky quotes it in Italian.

"Jests" and "Fables" recorded in his writings there are two in which reference is made to women and both are contemptuous and sarcastic, the one of their morals and the other of their physique (Richter, Vol. II, p. 291, No. 1290, No. 1292; Forster II part 1, 30 v., F, o '). Fumagalli (p. 106) reports that in Leonardo's library there was a book, *Il Manganello*, that breathes the air of extreme repugnance of women.[2]

In view of the relative scarcity of statements referring to women and of the almost total absence of any utterance that would suggest appreciation of the female sex in the 6,000-odd pages extant written by Leonardo, one is compelled to view seriously the references about the enigmatic Caterina. Few as they are, one feels behind them a concrete personal being. Whether she is proved one day to have been mother, wet nurse, or maid, she held a unique place, and the psychological importance of her name's being recorded in Leonardo's papers can scarcely be overrated.

A Point of Methodology

Before proceeding further I have to justify a method which I will apply to the Caterina and other problems. This method has been introduced into the Leonardo literature by Marie Bonaparte (1927, p. 29, n.). Apparently she considered it a matter of psychoanalytic common sense for she did not explicitly justify its use. Although most analysts will regard the procedure as a corollary of basic psychoanalytic tenets and therefore as not in need of further explanation, I still feel inclined to justify its application in view of the broad conclusions I will occasionally infer therefrom.

Nineteenth-century academic psychology was dominated by the concept of association. One of the main efforts then went in the direction of establishing the laws of associations which were the laws of similarity, of difference or contrast, of succession, and of coexistence

---

[2] Two instances, however, of friendly sentiments for women are attributed by some historians to Leonardo. One is the beginning of the draft of a letter to Cecilia Gallerani, mistress of his master Lodovico, whose portrait he has painted. It runs in its entirety as follows: "Cecilia—My dearest Goddess, having read your most gracious . . ." (Richter, Vol. II, p. 340, No. 1356A; C.A. 297 v.). The other instance is the beginning of a draft of a letter of July 5, 1507, to his family. It starts: "My dearly beloved mother, sisters, and brother-in-law" (Richter, Vol. II, p. 387, No. 1559; C.A. 132 r.). The letter would be remarkable because it would have been written at a time when he was involved in litigation with his family. Carlo Pedretti, however, assured me in a personal communication, that neither of these drafts is in Leonardo's handwriting; therefore they can safely be dismissed.

—in short, the law of contiguity. The underlying idea was that a numerical index decided which association would follow an idea or percept. That is to say, a perception or an association will be followed by the one with which it has previously been connected most frequently through one of the categories (similarity, contrast, etc.).

Though this idea has been proved wrong since then, at least in the form in which it had been accepted (Bühler, 1927), the concept of association did not lose its eminent position in Freud's psychology. Parenthetically I wish to remark that this is a surprising fact usually neglected by the historian who is prone to look upon Freud only as an innovator, whereas Freud's psychology is, as far as I know, the only twentieth-century psychology that, despite all its innovations, also assigns a central position to the old concept of association. However, this concept, as can be imagined, found a redefinition or remodeling in the edifice of psychoanalytic theories. Without denying the possible validity of the classical laws of association, Freud postulated and proved empirically that behind the sequence of associations as described in classical psychology there are other interconnections. The peripheral connections based on frequency and similarity or contrast cover a deep, repressed connection that is meaningful, based on an emotional nexus, and relevant in terms of the history and structure of the personality (Freud, 1900, p. 530f.; 1905c, p. 39). Thus a mechanical law was replaced by a dynamic genetic law.

In many pages filled with Leonardo's *Notes*, the majority, I suppose, cover a reasonable universe of discourse. Much of it may no longer impress us as reasonable, but deepened historical knowledge will teach us that a large part of it deserves this attribute. Thus, if, as we look at a page in Leonardo's anatomical work, we find that the mass of drawings and remarks refer to the same anatomical topic (or a logically allied one required by a reality context), that there are no parapraxiae, and that the factual information is as correct as historical factors permitted, then no conclusions of relevance to Leonardo's personality structure can be drawn. Of course, the premises for such conclusions may be amply contained on that page. If the subject could be interrogated and he told us his associations to that page we might derive a wealth of relevant information from the same item. Without the live associations, however, the piece is psychological deadwood.

Conversely, if in the universe of discourse of a page or set of pages, a topic or a remark appears that is alien to that universe of discourse, then we have to look—even if the relations of similarity, contrast, succession, and coexistence are present—for an unconscious, meaningful, emotional nexus relevant in terms of structure and development. I do not wish to enter into a discussion here of whether this is an empirical or an axiomatic rule. Suffice it to say, it is so closely related to Freud's law of free association that I regard one as the consequence of the other. Two situations have to be distinguished. The remark or set of remarks that does not fit into the universe of discourse may have been written at the same time as the rest, or it may have been added later. In my estimation the psychoanalytic principle of simultaneity and proximity ought to be applied to *both* instances, although it probably will have more weight—if any—with the historian only in the former instance. To be sure, it is conceivable that when Leonardo was seized by a thought and groped for paper he grasped at random and jotted down his idea without any awareness of the rest of the topics dealt with on that sheet. In that case, concurrence of two disparate topics was entirely a matter of chance. (It is, further, conceivable that a concurrence that was accidental should still appear from the point of view of psychology to contain a subterranean unconscious nexus. The psychologist would then be the victim of the accident of an accident. The chances, of course, are much greater that accidental concurrences will not yield to interpretation. In view of the small degree of probability that such coincidences may occur, I have neglected this potential source of error.)

In investigating some pages of Leonardo's *Notes* I have found some instances of the concurrence of disparate subjects that, as far as I could see, did not yield any psychological insight; that is to say, I could not guess at the unconscious nexus between the two disparate notes.[3] But besides these I have found others that proved valuable, and I shall report on them. I am convinced that this tool that Marie Bonaparte has introduced into the research on Leonardo will one day prove most valuable. In view of the way in which these notes probably came about (which will be discussed later) a scrutiny of this

---

[3] Of the many examples I could give one may suffice. On Q. II 12 r. (Vangensten et al., Vol. II, p. 25) Leonardo elaborates on the physiology of the heart and its valves. Suddenly we meet the entry: "bad company." I would be incapable of making any explanatory suggestion about such sequences.

sort may open up unsurmised insight into Leonardo's unconscious. Of course, the first premise for the undertaking is a full command of Leonardo's Italian. Also, we may hope that the future researcher who undertakes this arduous task will be better prepared for it than we are today. Our present relative ignorance of the key with which to transpose connections of cultural-science items into those of structural and genetic psychology prevents us from making maximum use of this potential treasure trove.[4]

After this preamble I will apply the psychoanalytic principle of simultaneity and proximity to the fourth instance I have enumerated of Leonardo's making mention of Caterina. This is the instance of the incomplete sentence: "tell, tell me how things are passing yonder and whether Caterina wishes to make . . ." Of the many other things Leonardo wrote on the recto and verso of this page (C.A. 71 r. a) and that could be brought into meaningful context with the sentence I quote only Leonardo's paraphrase of Ovid's *Metamorphoses,* Book XV, lines 232-36 (MacCurdy, 1956, p. 62, n.).

> O Time, thou that consumest all things! O envious age, thou destroyest all things and devourest all things with the hard teeth of the years, little by little, in slow death! Helen, when she looked in her mirror and saw the withered wrinkles which old age had made in her face, wept, and wondered to herself why ever she had twice been carried away.
> O Time, thou that consumest all things! O envious age, whereby all things are consumed! [MacCurdy, p. 61f.].

To find Helen on this page is of extraordinary importance, for there is a similarity between Helen and Leonardo's mother in one biographical detail. Helen was married and subsequently carried off (raped); Caterina was seduced (which also means raped in the boy's fantasy) and subsequently married. Leonardo's reference to an element common to Caterina's and Helen's experience on a page in which he also writes of a Caterina proves satisfactorily that he had his mother in mind when he wrote and thought of Caterina.[5] The idea seems to

[4] It may be of interest to note that a historian as innocent of psychoanalysis as Sir Kenneth Clark made use of the same method in his attempt at trying to find an explanation of Leonardo's choice of the *Leda* theme (Clark, 1939, p. 124). More about this later.

[5] Leonardo's identification of Helen and his mother may indirectly confirm Freud's selecting among the implications inherent in Mona Lisa's smile the one of ambiguity, "the promise of unbounded tenderness and at the same time sinister menace" (quoted from

have been a belated regret that his mother had been a sensual person victimized by her impulses (and male superior force). This is expressed by a pretended identification with the aged Helen whose beauty was brought to naught by age.

MacCurdy (p. 62) is right in saying that conclusions drawn from this coincidence are nothing but conjectures. The context does not permit certainty in identifying the Caterina in Leonardo's *Notes* with his mother. The Helen entry increases the probability thereof but does not prove it. The most we can draw with *certainty* is the minimum conclusion that the name Caterina, even if she was his maid, evoked the image of his mother; that is to say, that an identity was established unconsciously between his mother and the maid.

Here a principal issue has to be set forth. I believe that Freud to a certain extent argued against the purpose he had in mind when he used the Caterina entries to prove Leonardo's attachment to his mother and his pathological way of mourning. If, as Freud, in agreement with Merezhkovsky, assumed, the Caterina of these notes was Leonardo's mother and in later years visited him, fell sick during her stay, died there and was buried at her son's expense, these facts would not be particularly remarkable. What else should Leonardo have done in such circumstances? Unless he gave way to old feelings of resentment, this, in accordance with his filial duty, was how he would have been expected to proceed.

If, however, Caterina was a maid, then the entries take on greater psychological significance. Then we are entitled to assume that she was selected from among the applicants because of her name, and that her name, perhaps also her appearance and age, and her function in the household served to render her a maternal substitute. It would prove that it was the inordinate longing of the adult to enjoy the presence of a mother, at least in this form, that induced him to take a maidservant with his mother's name.[6]

Pater, Freud, 1910, p. 115; cf. Pater, 1873, p. 124), for Helen is the woman who promised and bestowed upon men unbounded pleasure but also brought upon them destruction. By the introduction of the Helen association the circle—Mona Lisa-Helen-mother—is closed and Freud's reconstruction obtains increased probability. I have not been successful in determining whether or not on the verso of the page on which Leonardo wrote of Helen and Caterina there is his short remark about his father's death. If this is the case, a powerful argument can be added in favor of the, at least unconscious, identity of the Caterina of Leonardo's *Notes* with his mother.

[6] Caterina, it is said, was rather an unusual or rare name in Leonardo's times.

Anyone who knows the archaic meaning of names, the indomitable emotions they can elicit, the superstitions attached to them, and the magic powers believed to be inherent in them will not doubt that the identity of names of the mother and the woman who appears in Leonardo's writings must be more than a coincidence but rather the expression of a central issue in the artist's personality.[7]

[7] Withal I do not mean to say that if it should turn out that Caterina was Leonardo's natural mother, this would disprove Freud's observation of Leonardo's attachment to her; I only say that if Caterina was Leonardo's maid, this would prove his (unconscious) attachment to his mother even more strikingly. Neither alternative has any bearing on the fact of pathological mourning in Leonardo. The death of the real mother as well as of the substitute mother would have required a full outbreak of grief of which Leonardo apparently was not capable. I take up the Caterina problem once more in Appendix C.

9

Leonardo's Father and Problems of Illegitimacy

I shall now turn to Leonardo's relationship to his father, Ser Piero. Freud presumed that grave damage was caused to Leonardo's psycho-sexual development by Ser Piero's absence during the early years of the boy's development, that is to say, by the lack of an adequate, virile object with which to identify (1910, p. 121). Freud connected with this factor Leonardo's aversion to carnal relations with women.[1] The essential part of Freud's reconstruction appears highly probable, although I believe that some factors in Freud's reconstruction require changes. As I noted earlier Cianchi (1952a, p. 79) draws the conclusion that Ser Piero must have taken up stable residence at Florence shortly before or after his first marriage in 1452 (cf. Christensen, 1944, p. 160f.). Indeed, in view of his activity before 1452 outside of Vinci, his marriage to a wealthy Florentine woman, her death in Florence in 1464 (Cianchi, 1952a, p. 49), his rise in Florence, it is most un-

[1] Freud thought Leonardo's identification with his father revealed itself in other areas, such as in his alleged fondness for fine clothes, his magnificence, etc., areas which in that phase of Freud's theories, were considered nonerotic (1910, p. 121). Schapiro (1955-56), following Calvi, rightly points to the bearing his father's profession had on Leonardo: the exactitude and concern with dates and small expenditures. Here would be another area of identification (p. 6f.).

likely that he could have spent much time in Vinci in those years. It has commonly been assumed that he left Vinci only after his father's death (c. 1468), but from what we can guess about his character and temperament, it is most unlikely that he was a man who would have suffered a delay in his ambitions out of consideration for his father. Thus we have to conclude that Leonardo did not see very much of his father prior to his departure for Florence, and we have to agree with Cianchi (1952a, p. 50) when he says that Leonardo was largely confided to the care of the grandfather, the grandmother, and Ser Piero's younger brother, Francesco. Thus, the main objects of identification were a grandfather eighty years old when Leonardo was born, a grandmother fifty-nine at that time, and an uncle sixteen years older than the boy. Ser Antonio as a father substitute did not serve this function well for obvious reasons, and this may have contributed to the grandchild's relation to women.[2]

The relationship to the grandfather is hypothetical, but Leonardo's closeness to his uncle Francesco, eight years younger than Leonardo's father, is documented. Ser Antonio made a sarcastic remark about this son in one of the tax rolls, describing him as not contributing to the household. The correctness of this remark has been doubted, but the record of Francesco's life does not reveal an energetic person. He stayed in Vinci most of the time and administered his own and his brother's property after their father's death. In 1498 he wrote in his tax return the same as he had forty years earlier: "sto in villa senza avviamento o esercizio [I am in the country without prospect or employment]" (Seidlitz, 1909b, p. 14). One gets the impression of a person who is quite ready to accept a subordinate role in life. I presume he was a welcome playmate of the boy Leonardo; he, no more than the grandfather, served as a person propitious for a virile identification.[3]

Thus, although the detail needs revision, Freud's reconstruction of Leonardo's youth having, for external reasons, been without an adequate father figure with which to identify has not been refuted by recent research.

[2] The death of Leonardo's stepmother in childbirth must also be considered.

[3] Leonardo's relationship to Francesco must have been a very live one and when Vasari in the first edition of his *Lives* wrote that Leonardo was the nephew of Ser Piero, this was an error but one which in my estimation expressed a deep truth. See later for Francesco's preference for Leonardo by making him his heir.

Freud emphasized the bearing his illegitimate birth had on Leonardo and this has been disputed by critics and others. This factor was of a general interest to Freud since he thought it to be particularly suitable for demonstrating the relevance accidental circumstances have to development. Freud assumed a close connection between the supposed vulture fantasy and Leonardo's illegitimate descent: since the vulture was believed to propagate parthenogenetically, it could well stand for a childbirth without previous cohabitation. We would now say that a vulture fantasy in such circumstances would have served the function of denial, as if to convey the idea that the child was born of a mother who had not contravened prohibitions but was a virgin. But we know that the fantasy Leonardo formed was not about a vulture, and this part of Freud's reconstruction was wrong as it stands now. During the last half-century, however, psychoanalytic theory has developed further, in that Freud and his co-workers have discovered a new phase in infantile development (Brunswick, 1928; Deutsch, 1930; Fenichel, 1930; Freud, 1931a; Lampl-de Groot, 1927). This is the *preoedipal phase,* which is characterized by its being dominated by the mother or her substitute to the exclusion of the father. It was first discovered in the psychosexual development of women but later also acknowledged in male development (cf. Brunswick, 1940). In this phase only the mother counts as a valid object; the father, if he acquires relevance at all, is experienced as nothing but an intruder. I think most analysts nowadays would look upon Leonardo's kite fantasy as a preoedipal one.

Freud stressed the biological factor underlying the childhood memory: the infant's pleasure in being suckled, and the equation of penis with breast which is formed some time later. But the biological concept of infantile orality covers a smaller area than that of the preoedipal phase. Freud required orality plus absence of the father—that is, a biological factor plus an accidental, environmental one—in order to fashion the memory, whereas the preoedipal phase alone suffices in order to account for it. In terms of practical research this means that Freud's explanation applied only if Leonardo's memory was in relation to a vulture, whereas the discovery of the preoedipal phase broadens the conceptual framework so far that any avian species, as long as the infant's relationship to the bird was of the type Leonardo described, can be fitted in.

The only aspect that remains to be explained is the reason for Leonardo's fixation to that phase, for it is reasonable to assume such a fixation in view of the absence of any other childhood memory and the consequent prominence of the kite recollection. It is this very fixation that speaks strongly in favor of there having been an intense, though possibly short-lasting, being together of mother and child and a subsequent disappearance of the mother, the situation being aggravated by the absence, or, at least, only rare presence, of the father. Thus the fact of illegitimacy had its bearing on the formation of the memory, though possibly in a more indirect sense than Freud assumed.

Be this as it may, there seems to be a tendency now to minimize the general effect of Leonardo's illegitimacy. Some authors, like Douglas (1944) and Vallentin (1938, p. 7),[4] deny any untoward effect. Wohl and Trosman (1955) even accuse Freud of carrying nineteenth-century feelings into the matter and dramatizing and sentimentalizing a subject that was looked upon quite differently in the Renaissance (p. 34f.).[5]

It appears to me that the ineptitude of the sociological trend within modern mental science can be demonstrated just in this instance. As is well known, Freud's theories of the human mind are assailed principally from two quarters. One school of thought, of less concern in this context, tries to reduce the observable data to the result of biological forces, such as the contest between the two principal drives, Eros and death instinct; the other, to the result of societal forces. In fact, Freud's theories explain the blending of the two.

In regard to Leonardo's illegitimacy, it seems that Wohl and Trosman were greatly misled through their lack of concern about the social structure of Renaissance society. In support of their thesis they cite historical instances such as that of Caterina Sforza, the natural daughter of Galeazzo Sforza, whose illegitimacy stood her in good stead. These authors forget that illegitimacy means something quite different among the powerful and noble from what it does with the commoner. Sarton

[4] Vallentin, however, assumes some psychological effect: she states that Leonardo felt that he was "in some way" not one of the family, although "he had been admitted in all external respects" (p. 7).

[5] The authors base this strange criticism on Freud's assumption that Leonardo's mother felt deeply disappointed at being abandoned by her lover and that she consequently turned with all the greater affection toward the infant (Freud, 1910, p. 116f.). From what sources these authors learn that women in the Renaissance period did not mind being deserted by a lover after having been made pregnant, is not known. For an important contribution to the history of Renaissance gynics, see Kelso (1956).

(1957, p. 32) reports that Cardano, born in Milan in 1501, was denied admittance to the College of Physicians in Milan because of his illegitimacy, and Cianchi (1952a, p. 54) asserts that Leonardo would not, because of his descent, have been permitted to follow his father's profession even if he had received the latter's full support.[6]

As so often, folklore conveys man's true feeling. There was a rather touching belief that clearly demonstrates the feeling about legitimacy and illegitimacy in those centuries—a belief that still persists in our time. A legend often depicted between the twelfth and seventeenth centuries can be cited here. Its general moral was that only illegitimate sons would shoot at their father's corpse (Stechon, 1942). The meaning of the fable reflects the feelings the father as well as the son were supposed to harbor toward each other.

As a matter of fact, Ser Piero died intestate and Leonardo was excluded from a share in the inheritance.[7] Francesco, the uncle, however, passed on to Leonardo the usufruct of all his property, which was to come into the possession of Ser Piero's legitimate children after Leonardo's death. The lawsuit Leonardo started against his siblings after his uncle's death shows that Leonardo did not take his illegitimacy with equanimity; this at least is the opinion of the historian Beltrami (1921b).

The mistake Wohl and Trosman make in evaluating Leonardo's illegitimacy seems twofold. First, they apply to the middle class something that was valid for the noble (see Seidlitz, 1909b, p. 10). Throughout the Middle Ages—and, indeed, until recently—illegitimate descent from a king or any person high in the feudal hierarchy was considered honorable. In medieval times cities even vied with one another to see which one a sovereign would choose his paramour from, although in general a woman who indulged in illicit intercourse was stigmatized. Much historical material can be cited that demonstrates the sexual privileges of those who were close to the top of the hierarchi-

6 Cianchi writes: "His [Leonardo's] condition [of birth] precluded or at least hampered greatly any career and perhaps the access to studies. Not even Ser Piero could have associated him to his profession" (1952a, p. 54). Cf. also Christensen: "It was not customary in middle class families to bring up illegitimate in the same household with legitimate children though this happened at the courts among the ruling upper classes" (1944, p. 160). Too late to make full use of it, I came across Doren's book. Cf. his statement that illegitimate sons were excluded from Florentine guilds at that time (1908, p. 143f.).

7 It seems that the law would have made it impossible for him to inherit any of his father's property, even by testament.

cal pyramid. But in the middle class the situation was different. Here, there was nothing honorable about the condition of illegitimacy for anyone involved: father, mother, or offspring. Secondly, in so far as there is a difference between illegitimacy for classes below the nobility in the Renaissance and in recent times, the difference is greatest for the father, least for the mother. Whereas in the Victorian age, for example, a man would have tried to conceal the fact that he had an illegitimate child, in the Italian Renaissance he would have feared no stigma—indeed, he might have been proud of it.[8] For his child, while he might, as in Leonardo's case, acknowledge him, take him into his household, and even win some degree of social acceptance for him in his circle more readily than later, he was powerless to surmount the juridical and institutionalized obstacles to his son's full integration into the community, e.g., as a fully legal heir, as an eligible entrant into a profession. The status of the mother was even more dubious: except by marriage, there was no way she could achieve even partial acceptance. A man might live fairly openly with a mistress, but she would be hardly any more respected then than in the nineteenth century; a castoff mother of an illegitimate child would be no better off than in the age of Victoria—nor would the child so long as he was with her. That the mother had to bear a considerable load of shame is borne out by Pierpaccini's assertion that the identity of the mother was concealed in such a situation. Thus Freud was possibly right in presuming a strong reaction in Caterina, although he too knew well that illegitimacy was not considered "a grave social stigma [schwerer bürgerlicher Makel]" in those days (1910, p. 81).

What are the facts of external evidence in Leonardo's case? When Leonardo's father died he left eleven legitimate children (nine sons and two daughters), one of them born shortly before (or after?) his death at the age of seventy-eight. Circumstances permit the assumption that progeny (particularly male progeny, as is usual in the case of ambitious men, and particularly in a historical period of emphasized individuality and in a family of long tradition) played a major role in Ser Piero's outlook on life. If one takes note that his first legitimate child was born of his third wife in 1476, when Leonardo was twenty-four years old—that is to say, that for twenty-four years Ser Piero

[8] This apparently was peculiar to Italy, for Vallentin (1938, p. 7) reports the surprise of Philippe de Comines, who was envoy of Louis XI, to learn of this custom.

did not know whether or not he would have legitimate progeny—
he must conclude that Ser Piero during that time experienced severe
frustration. That he might, in such a situation, have preferred certainty to uncertainty, and tried to legitimatize his first-born, seems
reasonable.

Was it at that time legally possible to accomplish this, aside from
marriage with the mother, if Ser Piero desired to do so? It seems that
several legal possibilities would have been open to Ser Piero,[9] such as
adoption or *legitimatio per rescriptum papae*. Ser Piero was a man
familiar with the law and he had excellent connections. There must
have been a strong personal reason at work to estop him, since, so far
as is known, no endeavor along these lines was made. After all, Leonardo's Renaissance biographers mention his illegitimate birth, and if
there had been an attempt at undoing it (even an unsuccessful one),
it very probably would have been recorded.

Indeed it seems that from the beginning the boy was destined to
take a station inferior to that of his family. He did not receive what
would today be called an education,[10] and he remained his whole life
un uomo senza lettere (Sarton, 1957, p. 230). However, I doubt that
Sarton is right when he goes on to say that Leonardo "paid but little
attention to books." His endeavors, probably futile, to learn Latin are
well known,[11] and I assume he had the difficulties so many people

[9] I wish to thank here Professors Frederick Kessler, Stephan Kuttner, and Anton-Hermann
Chroust for their courtesy in giving me their expert opinions on this legal problem. See also
McDevitt (1941) and Smiraglia (1900, pp. 19-21).

[10] Olschki (1919-27) says that Leonardo's education was no different from that of other
youths who came from prosperous bourgeois families in Tuscany of that time (Vol. I, p.
25). Is this really correct? Alberti, born in Venice in 1404, certainly received a far superior
education. Cf. Olschki's comments to this (Vol. I, p. 46ff.). I wonder if Leonardo's father
would, if his son had been legitimate, have left him in Vinci till the age of sixteen or
seventeen, or would not have provided the educational opportunities of Florence, which
must have been far superior to those of Vinci. Sarton believes that if Leonardo "had been
well born, his father would probably have provided for his education and sent him eventually to the University of Florence" (1957, p. 220). Sarton believes this would have had a
detrimental effect upon the genius, but in our analysis of the feelings the father presumably
harbored for his oldest son this viewpoint, correct as it may be in itself, is not relevant.

[11] MacCurdy (1956, p. 17), however, suggests the possibility that Leonardo was hired
to give Latin lessons to Lodovico Sforza's sons and this was the reason he underwent the
trouble of studying the language. I have nowhere else found such an opinion. Cf. de
Santillana (1953, p. 46) for an opinion that is far more probable. Olschki (Vol. I, p. 290)
claims that Leonardo had read more and with greater understanding than his contemporary
scientists. He also asserts that Leonardo was fluent in Latin (Vol. I, p. 319). For a thought-
provoking explanation of the numerous pages among Leonardo's *Notes* devoted to Latin
grammar and vocabulary, see Olschki (Vol. I, pp. 320-325).

encounter in later years when they did not learn opportunely how to handle the machinery of scholarly pursuits smoothly. Although the fact that Leonardo was largely an autodidact stood him in good stead, and with traditional education he probably would not have developed into the great scientist he was, we still should not overlook that Ser Piero had been withholding an education from the boy. It is scarcely believable that Ser Piero would have encountered resistance to learning in him. Valentiner (1949a, p. 45) is reminded of Goethe and his father when writing of Leonardo and Ser Piero. But whereas Goethe's father found his own fulfillment in his son's rise, Ser Piero's putting Leonardo as apprentice in Verrocchio's workshop impresses me as a step intended to solve an embarrassing situation. At that time—and Leonardo was to play a not minor role in changing this state of affairs[12] —the artist did not yet have anything of that almost charismatic prestige that he acquired in the high Renaissance. Artists were still regarded "as higher-grade craftsmen and their social origins and education do not make them any different from the petty bourgeois elements of the guilds" (Hauser, 1951, Vol. I, p. 311).

When Ser Piero gave his son to Verrocchio, he must have felt he was helping him to start the career of an ordinary craftsman who, if he turned out to be unusually talented, might reach a top place in his group but would never acquire a social status that could match that of his anticipated legitimate progeny. This, at least, is the impression one may easily form in view of the social status an artist was accorded at the time.[13] Posterity, knowing what a stroke of good luck it was that Leonardo was given into Verrocchio's care, might easily overlook that an event, proved later most propitious, was not necessarily brought about by love and affection.[14] It seems that despite his rise and although he even associated with kings, the mark of his birth

[12] Cf. Hauser (1951, Vol. I, p. 324): "The gradual ascent of the artist is mirrored most clearly of all in the career of Leonardo."

[13] I have not been able to find out why Leonardo's illegitimate origin did not militate against his entrance into the Guild of St. Luke, whereas he would have been obstructed in the vocation of a notary. This little detail may again reflect the relatively low social prestige of the artist around that time. Were more illegitimately born engaged in careers as artists at that time than in other vocations? Aside from Leonardo, I know of Alberti, Ghiberti, Giorgione, and Filippino Lippi.

[14] Michelangelo, born 1475, that is, thirteen years after Leonardo, had to overcome his father's fierce opposition in order to enter the career of an artist.

was not forgotten either by him or his brothers. As I have mentioned, he and his brothers were involved in a court suit the object of which was Leonardo's inheritance from his uncle Francesco. The background and details of this litigation cannot be reconstructed as reliably as one would wish (Beltrami, 1921b), but the present assumption that it rested on Leonardo's illegitimacy seems to be well founded. Significantly, this would have worked in a twofold way: first, Francesco's will, according to present reconstruction, was contested because Leonardo, being illegitimate, had, in the eyes of his family, no right to the inheritance, and, second, Leonardo put up a fight the intensity of which was out of proportion to the small value at stake just because the effect of his birth was involved. Thus even in his sixth decade, after dukes and kings had vied for his favor, Leonardo was still quite sensitive and vulnerable when reference was made to his birth, and his brothers and in-laws apparently united against him as an outsider who was not entitled to consider himself one of the clan. Consequently, whatever the social, legal, or moral consequences of illegitimacy may have been at that epoch, there is historical evidence of Leonardo's ill feelings. Francesco's preference for Leonardo, as appears in his will, has been cited as proof of the harmlessness of Leonardo's illegitimacy. The ensuing litigation disproves this interpretation. It seems to me that Francesco may also have felt like an outcast, since he apparently did not fit into the general family pattern. A rivalry with his older brother may safely be assumed, and here he had an opportunity pointedly to satisfy old resentments. His preference for Leonardo may show precisely how much he was aware of Leonardo's descent.[15]

There is a remark by Leonardo written on a sheet with anatomical drawings which it is possible to interpret as expressing revenge for the injustice of illegitimacy. It reads as follows:

> The man who uses coitus with contention and with depreciation makes irritable and untrustworthy children and when the coitus is made with great love and great desire of the partners then the child will be of great intellect, spirited and lively and lovable [Belt, 1955, p. 47].

[15] To what extent his estopping Leonardo from the free disposal of the property and limiting his access to usufruct may still have reflected a negative response to illegitimacy and to what extent it may have been enforced by legal necessities I cannot decide.

That Leonardo was of great intellect and lovable was not only the opinion of those about him but must have been part and parcel of his own self-evaluation. That bastards are conceived in passion has been a widespread belief. Perhaps in this remark (the source of which should not be too difficult to find) we may see a dig at his siblings and the conversion of a stigma into a mark of excellency.

10

Problems of Homosexuality and Object Relations

Here is the place to add a few words about that episode in Leonardo's life that suggests his possibly having had homosexual relations as a young man.

In Florence, the anonymous denunciation of citizens was institutionalized. Leonardo and two other Florentine youths were alleged to have had carnal relations with one Jacopo Saltarelli, seventeen years old and known for homosexual prostitution. Two hearings were held, on April 8, and June 7, 1476. The defendants went free. It seems that no final verdict was reached but the whole matter dismissed on the basis of insufficient evidence. Fumagalli (1952) intimates that there probably was a dismissal because the scion of a leading Florentine family, Tornabuoni, was implicated (p. 98). Since the investigation was brought about by anonymous denunciation, the veracity of the accusation has rightly been doubted by most writers. However, in instances that I have been able to follow up I have been surprised by the frequency of an observation I can best summarize as "the gossiper is right." I mean by this an observation not unlike one that Freud made when inquiring into the projections of the paranoid. Despite the delusional nature of the paranoid's effusions, he is not arbitrary in the selection of the area into which he projects; that is to say, his projection is guided by external circumstances into which his projection fits (Freud, 1922, p. 236). Likewise the gossiper, unless he is quite pathological, does not select his victim and the kind of denunciation arbitrarily, but is intuitively guided by the psychology of the person he maligns. The fact, so unfortunate for the historian, is, however, that one cannot learn from gossip whether it refers to the conscious or unconscious of the implicated person—to an action or to an unconscious wish. In the instance of the denunciation Leonardo was subjected to, the utmost we would be permitted to derive with certainty would be that Leonardo had homosexual wishes or tendencies. However, for this conclusion we do not need to rely on the accusation raised against the young Leonardo for, as we shall later see, there is direct evidence thereof available from Leonardo's notes. The historical record in connection with the affair of 1476 would be of interest only if we could learn from it whether or not Leonardo actually engaged in manifest relations at that time. This, however, cannot be determined from these documents.

There is, however, another report that may encourage some investigators to draw definite conclusions. On a dated drawing that shows two Profiles and Studies of Machinery (Plate 11), and that unquestionably stems from Leonardo, one finds the following inscription:

Fieravanti, Domenico's son, in Florence who showed himself as extraordinarily affectionate towards me as a maiden, I could love [Thiis, 1913, p. 151; F.U.].[1]

and underneath:

In Sept., 1478, I began the two Madonnas . . . and a similar one in Pistoja [Thiis, p. 151].

Leonardo's handwriting in this paragraph is particularly difficult to decipher, more so than usual. This is possibly one of the reasons why the relevant passage has been translated by Richter as:

. . . at Pistoja, Fieravante di Domenico at Florence is my most beloved friend, as though he were my [brother] [Richter, Vol. II, p. 350, No. 1383].[2]

[1] The Italian transcript is as follows: ". . . e che aparve amantissimo quanto mi e una vergine che io ami" (Thiis, p. 151). Dr. R. Almansi informs me that this statement may be understood slightly differently, namely, that Fieravanti impressed Leonardo as such a person.

[2] For a critical discussion of Richter's translation see Thiis (1913).

Since Thiis reacts almost with fury to the idea that Leonardo's purity was soiled by a contemporary's denunciation (p. 134f.), one can be sure that the reading of this suggestive inscription is not the result of any bias in favor of homosexuality. The author does not consider the possibility of such an interpretation and is mainly concerned with the question of how Leonardo ever got to Pistoja in 1478. The psychological interpretation of the passage is not easy since it depends on fine linguistic shades. Does "I could love him as a maiden" mean that he did not, but that it was a possibility if he let himself go? As strongly as the entry may suggest that a physical incident had occurred, someone familiar with the language of the time may demonstrate that affectionate relations were described in physical terms. If the physical aspect could be verified, one would think of a mainly passionate relation with inhibition or repression of the personal attachment that we would call object relation in the narrower sense of the word.

The little that can be said about this sentence is that it weights the scales in favor of assuming a physical relation in Leonardo's younger years, but it does not prove it beyond doubt. More important is the fact that the inscription was made on a sheet on which there are the profiles of an old and a young man, a theme that runs consistently through Leonardo's drawings (cf. Popham, 1945, p. 4) and about which I will have to say more later. It may throw a light on the meaning of homosexuality to Leonardo when he was old himself—namely, as a vehicle for rejuvenation. That we find it on a drawing of the young Leonardo combined with a sentence that suggests active homosexuality may indicate that he was motivated by repressed passive wishes.

The reference to the paintings of Madonnas is suggestive of: (a) an attempt at redemption by a turn toward the asexual mother, (b) the necessity of keeping the sexual drive free from longings for the female, who is to be preserved in consoling purity. The aggression against the female, inherent in homosexuality, is thus denied and the claim set forth that respect and esteem for women force the subject to seek gratification with the coarser sex.

Yet it can hardly be denied that, all in all, the ingredients of homosexuality as asserted by psychoanalysis are gathered on this sheet: the active impulses toward an effeminate contemporary that disguises a conflict in the parental relation, the passive submission to a father figure, and a distant adoration of a revered mother.

Returning to the episode of 1476, it can safely be stated that, whatever the conclusion regarding latent or manifest homosexuality may be, the denunciation did not depend only on the anonymous delator's envy, righteousness, and viciousness—or whatever may have motivated him—but also on the behavior of Leonardo himself. To be sure, he was not singled out but was one of four young men who had to appear before the magistrate. From clinical experience one knows that, rare exceptions aside, a person does not become involved in such a situation without some internal cause that has a bearing on external behavior. Consequently, we ought not to neglect the fact that, in the same year in which Leonardo had to defend himself before the magistrate, his father's first legitimate child, Antonio, was born.[3]

This event must have had a great effect upon Leonardo. His father's first wife, Albiera di Giovanni Amadori, had died on June 15, 1464, in childbirth (Cianchi, 1952a, pp. 49, 76). Evidently the child was born dead, since Antonio, son of Ser Piero's third wife, born in 1476, is listed as the father's oldest legitimate child.

In view of the confusion about birth necessarily brought about in the infant's and growing child's mind by his illegitimate status, and the death of his first stepmother caused by childbirth, we can be certain that a new pregnancy and birth must have elicited an intense reaction in Leonardo. As a matter of fact, I once observed a patient whose only manifest homosexual experience as an adult occurred during the night his wife gave birth to his first child. It is understandable that a man for whom pregnancy and childbirth constitute traumatic events turns away from female objects when exposed to the unbearable pressure of a repetition of the trauma. I also wish to emphasize vigorously here that Ser Piero in his four marriages usually chose a young girl as spouse, which must have set aflame Leonardo's oedipal conflict even more than it unavoidably would have in any circumstances.[4] This in turn must have heightened the feelings of

[3] Antonio's birthday was on February 26, 1476 (see Möller, 1934, p. 387).
[4] The consequences of this factor cannot be discussed here. This much only may be said, that the creativity of the genius requires that the oedipus conflict remain alive. To be sure, this does not depend on accidental factors, such as the youthfulness of Leonardo's stepmothers. Leonardo found himself here in a situation that might have impeded the creative process, since what usually is fantasy or repressed memory in the genius, in Leonardo's life

guilt immensely. It is not quite easy to predict whether a conflict-ridden situation such as that in which Leonardo found himself in 1476 would make a subject turn toward active or passive homosexuality. In the artistically creative or endowed man one may anticipate an upsurge of passive homosexuality. This is suggested by the rivalry with maternal creativity which, as a secondary factor, plays a prominent role in very many of the most creative personalities (cf. Kris and Kurz, 1934, p. 114). But the external circumstances asserted in the denunciation make active homosexual acts, if any, more probable.

The appearance of a legitimate child must also have reactivated an old conflict in the young man. Was he not hopelessly disinherited, if not disowned, when a legitimate sibling started to divert paternal affection away from him? The father's unrelenting effort at legitimate progeny must have been experienced by the first-born as an aggression against and disapproval of him.

Homosexuality was not infrequent in that time and place. Fumagalli (1952) makes a remark about sodomy within the elite of the fourteenth and fifteenth centuries; apparently it was frequent among the high clergy, humanists, literati, and higher nobility. Thus one must say that it was not eschewed, although it was punishable by burning at the stake (Fumagalli, p. 102). Apparently, as in the present, it was condoned as long as it was practiced clandestinely. Once brought to public attention, I presume, it not only endangered the accused but also brought shame and embarrassment upon his family. Thus as a secondary element conducive to his homosexuality there may be conjectured the following two factors: (1) an aggression against the father by endangering his professional prestige, and (2) a cry for help in a situation of unbearable internal conflict. Since the father, a man of law, may have given him his assistance under the pressure of the reality situation, the secondary motive may have been fulfilled by the procedure.

I am inclined to assume that at that time Leonardo, at least for a short while, indulged in manifest homosexual relations. Of course,

---

repeatedly became a reality factor. The father's marriages and his wives' pregnancies not only fanned the unconscious part of the oedipus complex but re-created the corresponding reality situations and thus repeated actual past traumata in actual present reality. Much as the persistence of the tension created by the infantile and childhood conflict may contribute to the momentum of artistic creativity, so perilous may it be to the creative potential when the psychic apparatus has to bear the literal repetition of past traumata.

this rests on conjecture and no proof can be adduced. At any rate, it is not a matter of importance. Whether the indomitable drives typical of his years, to which was added a desperate reality situation that resulted in jealousy and anger toward his father, actually led to manifest homosexual relations or, instead, led to behavior that suggested such activities to others but did not involve actual sexual contacts, is psychologically not relevant. If there was manifest activity, it cannot have lasted long.

Of far greater importance is Leonardo's sexual behavior as a mature man. Here one has to speculate about what his relation was to Gian Giacomo de'Caprotti detto Salaij (1480-1524), as his name is spelled in documents (Möller, 1928, p. 140). Until 1491 he appears as Giacomo and from then on as Salai in Leonardo's *Notes*. When the boy was ten he was taken by Leonardo into his household not to leave him again until the master left Italy for France. Salai was a waif and Leonardo has many bitter words about his thievery and bad character. But he was a charming child who developed into a handsome young man, and despite all the unrest he brought into the household Leonardo could not let him go. Möller (1928) gathered all the instances in Leonardo's work where Salai was used as a model. We shall see that Leonardo's relationship apparently changed essentially later.

What is so striking in this relationship is a factor that can often be observed in the heterosexual relations of a man who is endowed with a great creative potential. Since his creative work requires an excessive degree of sublimation, it deprives him of adequate physical gratification; accordingly, he attaches himself compensatorily to a woman who is impulse-ridden and uninhibited in her instinctual life. Thus he can undo the lack of intense gratifications which prevails in his own life by experiencing them vicariously in the object's release. I surmise that Salai had a function of this sort in Leonardo's life. Observing the misdeeds of this charming delinquent rascal may have softened the sting of Leonardo's excessive renunciations. But the subject who might have been destined to make renunciation palatable switched in turn into its opposite and became a source of almost irresistible temptation.

There is a drawing by Leonardo, the so-called Oxford Allegory of *Pleasure and Pain* (Plate 12), which shows two men with trunk and legs in common. I doubt Popham is correct when he describes it as:

"A nude figure with four arms and two heads" (1945, p. 118), for the essential feature seems to me to be a (temporary?) unification of two men. Leonardo's own description of *Pleasure and Pain* as twins supports this view. The man in front is the older one; the young man in the back, according to Möller (1928, p. 145), has the features of Salai. He is holding a reed in his hand. The object which the older man is holding has not been identified (Möller, 1928, p. 146). With his left hand, which is stretched out to the back, the young man lets drop gold coins. Leonardo's detailed account of the Allegory is not important in this context. The opening paragraphs convey no more than a firm assertion that pleasure is objectionable:

> Pleasure and Pain are represented as twins, as though they were joined together, for there is never the one without the other; and they turn their backs because they are contrary to each other.
> If you shall choose pleasure, know that he has behind him one who will deal out to you tribulation and repentance [MacCurdy, 1956, p. 1097; Ox. 107 v.].

There are other passages in Leonardo's notes that assert the same rejecting attitude of pleasure. Fortunately, there is on the same page still another comment by Leonardo referring to the Allegory (cf. Popham, p. 118, text of illustration No. 108). It says:

> This is pleasure together with pain, and they are represented as twins because the one is never separated from the other.
> They are made with their backs turned to each other because they are contrary the one to the other. They are made growing out of the same trunk because they have one and the same foundation, for the foundation of pleasure is labour with pain, and the foundations of pain are vain and lascivious pleasures.
> And accordingly it is represented here with a reed in the right hand, which is useless and without strength, and the wounds made with it are poisoned. In Tuscany reeds are put to support beds, to signify that here occur vain dreams, and here is consumed a great part of life: here is squandered much useful time, namely that of the morning when the mind is composed and refreshed and the body therefore is fitted to resume new labours. There also are taken many vain pleasures, both with the mind imagining impossible things, and with the body taking those pleasures which are often the cause of the failing of life; so that for this the reed is held as representing such foundations [MacCurdy, p. 1097; Ox. 107 v.].[5]

[5] In what Leonardo says in general terms about pleasure and pain he follows to a certain extent a historical pattern (see Panofsky, 1939, p. 217). The additional comment no doubt reveals a personal feeling in a personal matter.

I take some of these passages as Leonardo's free associations to the Allegory. Its substance refers to the fantasies Leonardo had while lying in bed, the sexual excitement in the early morning hours when he indulged in sexual daydreams about Salai. Literally, the text may suggest that he observed Salai lying idly in bed, which may have been the case, but it also conveys the impression that the imagining of impossible things and the pleasures that cause life to fail were known to Leonardo by his own experience. Notwithstanding the historical antecedents of the imagery used by Leonardo to visualize his thoughts about pleasure and pain, I shall try to analyze the sketch in terms of Leonardo's personal relationship to the body of the youth.

A very striking feature is the lack of clarity in the drawing—as well as in Leonardo's comment—as to whether the fusion is meant to include the young man's genital. The drawing permits either the interpretation that there are two male bodies united at their backs and ending in one pair of legs, the individual genitals being preserved, or that there is only one full body, with buttocks, genital, and back ending in two heads.[6] When Leonardo writes "they are made with their backs turned" he suggests the former interpretation; when he speaks of "the same trunk" and "the same foundation" he suggests the latter. But it may strike one as strange that just that twin which symbolizes pleasure would in the latter case be deprived of a penis (the penis of the older man who represents pain is visible). At any rate, Leonardo is lacking in clarity here, contrary to Socrates who said in *Phaedo* of pleasure and pain that "their bodies are two, but they are joined by a single head" (Jowett, 1892, Vol. I, p. 443).

It is possibly just this ambiguity that is one of the characteristic features. Greenacre (1953, p. 91f.) recently called attention to the fact that the child is actually impeded in gaining clarity about the physical structure of that part of his own body that is not accessible to visual inspection; that is to say, this is an area where infantile fantasy is less restrained by reality in imagining that which it desires to imagine. In the instance of the aging Leonardo, it was the rejuvenation by fusion with the young, the carefree, the unencumbered, and the beautiful—in short, all that he lacked in order to feel physically blissful

---

[6] The motif of double head appears also in *An Allegory of Statecraft* (Oxford, Christ Church; Popham, 1945, Plate 105). Prudence is depicted "with a double head and body, half man, half woman" (Popham, p. 117).

—and this was integrated by imaginary reorganization of visually inaccessible parts of the body. It seems important that in this drawing the port of entry is the anal zone. Whichever alternative of the aforementioned ambiguity is valid, the emphasis on the anal factor is unmistakable.

The anal factor is strongly represented in Leonardo's character by derivatives as well as reaction formations: stress on and pride in cleanliness; desire for order; aversion to dirt, bad odors, and noise; unconcern about money and wealth combined with occasional pettiness in monetary matters.[7]

In the allegorical drawing the buttocks become the leading physical zone of a narcissistic relationship to an object.

What is further striking is the maintenance of genital integrity. Despite the fusion—whether merely attempted or actually fulfilled—the object cannot be reached genitally. It looks almost as if one function of the imagery were to make sure that the genital can be protected against any encroachment by the object. The position of the arms suggests imagery of mutual masturbation or the defense against it—but more of that later.

The general idea of the drawing may rest on an excessive longing for a homosexually loved object and the simultaneous impossibility of ever reaching it, for in the Allegory the two men, despite their maximum closeness, are forever separated by the impossibility of seeing each other. I surmise that fusion with an object was viewed as a process of the greatest bliss, which, however, must not be attained because of the unspeakable grief that sets in as soon as the fusion ends. The longing for fusion is part of instinctual life, and the way nature affords for satisfying the longing is genital union. Genital union, however, involves the rise of tension to the highest level and its drop to a low level within a relatively short time span. If life processes are viewed in economic terms, it may be said that it is perhaps the genital gratification that puts the greatest demand upon the psychic apparatus.[8]

When, after the orgastic relief, tension is reduced to zero, this often

[7] Much evidence could be adduced to demonstrate Leonardo's anality. I will set forth just one example. Leonardo raises the question: *Perchè li cani odorà volentieri il culo l'uno al l'altro* [Why do dogs like to smell one another's arse] (F 47 r.). His explanation refers exclusively to the smell of feces.

[8] We shall later see that it was perhaps this strain that resulted in a grave impediment to an unencumbered genital excitement in Leonardo.

leads to the feeling of an object loss, or, at least, it may destroy the previous idealization of the object.[9] At the same time, it may lead to a desire for a permanent object attachment on a pregenital basis independent of "genital arbitrariness," a factor that was of importance in Leonardo's life as can be demonstrated from extant source material (see later). It seems that such a permanent attachment to the object required, for Leonardo, the exclusion of the object's visual representation. As long as the object is visually represented, the relation to it is subjected to a varying degree of stimulation, and the beholder is aware of the object's weakness.

Leonardo wrote:

The body of anything whatever that takes nourishment constantly dies and is constantly renewed [Richter, Vol. II, p. 103, No. 843; W. 19045 r.]. Man dies and always partly generates again [Vangensten et al., Vol. I, p. 32; Q.I. 12 r.].[10]

In life beauty perishes and does not endure [MacCurdy, 1956, p. 91; Forster III 72 r.].[11]

The object's approach to death and the diminution of its beauty by the mere process of life were, apparently, two indelible marks that marred the pleasure of normal object relations.

Leonardo's extreme sensitivity can be demonstrated in many areas and it is reasonable to assume that imperfections—of which the object's liability to die and the transitoriness of its beauty are not the least—made object love painful for him.[12] The Studies of Heads in the Uffizi (Plate 13) may be used as evidence of this factor in Leonardo's relationship to Salai. The right head unmistakably has Salai's features and the old man to the left impresses me as a transcription of the young face into the anticipated pattern of old age.[13]

[9] See Freud's concept of sexual overvaluation (1905a, pp. 151-154).

[10] This awareness of the process of constant death and renewal in the object is re-encountered in Leonardo's general view of nature. See Richter (Vol. II, p. 258, No. 1219; B.M. 156 v.). For time as a power causing cycles of procreation and destruction, see Panofsky (1939, p. 82).

[11] For a discussion of the Neoplatonic view of beauty, see Robb (1935, p. 113ff.). Cf. also Panofsky (1939, p. 134). The line occurs in a sonnet by Petrarch.

[12] How far Leonardo's fear of transitoriness went can be seen also in the advice he gave himself: "Avoid studies of which the result dies with the worker" (Richter, Vol. II, p. 244, No. 1169; Forster III 55 r.).

[13] Here it seems as if the two bodies are fused by their upper extremities. See also the Windsor Studies of Heads (Bodmer, 1931, Plate 114) where a diagonally drawn series of three male heads seems to visualize the same problem. The Uffizi drawing could be

According to my interpretation we would have to conclude that Leonardo tried to solve the conflict inherent in his relationship to love objects by anal incorporation with the exclusion of visual and genital excitations.

But in the second comment regarding the Allegory of *Pleasure and Pain* that I have quoted Leonardo speaks of "pleasures which are often the cause of the failing of life." Does this refer to the forbidden pleasure of sexual daydreams, or of actual orgastic release?

The fear Leonardo expresses here, when encountered in clinical examination, regularly refers to the fear of having caused irreparable damage by masturbation. If we wish to understand Leonardo's psychosexual economy, we must try to discover whether the feeling of guilt that he refers to here originated in infantile masturbation and was secondarily attached to the sexual daydreams of the adult, or whether it was caused by adult masturbatory acts that led to ejaculation and orgasm. On the clinical level such fears usually are indicative of masturbation during the years of adulthood without excluding previous childhood masturbation, but the common clinical experience is not necessarily applicable to the genius, who functions in a way that is not comparable to anything expected from patients who come to psychoanalytic or psychiatric observation.

In Leonardo's case the hypercathexis of the hand is to be considered (Hermann, 1922). It is said he went out with his notebook and put down on the spot what was noteworthy. At any rate, it may be said that his life was one of drawing and thinking, if "thinking" is defined as comprising all the steps (such as experimenting and observing) that are necessary for the acquisition of reliable knowledge. In this context the part the hand played in drawing is of importance. It was, after all, that organ that was ever ready to fixate the fleeting sense impressions. I mentioned earlier that Leonardo may have had the feeling he "knew" an object only after he had drawn it to his satisfaction.

The combination of drawing and knowing is well known in Goethe's life. In his case, however, the talent for the graphic art never de-

---

interpreted as a sketch of what Leonardo's mentally associated image was in view of the handsome Salai's appearance. Cf. Clark (1935, p. xlix): "Two types in particular, the pretty boy and the aged warrior with a forbidding nutcracker profile, seem to have been those which came first to Leonardo's pen whenever he wished to draw a face."

veloped to any very high degree and was not able seriously or for a long time to divert him from the literary art. In moments of emotional importance he resorted to the verbal channel for expression. Also, his defense against emotions was per se less radical or intense than Leonardo's. In the latter's instance, the hand apparently was the organ of choice that assisted in converting the emotion into objective images; the hand was the principal agent of both defense and fulfillment. As he repeatedly stated, no other skill could match the graphic arts, and he wrote about a drawing of the heart (O'Malley and Saunders, 1952, Plate 173):

> With what words O writer can you with a like perfection describe the whole arrangement of that of which the design is here?
> For lack of due knowledge you describe it so confusedly as to convey but little perception of the true shapes of things . . .
> I counsel you not to cumber yourself with words unless you are speaking to the blind [MacCurdy, 1956, p. 166f.; Q. II, 1 r.].

In view of the supreme role the hand played, I surmise that there was a severe prohibition against defiling that all-important instrument. It is possible that the urge to touch the penis was totally displaced upon the urge to draw and paint.

The strong repulsion Leonardo felt about the sexual organs is well known. He wrote:

> The act of procreation and the members employed therein are so repulsive, that if it were not for the beauty of the faces and the adornments of the actors and the pent-up impulse, nature would lose the human species [MacCurdy, 1956, p. 97; Fogli A 10 r.].

The fact that this remark is found on a folio[13a] on which four of the ten intended demonstrations of the myology of the hand are drawn is of incomparable importance. Marie Bonaparte (1927) has drawn far-reaching conclusions from what looks like mere coincidence.[14]

> From the psychoanalytic point of view it is conceivable that this contiguity is not accidental and that there existed an unconscious connection between his undoubtedly extreme repression of infantile masturbation and

---

[13a] See O'Malley and Saunders (p. 154, Plate 57). These authors do not quote Leonardo's remark about the repulsiveness of the genitals.

[14] It is the instance with which she introduced the aforementioned method (p. 88f.) into the research on Leonardo.

his subsequent disgust of sexuality. This may even be true also of the fact that he was left-handed, or at least preferred the left hand for drawing, painting, and writing. For it is remarkable that the hands Leonardo drew on the page on which he set down his thoughts about the disgust prompted in him by the sexual act are *all right hands*.

[Il est permis de penser, du point de vue analytique, que cette contiguité n'est pas un hasard, et que quelque lien existait, dans l'inconscient de Léonard, entre la repression sans doute extrème de sa masturbation in-fantile et son dégoût ultérieur de la sexualité. Peut-être même avec le fait qu'il fût gaucher ou du moins se servit avec prédilection de la main gauche pour dessiner, peindre et écrire. Car il est remarquable que les mains des-sinées par Léonard sur le feuillet où il nota la pensée relative au dégoût que lui inspirait l'acte sexuel soient *toutes des mains droites*] [Bonaparte, 1927, p. 30, n.; author's italics].

Indeed, on the verso of this folio the bones and tendons of left hands are represented (O'Malley and Saunders, p. 58, Plate 10).

In studying the anatomy of the hand—and Leonardo's study also included function and movement—an archaic impulse to masturbate was probably reawakened. This impulse led to the visualization of the genitals. The impulse was restrained and probably repressed by a feeling of disgust regarding the sight of the genitals, a moral feeling thus being attached to the visualization of an external object. A re-versal is also noticeable in another passage of the same folio regarding the touching of an object with the fingers crossed and the resulting sensation:

> If you cross the digits c d (right and middle fingers) so that a (ulnar border of ring finger) and b (radial border of middle finger) touch one and the same object between them, and this object stimulates them so that the 2 fingers are made painful, I say that the object will give rise to pain in 3 places although applied to 2 [O'Malley and Saunders, p. 154; Fogli A 10 r.].

In view of the context I interpret this observation—very tentatively —as indicating that pleasure experienced in masturbation was con-verted into a pain felt in the fingers. Here we encounter some of the safeguards that are supposed to protect the regression of sublimation to its instinctual sources. Masturbation was a particularly great danger since it could be performed without exposing to sight the offensive genitals. Here we are dealing with what may have been an important link between the eye and the hand, sight permitting the mental grasp of objects without the necessity of touching them. Sight was thus not only the preferred channel through which the external world flowed into the psychobiological system (Fenichel, 1935) and through which it could be appropriated, but also the ideal channel that kept objects at a distance and prevented contamination and defilement. The hand was the organ that, by drawing, put reality back whence it had come. Involuntarily, one is reminded of Freud's account of the schizophrenic's withdrawal of cathexis from the world and reinvestment of it in the delusional system that now replaces reality lost (Freud, 1914a, p. 86).[15]

When one now views the Allegory of *Pleasure and Pain* in terms of the relation of the four hands to the exposed genital, one may say that their four positions strike one as the result of fumbling around with the intention of avoiding touching the penis, despite its attraction. Recalling Leonardo's intimation that certain pleasures "are often the cause of the failing of life," I suggest that because of the total displacement of the urge to touch the penis upon the urge to represent graphically, the sexual urge became so excessively pent up that there was the danger of a release by concentration upon sexual imagery, an instance of true "omnipotence of thought" (Freud, 1913a, pp. 75-99). Some of Leonardo's advice sounds like countermeasures to protect against this eventuality, which, in turn, would endanger the defense against instinctual gratification. Thus he wrote:

STUDYING, IN THE DARK, WHEN YOU WAKE,
OR IN BED BEFORE YOU GO TO SLEEP

I myself have proved it to be of no small use, when in bed in the dark, to recall in fancy the outlines of forms previously studied, or other noteworthy things conceived by subtle speculation; and this is certainly an admirable exercise, and useful for impressing things on the memory [Richter, Vol. I, p. 307, No. 496; Ash. I 26 r.].

When we compare this passage with Leonardo's comment, when he is writing about the allegory, on the dangers of the morning hours, we may conclude that at night the ego, still under the impression of the past day's pursuits, was well prepared to use these very impres-

---

[15] Freud noted these two trends in the artist: "An artist is originally a man who turns away from reality. . . . He finds the way back to reality . . . by making use of special gifts" (1911, p. 224).

sions for defensive purposes, whereas matutinal awakening found the ego defenseless and victimized by the sexual excitement so far accumulated. Evidently the mind had to be kept in a state of constant preoccupation with contents derived from external reality or else it might be overwhelmed by internal excitement and the imagery attached to it.

The great artist uses the imagery that flows from his preconscious or unconscious. In view of the dangers inherent in such imagery, Leonardo discovered an ingenious technique with which to get its support without risking exposure to its dangers. The famous passage reads as follows:

> I cannot forbear to mention among these precepts a new device for study which, although it may seem but trivial and almost ludicrous, is nevertheless extremely useful in arousing the mind to various inventions. And this is, when you look at a wall spotted with stains, or with a mixture of stones, if you have to devise some scene, you may discover a resemblance to various landscapes, beautified with mountains, rivers, rocks, trees, plains, wide valleys and hills in varied arrangement; or, again, you may see battles and figures in action; or strange faces and costumes, and an endless variety of objects, which you could reduce to complete and well-drawn forms. And these appear on such walls confusedly, like the sound of bells in whose jangle you may find any name or word you choose to imagine [Richter, Vol. I, p. 311f., No. 508; Ash. I 22 v.].[16]

Here we get a glimpse of the cooperation between various ego functions and the provinces of the personality. The ego constantly has to withstand the pressure of the repressed. It does not dare give access to it in the form of free-flowing fantasies, ascending directly from the unconscious as derivatives of the repressed. The detour used is perception safely anchored in neutral external contents. Within this framework projected imagery is less liable to get out of bounds. Thus the creative power of unconscious imagery can be used for the purpose of artistic inspiration without the danger of arousing undue excitement or anxiety.[17]

[16] See also *Trattato* Parte II, 189, Ludwig, Vol. I, p. 223f., where Leonardo gives the same advice but emphasizes more the structure than the raw sense data obtained through the act of perception. Kris correctly asserted a connection between Leonardo's procedure and the Rorschach experiment of our days (Kris and Kurz, 1934, p. 55).

[17] Here may be the link to a psychological explanation of what Clark described as the "sudden unannounced swings from observation into fancy" in Leonardo's imagination (1929, p. 126). Indeed, Leonardo's procedure is most perplexing except on the basis of

In asking the question "Why does the eye see a thing more clearly in dreams than with the imagination awake?" (Richter, Vol. II, p. 238, No. 1144; B.M. 278 v.), Leonardo was perhaps the first to perceive the problem with such clarity—the answer would have to wait for four centuries—and the objective, scientific merit of posing the question in correct terms is by no means reduced when I suggest that a subjective problem underlay his asking it. It sounds like a regret that the clarity and distinctness with which subjective imagery imposes itself upon the mind, comparable to perceptions of reality, should occur when the ego is paralyzed and incapacitated by sleep. Thus there are situations in which the ego may become a victim of its unruly repressed.

Consequently, I suggest that depicting, a leading creative ego function in Leonardo, derived its hypercathexis from the defense against masturbation.

The puzzling Allegory of *Pleasure and Pain* can be linked with another statement of Leonardo's. In a paragraph entitled "On the life of the painter in his studio," we find the following statement: "While you are alone you are entirely your own and if you have but one companion you are but half your own" (Richter, Vol. I, p. 307, No. 494; Ash. I 27 v.).

In my opinion, the statement that the self is reduced to a half by the presence of a companion contains one of the keys to Leonardo's psychopathology of object relations which is represented in the Oxford Allegory. That drawing can be viewed as, in one aspect, a pictorial representation of the process of self-reduction that Leonardo adumbrated in the simple words of advice to the tyro of the graphic arts. Salai was the preferred object of the adult Leonardo's libidinal strivings and a consummation of that love, whether physically or purely emotionally, would mean ceding half the personality to him. Leonardo is really representing himself in the Allegory with a hunch he would have to carry on his back if he permitted himself to love. "Do not reveal, if liberty is precious to you; my face is the prison of love"

---

such an explanation. Why should a person whose imagination was exquisite and rich—as can be seen from his *Trattato*, which abounds in vivid expositions of how to depict various subjects—have to resort to the projection of his imagery into neutral external configurations? Why should he be afraid of or inhibited about direct contact with the products of his fantasy?

(Richter, Vol. II, p. 343, No. 1367).[18] Consequently the person in love is unfree and is prevented from thinking and creating freely.[19]

Notwithstanding their great scientific value and meaning, Leonardo's notebooks convey a moving, subjective impression. Endlessly he wanders through the whole universe as it offered itself to his senses and works his way patiently through almost all observable phenomena, resting with one for a while before turning to the next; returning to the former perhaps, even after many years, or dismissing it forever. But he never reaches a final conclusion; not only does his labor not lead to a publishable manuscript (cf. Sarton, 1953, p. 18), but almost nothing is thought through in a way that would lead to a final settlement. One gets the impression that a mind was at work here that, with but few exceptions, almost deliberately left everything in suspension so that he could return to it at any moment and continue. Despite his enormous concentration on some topics—such as anatomy, the flight of birds, and the nature of water—one still retains the impression that here too everything was kept in flux. No doubt his mind had forever to be kept in motion, and the assertion of an extensive realm of unknown things was to assure him of the vastness of a territory in which to travel endlessly.

As in his relation to objects no final settlement was permitted to occur, likewise there had to be no resting point found in his never-ending scientific inquiries. It is conceivable that his fear of being crushed by consolidated knowledge was a counterpart of his fear of being crushed by a love object.

We have to proceed now to another interpretation that is suggested by the Oxford Allegory, namely, that it also contains birth fantasies. This is suggested, in my opinion, by comparison with other works of art. One example from among the many that, I am sure, might be cited is a panel in the bronze door of the Cathedral of St. Sophia in Novgorod, probably produced in the twelfth century, which depicts the creation of Eve (Plate 14). Here too a man is shown in upright position, another person growing out of his back. Oddly enough, the features of Eve look quite masculine and those of Adam appear rather

18 MacCurdy (1956) translates this passage: "If liberty is dear to you, may you never discover that my face is love's prison" (p. 1129; Forster III 10 v.).

19 Cf. Freud (1921, pp. 111-114) for a genetic and metapsychological account of such a state.

feminine and are almost identical with those of Eve in another panel (Leisinger, 1956, Plate 3) of the same door. I cite this instance of emblematic similarity because here the birth fantasy is quite openly represented.[20]

Thus the Oxford Allegory may also express the latent desire of the genius to create children (cf. Jacobson, 1950). Leonardo had initially a maternal attitude toward the boy Salai; he fed and cared for him, and, despite a later significant change of relation, he preserved his loyalty and devotion to him, as can be seen from his last will in which he bequeathed "the moiety, of his garden which is outside the walls of Milan . . . to Salai his servant" (Richter, Vol. II, p. 389, No. 1566). In Leonardo's case the particular infantile roots of this urge to produce children are not known. The urge is to be presumed per se in most geniuses of great creativity, and can be demonstrated directly if sufficient biographical data are preserved.

EXCURSUS ON FREUD'S THEORY OF LEONARDO'S RELATIONSHIP TO HIS CREATIONS

According to Freud, the way Leonardo treated the works of art he created (1910, p. 121) echoed the neglectful treatment he had received from his father, thus showing the same genesis one can so often recognize in the disturbance of the parent-child relation when a parent's behavior reflects the way he had been treated when he was a child. However, as right as Freud was, in my opinion, in asserting this general principle of Leonardo's relationship to his works, he may have been mistaken in applying it specifically to the period of Leonardo's life that was dominated by his patron Lodovico Sforza (cf. Schapiro, 1956, p. 177). Freud thought that Leonardo's most productive artistic period occurred in Milan "where a kindly fate enabled him to find a father-substitute in the Duke Lodovico Moro" (1910, p. 133).[21]

We touch here on a question that like almost no other demonstrates both the contribution psychology may potentially make to a historical inquiry and also the sheer insurmountable obstacles it encounters in

[20] Although I would consider Leonardo's Allegory a genuine product of his imagination no matter what sources may have stimulated him, I still think the study of emblematically similar works is useful for the discovery of concealed aspects of meaning.

[21] Hildebrandt regards Leonardo's Milan period as perhaps the peak of his creativeness (1927, p. 155).

endeavoring to do so. The genius's relationship to his creations as if they were his children is observable in Leonardo and is well documented in other instances, such as Goethe's. A qualitative comparison of a genius's creativity during the different phases of his activity is quite difficult, and historians will probably not reach agreement in this area within the near future.

As long as the psychoanalyst does not obtain reliable data from the expert in the field to which psychoanalysis is being applied there will be a fringe area of seeming arbitrariness, as can be seen in the instance under discussion. I think, however, it would be a serious interference with the furtherance of applied psychology if the psychologist were forbidden to fill with tentative conclusions the gaps that exist where special studies have not yet provided the desired certainty.

Douglas (1944), for example, believes that the six years following Leonardo's stay in Milan were more productive than the sixteen spent there (p. 25). Clark (1939), too, believes that Leonardo's second stay in Florence was more productive than his Milanese years, and he gives a challenging explanation of it. He believes that the popular enthusiasm that Leonardo met in Florence, as Vasari reported, would hardly have been possible in Milan, and this helps us to understand why the five or six years spent in Florence were so much more productive than the thrice longer period spent in North Italy (p. 107).[22] To be sure, it is a foregone conclusion that success or failure have their bearing on the artist, but do they have really such deep-going effects as Clark seems to assume? The psychoanalyst would feel inclined to see in them only secondary factors, and to search for motives of the order Freud proposed. However, we may be able to dispense with specific evaluations of productivity and study Freud's general proposition in particular situations, namely, the change or stability of attitudes in the course of modified reality situations.

The final evaluation of Freud's remark will depend on what we have to assume the relationship was between Leonardo and Lodovico. Freud was well aware that the duke was "a man of ambition and a lover of splendour, astute in diplomacy, but of erratic and unreliable character" (1910, p. 121). This picture, which is how the historians show him,

[22] However, at another point Clark seems to limit this period to a later part of Leonardo's second stay in Florence, namely the three years following his service for Cesare Borgia (1939, p. 114).

would, however, not yet tell us what type of relationship existed between patron and artist. According to Vallentin (1938), one can hardly think of a worse one; but her inclination toward the biographical novel and consequent dramatization should warn against unchecked acceptance. Yet a sober-minded historian like Seidlitz, who speaks in gentle terms of the way Leonardo was met in Milan, produces sufficient evidence to warrant the assumption that Leonardo experienced in Lodovico a rather stern father substitute (Seidlitz, 1909b, pp. 183, 208f.), who did not reveal anything like an understanding of the genius despite the great praise he bestowed upon him shortly before his downfall (p. 211). Thus Lodovico, who, just because of his external splendor, ruthlessness, and initial success, served as a particularly suitable father substitute, may have provoked considerable ambivalence in Leonardo toward his artistic creations, an ambivalence that perhaps manifested itself sharply in *The Last Supper* and the monument for Francesco Sforza, the two greatest achievements of the Milanese period. One of these has almost perished, and of the other nothing has reached us. Consequently, it appears as if Leonardo's general ambivalence was heightened by the ill-treatment he may have found reason to complain about at times in Milan. If this reconstruction is valid, then Lodovico's downfall might have had the effect of setting free creative impulses that had previously been inhibited by the conflictual relation to the duke. One may even make the guess that the downfall or defeat of a father substitute, with or without any particular previous provocation, may quite generally have had such an effect on Leonardo.[23]

The devaluation of father or father substitute may have led to a temporary reduction of the effect of Leonardo's father identification and thus have supported the reawakening of his artistic creativity as described by Freud (1910, p. 122). Yet, just during the second Florentine period an observation is reported that would suggest a peak of

[23] If Leonardo's undated letter to his father in which he expresses his pain at hearing of the troubles his father was subjected to (Richter, Vol. II, p. 344, No. 1373A; C.A. 62 v.) was written during his second stay in Florence, I would surmise that the increase in artistic creativity during that period was caused not only by the escape from and defeat of Lodovico Sforza, but also by a temporary setback in his father's affairs. Vallentin thinks this letter refers to the death of the father's third wife (d. before 1485). My interpretation would make sense only if Leonardo's reference to difficulties in the father's life pertained to a situation in which the son had an opportunity to feel superior to his progenitor. (Mr. Pedretti recently informed me that the letter in question was written by Leonardo between 1500 and 1504. This is welcome additional evidence in favor of my hypothesis.)

aversion in Leonardo against painting at that time. I refer to the two so-often-cited letters Fra Pietro da Novellara wrote (April 8, and 14, 1501)[24] to the Marchesa Isabella d'Este of Mantua (Goldscheider, 1944, p. 19). Being most eager to collect works of art, she had instructed Fra Pietro to make Leonardo accept a commission. The two letters describe in all desirable frankness and clarity Leonardo's lack of "patience for painting"; the informant even reports "his [Leonardo's] mathematical experiments have made painting so distasteful to him that he cannot even bear to take up a brush." Oddly enough, this clear-cut description refers to Leonardo just during a period that Clark and Douglas regard as a particularly creative one in Leonardo's life. Was this aversion a passing whim, the mood of a few weeks? Are we confronted here with a problem of psychology? Are we to assume that the master was capable of the greatest artistic production only when he had to fight off a strong inner resistance? Or, again, was the whole report of Fra Pietro a clever excuse? I do not wish to go into Leonardo's relationship to Isabella d'Este (cf. Seidlitz, 1909b, p. 171, et passim), but it seems that he did not want to work for her, and Fra Pietro may have known that his mission was destined to failure. His two letters exculpate him for the failure and avoid any offense to his mistress, so it seems questionable whether the friar's letters are to be treated as documents regarding Leonardo's psychopathology or as a piece of diplomacy (cf. Clark, 1939, p. 107). If the friar was reporting truthfully, as all historians seem to agree, it may reduce the probability of Clark's explanation of Leonardo's increased artistic creativity during his second stay at Florence. A Leonardo who was greatly encouraged

[24] I have not been able to ascertain the exact date of these two letters. Goldscheider (1944, p. 19, No. xi) gives as the date of the first letter April 8, in the caption of the second, No. xii, April 14, but at the end of the letter April 4. Clark (1929, p. 112) says the interval between the two letters was "a few weeks." In his list of dates for which there is documentary evidence (p. 182) he dates the first letter as April 8, and the second as April 14. Douglas (1944) says Fra Pietro's "first visit" occurred on or before April 3. He further claims that the second letter was written the following day (p. 28). Beltrami (1919) dates the first letter (No. 107, p. 65f.) April 3, and the second (No. 108, p. 66f.) April 4. To make things more complicated, Fra Pietro wrote that he had visited Leonardo during Passion week. Mr. T. D. Nicholson of the Hayden Planetarium was kind enough to inform me that in 1501, by the Julian calendar, Easter Sunday fell on March 28, which creates a new contradiction. After finishing this manuscript, I found in Julia Cartwright's book on Isabella d'Este a reference to this problem. She dates the first letter April 3, 1501, and believes that the second letter was written on April 14. However, her conclusions are based on the assumption that "Easter Day fell on the 11th of April in that year," which apparently is erroneous (Cartwright, 1903, Vol. I, p. 320f.). For another important comment on the irreconcilability of the various dates, see Gronau (1910, p. 439).

by public success and therefore producing more artistically than before, but who at the same time had a marked aversion against painting, does not seem to add up.[25]

The conclusions will depend on the place that is accorded in the time sequence to some pertinent events. There is first Vasari's report of Leonardo's triumphal success. The cartoon of *Anna Metterza* which Leonardo after long procrastination produced for the Servites "filled every artist with wonder" and after it was finished it was shown publicly, whereupon "men and women, young and old, flocked to see it for two days, as if it had been a festival" (Vasari, p. 11).

Furthermore, we have the two letters of the friar. In the first one, besides a few remarks about Leonardo, there is mainly a description of iconographic details of his *Anna Metterza* cartoon. In the second letter, of a week later, he reports inquiries he had made with friends, contact with Salai, and a visit with Leonardo. He makes mention of paintings in Leonardo's studio. In both letters Leonardo's aversion is set forth.

The question I raise is whether the public showing of the *Anna Metterza,* and Leonardo's great success which Vasari reported, occurred before or after the friar's meeting with Leonardo. It is usually taken for granted that Fra Pietro had met Leonardo before the public exhibition, because in his first letter he wrote that "the sketch is not yet complete." Further, it may make a difference whether we assume that the friar had seen the cartoon himself or was conveying secondhand information in his first letter to the Marchesa. The general view is the former.[26] However, the documents do not seem to favor this conclusion. On March 17, the Marchesa had written to Fra Pietro asking him to get information about Leonardo if he was in Florence, whether he had started a new painting, and also whether he was expected to stay in Florence for a while. And then Fra Pietro was "as if on [his] own account" (Vallentin, p. 284) to ask him whether he would be ready to do some work for her (Seidlitz, 1909b, p. 239). The two letters in which Fra Pietro answered seem to be correlated to her two requests.

[25] Clark describes Leonardo's taking service under Cesare Borgia in 1502 as an outright "escape from painting" (1939, p. 113), which would not make sense in view of the hypothesis that the public success in Florence spurred Leonardo's creativity.
[26] Clark (1929, p. 107) leaves the question open by referring to a description of the cartoon. Douglas (1944, p. 28) speaks of the friar's first visit. Seidlitz (1909b, p. 239) speaks of an eyewitness.

First he reported what he knew about Leonardo, and in his next letter he communicated the result of his quasi-spontaneous visit. Also in this second letter the friar reported what he had done in order to inform himself about Leonardo, which in itself indicates that his first letter did not contain direct information. If these premises are correct, then the first letter would reflect what was common knowledge in Florence or the talk of the town. Yet, since this letter is replete with details of the St. Anne painting, this would speak strongly in favor of there having been a previous public showing. If, conversely, Pietro actually had seen the cartoon when he wrote to Isabella, he had seen it either at the public showing or in Leonardo's studio. If the latter is to be assumed, then one should expect that he had also met Leonardo on that occasion, in which case he would have been bound to mention it in his first letter. Again, the fact that after he had visited Leonardo (as recorded in his second letter) he does not mention the cartoon, although he does mention other paintings, allows the conclusion that the cartoon was no longer in Leonardo's studio, which in turn speaks in favor of the previous public showing.

I have gone into all these details because two interpretations of Leonardo's aversion against painting at that time are possible. It was either caused by a reaction of guilt elicited by his great success, or it was an inner revulsion that occurred at a time when he was actually engaged in creating a great painting. The second eventuality, which is psychologically the far more puzzling and interesting one, I will suggest an explanation for later. In this section I will discuss the matter on the assumption of a guilt reaction. The historical record is not clear enough to be certain one way or the other.

In order to find at least a tentative orientation among these seemingly contradictory details, we have to recall that, during his second stay in Florence, Leonardo served for a while (about eight months in 1502) an autocratic sovereign, Cesare Borgia, whose rise and misfortune he witnessed. That is to say, the Florentine period was in turn divided by the appearance of an autocratic father substitute who, by the fickleness of history and his own intemperance, suffered a fate similar to Lodovico's and thus may have found profound devaluation in Leonardo's esteem and respect.

Consequently we may tentatively propose the following sequence. Lodovico's defeat resulted in a potent stimulus of Leonardo's creativity.

The popular success, so different from what apparently he had to bear in Milan, aroused a feeling of guilt and depression—which is not at all unlikely in such a personality as Leonardo's. After he had served for a short time with Cesare Borgia, the artistic impulse may have regained its former momentum when this father substitute also suffered a downfall.[27]

Last but not least we have to consider the fact that the death of his father also occurred during the time of Leonardo's second stay in Florence (July, 1504).[28] Thus the period of the artist's increased creativity, if Clark's and Douglas's evaluations are correct, was initiated by the devaluation of a father figure and, further, was accompanied by two other instances of the same type of event. Two remarks Leonardo wrote, which I consider here in passing only, indicate the kind of relationship he entertained to patrons. After Lodovico's downfall he wrote: "The Duke lost the state, property, and liberty, and none of his enterprises was carried out by him" (Richter, Vol. II, p. 354, No. 1414; L cover v.). This last (the failure to carry enterprises to completion) was one of Leonardo's own misfortunes (cf. Freud, 1910, p. 122), and thus we notice the factor of identification within an area of defeat. The second remark, "The Medici created and destroyed me" (MacCurdy, 1956, p. 1123; C.A. 159 r. c) is indicative of the ambivalent father transference he made upon authority.[29]

If we compare once more the sociological explanation of the historian, namely, the effect of public enthusiasm, with the type of motive Freud suggested, to wit, conflicts within the relationship to a father substitute,[30] we may discover an aspect that to a certain extent is shared by both. The Florentine government, somewhat republican in structure

[27] Clark subtly proposes the features in Cesare's personality that may have lent themselves to idealization. It has always seemed to me that there was a remote similarity between the head of Cesare Borgia as drawn by Leonardo (Turin; Popham, Plate 189) and his head of Christ (Venice Academy; Popham, Plate 171B). In a footnote in Valentiner's study I have found a partial confirmation of this impression (1930, p. 60, n. 32).

[28] The historical record, in this instance also as in so many others, is incomplete, telling us only of the date of death and nothing about the preceding sickness and its length. In inquiring into Leonardo's reaction to his father's death it would be important to find out at what time the father became in the son's eyes a person marked by death. A release of creativity precipitated by the father's actual or impending death is not exceptional in the life of a genius.

[29] Leonardo's words, "li medici," however, have also been held to mean: the physicians (cf. MacCurdy, loc. cit., n.).

[30] Since what I am discussing here is types of explanations, it is to be disregarded to which period Freud applied his explanation.

with a weak gonfaloniere at its head, may appear, when compared with the dukedom of Milan governed by an oppressive sovereign, almost like a fatherless society (cf. Federn, 1919), and may therefore have relieved the artist by a reduction of both outer pressures and also an inner one. But it is noteworthy that Leonardo left Florence so quickly to serve Cesare, another tyrant, and that after his return to Florence he again did not stay for long but went on to Milan, where he again served an autocrat, the King of France or his representative. All this seems to me to reduce the explanatory value of the public-enthusiasm theory and to favor the application of the genetic aspect of psychoanalysis.

At any rate, it is noteworthy that Leonardo apparently was inhibited at times in his artistic creativity but "uninhibited in his scientific inquiry." In view of well-proved psychoanalytic observations it may be stated in general terms that the creation of objects probably had a feminine meaning to him and that a serious conflict about his femininity prevented him at times from tapping his creative artistic potential to its inherent maximum. We notice a free flow of drawings; that is to say, he was free to do the preliminary steps that should have led to a final accomplishment, but more often than not he did not achieve it at all, or achieved it in a way that made the finished work a short-lived one. But more about this particular problem later.

Apparently because of Leonardo's personal aloofness from women Douglas (1944) considers it "a strange psychological fact that in this portrait [of a Musician in the Ambrosiana, Milan; see Plate 15] as in the representations of men in his large compositions, Leonardo does not show such revealing insight as he does when he paints women." And he continues to praise Leonardo's "intuitive understanding of women—girls, wives and mothers" (p. 89). In view of what is known of the psychology of many latent as well as manifest homosexuals, this is not strange. Repeated clinical observation shows that the homosexual has a relatively poor understanding of male psychology but an eminent, even tender, empathy with women. Douglas's observation sets forth a point that subtly proves the essentially homosexual nature of Leonardo's mind. But evidently the ensuing conflict led not only to a sporadic relative standstill of artistic creativity but also to a drawn-out struggle against homosexual love objects. He apparently really loved Salai. He bought him a necklace and ring and expensive garments (Möller, 1928, p. 141). Suggesting an imagery of a nursing mother he wrote to him once: "I raised you with milk like a son" (Möller, 1928, p. 141; C.A. 220 v. c). And nevertheless when Leonardo traveled to Rome in 1513, Francesco Melzi (1491-1568), his new noble pupil friend, held first place, and, as Möller (1928, p. 143) believes, Salai did not accompany Leonardo to France. Yet Melzi was a sublimated love object; refined, reliable, devoted, handsome, courteous, he united all the virtues a master could expect from a pupil. Melzi's victory over Salai found its lasting record in Leonardo's will which made him executor and heir of his most precious belongings. Thus the development of Leonardo's relationship to the men he preferred reflects the history of his conflict about homosexual impulses; the high quality of the last object appears to me to be the sign of the sublimation he ultimately was capable of in this area too.

Yet in order to appreciate the Oxford Allegory fully one has to turn to Michelangelo and study his way of representing the equivalent conflict. As is known, Michelangelo was prone to fall in love with young men: Gherardo Perini (1522), Febo di Poggio (1534), Cecchino Bracci (1544) (see de Tolnay, 1943-54, Vol. III, p. 23). His most intense friendship, which was also of an enduring nature, was that for Tomaso de Cavalieri, whom he met in August of 1532 when Michelangelo was fifty-seven. Tomaso was a beautiful, gifted Roman of noble descent. Michelangelo made drawings for the young man, who, according to Vasari, was to use them as models from which to learn drawing. But they were actually declarations of love (ibid., p. 111). Two of them are of importance here. They are mythological representations: one of Ganymede (not preserved in original but as a copy; see Plate 16), the other of Tityos (Windsor Royal Library No. 115; see Plate 17).

About the Ganymede drawing, de Tolnay (1943-54) says:

Michelangelo confers on the eagle an anthropomorphic expression of passion. The bird seizes avidly in his talons the delicate body of the youth and the bird's neck is stretched around his torso. . . . The boy submits passively to the abduction and seems to be plunged in a dream of delights. From a distance the pair seem to form a single winged being—expression of that mystic union of which Michelangelo speaks in some of his poems [Vol. III, p. 112].

In the Tityos drawing the delights of love are replaced with the unbearable pain love causes. Tityos was the giant who threatened to violate Latona, the mother of Apollo and Artemis, but was slain by their arrows. In Hades he was tortured by a vulture who devoured his liver. Lucretius says about him: "But our Tityos is here, grovelling in love, and the winged things[31] that tear him (anxious anguish eating him up) or rend him with some other lust, are his passions" (Lucretius, p. 239).[32] Panofsky sets forth the Neoplatonic meaning of the two drawings. They are Michelangelo's presentation of *Amor Sacro e Profano*. The one symbolizes "the ecstasy of Platonic love, powerful to the point of annihilation, but freeing the soul from its physical bondage." Tityos "symbolizes the agonies of sensual passion, enslaving the soul and debasing it even beneath its normal terrestrial state" (Panofsky, 1939, p. 218). This may have been the conscious or preconscious imagery, but it can scarcely be overlooked that (if the copy is accurate) Ganymede's penis comes forth from a female genital, which proves— independently of whether the relationship was ever consummated physically—that Cavalieri was for Michelangelo also the object of a direct, sexual, unsublimated impulse. De Tolnay points to the patterns of friendship that were customary half a century earlier at the court of Lorenzo de' Medici, but adds that Michelangelo's drawings are characterized by "a new expression of the idea of inexorable fate" (1943-54, Vol. III, p. 114). This inexorable fate, expressed in the work of art, is the reflection of the feeling of doom caused by an indomitable drive that is rejected by conscience.[33]

The Ganymede drawing depicts the gratification of active homosexual love. The factor of fusion with the object is present as de Tolnay describes it. One may also think of a genitalization of the youth's body (Lewin, 1933), the male body being integrated in the form of a huge phallus. But the leading theme, of course, is the youth's passively abandoning himself to such a degree that he is appropriated by the active bird without resistance. In the Tityos drawing the punishment

---

[31] According to Homer, Tityos was tortured by two vultures. For the history of the myth, see Panofsky (1939, p. 217, n.).

[32] "sed Tityos nobis hic est, in amore iacentem
quem volucres lacerant atque exest anxius angor
aut alia quavis scindunt cuppedine curae"
(Lucretius III 992-994).

[33] From 1539 on Michelangelo took refuge in his love for Vittoria Colonna (1490-1547).

for forbidden wishes is represented. But it is not a matter of pure superego imagery; it is eroticized and also expresses a masochistic fantasy. Though the bird is now a vulture, it is still the same type as in the former drawing and represents a man, this time probably the youth himself who returns and proffers passive gratification in the form of revenge. The paralyzing effect of the masochistic wish is symbolized by the shackles that tie Tityos to the rock.[34]

The same universe of discourse is here encountered as in Leonardo's allegory. The meaning, however, is expressed visually with greater clarity and definiteness. The relationship to the body of the love object is quite different. It is not fused with the body of the lover; it is squarely faced and visually enjoyed. The sexual unconscious imagery probably refers to coition from the back. The full contrast to Leonardo's imagery, with its stress on the invisibility of the love object, is discerned when it is observed that the eagle is in a position of watching the youth from the front during the act. It is also possible that what is ostensibly the youth's erected penis, with its peculiar rise from a female genital, really means the eagle's penis which pierces the boy's effeminate body. Here the narcissistic component would be observable with particular clarity, since the wish to watch the passive gratification of the youth[35] would be combined with the wish to observe one's own genital.

In a comparison of Leonardo's and Michelangelo's drawings we encounter what are probably the essential differences in the roots of their artistic work, the vastness that separates them in terms of views of the world and relationship to the human body.

It is a rare occasion when one can perceive so distinctly two forms of homosexuality, in both instances rejected by the self (although with what success is not known for either), in the one leading to a restriction of the self and the replacement of the lost part with the object, in the other widening the self by appropriation of the object. Summarily one may tentatively say that homosexuality was connected with Leonardo's increased isolation, whereas in Michelangelo it probably precipitated new turns toward the world and had an activating effect.

[34] For the symbolic meaning of the liver in the Prometheus myth, which is also applicable to that of Tityos, see Freud (1932, p. 292).

[35] Dr. Anna Freud demonstrated in a lecture (1950) that the main function of active homosexuality is a defense against passive wishes.

From the Allegory of *Pleasure and Pain* I tried to deduce various aspects of Leonardo's object relations. It still behooves me to discuss another allegory, which, to a certain extent, may be looked upon as a counterpart of this one. This is the allegory of *Virtue and Envy* (Ox. 108 r.) (see Plate 18). There are two bodies facing each other growing out of one pair of legs. The drawing could also be described as of two persons pressing their pelves against each other, only the right body ending in lower extremities. Leonardo's comment on this drawing is short:

> No sooner is Virtue born than Envy comes into the world to attack it; and sooner will there be a body without a shadow than Virtue without Envy [Richter, Vol. I, p. 386, No. 677; Ox. 108 r.].

Fortunately, we have the comment of G. P. Lomazzo, who transmits information he obtained from Melzi, who was passing on what he had heard from Leonardo himself. From Lomazzo we learn (Pedretti, 1953, p. 56f.) that Virtue is represented in the form of Apollo, whose face has male and female features, whereas the rest of the body looks like that of Minerva. Envy is a strikingly pale female who tries to deprive Virtue of its strength, which is represented by arrows. Envy is in the act of setting fire to Virtue's hair and crown in order to take away honor and beauty, and is trying to poison Virtue's face with its tongue, which is like that of a snake. Envy is devoid of love and charity, venomous and pestiferous. It has a scorpion's tail and its hair is straight. "Masculine virtue as it is called by wise people" gouges out the eyes of Envy and pushes an arrow into its right ear.

Lomazzo adds to these details their symbolic meanings. These are not necessary for our purpose. The Allegory, when scrutinized for its sexual symbolism, reveals the imagery that is activated in Leonardo's unconscious when man and woman are sexually united. Mutual destruction breaks out. All the good is in the male and all the evil in the female. The female destroys the male for base motives; the male destroys the female in self-defense and for moral purposes. The female tries to castrate the male. The abundance of penis symbols (the snake-like tongue, the straight hair, the scorpion's tail) in the female is striking. From analytic observation it is justified to conclude that this type of symbolism refers to the preoedipal mother, who, in the child's imagination, is endowed with a male genital. Freud, in his analysis of Leonardo's cover memory, conjectured such symbolism to have been active in him (1910, pp. 93-95).[36] The Allegory is almost an illustration of this very interpretation. At the same time, it also reveals the castrative aspect of female anatomy, inasmuch as the female person has no legs of her own, the only pair of lower extremities belonging to the person identified by Lomazzo as Apollo.

The reason for representing envy as female can be found in Leonardo's projection.[37] In view of the overestimation of the male genital the conclusion becomes stringent that a being without a penis must necessarily envy one who is endowed with one and must harbor the most hostile impulses aimed at appropriating the cherished organ (envy stealing virtue's arrows). This projection contributes much to the anxiety of physical contact with females, but it also arouses feelings of pity, considering how terribly such a deprived being must suffer; it is an important root of the homosexual's empathy with and understanding of the female.

In the Allegory the most archaic imagery is represented. Its moralistic, intellectual meaning serves well as a rationalization of the repressed. What it says is that the female components of male virtue are good, whereas the male inclusions of female envy are evil. The self is purified by the projection of all objectionable features onto the female object. By means of the peculiar capacity of art to condense, the female object is set forth as simultaneously having and not having a male organ, arousing male hostility in either case. This, unless I am mistaken, is found but infrequently in clinical experience. There one can study, strictly separated from the disgust and pity with the castrated mother, the archaic fear of the preoedipal mother, so often endowed with a penis and imagined to be utterly cruel, usually because fantasy endows her with a determination to devour the small helpless male child.

Yet more important than this interpretation, it seems to me, is a conclusion that becomes necessary from a comparison of the two allegories. In the first, there are two males; in the second, male and female. Now, in the first, the two persons cannot see each other. The contrast between the relative peacefulness of this first with the wild hostility in the second is remarkable. I am inclined to refer this out-

[36] The avian species is immaterial to this interpretation.

[37] Leonardo's equation of the sinful and evil with the female had, of course, a long tradition in the Western orbit that goes back at least to Plato (see Kelsen, 1933).

break to visual stimulation. The sight of the object apparently is the trigger that makes the hostile impulse unrestrainable. The object imagined in fantasy has far less power to create this effect than the object seen. It seems to me probable that we are dealing here with another factor that may have contributed importantly to Leonardo's urge for artistic creation. The hostility aroused by the sight of the object is shunted into depicting the object; that is to say, the danger that he might attack the object on sight is averted by draining the impulse into making a counterfeit. In Leonardo's famous caricatures the hostile elements of the original impulse are quite evident. Here we may also find an additional explanation of Douglas's observation of Leonardo's greater capacity to depict women than men. The foregoing makes it understandable that the conflict aroused by the sight of the object is greater in the instance of women than of men. More elaborate measures are then necessary when the artist is dealing with the former, and the depth of conflict may be reflected in the quality of Leonardo's superb portraits of women, which have so far remained unmatched.[38]

---

[38] A comparison of the Allegory of *Pleasure and Pain* with the copy of Leonardo's drawing "Old Woman and Paramour Youth" (Möller, 1928, p. 153), where Salai makes love to a disgusting-looking old woman for money's sake, may confirm some of the interpretations I have set forth.

11

The Problem of the Leda *Painting*

There is one painting that is particularly puzzling in view of the interpretation that has just been set forth. This is *Leda and the Swan*. Except for an Adam and Eve cartoon that has been lost, it is, I believe, the only instance of a painting by Leonardo of a nude female.[1]

Before going into the psychology of this painting it is necessary to participate in a controversy which *ex lege* should be left to the historians of art but which the psychologist is drawn into against his taste and preference by the fact that the historians have left the question undecided. Leonardo's *Leda* painting is not preserved. There are extant only a few sketches of details and compositions by Leonardo and copies of the final painting by others. The psychological analysis will vary

---

[1] In this context it may be worth while to mention the paucity of female nudes in Leonardo's drawings as well. There are compositional and positional sketches of the *Leda* painting which cannot rightly be called studies of nudes. There are anatomical drawings of female anatomy. There are, further, female nudes in W. 12641 r.; a drawing in the Musée Bonnat; C.A. 98 r. Mr. Carlo Pedretti informs me that some of these are by Melzi. A drawing of a nude (Paris Ecole des Beaux Arts; Popham, Plate 48) is thought by von Bode (1921) to be a sketch for the *Adoration*. Most of these drawings apparently serve the purpose of clarifying parts of a composition, and I know of no study of a female nude comparable to the male like the W. 12594 (Popham, Plate 231). The nude in an allegory in the British Museum (Popham, Plate 103) cannot be called a study of a nude either.

considerably depending on which copy is considered the closest to the original.

There is the Leda drawing by Leonardo in Rotterdam (Plate 19) in which Leda, kneeling on her right knee, the left one half raised, turns toward the swan at the right of the drawing and one pair of twins lies in the left corner. Two similar compositions, very much smaller, are found on a drawing at Windsor (W. 12337 r.; Popham, Plate 202). There is a painting by the so-called Giampietrino (Plate 20) that copies *Leda* freely in which Leda is in a similar posture with two pairs of twins without a swan. Whether Leonardo ever made a painting showing Leda in that position can be questioned. If there ever was such a version, it will not occupy us any further here; in my estimation it can have been only a step toward that composition in which Leda is standing upright, the swan to her left. Leonardo's tendency to sketch in diminutive proportions the final composition of his paintings has come to attention. Müller-Walde (1897, pp. 137-154) has discovered accidentally just such a diminutive sketch of a standing Leda in the *Codice Atlantico* 156 r.[2] Also Raphael's sketch copying Leonardo's *Leda*, which must already have been made prior to 1504 (Clark, 1939, p. 122), shows Leda standing (Plate 21). From all this I conclude that the standing Leda was Leonardo's final composition. The difficulty is to make the right choice between two copies concerning which the opinion of the foremost experts clashes: the copy in the Borghese Gallery (Plate 22) and the one in Wilton House (Plate 23). Of the former Heydenreich (1954) has the following to say:

> Of the chief replicas in which Leonardo's original draft for the picture has been preserved, that in the Galleria Borghese is the most important; in the surrounding spaces in the representation of the Dioscuri and above all in the general quality it is undoubtedly the one which most closely approximates to Leonardo's conception [1954, Vol. I, p. 190].[3]

Clark (1939, p. 123), however, takes the copy at Wilton House, probably the work of Cesare da Sesto as the closest to Leonardo.[4]

[2] A similar sketch was found on one of Leonardo's anatomical drawings (see later).

[3] However, he adds the reservation that Leonardo had made but a cartoon "in which only the group of the principal figures was sketched out," since the group of children and the landscape vary from one copy to the other.

[4] Whether the Wilton House or the ex-Spiridon copy (Goldscheider, 1944, p. 31, Fig. 61) is closer to the original is not of consequence for the following discussion.

I feel very strongly that the Borghese painting is an almost faithful, if not indeed even an exact, copy of Leonardo's original except for details of landscape. Of course, it is not easy to derive convincing psychological conclusions from a painting that is considered by experts to deviate in essential details from the original.[5] Sir Kenneth Clark, in a personal communication for which I wish here to express my thanks, admits the un-Leonardesque landscape in the Wilton copy but writes that, though the Borghese copy is the work of a superior artist and makes in general a better impression, it is not very Leonardesque. The arguments Clark adduces in favor of the Wilton copy are powerful (1939, pp. 121-125). They are based on written historical records, a study of the details, and the identity between some of Leonardo's sketches and details of the painting.

For my interpretation it is decisive whether one or two pairs of twins were represented in Leonardo's painting. The myth says that Leda gave birth to two eggs, each of which contained twins: the one Castor and Pollux, the other Helen and Clytemnestra. The Borghese copy shows only the male twins, whereas the ex-Spiridon copy and the Wilton House copy have two pairs. Leonardo's original was said to have been taken to France, and one of Clark's arguments in favor of the Wilton House copy is the following description by Cassiano del Pozzo who saw the picture at Fontainebleau in 1625.

A standing figure of Leda almost entirely naked, with the swan at her feet, and two eggs from whose broken shells come forth four babies . . . [quoted after Clark, 1939, p. 121].

This record seems to support strongly the view that Leonardo's original showed the twins and eggs as they are seen in the Wilton House copy. Yet when Pozzo tells us that Leda was "almost entirely naked" whereas the paintings that have come down to us so obtrusively show complete nakedness, and when he speaks of "the swan at her feet" whereas such a description is most inappropriate in view of the Borghese or Wilton House copy which permit only the description: the swan at her side, then we may conclude that the Fontainebleau painting seen by Pozzo was of a different iconographic type. Pozzo seems to have been a very conscientious scholar. At least the picture

[5] Berenson also expressed himself in disfavor of the Borghese copy (1903, Vol. I, p. 162).

one gets of him in Miss Steinitz's publication (1958, passim) is that of a reliable, devoted person highly interested in scholarly pursuits. It is to be assumed that he described the painting correctly. It strikes me that his description would fit a combination of several iconographic types. In the painting by Giampietrino Leda is "almost entirely naked," in the Rotterdam sketch the swan's spatial relation to Leda can be approximately described as "at her feet," and in the Wilton House and ex-Spiridon copy Leda is standing and there are "two eggs, from whose broken shells come forth four babies." What the painting into which these three types were possibly integrated really looked like I cannot imagine, but the Fontainebleau version—Pozzo's reliability as an informant always presupposed—cannot have been of any of the iconographic types extant.

I wish to adduce another argument against the assumption that Leonardo represented two pairs of twins crawling out of eggs. Though standards and taste change so rapidly in Western culture and art, it is still remarkable that almost everything we have from Leonardo agrees with a present-day sense of decorum and with contemporary taste. Moreover, throughout his paintings, Leonardo succeeds so well in introducing naturally the details of iconographic import that they are comprehensible to everyone, including those who are not conversant with the religious mythology of that time.[6] Halos and crosses disappear, and his paintings, though they contain a wealth of symbolic and special iconographic details, are still constructed in such a way that the general human aspect is preserved. Thus the *Adoration*, the *Cenacolo*, the *Anna Metterza*, the *Anghiari Battle*, the *St. Jerome* paintings can be viewed, understood, and appreciated independently of the very special iconography they contain and any knowledge of history. If, however, the Wilton House copy reproduces correctly the iconographic detail of the original, we should be confronted unexpectedly and quite surprisingly with a Leonardo who gathers details quite meaningless to the uninformed and of a kind that strikes us today as bizarre or even preposterous.[7]

It contradicts, in my opinion, everything we know of Leonardo's art

[6] The retrenchment of direct religious symbols even in Leonardo's early paintings has been noted by Müller-Walde (1889).

[7] The *St. John* (Plate 24) perhaps does not live up to some of the features I have presented as characteristic of Leonardo's paintings. In his drawings, such as the Allegories, he did not apply this principle.

to assume that the disarray of the four babies with the four shell halves encountered in the Wilton House copy could have been even a distorted replica of something created by his brush.[8] Also the imbalance of the whole painting due to the unharmonious weighting of the left side by the crowd of babies, who remain disconnected from the rest and without counterpoise, is inacceptable in view of the fact that all Leonardo's other paintings are constructed with such excellence that the smallest detail finds its most dynamic integration into the whole composition.

When we turn to the Borghese copy we encounter an atmosphere unencumbered by any of these implausibilities.[9] What strikes me in the Borghese copy is the structure of the composition. I find in it the triangular motive, as we know it from other of Leonardo's paintings, more strongly than in any of the other copies. The whole group forms a formidable triangle from the tip of the swan's left wing, up to Leda's head, down to the right foot of the left twin. This structure obtains stability by the vertical of Leda's body. The superimposed triangular structure is built up by means of subordinate triangles, the twins forming one and Leda with the swan the other; but the composition can also be resolved into two triangles formed by the twins and the swan revolving around the vertical female body.

The Borghese copy is also the only one, as far as I know, in which an essential detail can be found: the strict parallel between the outer border of the swan's right wing and the curvature of Leda's pelvis and right thigh. This detail is present in Raphael's sketch (Plate 21) and in the drawing in the Louvre (Plate 25) which is after Leonardo by an unknown artist.

It is essential to consider a formal element that Heydenreich (1954, Vol. I, p. 47, et passim) has found in many of Leonardo's paintings. Often Leonardo seizes a transitory moment, the split second before action sets in. The presentation of such a moment is apt to produce the maximum tension in the beholder, for he is compelled to feel the

[8] In the Borghese copy an egg is hidden, barely visible, in the left lower corner. One should also consider in the Wilton House copy such details as the disproportion of the left and right breasts, the clumsy pressure of the right arm on the breast that has been drawn too small.

[9] See Douglas (1944, p. 40) for Edward Wright's report on the Leonardo cartoons he saw when visiting the Marchese Camedi in Milan in 1721: "A Leda standing, naked, with cupids in one of the corners." This, I believe would fit the Borghese copy.

dynamics of the ensuing action in a situation that is still at rest. Whereas for expressive purposes the actor favors situations in which action is set going (Bühler, 1933, p. 43), Leonardo chooses the last moment before the initiation of the new movement. In the *Anna Metterza*, for example, the expected new movement is St. Mary's drawing back the Christ Child, but the moment seized in the painting is the end of St. Mary's action of reaching out for the child. It is this overlay of two opposite trends in the moment that separates them that gives some of Leonardo's pictures their inner dynamic tension.

Returning to *Leda*, we observe that the parallel between the swan's right wing and Leda's body transforms the wing into a prehensile organ. When we seize or lay hold of an object, some organ, usually the hand, must take a shape accordant with the object grasped or with part of it. In my evaluation of the painting this accordance between wing and body is an essential feature without which the whole composition would lose its inner tension and fall flat. In the copies other than the Borghese, the swan is seductive, he is pleading and trying to come closer to the female body. In the Borghese copy the seductive element is preserved in the upper part of the swan's body, the neck and beak being engaged in action that apparently aims at exciting the female, but the right wing grasps the body. In the next moment this right wing will force Leda into cohabitation. Again we encounter the seizing of the most dramatic moment, the last one before action sets in.[10]

The *Leda* painting is striking to behold, for its beauty shows not a trace of all the horror the Allegory of *Virtue and Envy* seemed to me to contain. Whither did all the fear of the female body vanish? In superb female beauty Leda stands, the twins Castor and Pollux symbolizing Concord at her feet to the right, playing, and to her left the swan in evident excitement pressing against her.

The distribution of curved lines evokes a pattern of tension, without, however, disturbing the menacing calmness that dominates the whole composition. The area to the left of Leda is filled with the wild curvatures of the swan counterpoised by the bulging outline of the

[10] This feature is so significant of Leonardo that I feel reasonably sure I am not the victim of bias. Of course, such points cannot be proved with that exactness which we expect from scientific statements. At any rate, the Leonardesque composition in the Borghese copy may be permitted to outweigh in importance some of the details, such as Leda's hairdo and the plants, which, as Clark points out, follow exactly some of Leonardo's sketches in the Wilton House copy. Cf. Clark (1935, Vol. I, Notes to 12419 on p. 50f., and 12516 on p. 77f.).

right contour of Leda's body. The excited movement that dominates the left is additionally balanced by the swan's right wing following the outline of Leda's pelvis and thigh. By means of this simple formal element the swan and Leda are transformed into an inseparable unit.

If Leonardo's Leda is compared with Michelangelo's (Plate 26), this effect becomes particularly appreciable. Michelangelo shows Leda in the state of being possessed, or, as one feels inclined to say, of forfeiture. Resistance is absent on her side. She is succumbing and nothing will ever arouse her from the state of ecstatic repose. Leonardo's Leda preserves her narcissistic independence. Turning away and being attracted—both are equally present. The gesture of the outstretched right arm can be interpreted as defense and holding off as well as seduction and enticement. Although I am well aware of the objections to using the personal impressions left by works of art for scientific purposes, I still venture to say that there is something terrifying in Leonardo's painting.[11]

The expressive quality of the swan is not puzzling. It is referable to sexual excitement; no sign of hesitation is visible. Whereas in Michelangelo's painting the female body, at least according to the preserved copies (Plate 26), holds the principal place and the swan appears more like a decorative supplement,[12] in Leonardo's painting the swan holds a place at least as conspicuous and essential as Leda.

The puzzle lies in Leda. Does she reject force or submit to it, or does she surrender voluntarily without participation? Does she long for her paramour? Is she excited or frigid? At any rate, I doubt the correctness of Vallentin's description of voluptuous surrender (p. 431), which would be applicable to some of Correggio's females, whose passions are one-dimensional. The ambiguity observed in Leda is not caused by Leonardo's deficiency. It is one of his greatest achievements that he was capable here again of limning a state expressive of two or more opposing trends, just as he succeeded in the Mona Lisa. I should be able to proceed in a discussion of the Leda painting with greater certainty if I knew more about two iconographic details, the swan and

[11] Vallentin (1938), who gave an extremely sensitive analysis of this painting, received a comparable impression (p. 430f.). However, it is of course possible that the copyist carried some elements into the painting that were alien to the original.

[12] Cf. de Tolnay (1943-54) about Michelangelo's painting: "Leda predominates, the swan seeming to take on form only secondarily, so to speak, as a sort of fulfillment of her dream wishes" (Vol. III, p. 106).

Leda's erect position. It may be worth while to consider for a moment the concomitants of the swan's anatomy. The swan's foot is not suitable to functioning as a prehensile organ. Ancient iconography disregarded the fact and the sculpture in Venice (Plate 27) shows a bird grasping Leda's leg. Leonardo, who was not inclined to deviate from nature in his paintings, would not, I believe, have resorted to a presentation that contained elements conspicuously contradictory to observation. As a matter of fact, the relative dependency of the beast enforced by a deficit of aggressive equipment is reflected, as it seems to me, in an intimation of helplessness in the swan's behavior and expression. This relative helplessness is counterbalanced by the dynamics of the right wing, which functions here as a means of aggression that potentially can make the female submit.

Now, there is an anatomical drawing by Leonardo, which will be discussed later, that shows man and woman copulating in a standing position (Plate 28). Though, as I believe, the proximate cause for this choice of position in the anatomical drawing was a practical one dictated by representational-didactic considerations, it still suggests that Leonardo did not feel bound by the horizontal position traditional in the Western world. It is noteworthy that in Greco-Roman art there are many Leda sculptures in erect position (Plate 27, de Hevesy). The iconographic development in Leonardo seems to have gone from a half-rising Leda to an erect one, and he thus came close to an ancient iconographic type. However, I am thinking here rather of a coincidence than of voluntary selection as was the case with Michelangelo, who patterned the iconographic type of his *Leda* in accordance with a Roman funerary prototype (de Tolnay, 1943-54, Vol. III, pp. 190-193). The ancient *Leda* (Plate 27) and Michelangelo's *Leda* are two extremes, the former of bewitching erotic charm, the latter pervaded by the tragic aspect of love.[13] Neither conception would have satisfied Leonardo. The kind of undisguised naïve sensuality that had existed in the ancient world was no longer accessible to the artist who had grown up in a Christian community. The tragic aspect of sexual lust and love was an implication that Leonardo, in my estimation, did not wish to represent directly. Therefore, he was compelled to choose the moment before the act, when the relationship of the two sexes is not

[13] Michelangelo had used the almost identical design without the swan, as a figure representing *Night* on the tomb of Giuliano de' Medici (Wind, 1958, p. 129f.).

yet structured according to superiority and inferiority but when they are still on an equal footing. Actually, nothing in his composition asserts the primacy of activity over passivity. Yet, by choosing the moment proximate to what evidently meant for him an outbreak of hostility, he anticipated the tension of the subsequent act and projected it into the moment that is captured on the canvas.

The gruesome imagery of the Allegory of *Virtue and Envy*, however, is potentially embedded in the *Leda* painting, although we probably would not be able to decipher it without Leonardo's allegorical sketch, for in the painting the horrible imagery has been purified, sublimated, and poured into the beautiful. In my work on Goethe (1961) I have tried to prove that he presented on a lower plane, in farcical, often bizarre, plays of seemingly little aesthetic or literary interest, problems he was to deal with in a parallel fashion in classical plays of great beauty. These "unaesthetic" plays actually reveal with greater clarity than the aesthetically superior works the raw material originating in the unconscious. The secondary transformation, the adjustment to the requirements demanded by the self, the evocation of aesthetic pleasure to make the repressed palatable, all this had not yet been sufficiently evolved in those minor plays.

The creation of beauty seems in many instances to be an extremely difficult and well-nigh painful process that arouses destructive impulses. The self apparently needs a discharge of these demonic forces that constantly threaten the self's striving toward synthesis, integration, and harmonious organization. The Allegory, whatever its historical background or the conscious purpose of its creator may have been, may have supplied a vent for these destructive forces.[14] After the unconscious had been discharged in crude forms the self was free to form a higher configuration in which the horror of the former production is no longer visible but can be felt on the one hand in the tension produced in the beholder and on the other in some subordinate details (which, however, have now lost all offensiveness).

I will now discuss one of these details which proves to my satisfaction that the series of problems contained in the Allegories of *Virtue and Envy* and *Pleasure and Pain* are submerged in the beauty of the *Leda* painting.

[14] However, the dating of Leonardo's *Leda* makes it highly improbable that the interval between the Allegory and the painting was short.

I turn to the male twins in the Borghese copy. The myth suggested their inclusion, but it is not probable that Leonardo felt bound by pagan iconography. The subject per se would permit their deletion, since, after all, they were born after Leda had succumbed to the swan. Michelangelo evidently felt safer without them.[15]

Confronted by the impossibility, as it appears to me, of integrating four babies with a woman and a beast into a composition that would live up to Leonardo's strict artistic demands, it is tempting to regard the two babies as simply a convenient counterpoise against the swan, as in the Borghese copy. But when I consider that Leonardo's ingenuity would certainly have been equal to finding a solution to the composition problem without recourse to the two infants, I am bound to look for a psychological factor that may also have been involved and I think there is one.

The *Leda* painting is, after all, unusual if viewed within Leonardo's total work, as far as we know it from original paintings and copies. An additional explanation is necessary for his choice of subject and the way he presented it. Clark (1939) finds the special meaning the Leda myth had for Leonardo in "its analogy with the creative process of nature. His Leda symbolises the female aspect of creation" (p. 124). He supports his suggestion by referring to intrinsic factors such as the elaborate coils of Leda's hair, the exuberant burst of new life in Nature as found in the Wilton House copy, and the four babies emerging out of the eggs. He further adduces an external factor which he finds on Q. V 24 r. (Plate 30).[16] Close to the right margin of that folio there is visible in faint lines a sketch of a standing Leda with approximately the posture we know from the various copies. But at the left margin there is an anatomical study which, according to Clark (1939), can be directly related to some of Leonardo's drawings which deal with generation, one of which "bears a study of female anatomy very similar to the Leda and evidently of the same date. And in the drawing the creative process symbolised in the Leda is examined with scientific detachment" (p. 124).[17] Clark here applies the method in which I

[15] See, however, Plate 29, for an engraving by Cornelius Bos that presumably was produced as a copy of Michelangelo's painting and shows Castor and Pollux as well as an egg in which transparently the outline of an infant or infants can be seen.

[16] See Clark (1935, Vol. I, notes to 12642, p. 116f.).

[17] Clark refers to MS. B as he does also in his notes to 12642 (Clark, 1935), but I have been unable to find in MS. B the drawings with which the Leda sketch of 12642 is to be connected.

myself have put so much faith, but I cannot agree with the conclusion he draws, for the anatomical study is a rough sketch of the alimentary tract *in situ*. Esche (1954, p. 160) believes it to be the alimentary tract of an animal, probably a pig, that Leonardo drew within the outline of a human figure.[18]

The association of the beautiful Leda with the alimentary tract of an animal (though it too points to generative processes since the boy usually equates them with those of digestion and elimination) expresses contemptuous feelings toward the female and the archaic desire to tear the female body open and look inside it (cf. Klein, 1932, passim).[19] This is made even more probable when we turn to Leonardo's advice on how to proceed in the study of the intestines. This ends:

> But first take away with the chisel the pubic bone and the bones of the hip to note well the site of the intestines [Vangensten et al., Vol. V, p. 17; Q. V 24 r.].

Now all this is not meant to deny that the generative aspect has its bearing on the *Leda* painting. Womanhood and the generative process are so closely associated that a symbolization of the breadth and intensity realized in Leonardo's *Leda* must necessarily imply this aspect also. Yet I doubt that it is so penetrant here that it can truly be regarded as the central theme and be put into connection with Diana of Ephesus as Clark does.[20]

My own idea, which approaches the matter from a different direction, also contains something of the generative aspect without making it the central theme. I cannot escape the impression that here Leonardo, on the threshold of old age, returned to perhaps his earliest childhood memory, that of the bird who visited him in the cradle. That bird had struck him with its tail inside of his lips many times, and there seems agreement that this was recalled as a hostile act—and, as we insistently add, one performed by the mother.

[18] If the sketch were looked at as if it were a Rorschach test figure, I surmise it would be associated with the female genital by many.

[19] If I am not mistaken the outline of the body in the anatomical part of Q. V 24 r. indicates a female body, which would be quite exceptional in Leonardo's drawings. His anatomical demonstrations usually show a male body unless he is explicating the female generative system. An exception to this rule is on Q. IV 7 r.

[20] Here it may also be recalled that in the Renaissance the Leda theme, the name derived from Leto, was also part of a myth of death (see Wind, 1958, pp. 129-141, Amor as God of Death).

Was not Leonardo now trying to undo this childhood memory by subjecting the woman to the very act he thought he had had to submit to from her when he was a helpless infant lying in his cradle? To do actively what has been experienced passively is a widespread defensive maneuver and often helps in healing a traumatic effect (cf. Freud, 1920a). Indeed, in consideration of the presence of the twins we can go a step further. In the original childhood memory the infant submitted. In the painting a child witnesses what the bird will do to the woman. We know that the next moment will bring into the child's life the trauma of a primal scene (cf. Freud, 1918). One need not go far to surmise that the child is Leonardo himself. In other words, the *Leda* painting may go back to a trauma Leonardo suffered in early childhood when he witnessed a primal scene. In view of his childhood recollection one feels inclined to guess that what he witnessed was a fellatio.

To the many meanings attributed to this recollection I have consequently to add two more: (1) the desire to be in the place of the woman, prompted by the sexual excitement when beholding the sexual scene, and (2) the pity for the woman who is treated disgustingly and the subsequent desire to help and offer himself as victim in order to free her. Both meanings are connected with the child's passivity. The fact that the passivity was converted into activity, as I demonstrated earlier, would indicate that an identification occurred also with the active male. But we know from the course his life subsequently took that this identification did not grow strong. The introduction of the twins now adumbrates this in an aesthetically very satisfactory way. Castor and Pollux are the heralded symbols of sublimated homosexual friendship, a type of relationship to which Leonardo became fixated. I do not know whether I interpret the facial expressions of the children correctly, but it seems that the one on the right, who is looking at the group, has a fearful expression and the other, who is looking at his twin, looks quite happy. The presence of Castor and Pollux would then mean, translated into genetic terms: "Because as a child I witnessed a terrifying scene, I had to turn away from women and pursue forever the beauty of my mirror image." Thus the painting may recapitulate Leonardo's story and tell us why he had to become a Dioscuros.

The introduction of the homosexual theme into Leonardo's *Leda* painting makes me believe that the two Oxford Allegories have indirectly found expression here. But I wish to add a general remark at this point. A mind so wide and so eminently differentiated as Leonardo's entertained, of course, a variety of relations to a subject that looms so broadly in a man's life as that of womanhood; that is, femaleness must have had a variety of meanings for him. But even where he is close to glorifying or, at least, to highly overvaluing it, his deep-seated ambivalence is still evident. Thus he wrote:

> As one mind governs two bodies, inasmuch as desires and the fears and the pains of the mother are common with the pains, that is the bodily pains and desires of the infant lying in the body of the mother, likewise the nourishment of the food serves the child, and it is nourished from the same cause as the members of the mother and the spirits, which are taken from the air—the common soul of the human race and other living things [O'Malley and Saunders, p. 484; Q. III 8 v.].[21]

Here the community of mother and fetus is emphasized and the mother is set up as the giver of the infant's soul; yet she is held responsible for the fetus's pains. In another passage Leonardo goes a step further:

> ... but [nature] puts within them [the bodies of the animals] the soul of the body which forms them, that is the soul of the mother which first constructs within the womb the shape of the man, and in due time awakens the soul that is to be its inhabitant. For this at first remained asleep, in the guardianship of the soul of the mother, who nourishes and gives it life through the umbilical vein, with all its spiritual members; and so it will continue for such time as the said umbilical cord is joined to it by the secundines and the cotyledons by which the child is attached to the mother.

---

[21] For a different and in some way clearer translation see McMurrich (1930, p. 233). On the same folio Leonardo demonstrates that "the seed of the mother is potent in the embryo equally to the seed of the father." This impresses me also as a defense of femaleness if it is considered that one theory of the ancient Greeks was that the male semen contains the whole child and the mother provides only a temporary habitat for it. Cf. Aeschylus: "The mother is no parent of that which is called her child, but only nurse of the new-planted seed that grows. The parent is he who mounts. A stranger she preserves a stranger's seed."

This theory pronounced by Apollo leads to Orestes' acquittal. For theories of generation in antiquity, see Lesky (1950). I have not found a satisfactory text on the history of the theories of propagation and therefore hesitate to draw definite conclusions from Leonardo's entry. Yet a passage I found in an article by Jean Rostand (1958) may be profitably quoted here: "In the Middle Ages, women were thought to be basically akin to animals, the active principle of generation being lodged in the man and his seed. The woman's role was simply restricted to receiving and nurturing man's seed. Woman was above all an *instrumentum*" (p. 56).

And this is the reason why any wish or intense desire or fright experienced by the mother, or any other mental suffering, is felt more powerfully by the child than by the mother, for there are many cases in which the child loses its life from it [MacCurdy, 1956, p. 179; Q. IV 10 r.].[22]

Here the mother is again set forth as the maker of the child. He owes her body and soul. The unit is described mentally and psychologically. Yet parallel with the glorification of the mother there is the accusation that her emotions may lead to the child's death.[23] Quite independently of the factual content of Leonardo's remarks and observations there are also presented here the adult's conscious and preconscious fantasies about motherhood within which one perceives hostile imagery of preoedipal origin such as I deduced previously from direct derivatives of the repressed in the form of the childhood recollection.[24] A detail that will perhaps demonstrate more convincingly Leonardo's ambivalence toward motherhood than the foregoing quotations can be found on Q. III 8 v., where Leonardo describes the mother as source of food and soul but also of desire and pain in the infant. On that folio there is a sketch of a figure with female outline possibly containing the male and female genitals with the three fetal navel vessels and navel cord (Plate 31).[25] It is perplexing at first to find a synthesis of the sexes on a sheet on which the unity of mother and fetus is set forth in detail. The surmise that they are associated by envy and that the synthetic view was born from the male desire to compete with maternal productive capacity is not far to seek. Yet, without denying these motives I suggest that this diagram is also an attempt at constructing an organism that would fulfill the generative functions with greater proficiency and less pain to the fetus than the maternal.

[22] Vangensten et al. (1915) translated the last sentence as follows: ". . . one will, one supreme desire, one fear which the mother has, or other mental pain, has more power on the fetus than on the mother; for many are the times that the fetus thereby loses its life" (Vol. IV, p. 17). For still another translation, see McMurrich (1930, p. 233).

[23] We encounter here, assigned by Leonardo to the fetal period, theories currently propounded by many analysts regarding the allegedly sinister influence of the mother on the child during the first years of his life.

[24] The foregoing theories of Leonardo's are not necessarily original with him. For the variety of theories that reached the Western world from antiquity, see Lesky (1950). In view of this variety of traditional views among which Leonardo could make his choice, one may assume, aside from Leonardo's observations and ratiocinations, an unconscious factor.

[25] This at least is Esche's interpretation (1954, p. 144). O'Malley and Saunders (p. 484, notes to Fig. 2) do not mention the bisexuality of the torso. Indeed, Esche's interpretation, though in my opinion correct, is open to question.

12

The Problem of Homosexuality and Trauma

Withal, the question has not been answered whether or not Leonardo had manifest homosexual relations in his adult years. Freud "without sharing in the certainty of his [Leonardo's] modern biographers" took it as more probable that Leonardo's relations to his pupils were not of a direct sexual nature (1910, p. 73). However, in 1910 Möller's article on Salai had not yet been published. Although this author castigates Freud and rejects the idea of even latent homosexuality in Leonardo, no one else has done more than he almost to compel the reader to assume the presence of manifest homosexuality in Leonardo. To be sure, this was by no means his intent, but perusing the record of that relationship, and in particular Möller's apparent proof that Salai is to be seen in the Oxford Allegory, makes the conclusion almost inescapable.

Furthermore, Dr. Gombrich kindly called my attention to the fact that "no personal letters such as were found in the Italian Archives from the pen of Michelangelo or Raphael have been discovered of Leonardo."[1] Gombrich takes this as another expression and proof of

[1] I owe thanks to Dr. Gombrich for this and many other instances of his help. Dr. Gombrich, in my opinion quite rightly, wonders that "the existence of a person of Leonardo's eminence and articulateness left so little trace in the Italian archives."

the deep isolation in which Leonardo lived. Indeed, this observation too favors the diagnosis of manifest homosexuality. From clinical observation one knows the type of personality isolated by iron barriers from the world and suffering deeply because of his prisonlike existence. The manifest homosexual relationship is then the only access there is to the world. Sexual pleasure is in such circumstances of moderate or little importance and by no means the primary motive. It is rather the temporary relief of a deep grief that holds such a man like a prisoner in restraint, that compels him to indulge sporadically in sexual relations with a mirror image of his past existence; it is the only access to the world that is kept free.

And still, my feeling is that Freud was right. Although Leonardo preferred solitude, he did not live a secluded life. He had plenty of enviers and rivals and gossip about him was rampant. If there had been manifest homosexuality, the rumor of it would somehow have reached us, I presume. It is even strange in view of his style of living that such a rumor did not arise no matter what kind of sexual life he actually had. Concealment of homosexual relations, particularly when habitual, is rather difficult; the environment responds sensitively to their existence.[2]

[2]This argument may, however, be proved at fault through the publication of a 1560 manuscript by Gio. Paolo Lomazzo (British Museum, Add. Mss. 12196), edited by Professor Eugenio Battisti, who has generously provided me with a transcript of a pertinent section. With Professor Battisti's permission I quote below a few passages that are relevant in this connection, in a translation prepared by Dr. Almansi; they are from a purported dialogue between Leonardo and Phidias.

Leo: . . . Salai, whom in life I loved more than all the others, who were several.
Phidias: Did you perhaps play with him the game in the behind that the Florentines love so much?
Leo: And how many times! Have in mind that he was a most beautiful young man, especially at about fifteen.
Phidias: Are you not ashamed to say this?
Leo: Why ashamed? There is no matter of more praise than this among people of merit [virtuosi]. And that this is the truth I shall prove to you with very good reasons.

· · · · · · · · ·

Leo: . . . Understand that masculine love is solely the product of merit [virtù] which joins together men of diverse feelings of friendship so that they may, from a tender age, arrive at manhood, stronger friends. . . .

[Leonardo continues in a long discourse to the effect that masculine homosexual attachments are the only ones that reflect a truly philosophical turn of mind; that heterosexual love arises out of a mere necessity—the continuation of the species—and is therefore second rate. He speaks disparagingly of women and cites instances of homosexuality in illustrious personages of antiquity. His speech concludes:]

Leo: . . . Besides this, all Tuscany has set store by this embellishment and especially the savants in Florence, my homeland, whence, by such practices and fleeing the

The argument in favor of manifest homosexuality as a defense against or escape from isolation, so convincing in a reconstruction of the sexual life of the average person, may lose its validity if applied to a genius. We are treading here on no man's land and tentative conclusions will depend on impressions rather than on experience and insight. The question is not per se an idle one but derives importance from the light it may throw on a singular phenomenon, genius, which, though rare, is characteristic of the human mind as is nothing else. That the general energic economy is in many instances of artistic genius essentially different from that of the ordinary man or the man of talent is very probable. The demand put upon the artistic genius is incomparable; he has to achieve the creation of a new universe that shall be as real as that which he observes with his senses and still be essentially different from the world into which he was born and in which he grew up. It is not surprising if he manages his store of libidinal energy differently from those who are spared the task that myth reserves to a creative deity. That Leonardo had impulses and wishes regarding Salai is highly probable; that he actually succumbed to temptations is questionable, although it is at present beyond a final decision.[3]

---

volubility of women, there have issued forth so many rare spirits in the arts, of whom in the field of painting I reminded you of some a little while ago and shall go on to remind you of more, whom the Neapolitans have adopted the practice of following.

I am not prepared to evaluate these passages. Those who are familiar with Lomazzo and his times will have to decide whether this work is (1) a reliable document although published forty-one years after Leonardo's death, (2) a facetious piece written for personal reasons, (3) reflections of a generation close to Leonardo's, or (4) an echo of gossip (or knowledge?) current among Leonardo's contemporaries. Be this as it may, the first and tentatively stated impression is that, notwithstanding psychoanalytic reasoning favoring the contrary, evidence seems to accumulate that Leonardo entertained manifest homosexual relations in his years of maturity. Nevertheless, even if it should be proved that Lomazzo was basing himself on information he received from Melzi, it still would have to be considered that Melzi may have been jealous of Salai, who after all seems to have been Leonardo's personal favorite up to the years of Melzi's own acquaintance with him. Lomazzo may also have set forth as fact what he was told in jest.

[3] Another side light is thrown on the question of Leonardo's homosexuality by the suggestion made by Mary McCarthy, in her book *The Stones of Florence*, that Verrocchio was a homosexual. She offers no basis for this suggestion other than the impression she derives from certain of his works, but even such an observation by a sensitive observer may be taken as worthy to initiate speculation. If her impression is valid, one must assume that Leonardo, who is described as of particular handsomeness in his youth, must have been exposed at least to seductive advances. Indeed, when one considers how long Leonardo remained in Verrocchio's household—including at least six years after he was accepted into the painter's guild (see Valentiner, 1930, p. 48)—some may think that manifest homosexual relations must inevitably have taken place. One might even speculate that the anonymous denunciation of Leonardo had Verrocchio as its real target, since the delator refers—perhaps

There is a passage in his writings which, in my estimation, contains the key to an understanding of his relation to male genitality.

> *Della verga.* This confers with the human intelligence and sometimes has intelligence of itself, and although the will of the man desires to stimulate it it remains obstinate and takes its own course, and moving sometimes of itself without licence or thought by the man, whether he be sleeping or waking, it does what it desires; and often the man is asleep and it is awake, and many times the man is awake and it is asleep; many times the man wishes it to practise and it does not wish it; many times it wishes it and the man forbids it. It seems therefore that this creature has often a life and intelligence separate from the man, and it would appear that the man is in the wrong in being ashamed to give it a name or to exhibit it, seeking the rather constantly to cover and conceal what he ought to adorn and display with ceremony as a ministrant [MacCurdy, 1956, p. 120; Fogli B 13 r.].

If one accepts this statement as a psychological record, one can derive from it in dynamic terms one basic aspect of Leonardo's unconquerable conflict about the male genital. McMurrich (1930, p. 202f.) and Esche (1954, p. 115) measure this paragraph in terms of physiological theories and link it historically with views of the Galenic school. Yet Leonardo expresses here, in the form of a scientific statement, a consternation that is often encountered clinically in men—that penile reactions are not accessible to the will. One perceives between the lines an expression of helplessness and despair about the defeat man may suffer when the organ of his greatest pride and pleasure refuses its cooperation just at the moment when it ought to carry out its greatest feats. One may discover this leading issue in the *Leda* painting, for Leonardo's imagery may have been drawn toward this subject just because the swan, being without a prehensile organ, is least prepared to perform the act mythology attributes to him. Indeed, Leda's sisters in fate, Danaë, Europa, and Semele, faced a more ap-

---

pointedly—to Leonardo's being in Verrocchio's house. Furthermore, if Leonardo did engage in manifest homosexuality initially and subsequently with his teacher, the feeling of guilt, the sense of humiliation, the reactive aggressivity, so frequently encountered clinically, must have been particularly intense. One could not then but wonder whether he would have wanted to subject Salai to the same conflictful situation in which he found himself as a young man. The temptation might have been inordinately strong, but in view of his past experiences the inhibitions and feelings of guilt might have been no less so. For the role of homosexuality in Plato's life and philosophy, see Kelsen (1933). It is my impression that many of Kelsen's views about Plato could fruitfully be applied to the problem of Leonardo's homosexuality.

propriate situation.[4] In this aspect of the physiology of male genitality may be found the ambiguous presentation of the bird as being simultaneously wild and passionate as well as helpless and dependent.

In the last sentence Leonardo recommends the full gratification of male narcissism: one should talk of the penis, adorn and display it. There is the intimation that such exercise will favorably predispose the organ; in other words, the priapic cult should be applied to the organ itself. Thus he indirectly expresses a psychological truth: that shame and fear may prevent the integration of the penis into the body image and cause the feeling of helplessness and prostration from which Leonardo apparently suffered. The first step toward recovery would have been the full establishment of the narcissistic cathexis of the penis. This, however, was blocked. Its physiological independence made the organ for him an object of aversion. By its spontaneous arousal under inappropriate circumstances and its passivity in situations of demand it leads to shame, embarrassment, humiliation, and fear.[5] Consequently, the penis becomes an organ of narcissistic defeat, a symbol of the self's limitation.

On the same page Leonardo writes about the bearing of the *will* on the movements of the lungs and the automatic function of the heart, the intestines, and glands (MacCurdy, 1956, p. 120; Fogli B 13 r.). Here the ego was well served: one group of organs, like the lungs, both working spontaneously and leaving a broad margin to ego control, as the case may be, and the other doing its work subterraneously and efficiently without bothering the ego by arousing its attention or interfering with the attainment of its goals. It seems that he longed for the genital to be obedient to either of these principles. Viewed under the aspect of ego control, it would make good sense if Leonardo secretly envied women, who were spared such suffering.

This factor may also have accelerated Leonardo's desire to achieve control by knowledge. Here, in the realm of experience, the ego could evolve its supreme potency independent of the vagaries of a self-willed physical organ and could build machine after machine, all of which would behave according to a predetermined plan and move in accordance with the commands received from man. Yet Leonardo's in-

[4] For an interpretation of the four women as the four elements, see Wind (1958, p. 139, n. 5).
[5] For psychopathology of male sexual function due to fixation to a passive phase of genital development, see Loewenstein (1935).

ability to publish his findings appears like an aftermath to the traumatic penile experience. Despite the stupendous mental potency he commanded, he still was inhibited in adornment and display in this area too. If Vasari was right, narcissistic exhibition was possible for Leonardo only in matters of outward decorum, such as servants and horses (Vasari, p. 6). Freud, as mentioned before, drew some conclusions from this one-sided and limited ability to identify with his father. The father's sexual behavior, the disloyalty to the son's mother, the early death of the first stepmother, all these conjoined to make Leonardo look upon heterosexuality with suspicion, aversion, and fright, whereas the additional factor of control made acceptable and even desirable such identifications as did not transgress the volitional sphere and manifested themselves in the choice of garments and outer paraphernalia of prestige. These paraphernalia became the carrier of beauty, but the genitalia, the physical essence of passion, were relegated to the realm of ugliness.

Leonardo's appraisal of male genitality is suggestive of a general factor that may have had an important bearing on the structure of his personality. Notwithstanding the actual existence of those psycho-biological processes characteristic of male genitality that impressed him so deeply, it must be presumed that his demand for control was excessive. Apparently he was able to generate confidence and trust only on the basis of absolute predictability. Did not his incessant search for knowledge have as its goal to render the universe a predictable one? But excessive controls and excessive demands for predictability do not evolve spontaneously; they are created for purposes such as protection against painful contingencies. It would be for reasons not far to seek if one assumed that these measures served the function of averting anxiety. This, at least, is the most frequent function of such counter-measures when they are encountered under ordinary clinical conditions. However, for reasons presently to be discussed, I tend to assume that Leonardo was excessively vulnerable to traumata, that is to say, that his psychic apparatus was so sensitive to sudden stimulation even by stimuli of relatively low intensity that it was most of the time on the verge of being injured. In other words, the margin of tolerable stimulation must have been a narrow one. The emotion against which he had to protect himself was therefore not anxiety but fright. I presume that he often or even most of the time felt on the verge of being overwhelmed by sudden fright or terror (cf. Reik, 1929, pp. 7-44).[6]

There is a short remark to be found in Leonardo's notebooks that of itself is almost convincing evidence in favor of this hypothesis: "Just as courage imperils life, fear protects it" (Richter, Vol. II, p. 248, No. 1200; C.A. 76 v.). This accords well with Freud's theory that anxiety protects against suffering a psychic trauma (Freud, 1920a). The courageous person does not mind the sudden upsurge of stimuli—he cannot be traumatized. But Leonardo, by putting himself into the position of the courageous person and imagining what he has to endure, draws the conclusion that this would go beyond what he, Leonardo, could tolerate. Fear, however, would protect against trauma. How well he succeeded in protecting himself can be learned from the following statement: "Fear arises sooner than anything else" (Richter, Vol. II, p. 248, No. 1199; L 90 v.).

If we consider in what way the genital became a source of trauma, we may conclude that his disappointment and distrust of the male organ may have been caused by fright as a boy precipitated by a sudden erection, or by the unexpected cessation of an erection while daydreaming (causing the feeling of loss of penis), or an orgasm for which the boy was unprepared by previous experience. Rarely as this last occurs in boys before prepuberty or puberty, it still does occur, occasionally at an early age, and has then always the extraordinary consequences of a severe trauma. The penis would thus have become a constant source of potential trauma, and Leonardo, in order to evade the threat inherent in the organ, may have had no choice but to divorce himself internally from being one with his generative system.

All of this of course is speculation. But we are on safer clinical grounds when we study Vasari's biography and notice with surprise how many incidents Vasari records of Leonardo's having tried to frighten others. The earliest seems to have been the following: On a round piece of wood that his father brought him to be painted for a tenant of his estate, Leonardo "resolved to do the Medusa head to terrify all beholders." He succeeded so well that when his father saw the head without previous warning he "started back . . . and was beating a retreat when Leonardo detained him and said, 'This work has

---

[6] For the bearing of trauma upon artistic creativity, see Lowenfeld's important paper (1944). The author approaches the problem from the viewpoint of traumatophilia, whereas in Leonardo it seems to me traces of traumatophobia can be discerned.

served its purpose, take it away, then, as it has produced the effect intended' " (Vasari, p. 7).[7] According to Vasari (p. 8), Leonardo later painted "a picture of the Medusa's head in oils with a garland of snakes about it, the most extraordinary idea imaginable."

On his way to Rome he constructed "hollow animals which flew in the air when blown up, but fell when the wind ceased." In Rome he fastened scales to a lizard "taken from other lizards, dipped in quicksilver, which trembled as it moved, and after giving it eyes . . . all to whom he showed it ran away terrified." With bellows he would blow up the guts of a wether until the room was filled, forcing anyone there to take refuge in a corner. "He perpetrated many such follies" (Vasari, p. 12). It is noteworthy that Leonardo's desire to frighten others is reported of his youthful years as well as of his later life (see Clark, 1939, p. 162). In Rome he no doubt was unhappy, unsuccessful, disappointed, and utterly defeated by his rivals, and it is of just these years that Vasari has much to say about this peculiar tendency of Leonardo's. One feels inclined to assume that Leonardo's desire to frighten others extended through all periods of his life. Freud cites such and other examples as signs that "Leonardo remained like a child for the whole of his life in more than one way" (1910, p. 127). Moreover, one may say, though it is not literally true, that we remain children in so far as we remain vulnerable to traumata. Leonardo's frequent desire to traumatize others by frightening them may demonstrate how much he was in danger of suffering the same fate.[8] We are dealing here with a principle Freud demonstrated first in children's play but which has general significance, namely, to do actively to others the unpleasant thing that has been suffered passively (1920a, p. 16f.). We

[7] It impresses me as revealing an understanding of the secret meaning of the incident, whether it be legend or real occurrence, when Vasari reports that the father, not wanting to turn over the valuable painting to the tenant, replaced it with another piece of wood on which "a heart transfixed by a dart" was painted. This symbolizes well the sensation frequently felt in a moment of fright or terror.

[8] Dr. O. Isakower was kind enough to call my attention to a different interpretation of this behavior of Leonardo's. Leonardo here was probably stepping out of his function as an artist and concretizing on a lower plane an aspect that is inherent in the effect a genius's work has on others, namely, the *tremendum* (defined by Lewis and Short [1879] as "that is to be trembled at, hence *fearful, frightful, formidable, terrible, tremendous*"). Lange-Eichbaum has described this aspect among the many others (*majestas, energicum, fascinans, sanctum*, etc.) which are observed in an analysis of the genius's effect on society (1927, pp. 114-134). Leonardo's need to act out in buffa what is part and parcel of the most serious pursuit opens new avenues of investigation that go beyond the limits of this study. Cf. also Gombrich (1953-54, p. 191).

will here think of various defense mechanisms, foremost of one described by Anna Freud as the identification with the aggressor (1936, pp. 117-131).

Excursus on the "Cenacolo"

I wish to add here one particular factor that makes me almost certain that this reconstruction may be appraised as more than hypothetical. This has to do with Leonardo's *Last Supper* (Plate 8). That fresco is unique among his pictorial creations for more than one reason. It is the only monumental religious painting he undertook. It is also the only complete large work about which there is no doubt that it was painted exclusively by him. But aside from these and many other external features that are bound to be special in a work of art of such excellence and consequence, there is one strikingly prominent respect in which the *Cenacolo* stands apart from Leonardo's paintings. From them one receives, rightly or wrongly, the feeling that they can (most of them with relative ease) be connected in one way or another with what is known of Leonardo or has been obtained by psychological reconstruction. Thus, for example, his paintings of St. Mary, whether with the Christ Child or in the *Adoration of the Magi*, the *Virgin of the Rocks*, or the *Anna Metterza*, can all be brought into a meaningful context as consequences of his illegitimate birth, of an attempt to idealize his own mother, or of his homosexual impulses.

The painting of St. Jerome, particularly in view of Leonardo's unusual conception of this saint, may easily have given occasion to vent his own feelings of guilt, and the cartoon of the *Battle of Anghiari*, with its presentation of unleashed wildest fury, to vent his aggressive impulses, which must have been considerable in view of his strong reaction formations.

The various paintings of young men of his later period may have been the result of Leonardo's strivings to represent his ideal of youth, which synthesizes male and female and reaches the highest expression of human beauty.[9] In the projected paintings, too, the personal connection can, rightly or wrongly, also be discovered with ease: would not his *St. Sebastian* well have symbolized his own isolated standing

[9] For the *Medusa* and *Leda* paintings I have already suggested a connection with Leonardo's personality structure.

in the world and the enmity he thought confronted him; would he not, in painting *St. George and the Dragon,* have felt that he was like a St. George who wanted to defeat superstition and ignorance; would not his *Christ among the Doctors* have stood also for himself, wandering through the world like a Christ Child astounding and irritating professional scholars? I make these remarks not because they are necessarily correct but only to show the ease with which one can fit almost all the subjects in which he was interested into the psychological context of his life history. However, it is very different with *The Last Supper.* The iconological subject strikes me as almost a foreign body in his religious *œuvre.* It is not easy to guess at what personal problem loomed in the background of this work. In my opinion the relevant psychological factor is to be found in an iconographic element characteristic of the painting. Whereas traditionally the moment of the institution of the Eucharist had been chosen as the theme of the Last Supper, Leonardo's painting, as has often been pointed out, presents the moment after Jesus utters the words: "But behold, the hand of him that betrayeth me is with me on the table."

This shift was Leonardo's doing. There is no reason to assume he was acting upon a request or that it was imposed upon him. It was a shift from a moment of hope and promise and consolation to a moment of the greatest terror. Nothing more frightening could have been said by Jesus. Imagine: a revered person whose authority is absolute announcing during a solemn feast that his murderer is among the company. It is the most dismal moment in Jesus' life, and I wonder whether Leonardo was drawn toward the depiction of this moment because it contains a maximum of fright and terror in a setting that is itself significant. For the shocking event did not occur against a neutral background; the moment is particularly suitable for a traumatic effect in view of the solemnity of the preceding moment, replete with affection, object closeness, almost object identity. One can hardly imagine a combination of factors that would require the integration of a larger span of contrasts than the switch from the institution of the Eucharist to the announcement of the presence of the traitor. Through the Eucharist the group had become a solid unit, the magic medium of Christ's body and blood flowing equally through all present; the declaration that the betrayer is present makes the group fall temporarily apart into an aggregate of isolated parts each of which potentially may turn destructively against the rest. Had Christ announced the name of the traitor the effect would have been terrible enough but not truly traumatic, for the coherence and integration of the group into a unit would not have been threatened. Group wrath would have turned against one of its members doomed to be expelled, but the aggression thus evoked would have provided an appropriate channel to drain off the emotion. However, we read: "And they began to inquire among themselves, which of them it was that should do this thing." This indicates that any of them could be the traitor. The ambivalence of the apostles is expressed in the immediately following events at Gethsemane. Thus as soon as Christ had announced the presence of the traitor not only did the group temporarily dissolve and panic threaten as a result of the sudden freeing of all libidinal cathexes (see Freud, 1921) that were invested in the ties to the other group members and Christ, their leader, but they were suddenly confronted with the task of searching their own souls. Thus a situation of the greatest security was changed from one moment to the next into one of the greatest insecurity, the individual member facing a task for which he was utterly unprepared and not equipped to deal with. It is the paradigmatic structure of a traumatic situation. Douglas (1944), admitting the disappointment he suffered when for the first time he looked upon *The Last Supper*, declares he had the same feeling when he saw Picasso's *Guernica* (p. 90), and this, in my opinion, may indirectly confirm my thesis, for Picasso tried in that painting to depict what is considered in our century as the greatest trauma.

Consequently, the psychologic quest underlying Leonardo's *Last Supper* appears to me to be the examination of how man is affected by trauma or can overcome trauma. Yet simultaneously it also represents the one being that was immune to trauma, namely Christ.[10] Heydenreich made the subtle and far-reaching observation that there is a factor common to Christ and Judas. "Outside the circle of the guiltless, he alone shares Christ's secret, and is the second isolated person, though isolated by guilt," whereas Christ "appears as the sud-

[10] Some may hold, of course, that, at Golgotha at least, Jesus was vulnerable to trauma. Even if this were certain, however—and theologians differ on this point—it would not disturb the proposition asserted here, which bears only on the Jesus whom Leonardo is depicting.

denly isolated Deity, alone in the knowledge of his fate" (1954, Vol. I, p. 18). That is to say, Christ and Judas are exempt from the traumatic effect and well protected by knowledge.[11] Yet simultaneously they are antipodes. Nevertheless, they both symbolize Leonardo himself: the one his ideal and the other what in dark hours he probably feared to be. Here knowledge is represented as supreme value, as the bringer of truth and peace, but it is also represented as the bearer of sin and execrable guilt, but in both instances it preserves from fright and therefore from trauma.

Douglas's criticism of the *Cenacolo* pertains to the impression it allegedly gives of "some carefully rehearsed scene in a great stage play, in which the characters had been posed by an experienced but unimaginative producer" (p. 93).[12] This criticism seems to me to go much too far; though a mild degree of artificiality or posing of the gestures of the Apostles can, I think, hardly be denied, it does not detract from the formal perfection of the painting. Still, the question may be raised whether this factor of posing militates against my thesis. Leonardo's two other groups, *The Adoration* and the battle scene, do not show any trace of posturing but are famous just for the superb expressiveness of movement. Would one then not expect to observe this quality even intensified in a scene in which the effect of trauma is asserted to be the principal issue?

To bridge this contradiction I have to refer to a subtle observation Clark made when following up what comes "between the sketch and the picture" in Leonardo's instance, namely the conflict between spontaneity and perfection (1939, p. 18f.; see also pp. 95-99). If we look at the only two studies for the composition that have survived among the many that must have preceded the final work (Plates 32 and 33), we may get a glimpse of what I have propounded as the basic issue of Leonardo's *Cenacolo*. Clark had said about the study in the Venice Academy (Plate 32): "[it] is one of the most puzzling of all Leonardesque relics. It is badly drawn—the Christ's right arm and hand are childish; and in spite of the factitious animation of the figures they

[11] Although Judas if for no other reason than because of the revelation that Christ knew of his betrayal would be expected to show fright, he remains singularly calm and only the peculiar position of the left hand betrays tension and what may be called a suppressed startle reaction. But there are no signs of weakened control visible in him.

[12] Douglas reports that the contemplation of Christ mitigated his disappointment.

lack the inner life which redeems Leonardo's most careless scribbles: they are stiff, almost archaic" (p. 95).[13]

Although it may be bold for an outsider in the field to disagree with such an authority as Sir Kenneth Clark, still I venture to say that this early study conveys something of the effect I have in mind, particularly in the figure of Bartholomew. His benumbed torpidity may be the congealed state of stupor, whereas John, reacting in the opposite way, is in complete collapse. These are the extremes with which man may react to trauma. The little study at Windsor (W. 12542) conveys the impression of a mad, frenzied rush.[14]

Both these studies are evidently far from the composition that emerged as the final product. There apparently each figure was constructed in such a way as to express its most personal reaction while integrated into the rhythm of a subgroup of three, which in turn is integrated into the rhythm of the half on each side of Christ, the half, in turn, again being integrated into the rhythm of the opposite half. Thus each single member of the twelve, aside from holding his own place as a distinct individuality, is assigned a dynamic value felt in three different formal contexts, the whole revolving around the center in supreme repose (cf. Clark, 1939, p. 94f.). This is the opposite of the Venice study, where the disciples are isolated, essentially without communication, rigid and frozen. The impression of childishness and

---

[13] Cf. Richter (Vol. I, p. 373): "Here the disciples are seen to express consternation. . . . The artist's preoccupation seems to have been . . . with the individualization of a variety of characters." Miss Kate Steinitz informs me that at present most Leonardo scholars deny Leonardo's authorship of this sketch. Cf. Hildebrandt (1927, p. 336).

[14] Now that I have inspected the study in the Academy in Venice I feel better prepared to make a comment—without losing sight of the fact that what I am saying is strictly hypothetical. Others too have probably noticed that what may be traces of another hand are visible in this sketch. Still, it is my feeling that this drawing is mainly by Leonardo. It would really be a coincidence of the strangest sort if a drawing by a left-handed artist that fits so well into a well-circumscribed psychological pattern were not by Leonardo. Yet in leaving external probability aside some of the best experts rightly find un-Leonardesque traits in this drawing. If, however, it is considered that there is presented here a subject, a mood, an atmosphere, against which—according to my thesis—Leonardo fought all his life and of which he was in terror, then we may have to admit that this is an extraordinary, so to speak, an un-Leonardesque situation. It may have been one of those unique moments when for a split second a defense breaks down, and something rushes forth that had ordinarily to be concealed. Is it not quite probable that the usual formal perfection would then have to be missing? Although it sounds paradoxical, I would claim this drawing for Leonardo just because the formal aspect is un-Leonardesque. This, at least, is what the psychological background I have constructed would require. When the accident of a moment forces a genius to express that against which he feels a supreme aversion it is not to be expected that his hand will have its usual masterly control and will not tremble. If my construction is correct, Leonardo would have lost control at the moment when he produced this particular creation.

archaicism appears to me to be the result of the artist's extraordinary identification with the sufferers of the traumatic blow. When Clark says that in the groups of Apostles there is still evident the labor that lies between the sketches and the final composition, he may be referring to an inner resistance Leonardo may have felt against converting the stunning or shattering effect of a paralyzing trauma into movement that should show at least some degree of control. It is just that the figures of the Apostles do not move freely. The labored quality of the style is, according to my reconstruction, the effect of the artist's identification with subjects that have been utterly defeated by trauma. Investigators agree that the figure of Christ is sublimely free of any sign of that labored quality, and I presume that this is also true of Judas.

If my suggestion to investigate Leonardo's seemingly discontinuous notes as free associations that are interconnected by a latent psychological meaning is accepted, it may be worth while to study two folios on which Leonardo wrote a comment on the iconography of the *Cenacolo*. The full text runs as follows:

> One who was drinking and has left the glass in its position and turned his head towards the speaker.
> Another, twisting the fingers of his hands together, turns with stern brows to his companion. Another with his hands spread open shows the palms, and shrugs his shoulders up to his ears, making a mouth of astonishment.
> Another speaks into his neighbour's ear and he, as he listens to him, turns towards him to lend an ear, while he holds a knife in one hand, and in the other the loaf half cut through by the knife. Another who has turned, holding a knife in his hand, upsets with his hand a glass on the table.
> Another lays his hand on the table and is looking. Another blows his mouthful. Another leans forward to see the speaker, shading his eyes with his hand. Another draws back behind the one who leans forward, and sees the speaker between the wall and the man who is leaning [Richter, Vol. I, p. 380, Nos. 665 and 666; Forster II 62 v., 63 r.].

Here one gets the impression of scattered gestures strewn all over the scenery and Leonardo's own words possibly confirm my earlier conclusion that the initial imagery referable to the *Cenacolo* was one of a previously united group torn asunder by an explosive event. But the folios are to be used here for a different purpose. On folio 63 r.

(Plate 34) on which the fourth paragraph of the above quotation starts, other entries are found. There is a sketch of a tree trunk from which a twig is sprouting. Leonardo wrote: "A felled tree which is shooting again." Then follows a multiplication $30 \times 40 = 1200$ under which is written: "I am still hopeful." The next two lines read, respectively: "A falcon," "Time" (Richter, Vol. I, p. 391, No. 697), the whole being put at the side of the sketch of a bird with widespread wings, seemingly flying upward and holding in its mouth a drawn-out linear object that has been interpreted as a serpent (see Pedretti, 1953). The tree trunk is identical with an emblem used in Florence; this, however, is thought to be a mere coincidence (see Richter, Vol. I, p. 391, n.).

It is surprising indeed to find the *Cenacolo,* a sprouting tree trunk, and a bird flying upward together suddenly on one page. If we consider the meeting of these three topics on the same page as purely coincidental, then it is without psychological meaning. But I take that which is spatially united as psychologically connected, space here replacing the time factor in psychoanalysis, where proximity of associations in time is taken as an indicator of a deep psychological connection. We have therefore first to venture an interpretation of each item.

The clearest seems to be the trunk of the felled tree that is sprouting again, a legendary theme of old age. In Richard Wagner's *Tannhäuser,* the Pope denies forgiveness unless the dead stick Tannhäuser carries as a staff leafs out as a green twig. Here the reference to sex is evident, since Tannhäuser has sinned in the Venusberg. The trunk of the felled tree in Leonardo's sketch can be deciphered as the stump of a penis injured by masturbation. The inscription "I am still hopeful" then would mean: "Although I masturbated and destroyed my potency, a new and uninjured penis may grow." If this interpretation is correct, whereas the trauma (masturbation) occurred first, followed by the resolution, by his choice of sequence of events for the *Cenacolo* Leonardo presented the reverse sequence there, first the institution of the Eucharist, followed by the traumatizing event.

We may here reconstruct the unconscious meaning the *Cenacolo* had for Leonardo. Judas's betrayal is the aggression against a father figure, and we may therefore conclude that the masturbatory fantasies of the boy probably contained elements of aggression against his father or that masturbation had a rebellious function.[15] Furthermore, in attempting to find a general frame of reference we may surmise that death was equated in the unconscious with castration. Easter, then, the time of the crucifixion and resurrection, gives occasion for infantile imagery symbolized by the sprouting of the felled tree.

A reconstruction of the meaning of the bird sketch seems more difficult and hazardous. Apparently Leonardo had a falcon in mind. Therefore, it may be helpful to gather the contexts in which the falcon is recorded in his *Notebooks*. In the tales of animals the falcon appears as a proud and courageous bird. Under the heading of *Magnanimity*, we find:

> The falcon never preys but on large birds; and it will let itself die rather than feed on little ones, or eat stinking meat [Richter, Vol. II, p. 264, No. 1230; H 10 r. See also No. 1264; H 101 r.].

or under *Pride:*

> The falcon, by reason of its haughtiness and pride, is fain to lord and rule over all the other birds of prey, and longs to be sole and supreme; and very often the falcon has been seen to assault the eagle, the queen of birds [Richter, Vol. II, p. 265, No. 1233; H 11 v.].[16]

In a fictitious letter to a Benedetto in which a fantastic tale of a gruesome catastrophe, a kind of fantasy of world annihilation, is set forth, the falcon is used in a comparison to demonstrate the particular plight of humans in such a situation when compared with animals. Leonardo wrote:

> In truth, the human species in such a plight has need to envy every other race of creatures; for though the eagle has strength sufficient to subdue the other birds, they yet remain unconquered through the rapidity of their flight, and so the swallows through their speed escape becoming the prey of the falcon . . . [MacCurdy, 1956, p. 1055; C.A. 96 v. b].

So much about the falcon in Leonardo's writings, as far as can be found in the indexes of the main publications. In view of these quotations one may say that there were two sets of images associated with

---

[15] See my earlier suggestion regarding the accusation against Leonardo for homosexuality in 1476.

[16] See also MacCurdy (1956, p. 418; Sul Volo 17 r.) for a similar reference to the falcon.

it in Leonardo's mind: one of a chivalrous, clean, proud animal that loves solitude and would attack only a peer and is pugnacious enough to fight with the far stronger queen of the birds; the other, of an animal that preys on ducks, by no means his equal, and would like to prey on swallows if they were not too quick. Also I should like to point out that in one set the falcon is thought of as the enemy of the eagle; in the other, by being given the same place in the comparison as the eagle it is assigned a functional identity or at least a parallel role, as if they belonged together. In the tale of annihilation, the falcon is, by analogy, put into the position of the fiend that causes the fantastic destruction and whose appearance is described as follows:

> The black visage . . . most horrible and terrifying to look upon . . . And believe me there is no man so brave but that, when the fiery eyes were turned upon him, he would willingly have put on wings in order to escape, for the face of infernal Lucifer would seem angelic by contrast with this [MacCurdy, 1956, p. 1054f.; C.A. 96 v. b].

We emphasize here the important reference by Leonardo to flying. "To put on wings" was, after all, one of Leonardo's cherished ambitions. Here he tells us one of the fantasies behind this ambition. It was associated with the desire to escape a fearsome danger.

We have thus discovered three different meanings which may be relevant for the falcon depicted on folio 63 r.: a chivalrous bird; a fiendish bird; and, finally, the artist himself, who would like to fly like a falcon. The material on which to base an interpretation becomes ambiguous here, so it seems wiser to break off at this point. Yet one more attempt, however hazardous, may be permitted. Could it be that the falcon at the bottom of the folio represents all three: the chivalrous, the fiend, and the artist? The first two are aspects of the ambivalently loved parents, probably the father: the father as hero and as fiend. Combined with the self, the falcon would then symbolize the integration of an identification with the father. After having discussed the meaning flying had for Leonardo I will add a remark about this folio. In any event, we have not so far found anything that would contradict my previous thesis that the psychologically relevant problem of the *Cenacolo* is that of trauma. The folio seems, if anything, to confirm it.

Excursus on the Meaning of Flying to Leonardo

A considerable portion of Leonardo's time was devoted to the attempt to realize man's ancient dream of conquering also the element of air. We can be sure that in this Leonardo was not only following a traditional and universal mythical dream of mankind but was also responding to the most personal motives. Freud based his reconstruction of Leonardo's motive on the interpretation of the frequent dream of flying, on mythology, and on slang expressions. He states that the bird is a symbol of the male genital, and the wish to be able to fly results from the infantile wish to be capable of the sexual act (1910, p. 125f.).

Although the clinician will agree with this interpretation, it may still be worth while to inquire to what degree the unavoidable margins of arbitrariness inherent in symbolic interpretations can be reduced by additional evidence. James Strachey in his superb *Standard Edition of the Psychological Works of Sigmund Freud* adds a footnote (1957, p. 86, n.) in which he points to anatomical peculiarities of the kite, which, after all, was Leonardo's favored bird of study during one part of his inquiry. The kite's long, forked tail is one of its prominent features, and, as Strachey cites from an ornithological account: "At times the tail is fanned out at right angles to its normal place." The following remark, from a special study of Leonardo's writing on this topic, is also of interest:

His [Leonardo's] special favorite among birds was the kite, especially because the kite may be taken to be the most perfect acrobat in flight without wing strokes and under the most difficult atmospheric conditions; he is so skillful that he can maintain himself aloft even when the wind is so gusty and irregular that it makes flight impossible for other birds [Cutry, 1956, p. 341].

Thus the phenotype of the bird and its particular ability make it well suited as a penile symbol. In view of Leonardo's sexual difficulty and his great sensitivity to the genital's inability or unwillingness—so to speak—to maintain itself "aloft" in circumstances when such service was expected, the kite may well have been selected as the most promising among all avian species from which to glean the secrets of its skills.

The historian, distrustful of unconscious motives, will, however. raise the question of what species Leonardo should have investigated if not that which is the most skilled in flying. An unconscious motive may support a rational one and the presence of a rational motive does not exclude the unconscious one. It is just the harmonious synthesis of both that creates the strongest motives in man. To be sure, Leonardo delved into an incredibly large number of topics and his mind was Aristotelian-encyclopedic, but outside the subject of art one can recognize three well-delineated topics that most aroused his zeal: anatomy, the nature of water, and flight. From all we know about the structure of man's mind, it is hardly feasible that this could occur without the support of strong unconscious motives.[17] If he had been asked why he selected just the kite as a paradigm, he might have referred to Pliny as Schapiro (1956) has suggested, but we may rest assured that this would have been a rationalization. For a man who makes himself an instrument of experience, it may be bitter to acknowledge the hidden bearing of an inadequacy upon seemingly rational choices.

We also know that Leonardo in the course of his inquiry dropped the kite as a flying model and replaced it with the bat: "Remember that your flying-machine must imitate no other than the bat, because the membranes serve as framework, . . ." (Richter, Vol. II, p. 225, No. 1123; Sul Volo 16 r.). Again we encounter well-chosen justifications, but about a decade earlier Leonardo had excerpted the following from *Fiore di Virtù*, published in 1488 at Venice (Richter, Vol. II, p. 259): "The bat, owing to unbridled lust, observes no universal rule in pairing, but males with males and females with females pair promiscuously, as it may happen" (Richter, Vol. II, p. 265, No. 1234; H 12 r.). I do not know whether knowledge of this passage resulted in the bat's becoming a symbol to Leonardo or whether the story impressed Leonardo as worthy of being copied because it confirmed an earlier associative connection of his; at any rate, the bat is pictured as unchaste,

---

[17] About the unconscious background of Leonardo's interest in anatomy I will have something to say later. Leonardo's interest in water, which was really excessive, I will not discuss. The psychoanalytic formula favors a history of severe bed-wetting. The excessive fear of trauma and the excessive demand for control could be meaningfully connected with such a history. Anyone who has had the opportunity to observe in detail the working of the defense mechanisms in a male patient in whose history prolonged bed-wetting was a source of repeated traumatization will agree that Leonardo's incessant preoccupation with water, his plans to curb its destructive effects, to channelize rivers—that all this combined with his unusually intense precautions against trauma permits the assumption that enuresis played a leading role in his childhood and probably throughout the years of latency.

and this association may well have served to support the unconscious equation of penis and flying animal.

Yet whatever we may rightly deduce from finding this animal story among Leonardo's notes, there is a structural element in the bat's way of life about which I feel more strongly that it may have made it an appropriate penile symbol. Leonardo, when he pondered upon the problem of the balance of the heart, was puzzled by the fact that the bat "when it sleeps always places itself upside down" (MacCurdy, 1956, p. 169; Q. II 17 r.), that is to say, when it relaxes its head is down and when it becomes active and flies it changes its posture and the head rises. This peculiarity may have been a strong stimulus toward penile symbolization.

Moreover, if we look at the paragraph preceding Leonardo's observation on the bat, we will feel even more certain of the interpretation:

> And if you say the testicles are made only to open or shut the vasa spermatica, you are mistaken because they would only be necessary to the rams or bulls, which have them very big; and if these testicles had re-entered into the body on account of the cold, the coitus could not be performed [Vangensten et al., Vol. II, p. 38, 17 r.].

Then follows abruptly the remark about the bat and a question regarding its heart.[18]

When writing "Of the Bird's Movement" Leonardo abruptly closes the section with: "Dissect the bat, study it carefully, and on this model construct the machine" (MacCurdy, 1956, p. 472; F 41 v.), and on another occasion, where he urges himself not to forget that "your bird [the flying machine] should have no other model than the bat," he compares the physiology of the flight of birds and bats. The wings of feathered birds are more powerful in structure of bone and sinew because the feathers are separated and air passes through them, "But the bat is aided by its membrane, which binds the whole together and is not penetrated by the air" (MacCurdy, 1956, p. 416; Sul Volo 16 r.). The condition of being penetrated by the air or not seems to have some bearing on Leonardo's shift from kite to bat, and here we reach

---

[18] I do not deny that these sequences may also be connected by meaningful associations derived from the subjects Leonardo investigated. Still it speaks in favor of the psychoanalytic interpretation when a reference to a condition that would make intercourse impossible is followed by a remark about the upside-down position of the sleeping bat.

an important point of contemporary physiology that may throw some light on the unconscious background of Leonardo's interest in flight.

The accepted theory of the penile erection in Leonardo's time was that it was caused by air. Air under pressure was believed to produce the hardness of the penis as well as of muscles under exertion (Belt, 1955, p. 54). Whether or not this view is a corrupted tradition of the ancients' attribution of erectile power to pneuma or vital spirit, as Dr. Elmer Belt states (see also O'Malley and Saunders, 1952, p. 496), I do not know, but evidence is extant of Leonardo's vigorously disputing this theory. Not only did he have practical experience with air under pressure, but his anatomical studies gave him firsthand evidence of the correct state of affairs. He wrote:

> What is it that increases the size of the muscles so rapidly? It is said that it is air [pneuma]—and where does it go when the muscle diminishes with such rapidity? Into the nerves of sensibility which are hollow? Indeed, that would be a vast amount of air, that which enlarges and elongates the penis and makes it as dense as wood, so that the whole great quantity of air [in the nerves] would not be sufficient for reduction to such a density; not only the air of the nerves, but if the body were filled with it, it would not suffice. If you will have it that it is the air of these nerves, what air is it that courses through the muscles and reduces them to such hardness and power at the time of the carnal act? For I once saw a mule which was almost unable to move, owing to the fatigue of a long journey under a heavy burden, and which, on seeing a mare, suddenly its penis and all its muscles became so turgid that it multiplied its forces as to acquire such speed that it overtook the course of the mare which fled before it and which was obliged to obey the desires of the mule [Belt, 1955, p. 54f.; O'Malley and Saunders, 1952, p. 496; Fogli A 18 r.].

Here Leonardo deductively and inductively adduces proof that the pneumatic theory of erection is erroneous.

The following paragraph contains the proof by direct observation that an afflux of blood is the causative agent:

> Of the virile member when it is hard, it is thick and long, dense and heavy, and when it is limp, it is thin, short and soft, that is, limp and weak. This should not be adjudged as due to the addition of flesh or wind, but to arterial blood. I have seen this in the dead who have this member rigid. For many die thus, especially those hanged of whom I have seen an anatomy, having great density and hardness, and these are full of a large quantity of blood which has made the flesh very red within, and in others,

without as well as within. And if an opponent contends that this large amount of flesh has grown through wind which causes the enlargement and hardness as in a ball with which we play, this wind provides neither weight nor density but makes the flesh light and rarefied. And again, one observes that the rigid penis has a red glans [*testa*] which is a sign of an abundance of blood, and when it is not rigid, it has a whitish appearance [Belt, 1955, p. 55f.; O'Malley and Saunders, 1952, p. 414; Fogli B 2 v.].

This paragraph was added by Leonardo between 1504 and 1506 on a folio on which he made several annotations about fifteen years previously. They are: (1) a reminder that he should inflate the "windings" of the intestines which he had sketched extremely cursorily on the sheet, in order to be enabled to study them more profoundly; (2) a note on the liver and the gall bladder; (3) the following remark on the nervous system, neuropathology, and the structure of the mind:

> How the nerves sometimes act of themselves without the command of other functions or of the mind.
> This is clearly apparent for you will see paralytics, cowards and the benumbed move their trembling member, such as the head or the hands, without permission of the mind. The mind with all its powers cannot prevent these members from trembling. This also happens in epilepsy and in members which have been severed, as in the tails of lizards.
> The idea or the imagination (*imaginativa*) is the helm or bridle of the senses, for the thing imagined moves the senses.
> To pre-imagine is to imagine things which will be. To post-imagine is to imagine things past [O'Malley and Saunders, 1952, p. 414; Fogli B 2 v.].

Again the question arises whether it was due to accident that Leonardo made his entry of about 1506 on this particular folio. The remark about the inflation of guts takes us directly to the problem just mentioned. It seems to me that Leonardo himself originally believed that air was the causative agent of erection. I do not know what the popular belief on this topic was in Leonardo's time, but I would not see, offhand, an objection to the assumption that only by observation and ratiocination did he convince himself of the physiological truth and until then took tradition for granted.

We may recall how Leonardo frightened others by inflating an animal's guts, and the unconscious meaning of the practical joke may have been the fantasy of terrifying or even destroying a person by a

1. *Portrait of Mona Lisa*

2. *The Virgin and Child and St. Anne*

3. *The Virgin and Child with St. Anne and St. John the Baptist*

4. *Luca di Tommè: The Virgin and Child and St. Anne (Detail)*

5. *The Virgin of the Rocks*

6. Masaccio: *The Virgin and Child and St. Anne*

7. *Gozzoli: The Virgin and Child with St. Anne*

8. *Raphael Morghen after Leonardo: The Last Supper*

9. *St. Jerome (Detail)*

10. *The Adoration of the Kings*

11. *Two Profiles and Studies of Machinery*

12. *Allegory of Pleasure and Pain*

13. *An Old Man and a Youth Facing One Another*

14. *Unknown Artist: Creation of Eve*

15. *Portrait of a Musician*

16. *Copy after Michelangelo: Ganymede*

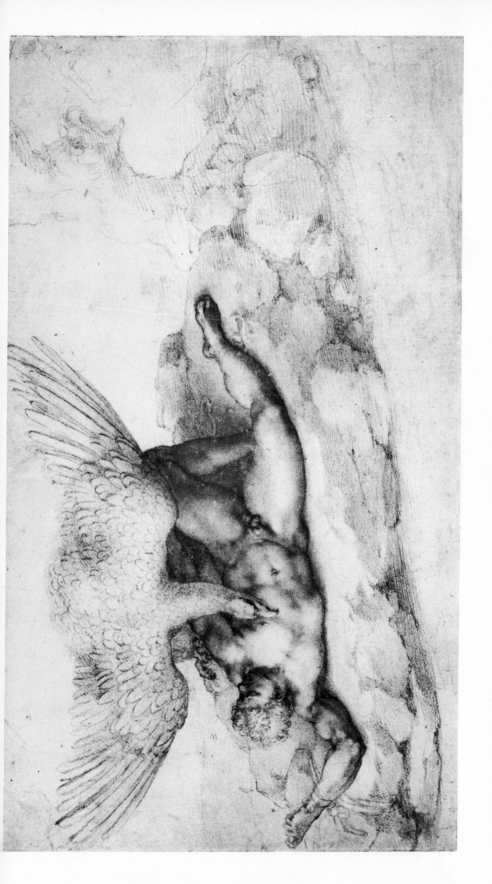

17. *Michelangelo: Tityos*

18. *Allegory of Virtue and Envy*

19. *Leda and the Swan*

20. *Giampietrino, free copy after Leonardo: Leda*

21. *Raphael after Leonardo: Leda*

22. *Unknown Artist after Leonardo: Leda*

23. *Cesare da Sesto after Leonardo: Leda*

24. *St. John the Baptist*

25. *Unknown Artist after Leonardo: Leda*

26. *Unknown Artist after Michelangelo: Leda*

27. *Hellenistic Sculpture: Leda*

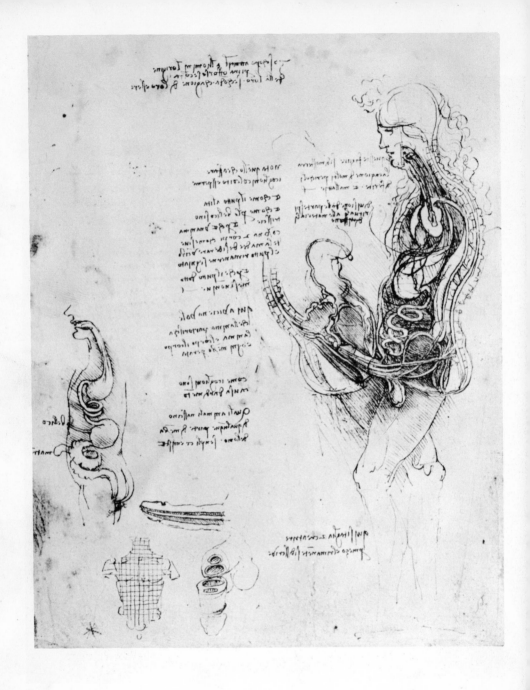

28. *Anatomical Representation*

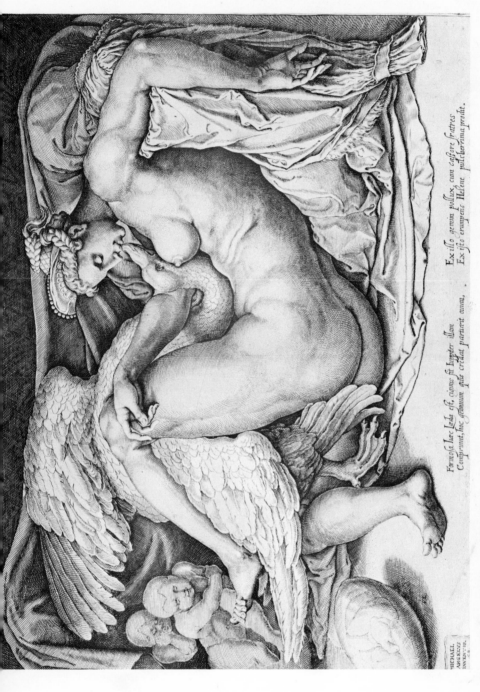

MICHAEL
ABIGENSE
INVENT DE

Formosa haec Leda est, cignus sit Iupiter illam
Comprimit, hoc geminum quae credit parturit ouum,

Exillo gemini pollux, cum castore fratres
Exifto erumpens Helene pulcherrima prodit.

29. Bos after Michelangelo: Leda

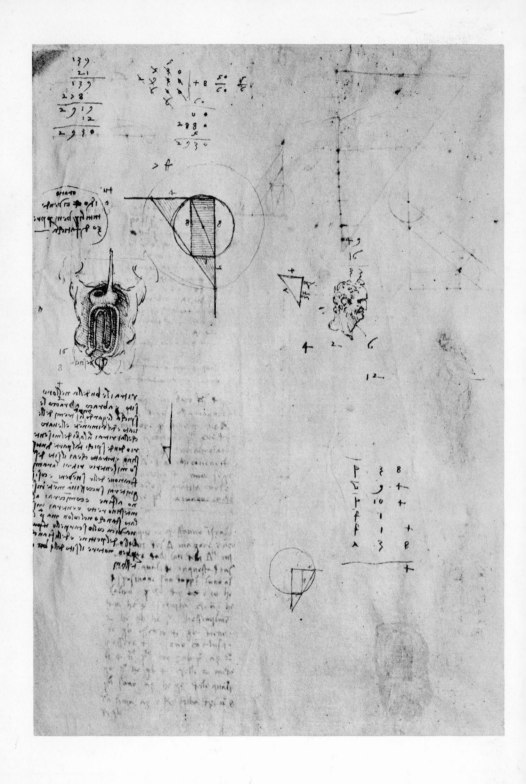

30. *Anatomical and Other Representations*

31. *Anatomical Representation (Detail)*

32. *Studies for the Last Supper*

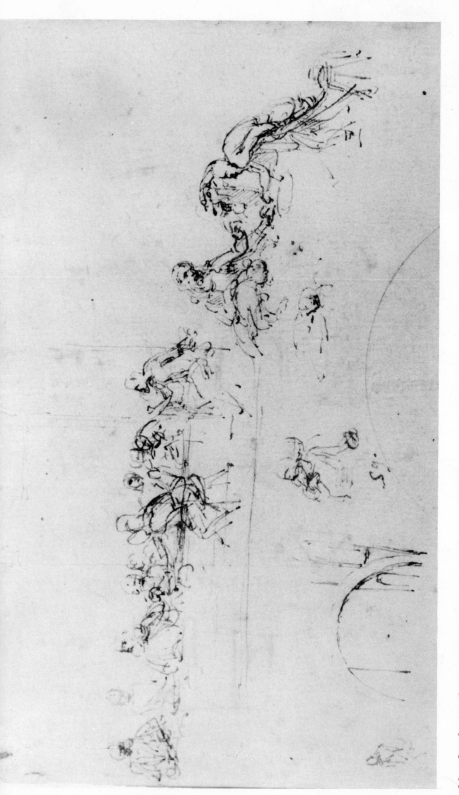

33. *Study for the Last Supper*

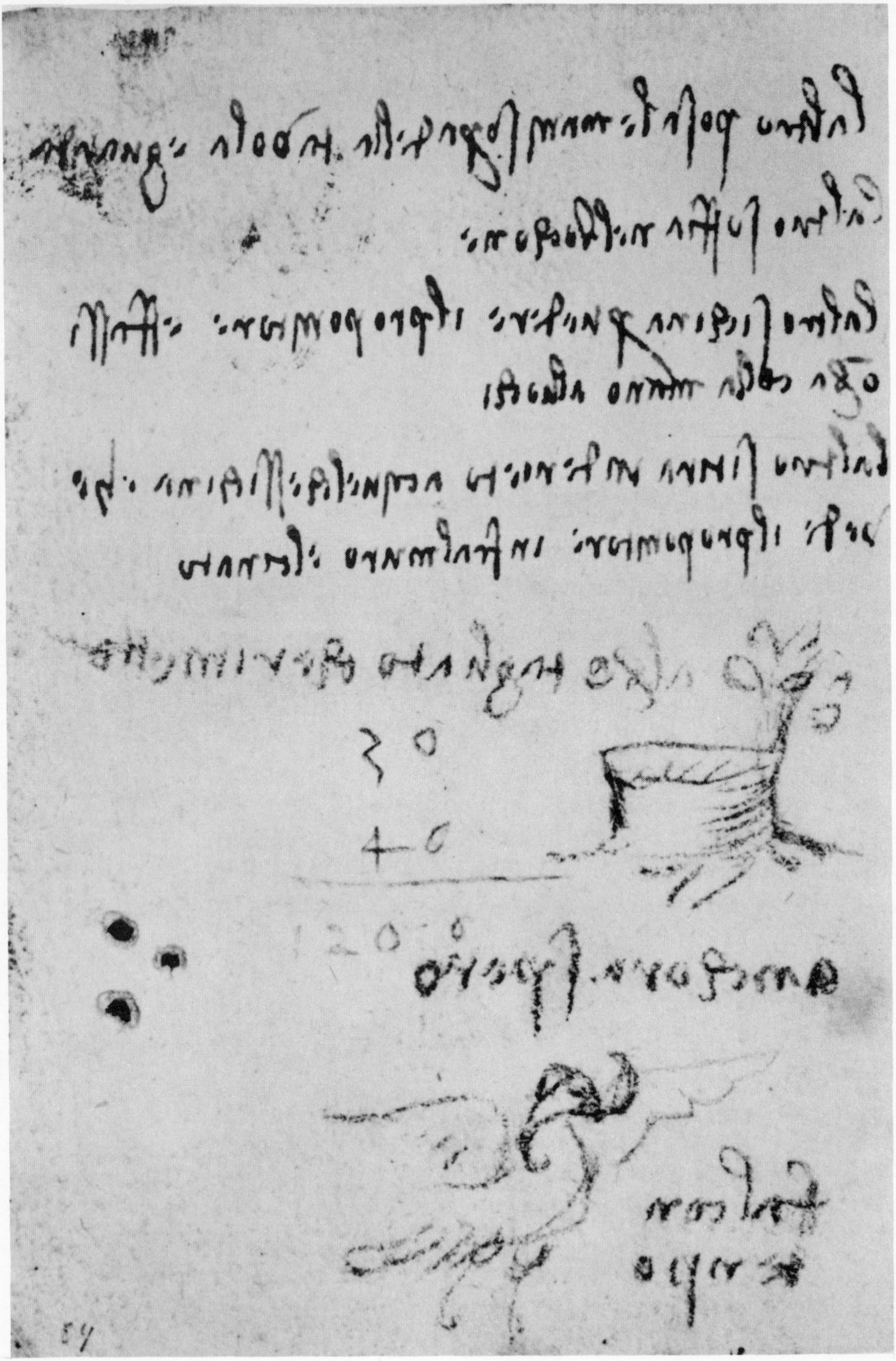

34. *Notes and Sketches*

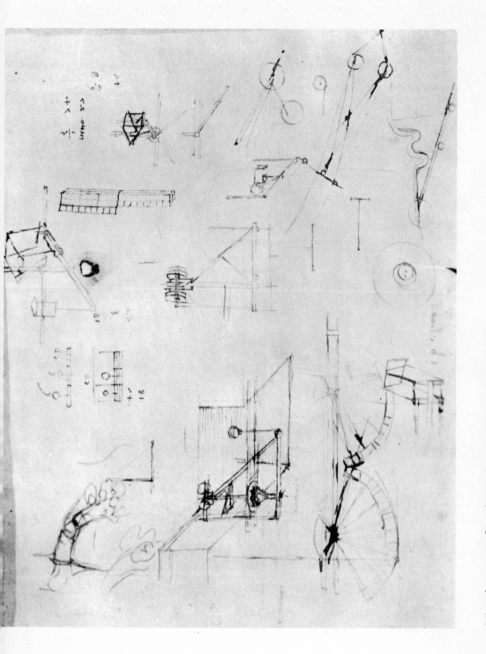

35. *Anatomical and Mechanical Representations*

36. *Anatomical and Mechanical Representations*

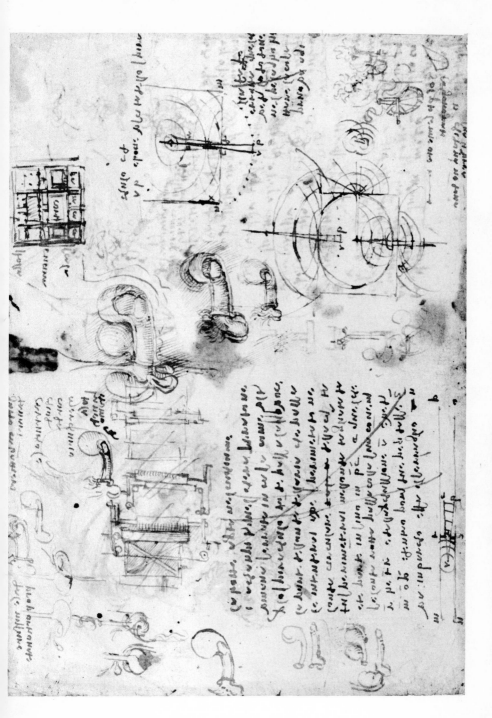

37. *Anatomical and Other Representations*

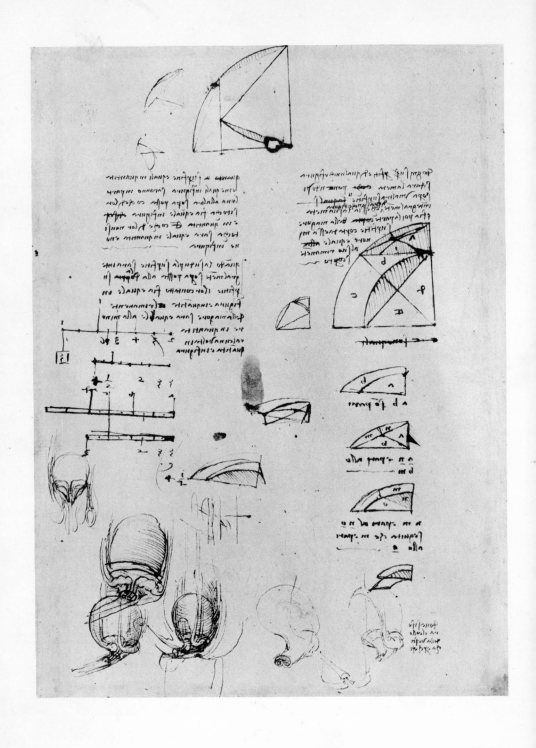

38. *Anatomical and Geometric Representations*

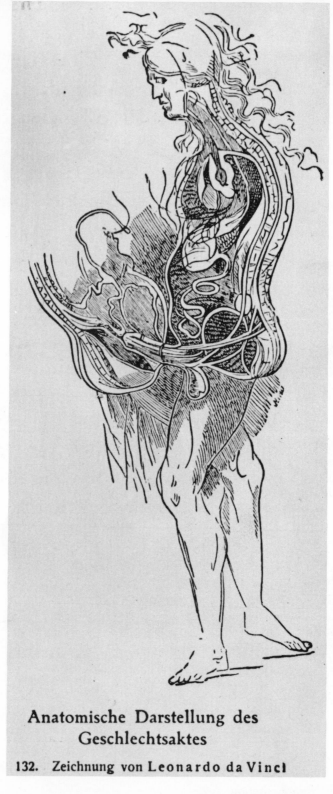

**Anatomische Darstellung des
Geschlechtsaktes**

132. Zeichnung von **Leonardo da Vinci**

41. *Anatomical Drawing purportedly after Leonardo*

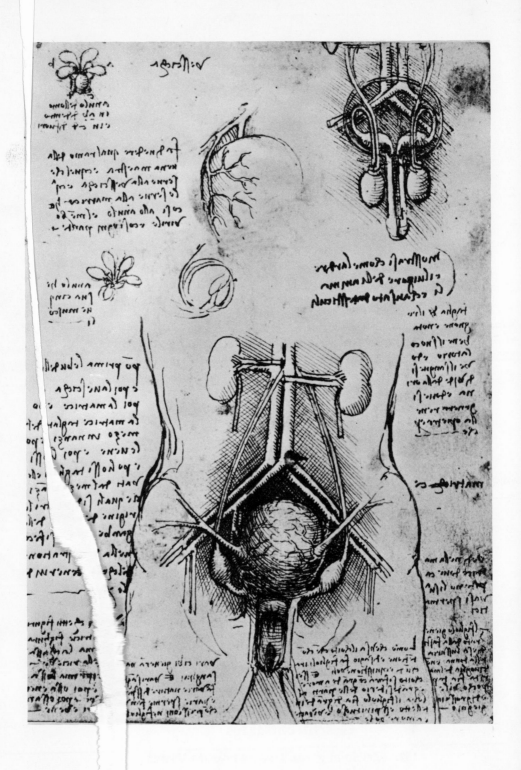

42. Anatomical Representation

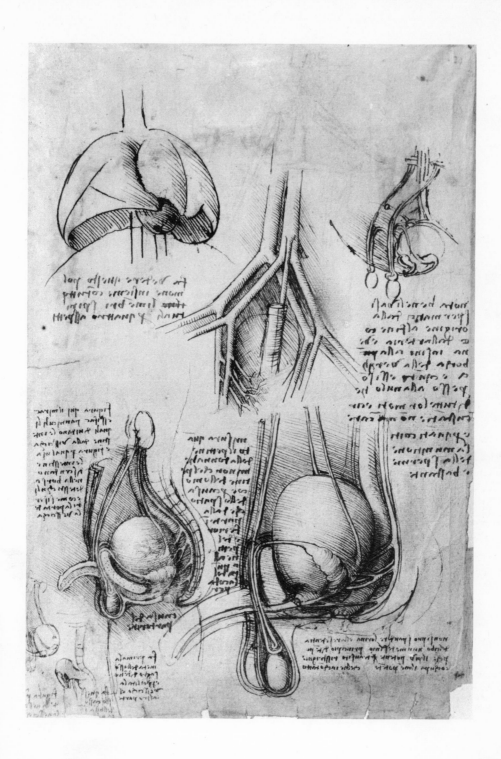

43. *Anatomical Representation*

44. *Five Grotesque Heads*

45. *Verrocchio: Baptism (Detail)*

46. *Portrait of Ginevra de' Benci*

47. *Rubens after Leonardo: The Battle of Anghiari*

48. *Michelangelo: The Victory*

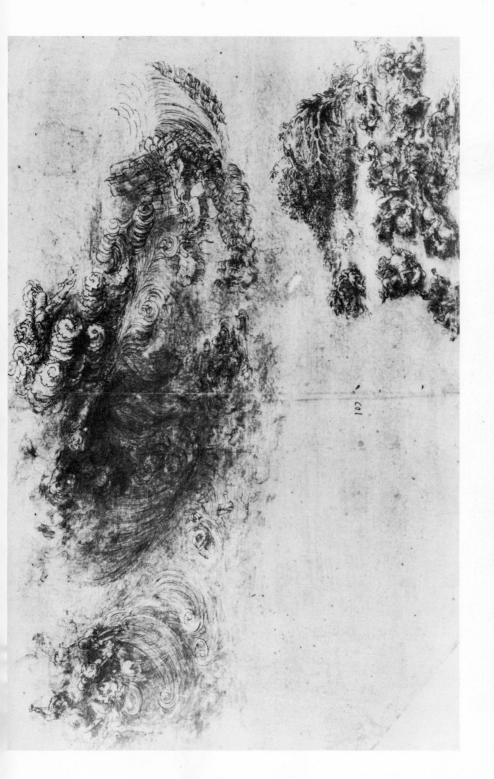

49. *A Hurricane*

50. *The Beginning of the Deluge*

51. *The Deluge*

52. *The Deluge*

53. *The Deluge*

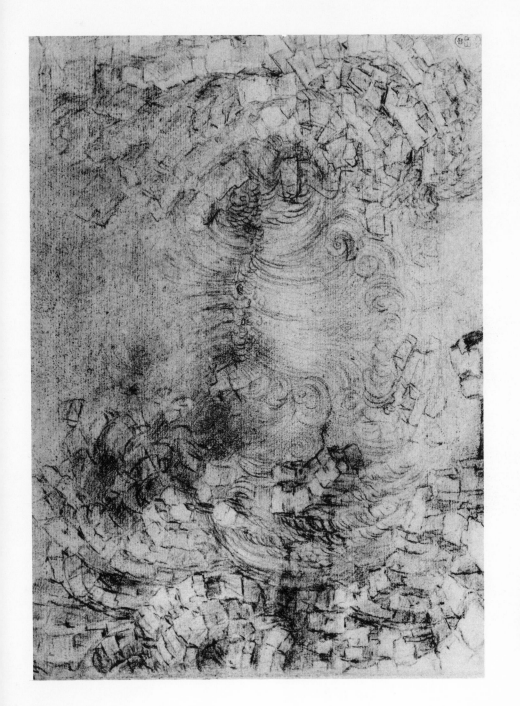

54. *The Deluge*

55. *The Deluge*

56. *The Deluge*

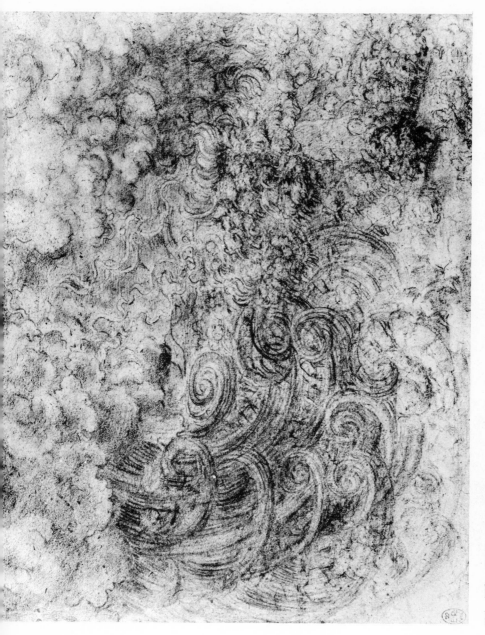

57. *The Deluge*

58. *The Deluge*

59. *The Deluge*

60. *Goya: Saturn*

61. *Destruction of a City*

62. *Emblematic Representation*

63. *Study of Drapery*

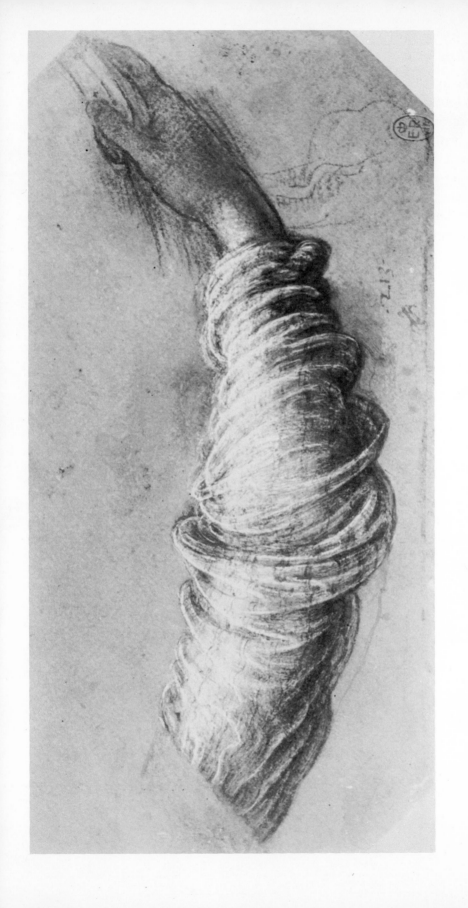

64. *Study of a Sleeve and Hand*

giant erection.[19] On that folio, then, Leonardo was suggesting doing with the intestines what he believed happened to the penis in the state of erection; the intestines *in situ* may have reminded him of a shriveled, vastly extended, unerected penis,[20] or the penis may have struck him as an extension of the guts.

The other note, about the nervous system, takes us right into the problem which seems to me of the greatest relevance to Leonardo's genitality. This "acting of the nerves without the command of the mind" was one of the structural elements inherent in male genitality that obstructed forever the integration of the penis into the body scheme. Consequently, observations on patients suffering from diseases of the nervous system that lead to automatic movements outside of ego control and obstruct the attainment of ego aims must have struck Leonardo deeply and could easily have become associated with the troublesome penile reaction.[21]

Leonardo's added remark about imagination, as I understand it, refers to the controlling agency with its two safeguards, the anticipation of the future and the recollection of the past. A reference to this agency at this point sounds like a question: How is it possible that the nerves sometimes act of themselves, when the mind possesses such a marvelous steering wheel?

Although Leonardo's remarks about the liver and gall bladder which, as mentioned above, are also to be found on Fogli B 2 v., are not correct but derive from Mundinus (see O'Malley and Saunders, p. 414), they can be fitted meaningfully into the rest. Leonardo calls the liver the distributor of vital food and the gall bladder the servant of the liver that carries off the filth remaining after the distribution of nourishment. Here there is set forth for a group of organs a physio-

[19] It is commonly known that impotent patients have exaggerated fantasies about the size of the erected penis.

[20] O'Malley and Saunders describe the two *Sketches of the Intestinal Coils* on the folio as follows: "These slight and inconsequential sketches of the intestines exhibit only the slightest acquaintance with the arrangement of the alimentary tract even if judged as no more than graphic reminders" (p. 414).

[21] Exactly the ego relevant that is resistant to ego control often has the deepest effect on the genius. Thus Freud's work starts out with an inquiry into the neurotic symptom, then the dream, parapraxia, laughter and mourning, the drive, the impact of masses—all these phenomena that are ego relevant but outside control. Only after the thirst to understand these areas has been satiated does the controlling agency move into the center of attention. Also in Goethe a period of surrender to emotional storms is followed by one during which a heroic effort is made to insure mastery over the irrational that incessantly threatened to upset organized ego pursuits.

logic and anatomic wisdom very much in contrast with the penis, which may be erect in the moment of death, when again it proves its independence of the vicissitude of the total organism.[22]

Thus the seemingly disconnected remarks, assembled on the same page as if by chance, here again show law and inner order. From the single organ over the group of organs that, though not accessible to will power, still reflexly work in support of the superordinate organization, Leonardo arrives at the mind, the supreme helm that gives order and command to the various executive organs by its own will. However, this marvelous state of freedom is threatened, as by disease, in which these organs start to act on their own, or by the inscrutable laws of the male organ characterized by uncalled-for arousal or limpness.

Both the kite and the bat were thus excellently endowed with capabilities by means of which they became symbols of a penis free of all the deficiencies Leonardo imputed to it. Neither animal rose through inflation by air, as Leonardo probably once thought the penis did, but it was surrounded by air and rose into air like the genital. It was never limp unless asleep or resting, and it rose in accordance with its will. Even under the most adverse conditions it was capable of speed and unimpaired movement. And what apparently impressed Leonardo most and made him marvel no end was the bird's ability to rise even without beating its wings. Leonardo returns over and over again to this phenomenon since here apparently was the crux of a tantalizing problem. He who succeeded in unraveling the secret of avian flight became capable of rising to high altitude himself. The secret fantasy of giant penis and giant erection became fulfilled.[23] When Leonardo writes:

> You will make an anatomy of the wings of a bird together with the muscles of the breast which are the movers of these wings.
> And you will do the same for a man, in order to show the possibility that there is in man who desires to sustain himself amid the air by the beating of wings [MacCurdy, 1956, p. 421; C.A. 45 r. a],

does not he, the man who is to await patiently the revelations of experience, anticipate impatiently the result of research and order nature

[22] This page is in essence an extended or more complete version of the previously cited page on which Leonardo wrote *Della verga* (see p. 227, Fogli B 13 r.). The repetition of structure in sequence of thoughts may exclude the factor of chance.

[23] Leonardo's idea of the whole body rising to great height by its own effort falls within the scope of the clinical material set forth by Lewin (1933).

to live up to his wishes?[24] It seems to me that such impatience is perhaps unusual for Leonardo and that Freud's explanation makes it understandable why Leonardo became unfaithful to his own principle just at this point. "To sustain himself amid the air" is also an image that is expressive of the difficulty it is presumed he anticipated in achieving and maintaining an erection. How much Leonardo may have been preoccupied with the specific problem involved in the seeming overcoming of gravity by the erected penis can be learned from two pages of his *Quaderni d'Anatomia*. On Q. III 2 v. (Plate 35) one finds, beside a rough sketch of the uterus, a drawing of the sex organs in the state of coition.[25] Yet on the same page mechanical drawing of cranes and pulleys is discussed. On Q. III 2 r. (Plate 36) there are three coition figures. This time the anatomy of increasingly deeper penetration apparently occupied Leonardo. On the same sheet there are again mechanical drawings and calculations, this time for a device of a chain of buckets used for raising water. Thus the idea seems to have been that, as pulleys and cranes overcome the pull of gravity, also the erection does or should. Yet the overcoming of the pull of gravity is also most conspicuously achieved in the flight of birds.

If we now return once more to Forster II f. 63 r., on which the comment on the *Cenacolo*, the sprouting tree stump, and the rising bird are found, we may feel more certain than before that the bird symbolized the fulfillment of Leonardo's most intimate wishes.[26] We may then look upon this page as representing three stages: the moment of trauma and the fright it involved; the acknowledgment of trauma; the achievement of full recovery and actual restoration of unscathed integrity and completeness by achieving a new equilibrium on a higher plane. According to this folio, the trauma may have been connected with the son's feeling of aggression against his father either by Leonardo's sudden realization of it or by his father's unexpectedly confronting him with an awareness of it. The effect of the trauma

[24] Cf. Leonardo's bitter words against impatience, which he calls "the mother of folly" (MacCurdy, p. 83; Q. II 14 r.).

[25] This sketch is of particular interest because the uterus is given almost the shape of a penis, so that the drawing looks like that of two erect penises touching.

[26] Unfortunately it cannot be determined what the object the bird is holding in its beak really is. Pedretti (1953) interprets it as a serpent. It is drawn like an S-curve and could just as well be an olive branch. See also Pedretti for an interpretation of stump and line as historical emblems.

would have been castration fear and impotence; this effect would have been undone by the invention of a flying machine. Thus, an inquiry into the unconscious motives of Leonardo's inordinate desire to fly also leads to his relation to trauma, though here to trauma in the context of a valiant but vain attempt at recuperation. Leonardo's course was not in reality as benign as he pictured it on the folio. "It may very well be," wrote Freud, "that the skill that he desired was no more attainable by him in its primary sexual sense than in its mechanical one, and that he remained frustrated in both wishes" (1910, p. 126).

13

Notes on Leonardo's Sexuality

It may be a potent stimulus to creativity for a genius when his wishes are not as profoundly satisfied as one feels inclined to want them to be for the ordinary man. What degree of frustration and what degree of gratification are optimal to creativity we do not know. That Leonardo's sexual life was most unsatisfactory when measured by the norm there cannot be much doubt.

A generally hypochondriacal disposition is to be tentatively considered. The clinical evidence for this hypothesis is not extensive. Among his notes is a poem, evidently a copy, in which rules for good health are set forth, such as to eat lightly, to chew thoroughly, to take no medicine, to beware of anger, to go regularly to stool, etc. (Richter, Vol. II, p. 106, No. 855; C.A. 78 v.). We also find an occasional piece of advice such as "Wine is good, but water is preferable at table" (MacCurdy, p. 72; I 122 v.). I would also include here Leonardo's contempt for physicians. There are several remarks that deride physicians and warn against them.[1] Such hostility toward physicians, justi-

---

[1] For an example, see Richter (Vol. II, p. 106, No. 856; W. 19001 r.). However, Leonardo found kind words about medicine when he could use it for the sake of a comparison to set his own abilities, as an architect, for example, in the right light. See the draft of his letter to the Works Department of the Cathedral of Milan (Richter, Vol. II, p. 330f., No. 1347A; C.A. 270 r.).

fied as it may appear retrospectively in view of their ignorance and adherence to ancient tradition in Leonardo's time, is also encountered occasionally in the present. It then often turns out that those in whom it occurs are hypochondriacal persons who deeply resent that medicine cannot protect them against any kind of disease and, chief of all, against death. Leonardo's contempt for physicians I am also inclined to interpret as a sign of hypochondriasis, in concealed form, of course: it seems he always enjoyed good health, was of unusual physical strength, and, what is very important, was unusually handsome.

When Leonardo wrote in reference to the two figures in coition (Plate 28; Q. III 3 v.) "Through these figures will be demonstrated the cause of many dangers of ulcers and disease" (O'Malley and Saunders, p. 460), his hypochondriasis comes quite clearly to the fore. Again it may be objected that in Leonardo's time venereal disease was rampant in Europe,[2] but this does not justify his pessimistic account of the generative process.[3]

The fear of venereal infection is based, as is well known, on castration fear. An anatomical remark of Leonardo's about the penis may well have been the outgrowth of this fear:

> The origin of the penis is situated upon the pubic bone so that it can resist its active force on coition. If this bone did not exist, the penis in meeting resistance would turn backwards and would often enter more into the body of the operator than into that of the operated [O'Malley and Saunders, p. 454; Q. III 1 v.].

Despite the partial correctness of this remark, one may derive from the teleological portion the direction of Leonardo's fear. The feminine identification thereby becomes particularly clear: if nature did not take special precautions an organ would penetrate into the male during coition. That this would be the male's own penis, may be additional evidence of the deficient integration of the organ into the body scheme.[4]

[2] It is uncertain whether Leonardo's drawing was made before or after 1495, when "syphilis began to assume epidemic proportions following the conquest of Naples" (O'Malley and Saunders, p. 460).

[3] One could repeat here, I suppose, what Bode said of Goethe who postponed intercourse for a surprisingly long time and also suffered from inordinate, though seemingly well-justified, fears of infection: "Goethe's cautiousness (prudence) was certainly laudable, but since he was exposed to the danger no more than other men, he must have been more apprehensive and more scrupulous than they" (1921, p. 38).

[4] For an instructive clinical observation regarding the pathway of the integration of the penis, and thus the points of developmental disturbance, see Loewenstein (1950, p. 47f.).

From another remark one may divine some of Leonardo's feeling about a basic incompatibility of the sexes. He wrote:

The woman commonly has a desire quite the opposite of that of a man. That is, that the woman likes the size of the genital member of the man to be as large as possible, and the man desires the opposite in the genital member of the woman, so that neither one nor the other ever attains his interest because Nature, who cannot be blamed, has so provided because of parturition. Woman has in proportion to her belly a larger genital member than any other species of animal [O'Malley and Saunders, p. 480; Q. III 7 r.].

This is then mathematically demonstrated by a comparison of proportions in the cow. I surmise that certain physiological assumptions which Leonardo derived from Arabic doctrines had their bearing on this passage. It was believed that the penis enters the cervix, and that the uterus increases in volume during coition (O'Malley and Saunders, p. 460). From some of Leonardo's drawings of coition (particularly on Q. III 12 v.; see Plate 37) one gets the impression that, in Leonardo's imagery, the uterine cavity was included in the space that is to be filled by the erected penis.

In Leonardo's reasoning regarding the opposite wishes of the sexes there seems to be an erroneous implication, although this is not spelled out. In view of the female's desire for the penis to be as large as possible, one would rather expect, as one can actually clinically observe, that women would want their own genital to be small, whereas Leonardo intimates that the disproportionate largeness of the female genital is the result of—or at least corresponds to—women's own wishes. A worry about disproportion of volume or size between the genital apparatus of the two sexes may be derived from Q. III 11 v. (Plate 38), where notes and diagrams concerned "with problems of surfaces of equal area but unequal shape and proportion" (O'Malley and Saunders, p. 446) are combined with sketches of the male genitourinary system. Actually, in an early drawing (c. 1503) of the female genital (Plate 39; Q. III 1 r.) the introitus is drawn widely gaping, the labia majora and minora being replaced by a protuberance shaped like a cylinder oval in section, and the clitoris missing. In a later drawing (c. 1510-12) (Plate 40; Q. III 7 r.) the labia majora and minora are drawn, the opening of the urethra seems to be visible, and there is possibly an indication of the clitoris; the introitus is not gaping but the genital is too large and the perineum too low.[5]

Leonardo excuses Nature for the proportional unfavorableness of the female genital since parturition is necessary and requires a large female genital, but his calculation that this factor is unfavorable only in the human species permits the suggestion that there is a specific reproach against women, possibly implying that they are insatiable creatures. At any rate, the interests of male and female are presented as opposed to each other and irreconcilable and this antagonism is referred to propagation.

An inscription on the verso of Leonardo's drawing *Aristotle and Phyllis* in the Kunsthalle, Hamburg (Popham, Plate 110B) demonstrates his conscious and deliberate resistance to sexual pleasures. We read there: "The accompaniment of voluptuousness displeases love. Jealousy [displeases] felicity. Envy [displeases] fortune. Penitence" (Valentiner, 1949b, p. 109, No. 75). Here voluptuousness, jealousy, and envy are contrasted with love, felicity, and fortune. The two series are incompatible. Giving in to the former is followed by remorse.

Yet despite sublimation, which figures so strikingly in Leonardo's life, despite powerful rationalizations, despite conscious repudiation, and despite an attempt to replace it in part by an intense desire to fly, the sexual drive may still remain quite alive and demand direct physical gratification.

On the early folio (Q. III 1 r.; Plate 39) on which the female genital is drawn, Leonardo wrote the following:

Let the cause be defined why in the female the labia of the vulva open on the closing of the anus, and in the male, in similar case, the penis becomes erect and ejects the urine or the sperm with force or, as you may say, in spurts [O'Malley and Saunders, p. 452].

This note, which in its kind is unique and solitary in Leonardo's writings,[6] is described by O'Malley and Saunders as reflecting "beliefs

[5] I wish to thank Dr. Bernard Berglas for his assistance in interpreting Leonardo's drawings.

[6] My claim that Leonardo's reference is unique and solitary requires qualification. I can only state that I have made a strong though futile effort to find similar statements in the publications I have studied. In view of the voluminousness of Leonardo's writings and my inability to check on those of his writings that have been published only in Italian, I am aware that more passages of this type may be adducible.

of the bagnio rather than scientific information" (p. 452). Nevertheless, I feel strongly that here possibly is the key to Leonardo's own sexual life.

I presume that jokes and stories about sexual matters were in Leonardo's time just as rampant as nowadays and, if anything, people were even freer in exchanging their views on and interpretations of the sexual process. Yet nothing of this kind is detectable in Leonardo's writings, at least in the commonly used texts. This reference to the bagnio is, therefore, out of place, since, if Leonardo had not been averse to setting down such things, there would have been bound to be more observations of this kind in his *Notes*.[7] Furthermore, is it probable that Leonardo would have included in his scientific work a problem that was presented in the form of a smutty story? The bagnio theory can safely be dismissed.

Further, the question of historical antecedent also arises. Was Leonardo following respectable tradition when he asserted the connection between anal contractions and erection? In Aristotle's *Problems* (Book IV, 876 b) we find:

> Why do both the eyes and the buttocks sink very noticeably in those who indulge excessively in sexual intercourse, though the latter are near to and the former far from the sex organs? Is it because both these parts obviously co-operate in the act of coition by contracting at the time of the emission of semen? . . . For it is impossible to emit semen without contracting the parts about the fundament, or without closing the eyes. The contraction of the buttocks forces out the moisture (just as the hand does from the bladder), while the contraction of the eye forces out the moisture about the brain [Aristotle, Vol. I, p. 109f.].[8]

The *Problems* as written by Aristotle have not reached us, but the extant manuscripts contain parts of the Aristotelian version. In 1438 a Latin edition of the *Problemata* was produced by Theodore Gaza

---

[7] I do not consider here sexual stories in the form of anecdotes which Leonardo apparently occasionally liked to jot down such as the following (Ravaisson-Mollien; C 19 v.) which is usually omitted. It concerns a man who after a visit to a prostitute wonders that he had to pay only five sous in order to have his whole body enter Modena, whereas in Florence ten ducats were required to have admittance for only a little part of him. It is immediately clear that the quotation under discussion is of an entirely different order and may not be equated with the few off-color stories that are found in Leonardo's *Notes*.

[8] I am deeply indebted to Dr. Owsei Temkin for this apt reference. He was the only one of the many authorities I consulted who was able to provide a reference that can be meaningfully connected with Leonardo's statement under discussion.

(Hett, in Aristotle, p. vii). Aristotle was cited nine times by Leonardo (Sarton, 1953, p. 18). Twice he contradicts Aristotle *expressis verbis* (MacCurdy, 1956, p. 286, F 84 v.; and p. 385, C.A. 279 r. b). The *Problemata* are not among the works by Aristotle he apparently used (see Richter, Vol. II, p. 371, n., and Index p. 424). All this, of course, does not prove that he did not have direct contact with the *Problems*, or hear the passage cited, or come upon the same view in some other source that is related to the *Problems*. Such and allied questions will have to be answered by the historian and the philologist.

In view of the conclusions I will draw from the passage in Leonardo's anatomical manuscript I wish to discuss first the probability that Leonardo read the Aristotelian or pseudo-Aristotelian passage. First, one may wonder why the visual organ system that was brought into connection with ejaculation by the Aristotelian writer was not mentioned by Leonardo. If he did read the *Problems*, one may also wonder why more of that text did not find its way into his *Notes*. There are many contentions that might have been taken up by him. Thus we read in the *Problems*:

> Why do both those who indulge in sexual excess and eunuchs who never do so, alike deteriorate in sharpness of vision [p. 111]?
> Why is it that bare feet are not good for sexual intercourse?
> Why is a man more slack after sexual intercourse than other animals [p. 113]?
> Why is sexual intercourse more rapid with men who are fasting [p. 115]?

I have selected a few of the *Problems* that Leonardo might have been expected to deal with if he had encountered them in this book. I am not aware that these or others were considered by Leonardo, but am not prepared to judge whether other parts of the *Problems* found their way into Leonardo's writings.

It will also come to our attention that there is a considerable difference between the views expressed in the two passages, the one by Aristotle and the other by Leonardo. The Aristotelian version speaks of a cooperation between the two organ systems, their simultaneous contractions at the time of ejaculation, whereas Leonardo's text clearly states a causal nexus, the anal contractions producing, so to speak, erection and ejaculation. Thus, if there was an actual connection with the Aristotelian text, it functioned only as a suggestion upon which Leonardo elaborated in order to evolve his own theory.[9]

Leonardo tried to be as exact in observations regarding sexual problems as he was in other fields. I wish to cite here the one example, noted before, of the mule that was quite fatigued and recovered all its strength on sight of a mare. That does not sound at all like a repetition of a traditional tale but breathes the freshness and directness of a personal observation.

Yet admittedly one finds in Leonardo's writings a lot of misinformation. This has been variously explained. The bulk of that misinformation, though not all, is in tales and stories, in which we encounter Leonardo in an aspect different from that we are thinking of when we speak of Leonardo the scientist. Still, even in his anatomical writings we do encounter misinformation, but it is misinformation of a special kind. When he draws pores in the cardiac septum we know he was victimized by erroneous tradition, as well as by an inner necessity to assume something that, in view of contemporary knowledge, appeared a *conditio sine qua non*. When he drew two penile canals it was because he had not dissected a penis, just as many other mistakes he temporarily adhered to resulted from lack of occasion for verification. There are, besides, many errors of theory. But these are of a different order. The interpretation of facts in the form of theories must be strictly separated from factual contents in this discussion. The general spirit that pervades this part of Leonardo's writings, his studies in anatomy, betrays a scientific temper, that is, the determination to verify what is accessible to verification under conditions at his disposal. Of course, there are fringe situations. Thus he wrote in Fogli B, 32 v.:

If you compress the four vessels m [carotids and jugulars] of either side where they are in the throat, he who has been compressed will suddenly fall to the ground asleep as though dead and will never wake of himself, and if he is left in this condition for the hundredth part of an hour, he will never wake, neither of himself nor with the aid of others [O'Malley and Saunders, p. 286].

[9] Also in the *Problems* a view is expressed that is in outright contradiction to Leonardo's account: "Why cannot those who wish to make water have sexual intercourse? Is it because the passages are full? What is already full of moisture cannot contain more moisture" (Aristotle, p. 123).

O'Malley and Saunders trace this observation back to Aristotle; it was denied by Galen; others explained it by pressure on the vagus: "Leonardo is thus echoing traditional information," the authors conclude (p. 286). Maybe they are right. Here, after all, was an area where experiment was dangerous, and Leonardo may have been at a loss as to how to verify it. On the other hand, the observation he puts down here cannot be called outright wrong though some details may be questionable; cases of death by pressure on the carotid sinuses are reported and it is possible that an instance of that kind had come to Leonardo's attention.[10] Nevertheless, the possibility that Leonardo here took over a traditional view without corresponding observation cannot be disproved, although it is not quite probable.

We know from Leonardo's *Notes* that he must have used self-observation or self-experimentation in his physiological inquiries. Thus he wrote:

> One cannot swallow and breathe or make a sound at the same time.
> One cannot breathe by the nose and by the mouth at the same time; and this is shown if one should attempt to play a whistle or flute with the nose and another with the mouth at the same time [MacCurdy, 1956, p. 94f.; Fogli A 3 r.].

He even may have gone so far as to experiment with the whistle and flute combination to verify this.[11]

An example of direct reference to self-experimentation occurs when he defends his own theory regarding the muscles from which certain cords arise.

> And if you wish to prove this, grasp the thigh with your hands a little above the knee and elevate the toes and you will perceive . . . [O'Malley and Saunders, p. 190; Fogli A 17 r.].

The following passage too (from Q. III 4 v.) must be the result of self-experimentation:

[10] I owe thanks to Dr. George C. Leiner for calling my attention to the following paragraph about "Sudden Death in Aortic Stenosis." As one of the reasons thereof the following is recorded: "A hypersensitive carotid sinus (i.e., hypersensitive to external pressure among others) may produce cardiac standstill and sudden death. In some patients this outcome may be the result of a combination of factors. Thus reflexes from a hypersensitive carotid sinus may more readily cause sudden death if there is already some degree of myocardial ischemia and conduction disturbance" (Friedberg, 1956, p. 702).

[11] In MS. G 96 v. Leonardo tries to prove the correctness of his claim in still another way (MacCurdy, 1956, p. 202).

One cannot expel the urine and the residue of the food at one and the same time, because the more powerful passage restrains and occupies the less powerful which is in contact with it [O'Malley and Saunders, p. 440].

How then can we explain the fact that Leonardo in his account of the effect of anal contraction makes a statement that simple self-experimentation would quickly have proved false? The only answer I can find is that Leonardo is here making a series of erroneous statements in a matter-of-fact way because these statements describe what actually was true of his own sexuality. What Leonardo wrote is false only as a general statement. Yet there are people whose sexual organs behave the way Leonardo describes. Then we are dealing with perversions. Whether he later read a source like the *Problems* and felt reassured that his was a general property of male sexuality or whether he had read prior to the onset of his perversion about a comparable procedure and found it confirmed through self-experimentation and therefore generalized it, is open to speculation. Consequently, I shall in the following discuss this dysfunction as if it were Leonardo's perversion and set forth its implications.

The disturbance is reminiscent of spermatorrhea, which, I am certain, is far more frequent than commonly known. In spermatorrhea the semen flows out either spontaneously or in conjunction with urination or a bowel movement. The penis is not erect and there are no ejaculatory spurts. In spermatorrhea the penis often seems excessively anesthetic and the discharge so much devoid of any sensation that the subject often does not even become aware of its occurrence but only notices the effect produced by the secondary irritation of the skin by the ejecta. Spermatorrhea is the most complete victory of forces hostile to sexual pleasure, since it results in a mechanical removal of semen without any participation of or reaction by the psychic apparatus. According to my clinical experience, however, it is not followed by any considerable decrease of sexual reactibility.

Leonardo's disturbance, if he really had one, was certainly not a spermatorrhea, but it is to be discussed in conjunction with this dysfunction in view of the anal sphincter contraction and urination that he mentions. What makes the two so different is that spermatorrhea is not a perversion but an inhibition that results in a physiological dysfunction; however, as can easily be understood, it occurs in persons endowed with strong perverted dispositions.[12]

The sexual behavior documented in Leonardo's anatomical *Quaderno* is definitely a perversion. By the excitation of a pregenital zone the erectile mechanism is activated. Oddly enough, urination and ejaculation are treated identically, although urination is not possible with a full erection. The person who performed the perversion, one may conclude, did not notice a difference in erective intensity whether the one or the other occurred. Further, there is another annotation (on Q. III 1 v.) which gives a hint of Leonardo's urethral fixation. He wrote:

> See which is the first in the urinary canal [urethra], either the mouth of the spermatic vessels [ejaculatory ducts] or the mouth of the urinary vessel [bladder]. But I do believe that of the urine is first so that it can then clean and wash out the sperm which makes the urinary canal sticky [O'Malley and Saunders, p. 454].

Here there is an intimation that the semen is dangerous to the urethra in so far as its stickiness may clog the canal, while urine is praised as clean and as having a beneficial effect upon the tissues through which it passes.

Yet though the urethral fixation as it shows up in this paragraph and other material that could be cited should not be underrated, the other remarks Leonardo put down on the folio on which he described the perversion emphasize his anal fixation, which, after all, is noticeable in the structure of the perversion per se. Other topics he discusses there, are: the ramification of sensory nerves into the muscles of the anus; the vulva; the definition of the operation of anal muscles; why the muscles of the anus are odd in number and, if an odd number was needed, why three or seven was not chosen rather than five; the appearance of the genitals in old, young, and middle-aged; the dilated and contracted anus, the definition of the shutting of the fissures of the skin, that is eyes, nostrils, mouth, vulva, penis, and anus—and heart, although that is not of skin (see Vangensten et al., Vol. III, p. 1). It should not be forgotten that almost half of the folio is taken up by the design of the female genital (Plate 39). Why should the perversion

---

[12] Hitschmann (1933) reports a case of spermatorrhea in a patient with strong feminine, passive tendencies.

and the anatomy and physiology of the anus be discussed just on such a folio? It is almost certain that the vulva was equated by Leonardo with an anus (cf. the earlier remark about the Leda sketch on Q. V 24 r.; Plate 30) and thus one meaning of the perversion may have been the integration of female and male components into one act.

Leonardo writes as if "the ejection of sperm in spurts" was exceptional, worthy of special mention and referable specifically to the effect of sphincter contractions. Again one may conclude that a person who describes his perversion in such a way never masturbated or had intercourse, for otherwise he would have taken it for granted that ejaculations occur in spurts.

However, a different, though less probable, interpretation is conceivable here. Possibly, it may be argued, this subject's ejaculation, when it occurred in masturbation or intercourse, flowed out in rather urinelike fashion and therefore when spurts were observed in the perverted act, this was specially noted. This possibility cannot be disproved. It is known that forms of genital activity that arouse anxiety lead to a flow of sperm (Abraham, 1917, p. 281), whereas a specific form that, for whatever reason, decreases anxiety, or perhaps even eliminates it, will then be followed by an unimpaired ejaculatory mechanism. I would still feel inclined to assume that the perverted form of sexual activity as described by Leonardo in terms of general physiology was the only one accessible to him. The hand, after all, was in his life an instrument of such overpowering magic that he may easily have succumbed to an excessively intense taboo against soiling it.

Of course, one would like to know the frequency of the perversion and the sensation it elicited. My guess is that it occurred only sporadically or, at the most, with increased frequency during short periods of inner or outer emergency. In view of Leonardo's general aversion to the pleasures of the body, I would assume that the ejaculation evoked only a subdued sensual response.[13]

The structure of the perversion may confirm an earlier conclusion. In a person like Leonardo, with his prevailing abhorrence of the animal part of human nature, one might expect that a disturbance like

[13] Withal I have not explained whence Leonardo may have derived his wrong belief about the effect of the closing of the anus on the labia. I would be at a loss as to how to explain this notion in any other way than to assume that it is a common-sense statement such as one may figure out by simple ratiocination, if Dr. Berglas had not called it to my attention that experimentation on the cadaver may lead to this erroneous conclusion.

spermatorrhea would be infinitely preferable to the coarser form he described. Yet, a person has no control over this dysfunction. It occurs against the will and is not predictable. One may deduce that the choice of perversion was dictated by Leonardo's aforementioned sensitivity to uncontrollable occurrences and the disposition toward traumatization by the uncontrollable. Leonardo then would by means of his perversion have experienced the ejaculation, that is, a reflex action, as caused by voluntary and purposeful sphincter contractions. I would surmise that a synchronization of these contractions with the ejaculatory spurts deprived the genital satisfaction of its last vestiges of an involuntary, reflex process. The morphology of the perversion, then, would have made it possible for the self to maintain the illusion that the orgasm too, or at least the ejaculation, was under the ego's control.

One can imagine that just the orgastic sensation itself, in the experience of which the ego is overwhelmed and recedes, was fear-arousing to a personality that wrote: "Whoso curbs not lustful desires puts himself on a level with the beasts" (MacCurdy, 1956, p. 90; H 119 v.), and "Where there is most power of feeling, there of martyrs is the greatest martyr" (MacCurdy, 1956, p. 67; Tr. 35 r.).

This last sentence above all reveals the principal issue. In a personality type like Leonardo's, the mere experience of feeling (and, as I believe, of sensation) created pain quite independently of what kind of feeling it was. Here we observe the psychic apparatus geared to the greatest sensitivity, rarefied and vulnerable to the extreme. We can then imagine how painful and how dangerous the experience of an orgasm would have become in such aggravating circumstances and how formidable the defenses that had to be erected.[14] Furthermore, the morphology of the perversion conspicuously shows the earmarks of omnipotence: no object is required; erection and ejaculation can be brought about at will. Thus nature is defeated and the penile independence is overcome.[15]

[14] This would be particularly understandable if Leonardo had an early orgastic experience (whose memory was repressed) at a time when his psychic apparatus was physiologically and psychologically not prepared to withstand the intensity of the experience.

[15] However, in weighing the various possibilities that might have led Leonardo to make this claim about male genitality, I did not consider the following contingency which was brought to my attention recently. A patient whose sexual life was reduced to nocturnal emissions, who complained of genital unresponsiveness to, and lack of sexual desires for, women but tender feelings for his own sex and inability to ejaculate by masturbation, told

Excursus on the Deontology of Psychoanalytic Pathography

Here I feel the urge to interpolate a general remark on psycho-analytic pathography, which was so vehemently criticized not long ago by Hiram Johnson (1956), on the occasion of the publication of a Beethoven study by the Sterbas (1954). I am bringing up Johnson's article not because of its scientific content—I did not find much science in it—but because it is a *document humain* that gives expression to a fear, anger, and regret about what psychoanalysis, so to speak, has made out of man and the evil effect it has had and will be having on our society. The abhorrence so eloquently brought forth by the author becomes acute when psychoanalysis is applied to persons who by the perfection of their achievements have become indelibly inscribed on mankind's memory as ideals worthy of imitation. A superficial scan-ning of psychoanalytic pathography may leave the impression that the analyst is firmly determined to prove at all costs that those "enshrined in the Pantheon of western civilization were voyeurs, sadists, inverts and what not" (Johnson, p. 36). My hypothesis about Leonardo's per-version may be used as an illustration of this alleged compulsion of the analyst. Leonardo in his quest for truth raises the question of the physiological mechanism of a perversion, and immediately I jump to the conclusion—gratuitously, as the critics will add—that this is Leo-nardo's own perversion.

I am aware of the hypothetical nature of my assertion. I am also aware that further research may demonstrate that this description of an alleged physiological mechanism was traditional in Galenic or Arabic medicine or was known to Leonardo from some other source. This, of course, would weaken the credibility of my construction though not

---

me that by contracting the buttocks the whole body is pushed forward and "the semen is pushed out." I at first took his words as a description of what he had observed in himself. It turned out, however, that he had only the feeling "as if" the semen were pushed out and that he was certain other men were capable of doing this. He complained about his inability to produce emissions by contractions in the same way that he complained about his masturbatory inability. It is to be conceded that a similar combination of circumstances may have been at work in Leonardo. He may have formed on the ground of certain sensations he experienced in himself, and assumptions regarding the sexual life of others (possibly aided by a story he heard or a passage he came across in his reading), the general conclusion he put forward on Q. III 1 r. The above clinical experience weakened the certainty I had felt previously about having found a record of a *manifest* perversion in Leonardo.

necessarily disprove it, for Leonardo, who was not inclined to accept tradition unchecked, could still have tested the physiological correctness of the report.

At any rate, it will be asked: what is the rationale of hypothesizing at all that the sexual life of such a genius assumed a form that is unaesthetic, to say the least, undoubtedly immature, and offensive to the moral feelings of Occidental man? The biographical material at hand is sparse and psychoanalytic constructions of the kind I have suggested are made against a background of doubt and hesitation. In view of the paucity of the biographical record one can only try to draw conclusions to the best of one's ability and knowledge and see in the end whether it all adds up to a fairly meaningful and sensible theory.

However, there are geniuses about whom the extant record is more complete. Whether or not the Sterbas were right in their explanation of Beethoven's psychosexual development, one fact remains assured, that his sexual life showed an unusually high degree of deformation. Goethe, whose phenotype of personality was quite different from Beethoven's, shows an unusual delay of psychosexual development and aversion to intercourse (Bode, 1921), and the presence of strongly perverted fantasies can easily be demonstrated from some of his poems. Thus we may say that there is a type of genius whose sexual life is most unusual, to say the least. Perhaps my reconstruction of Leonardo's sexuality is wrong. Still, a Leonardo who falls in love in early manhood, marries, settles down, has a family in accordance with the paternal tradition, is unthinkable. Under such conditions he would never have been capable of creating that which he did. But why not? Why is what is cursorily called a normal sexual life incompatible with a certain type of genius?

The tacit expectation which seems to be present in some critics of psychoanalytic pathography, that the sexual life of the genius will be normal, overlooks, in my opinion, the difficulty, pain, or, as one feels inclined to think, unnaturalness of the genius's creative act. I leave the question of skill aside. The genius forms with his skills a new world that is not comparable in its kind to anything he found present or existing before. The many shortcomings of this simplified statement may be forgiven. We sometimes forget the intensity of concentration and the incredible effort that go into those moments when a work of genius is created. The genius's contemporaries may turn away from him, but for thousands of years after his work will stand as perfect and unmatched before the eyes of a well-nigh unending sequence of generations. Customs, beliefs, religions, ethics, languages, political institutions, empires, all will be subjected to change and cease to exist, but these numerically few structures will still elicit the same awe, the same reverence, and the same admiration. Something incredible that is against probability and expectation has happened whenever such a work of art has begun its existence.

And what may we expect in a person who, aside from skills that many may have, possesses this particular originality that makes out of a beautiful painting the work of a genius? Here it is to be said that no compromise is possible for the genius. A total devotion, a total concentration, is necessary. I do not wish to go into the metapsychology of such a creative process here but rather stress that this total reaction takes place against high odds, the highest of which is the claims of genital sexuality. Here is a drive that most urgently requires physical gratification—and yet that gratification, if it is adequate, tends to draw the whole personality into its scope. The pregenital desires are far more manageable. In general, they endanger the devotion to creation far less than the genital drive. Thus, for example, we find that Goethe indulged freely in all kinds of oral pleasures. I even think that the relatively open access to pregenital pleasures is a compensation for or an adjunct to keeping genitality free for sublimation. The difference between the genius and the talent may depend upon what biological source it is that supplies the energy for the sublimatory process. The genius seems to obtain it from the genital.[16] This may be one of the reasons why this type of genius, as far as the record speaks, describes his existence as a painful one.

These tentative and cursory statements serve the purpose of making it understandable why, more frequently than not, an inquiry into the sexual life of a certain type of genius reveals a high degree of deformation of the *vita sexualis*. For this type, the maximally tolerable retrenchment of genital gratifications seems to be a prerequisite to maximum creativity. I write this *a posteriori*, after having discovered evidence of such deformation in Goethe, where I would least have expected it.

---

[16] Yet see Deri (1939) for objections to such a view. Lantos (1955, p. 286f.) discusses problems of the sublimation of genitality.

Then, of course, I started to consider how this deformation might be connected with Goethe's unusually great creative output.

But I do not see in what way the general theory of psychoanalysis would *require* the assumption of sexual deformation in a genius, as Johnson's article (1956) may lead the reader to believe. When he says of psychoanalysis that it is "a compound of *determinism, atheism, hedonism, fatalism,* and *mechanism*" (p. 38; author's italics),[17] I can only say: "Maybe." I personally think these terms are not properly applicable to psychoanalysis, but it is idle to speculate on the matter since the decisive question is whether psychoanalysis is correct or incorrect; that, after all, is what the scientist is primarily interested in. I can hardly think of any idea that lent more support to atheism in Occidental society than the heliocentric theory of our planetary system, and the Church was wise to attempt to forestall its general acceptance.

However, I would have felt inclined to agree with Hiram Johnson if he had proposed that psychoanalytic findings on genius should be made known only to the small group of experts. Since, however much knowledge we may gather about genius, any attempt to produce geniuses according to plan is probably foredoomed to failure and improved techniques of rearing or educating or what not can at best only lead to a greater frequency of talent but hardly of genius, not much practical harm would be done if the public remained ignorant of what the psychoanalyst may find in searching the genius's intimate life. The ordinary man, whose illusions have been so direly shattered, has only one little island left where he may indulge without punishment in the pleasures of illusion, and that is art. It may disturb him to know the life and tribulations of those who created so much beauty. As a father would not want to be reminded that the charming infant he hugs was born *intra faeces et urinam,* as one of the Fathers of the Church has put it, our society, too, perhaps, feels repelled when its attention is called to the abomination that surrounded the emergence of beauty. At least Dr. Johnson feels that way, and I sympathize. The genius invites identification, and the mere talent, that could well do without abominations, may easily exploit psychoanalytic findings for the purpose of rationalizations and false justifications.

[17] For the historically interested reader it may be advisable to read Hemmeter's essay (1924) on Freud's Leonardo study in order to observe how far the rejection of psychoanalytic pathography may go.

Yet, Lombroso's theory of genius is, in my estimation, a far greater blow to our cherished beliefs than all psychoanalytic writings on the topic together. I hope Dr. Johnson will read Lombroso's book with greater dispassionateness than he has the corresponding psychoanalytic literature and also take notice that, as I will intimate later, findings in the genius require an essentially different yardstick from that commonly used in the investigation of clinical cases.[18]

---

[18] I am well aware of the controversial nature of the stand I am taking here. In my work on Goethe (1961) I have presented other aspects of the problem in question.

14

Remarks on Leonardo's Anatomical Work

Leonardo's anatomical drawings, some of which I have discussed in the foregoing, are truly striking. To grasp the full impact of these folios one must know the state of anatomical knowledge and anatomical illustration in Leonardo's time. McMurrich (1930) has given us a splendid study of the chasm between Leonardo and his contemporary anatomists. As one examines Leonardo's work one of the greatest individual achievements unfolds before one's unbelieving eyes. Here one man, working alone, performed thirty dissections, taking the human body apart and relentlessly examining organ after organ, trying to guess its function and purpose, studying its surfaces and recording its various aspects so that no doubt could remain regarding its morphology. Contrary to what authority and textbook said, he put faith in the workings of his sense organs and created singlehandedly one of the most beautiful flowerings of the science of anatomy.

I do not want to linger over what this meant to culture and civilization, since this has been dealt with so very ably by others, but I marvel at the psychology underlying such a feat. To be sure, the dissection of bodies was performed in Leonardo's time, though relatively infrequently, and Leonardo witnessed semipublic displays of such procedures. A professor more frequently than not presided over the gathering from a pulpit, usually reading from a book what would be seen in the course of the dissection. A demonstrator directed a surgeon or barber where to proceed. Spectators stood around the table on which the cadaver was stretched out (McMurrich, p. 18).[1]

Although the dissection of bodies was institutionalized on certain occasions in the fifteenth century, one must not forget the strong inner resistances and aversions which almost every medical student must overcome anew even in our time, when dissection has become routine. It is at present rather rare for a student to be so deeply affected emotionally by dissection that he feels compelled to discontinue his medical studies, but we do not know how many abstain from studying medicine because of such an aversion. At any rate, the taboo against touching a cadaver, against doing violence to the body, which also includes dissecting it, is so very old and well known that I can spare myself the citation of sources. The Church did not object to dissection in Leonardo's time, but occasionally a ruling was erroneously interpreted as if it applied to dissections; however, it seems that in Rome Leonardo was prohibited by the Pope from continuing dissection.[2]

Yet, forgetting for the moment the inner obstacles to dissection, the external physical conditions under which such a procedure had then to be carried out must also be remembered. Nowadays a dissection is a clean, neat, technical task almost completely devoid of any implication of death, its mystery or horror; then the present-day preparation of bodies was not known. Sarton ingeniously re-enacted in his lectures the conditions to which Leonardo and Vesalius were exposed in the course of their anatomical work and he writes about the nauseating effect it had also on the contemporary (Sarton, 1957, p. 225 and p. 308, n. 23). Sarton adds that Vesalius's work was greatly facilitated by the assistance of the artist John Stephen of Calcar, so that he could proceed uninterruptedly with the dissecting, whereas Leonardo was entirely on his own and had over and over again to interrupt and turn to the artistic, recording part. All these facets taken together make

[1] In McMurrich's text a detailed presentation will be found of the history of anatomy in so far as it throws light on Leonardo's work as an anatomist and on his anatomical achievements. As is known, Leonardo was not the first artist of the Quattrocento who was interested in dissection. I have not been able to ascertain whether his teacher, Verrocchio, performed dissections himself or what the conditions were under which Leonardo's artistic predecessors interested in anatomy were able to pursue their studies.

[2] This probably occurred as a result of a denunciation of Leonardo by a personal enemy.

Leonardo's anatomical feats border on the incredible. The result, though it probably had little influence upon the historical progress of anatomy, was the scores of anatomical drawings in which the beholder is unable to make up his mind what is more to be admired, the artistic beauty or the scientific accuracy.

However, Reitler, an early student of Freud's, thought he had discovered an inaccuracy in one of Leonardo's anatomical drawings which, if verified, would prove that the sexual inhibition, so strikingly evident from his life history and a few of his notes, had actually also penetrated into his anatomical studies. Since Reitler's claim and his conclusions have been disproved (Bonaparte, 1927, p. 35, n.; Stites, 1948a, pp. 262, 266), and I believe that the anatomical drawings, to the contrary, demonstrate that in the scientific context Leonardo effectively excluded the bearing of his psychopathology (a fact of eminent importance to the historian of science), it may be appropriate to present the whole matter in detail.

In 1916-17 Reitler published a drawing by Leonardo of a man and woman in coition (Plate 41) which is remarkable for a conspicuous error: instead of a male right foot, as the diagram requires, there is a left one; in the female an equivalent error occurs. If Reitler's reproduction had been correct, some of his conclusions might have been valid, but he relied on a reproduction published by Fuchs (n.d.) in his famous *Sittengeschichte* without checking in the facsimile edition by Vangensten et al.[3]

Leonardo's original (Plate 28; Q. III 3 v.) does not show any trace of such a mistake, the lower extremities of man and woman ending above the ankles.[4]

---

[3] I have not been able to trace the history of the errors in Fuchs's reproduction. In an engraving by Fra. Bartolozzi published by John Chamberlaine (1796) the right foot of the male already shows a trace of the error that appears later so clumsily in Fuchs and Reitler. The female foot is reproduced in Chamberlaine's publication approximately as it is in the original. In my opinion, even in the original as we have it today the drawing from the knee down is an addendum by a foreign hand. Reitler's negligence may appear pardonable if it is considered that the six volumes of the *Quaderni d'Anatomia* were published between 1911 and 1916, the third (containing the drawing of the copulation) in 1913; it is possible that Reitler had no access to this edition. Moreover, in view of Eduard Fuchs's standing as a historian there was no apparent need to question the accuracy of the reproduction.

[4] In the second edition of his Leonardo study (1919) Freud, with a favorable remark, added, in the form of a footnote, the main part of Reitler's paper. In 1923 Freud added a concluding reference to the criticism Reitler's paper had encountered, namely, "that such serious conclusions should not be drawn from a hasty sketch, and that it is not even certain whether the different parts of the drawing really belong together" (Freud, 1910,

Yet Reitler's interpretation of the drawing as being indicative of "a sexual repression of quite special strength" (Freud, 1910, p. 72) was based on still other details than the alleged confusion about right and left. The standing position of the two figures cannot be considered as an expression of sexual inhibition, as Reitler regards it, since the coition drawing is a "controlled" one serving a strictly propaedeutic purpose. From this point of view the standing position is, of course, preferable, since otherwise the anatomical orientation would be greatly impeded.[5] The suffering facial expression of the male, which Reitler also calls attention to, becomes questionable in view of the original. In any case, traditional treatments of the facial expression of the medical phantom in anatomical illustrations are to be considered.[6]

The usual name of the drawing, "Figures in Coition," does not do justice to Leonardo, since it is a sagittal section through two such figures and aims primarily at demonstrating the sites of organs in man and woman during the act of copulation. To have rendered the faces of anatomical phantoms with a passionate expression would rather have betokened a dangerous deficit in emotional distance from the object of inquiry. Absence of sublimation would have made Leonardo's studies impossible. To be sure, Leonardo's added remark that the drawing shows the cause of diseases bears the earmark of his defense against sexuality.

Reitler, further, points to some anatomical inaccuracies in the drawing. Most of these were, however, traditional. Furthermore, one must keep in mind that, as noted before, and as Reitler seems to have been aware, the conditions under which Leonardo dissected were unfavor-

---

p. 72, n.). It is not clear from the addition whether or not Freud shared this criticism. Stites (1948a, p. 266) informed Freud of Reitler's error in 1924. The German edition was reproduced unchanged except for one insignificant word (Freud, 1910, p. 123, n.) in the *Gesammelte Schriften* 9:371-454 (1925). In the French edition of Freud's Leonardo study Marie Bonaparte commented on the problem and reproduced Leonardo's original and Reitler's version.

[5] In the first instance (1795) of documented commentary by a scholar on this drawing of Leonardo's, the scholar clearly shows that he regarded it as having a propaedeutic function (Blumenbach, p. 19, n.).

[6] See McMurrich (1930, p. 19, Fig. 2) for a reproduction of a dissection by Guido da Vigevano (1345) and (p. 47, Fig. 9) for a situs figure from the *Spiegel der Artzney* (1518) by Laurentius Phryesen, for two samples of the facial expression customary in the drawings in medical books. In my opinion this tradition culminated with an incredibly dramatic power in Rembrandt's *Anatomy of Doctor Jean Deyman* in the Ryksmuseum, Amsterdam.

able for exact observation and his early drawings naturally show many inaccuracies that disappeared in the course of his studies.

However, and this impresses me as extraordinary in his personality, Leonardo was quite ready to assume the correctness of tradition whenever his own experience had not taught him better.[7] In view of the many discoveries he made and the many instances in which he challenged traditional views, one might expect a pugnacious temperament that, by a kind of psychopathic constitution, tends a priori to take a hostile attitude toward opinions sanctified by a tradition that had lasted in many instances fifteen hundred years. It does not seem that Leonardo acted upon a compulsion or inner necessity to contradict. As long as he himself had not examined the cavity of the uterus, for example, he was quite ready to believe that, in accordance with medical tradition, it consisted of several cells (a view he soon abandoned). However, there is one surprising instance where theory, that is to say, tradition, overruled his senses and he drew what did not exist and could therefore not be seen but was, prior to Harvey, postulated by theoretical necessity (cf. Sarton's introduction to McMurrich, p. xix). In this instance he designed pores in the septum of the heart, which he called the "sieve of the heart" (O'Malley and Saunders, p. 226, Plate 91, Fig. 1; Q. I 3 r.; and p. 236; Plate 96, Fig. 1; Q. II 4 v.).

As shown in the coition figure, he likewise accepted Galen's teaching that there are two canals that pass through the penis, the upper and smaller one conducting the animal spirit or soul to the future embryo, the lower one for the passage of sperm and urine (O'Malley and Saunders, p. 460; Q. III 3 v.).[8] Belt (1955) claims that in the drawing at the Schlossmuseum, Weimar (Plate 42), "the canal through the penis is demonstrated as a single passage, not a double one" (p. 45),[9] but since this is an anteroposterior view it leaves the point in question moot.[10] On Q. III 4 v. (Plate 43) there are two longitudinal sections of the penis. The left one definitely shows one canal, but much broader

[7] Cf. Keele (1952), who discussing Leonardo's critical approach to Galenic theory says: "The fundamentals, however, which Leonardo thought he could verify, or at least, could not disprove, he retained" (p. 125). Cf. also Olschki (Vol. I, p. 329).

[8] Avicenna even describes three penile canals: *meatus urinarius, spermatis,* and *alquadi* (McMurrich, p. 202). Leonardo's sketch on Q. III 6 r. possibly intimates three canals, but this would be an exception.

[9] McMurrich (p. 202) writes as if Leonardo had not given up the idea of two canals passing through the penis.

[10] I owe thanks to Dr. Bernard Berglas for his kindness in interpreting and commenting upon this and the subsequent anatomical drawings.

than is anatomically correct. The section to the right shows two canals; it is not difficult to explain the one passage in the drawing to the left: by way of cursory or general diagram, Leonardo drew one broad passage instead of two narrow ones.[11]

Other figures of the penis that are found in his anatomical work likewise show him not to have been familiar with penile anatomy. Only the diagrammatic presentation at the bottom of Q. III 11 v. (Plate 38) may raise a doubt. O'Malley and Saunders describe it as a "Cross-section of the penis disclosing the corpora cavernosa" (p. 446, note to Fig. 5). However, it may be doubted that Leonardo here really meant the corpora cavernosa. The drawing possibly is intended to represent two tubelike passages within a surrounding hollow space. But this interpretation may be questioned. If Leonardo intended here to depict the corpora cavernosa, he was guilty of a couple of mistakes. First, at this distance from the neck of the bladder the two crura have already merged into the corpus cavernosum proper. Secondly, if Leonardo's diagram had been based on an observation of a penile cross-section, he would have been bound to observe the corpus cavernosum urethrae. He would also have observed that there was but a single passage and we should have expected to find it so shown in other figures. Furthermore, it is possible that Leonardo knew of the existence of the corpora cavernosa by palpation. The diagram on Q. III 11 v. (Plate 38) would not demonstrate that its author had knowledge of the anatomy of the penis either and therefore in all probability had not performed a dissection of that organ.

If this conclusion is correct, it would be of no minor psychological import.

That his castration fear was excessive one does not need to doubt. It would have been a triumph of his indomitable quest for knowledge if he had succeeded in abating this fear so much as he would have had to in order to bring himself to dissecting the penis. But it seems that here a limit was reached.

The picture I have formed of Leonardo in the course of my study would lead me to believe that there was no limit to his inquisitiveness and that no neurotic fear, nor any other for that matter, would have been able to detain him from a step necessitated by his service to

---

[11] There are other points in that diagram that are erroneous in regard to the anatomy of the penis.

science, but I have thought it appropriate to record the doubt that is left in this one instance. Even if he was not capable of taking this last step, it would not detract from his heroism. For if my conception of his times is correct, then I think he deserves the epithet heroic without a hint of empty idealization.

To fathom the full impact of Leonardo's deed in psychological terms, one has to tear oneself from exclusive contemplation of the intellectual scientific aspect and consider the following points. The account commonly given is that the Occident was dominated by tradition, such as that of the ancients, the Bible, the Fathers of the Church, and scholastic or other writers of great authority; these sources were uncritically accepted, and only gradually did Occidental man learn to rely on direct observation rather than on what was handed down.

But as a matter of fact dissections were performed and observational data were accessible. What is usually neglected in the histories of that epoch is the prevailing anxiety which, in my opinion, must have been a deterrent to checking on the correctness of tradition. Essentially, the child goes through a like phase in every era when he readily accepts parental assertions or explanations that are obviously contradicted by sense data. Clinical observation in our time then almost regularly shows that when the child accepts the illusion offered by the parent as truth he does so not only because of an identification with the parents or out of obedience and trust in the wisdom of superior authority but also because he is afraid of what he may learn if he acknowledges what is conveyed by his senses.[12] Consequently, I conclude that it was not only submission to authority that made anatomists conform to the erroneous

12 The conflict between belief in authority and evidence of sense data and conclusion from observation apparently centers in the problem of propagation. Yet it is to be considered that the facts of life were not kept from children in earlier centuries and that it was taken for granted that children knew of the relations between the sexes not only as far as biological facts were concerned but also social facts such as prostitution (see Elias, 1939, Vol. I, pp. 230-263). However, from the documents I know, it is not quite clear how far back the sexual knowledge of children was taken for granted. It seems—as is to be expected—that this openness referred to the latency period. The childhood sexual researches that supposedly contributed to Leonardo's insatiable quest for knowledge would have taken place prior to the age of six. Therefore, the historical fact of children's familiarity with the facts of life in earlier centuries would not interfere with Freud's reconstruction of the development of Leonardo's desire for knowledge and investigation from the sexual researches during early childhood or infancy. We see also in the present how the early sexual enlightenment of children that is customary in so-called progressive families does not help the child but in some instances even leads, if possible, to greater confusion and to no abatement of anxiety.

traditional claims but anxiety over looking into and observing the interior of the human body.

As remarked before, in the dissections which seem to have been conducted publicly the professor, strangely enough, read from a text whereas it was the assistant that did the work of dissection (McMurrich, p. 18). Evidently those who were responsible stood under the taboo not to look at what the dissection revealed. Yet every taboo is based on anxiety. I presume that the presence of a group reduced this anxiety, and it is to be doubted that a man would in those times have been able to perform a dissection at all when alone with a cadaver.[13]

Vesalius in the preface to his *De corporis humani fabrica* (1543) wrote of contemporary dissections:

> A detestable ceremony in which certain persons are accustomed to perform a dissection of the human body, while others narrate the history of the parts; these latter from a lofty pulpit and with egregious arrogance sing like Magpies of things whereof they have no experience, but rather commit to memory from the books of others or place what has been described before their eyes; and the former are so unskilled in languages that they are unable to describe to the spectators what they have dissected [quoted after McMurrich, p. 20].

Here is described exactly the taboo I have in mind. But such a taboo is quite puzzling, for the Renaissance was not a squeamish time. During the medieval and Renaissance periods, man in general was not afraid to stab, burn, or cut open the bodies of others, or to do any kind of abominable violence to the live physical structure. In those times the direct cruelty of man to man seems to have been far more widespread and to have taken far more atrocious forms than is the case in our times. Except for our present forms of mass destruction, our behavior and attitudes might be considered squeamish by Leonardo's contemporaries. It may therefore sound quite upside down when I stress so strongly that there then existed an anxiety barrier to the observation of the inside of the human body. However, there seems in former times to have been less inhibition about opening a live body than a dead one. To act in passion or to be driven by strong emotional impulses when attacking the human body was, after all, psychologically quite different from performing the same act with that coolness and

---

[13] I surmise that if instances of solitary autopsies occurred, perversions or necromancy may have been involved.

deliberateness of mind that is necessary in a scientific inquiry. When the live body was torn open it was under the urge to revenge or punish or attack; the sadistic impulse was then well protected either by the superego or by a reality factor that provided suitable rationalization. In the case of a dissection for an alleged scientific purpose, however, the sadistic impulse had to be excluded. Thus the psychological danger of the break-through of an impulse per se forbidden was quite great in such an instance. The appearance of the archaic impulse would have made impossible the detachment and coolness that are necessary in research.

Norbert Elias has most impressively shown the history and meaning of that process of civilization that, starting in the sixteenth century, culminated in the Victorian period. The direct joy derived from physical functions (including the pregenital ones) and the frankness about it, the direct gratification of aggressive, sadistic impulses, was gradually replaced with a refinement that almost denied the existence of a body at all.

It is difficult for us to imagine that there was a time not so long ago when it was taken for granted that prisoners of war were either killed because it was difficult to feed them or were mutilated before being sent home so that they could not be of help to one's enemy. I select here one example of the wealth of material Elias presents regarding the amazing change of attitude Occidental man underwent in his relationship to the body and its functions. In my mind there is no doubt that this change was one, and by no means a minor one, of the many prerequisites that had to be realized before the biological sciences could develop. Leonardo stood at the threshold of that process. Eleven years after Leonardo's death Erasmus of Rotterdam published his book *De civilitate morum puerilium*, which introduced that new concept of "civilité" destined to have such serious impact upon the customs and mode of living of European man (Elias, Vol. I, p. 66). Erasmus, of course, did not create that movement but conceptualized a historical mood or tendency.

But Leonardo had not yet benefited from that process. When, alone at night, he dissected bodies and studied the morphology of organs, he was performing a feat that not only was intellectually or scientifically far beyond his time but that required a degree of fortitude that was far beyond the temper of his time.

Without intending to belittle the factors I have so far set forth, I must still stress man's archaic anxiety regarding cadavers. I am not quite certain that even in our enlightened century there are very many who could fall asleep with ease in a room where there is a body. The psychology of the awe, the weirdness, the uncanniness, that surrounds a dead body has not yet been fully explained, though often investigated. I put it as a constant into the calculation I set up in discussing the truly incredible psychological accomplishment of Leonardo in preparing his anatomical drawings.

A personal passage of his about this subject follows:

> And you who say that it is better to look at an anatomical demonstration than to see these drawings, you would be right, if it were possible to observe all the details shown in these drawings in a single figure, in which, with all your ability, you will not see nor acquire a knowledge of more than some few veins, while, in order to obtain an exact and complete knowledge of these, I have dissected more than ten[14] human bodies, destroying all the various members, and removing even the very smallest particles of the flesh which surrounded these veins, without causing any effusion of blood other than the imperceptible bleeding of the capillary veins. And as one single body did not suffice for so long a time, it was necessary to proceed by stages with so many bodies as would render my knowledge complete; and this I repeated twice over in order to discover the differences.
>
> But though possessed of an interest in the subject you may perhaps be deterred by natural repugnance,[15] or, if this does not restrain you, then perhaps by the fear of passing the night hours in the company of these corpses, quartered and flayed and horrible to behold; and if this does not deter you then perhaps you may lack the skill in drawing essential for such representation; and even if you possess this skill it may not be combined with a knowledge of perspective, while, if it is so combined, you may not be versed in the methods of geometrical demonstration or the method of estimating the forces and strength of muscles, or perhaps you may be found wanting in patience so that you will not be diligent.
>
> Concerning which things, whether or no they have been found in me, the hundred and twenty books which I have composed will give their verdict 'yes' or 'no'. In these I have not been hindered either by avarice or negligence but only by want of time. Farewell [MacCurdy, 1956, p. 166; Q. I 13 v.].

[14] In 1517 Leonardo told Cardinal Luigi d'Aragona that he had dissected more than thirty bodies (Goldscheider, 1944, p. 20).

[15] The literal translation of Leonardo's earthy language conveys his own feelings better: "And if you have love for such matter, you will perhaps be impeded by the stomach" (Vangensten et al., Vol. I, p. 35).

This autobiographical passage most movingly conveys the great scientist's tribulations, and he rightly took pride in his accomplishment. And yet, in another of the *Quaderni* we find a definite sign of a feeling of guilt and Leonardo's way of warding it off. In Q. II 5 v. he wrote:

> O, Speculator,[16] of this machine of ours, you shall not be distressed that you gave knowledge of it through the death of your neighbour, but rejoice that our Creator has the intellect firmly on such excellence of instrument [Vangensten et al., Vol. II, p. 13].

Apparently the scientist, aware of the great narcissistic gratification he obtains from enlarging his knowledge, is for a moment on the verge of succumbing to guilt that this joy is bought at the price of death of a fellow man, but he finds consolation by declaring his doings to be part of a service to the Deity.

There is further a famous passage among his notes that was written possibly between 1470 and 1480 (see Richter, Vol. II, p. 329), that is to say, the decade in which his scientific inquisitiveness must have started to form and to show itself. It strikes me as a biographical annotation symbolizing in the simplest language the general conflict in which he found himself throughout his studies:

> And drawn on by my eager desire, anxious to behold the great abundance of the varied and strange forms created by the artificer Nature, having wandered for some distance among the overhanging rocks, I came to the mouth of a huge cavern before which for a time I remained stupefied, not having been aware of its existence, my back bent to an arch, my left hand clutching my knee, while with the right I made a shade for my lowered and contracted eyebrows; and I was bending continually first one way and then another in order to see whether I could discern anything inside, though this was rendered impossible by the intense darkness within. And after remaining there for a time, suddenly there were awakened within me two emotions, fear and desire, fear of the dark threatening cavern, desire to see whether there might be any marvellous thing therein [Mac-Curdy, 1956, p. 1127f.; B.M. 155 r.].[17]

This conflict of fear and desire that Leonardo felt when he peered into the dark cave must have arisen with manifold intensity when he

---

[16] Speculator here means researcher or investigator.

[17] Leonardo in this famous passage may have been describing an actual experience or a fantasy. In either instance a symbolic meaning is to be attributed to the dark cavern. The tale confirms that curiosity originates in the child's sexual research, as Nunberg (1960) has again demonstrated recently.

penetrated deeper and deeper into the human organism. He had gone far beyond the immediate needs of the artist, and studied layers of human anatomy that seem to have had no bearing on his artistic work. The function of observation had wrested itself away from the artistic one with which it appears originally to have been allied. What was it really that drove him on so relentlessly? And what made him such a superb observer?

15

Some Constructs

I have to go back to my initial construct that Leonardo's basic relationship to the world was a traumatic one, that is to say, that he was almost constantly on the verge of suffering a trauma unless he was geared to counter it by the proper measure. There are two ways of protecting the psychic apparatus against traumatization that are relevant in this context: one is to put the proper guards to the sense organs that are the portals of entrance of external reality; the other is to be capable of predicting the sequence of events and so to eliminate surprise.

PERCEPTUAL STIMULUS AND DEFENSE

For Leonardo the principal portal of entrance was the eye, and he never tires of praising the supremacy and excellency of that organ. To get an idea of how much this organ system was cathected, one has only to listen. He wrote:

> There is nobody so senseless who when given the choice of either remaining in perpetual darkness or losing his hearing will not at once say that he prefers to lose his hearing and his sense of smell as well rather than be blind [Richter, Vol. I, p. 66, No. 30; Ludwig, Vol. I, p. 55].

... whoso loses his eyesight is deprived of vision and of the beauty of the universe and may be likened to one buried alive in a grave where he can move and subsist [Richter, Vol. I, p. 67, No. 31; Ludwig, Vol. I, p. 57].

This almost equating of life and sight of itself shows the hypertrophy of the visual function. Indeed, it is necessary to assume a psychobiological factor that endowed Leonardo's eyes with an extraordinary degree of differentiation or sensitivity. The historian of art seems to draw the same conclusion. Thus Clark (1939) writes: "There is no doubt that the nerves of his eyes and brain, like those of certain famous athletes, were really supernormal" (p. 130) and on another occasion he speaks of Leonardo's "preternatural sharpness of eye" (p. 34) and inhumanly sharp eye (p. 179). Heydenreich (1954) also believes that the ordinary eye would have been able to see only with the help of optical instruments what this artist's keenness of eye and visual awareness was capable of perceiving (1954, Vol. I, p. 129).[1]

Whether this is a constitutional factor or a disposition fortified by early stimulation or trauma one can only speculate. Mozart's auditory system seems to have been physiologically endowed with singular capabilities and I am inclined to assume the same about Leonardo's vision. I leave aside other sense systems since the visual was undoubtedly the leading one.

Leonardo's *sfumato* technique, the chiaroscuro, the advice to paint figures in twilight, can be brought into remote connection with attitudes derived from the protective barrier against external stimuli. But hypercathexis of sense organs, constant watchfulness for the minutest changes and details of external reality, do not yet provide a reliable guard against potential trauma. The influx of stimuli may, after all, excite the psychic apparatus unduly unless countermeasures are at hand. Perception may, to be sure, be followed by dangerous consequences: it may convert the self into the object perceived, it may cause destruction. Here I wish to consider the danger only in terms of psychic economy, that is to say, as a potentially unbearable excitation.

[1] The biology of genius is a challenging topic. It is fascinating to observe how in the one instance the exquisiteness of a biological apparatus (Greenacre, 1957) makes it possible for an equally exquisite mind to create supreme values, how in others the exquisiteness of a biological function leads to unusual but mediocre or trivial achievements, and then again to observe an exquisite mind impeded in the creation of corresponding values by the dearth of biological endowment.

In Leonardo's case the change aroused by perception is immediately converted into an act of depiction—hence the stream of sketches, of which, I am sure, we have only a small part despite the large number preserved. In going through Leonardo's work one gets the impression of a man who is constantly geared to observation and depiction, the eye and the hand being integrated into a centripetal-centrifugal unit.[2]

Goethe describes how while he is taking a walk a stream of verses goes through his mind, evidently the stream of sense impressions being reflexly converted into verses. I presuppose a like process in Leonardo, but here the medium requires a stream of alloplastic actions in the form of sketches and drawings. The stream of verses going through the mind does not have a discharge value as high as the discharge in the form of drawings and sketches which require, in contrast with autoplastic thought processes, actual bodily movement.[3]

Despite important similarities between Goethe and Leonardo there is one principal difference: although Goethe too evolved his techniques for withstanding states of high-pitched emotional tension, we observe him for the first four decades of his life falling from one emotional crisis into another. The scanty data on Leonardo suggest a different course.

The impression one gains in Leonardo of a fixation to an optimal tension level enforced by hypersensitivity to oscillations is confirmed by the style of Leonardo's notebooks.[4] They are unique in many respects besides the external feature of having been written in mirror script. Heydenreich characterized them as follows: "His literary remains, numbering thousands of pages, which record the whole of his life as he lived it, down to its daily details, tell us nothing about any strong inclinations, predilections or aversions" (1954, Vol. I, p. 19; see also Clark, 1939, p. 179). The personally intimate, the emotional, the subjective, that is to say, messages about his inner life, are with very few exceptions excluded. Moreover, there is seemingly a great disorder in these notes. Remarks that seem to be disconnected appear

---

[2] This has been observed by almost every writer on Leonardo.

[3] The recoil of the drawn picture or sketch is also to be considered. Most of the verses that percolated through Goethe's mind were forgotten as quickly as they emerged.

[4] See Berenson for an important remark regarding the imbalance of verbalization and visualization in Leonardo (1903, p. 147), which is a key issue in the structure of personality. Cf. Johnson (1949, p. 147f.).

in closest propinquity; repetitions are very frequent. The Arundel manuscript in the British Museum starts as follows:

> Begun in Florence in the house of Piero di Braccio Martelli, on the 22nd day of March, 1508. This will be a collection without order, made up of many sheets which I have copied here, hoping afterwards to arrange them in order in their proper places according to the subjects of which they treat; and I believe that before I am at the end of this I shall have to repeat the same thing several times; and therefore, O reader, blame me not, because the subjects are many, and the memory cannot retain them and say 'this I will not write because I have already written it'. And if I wished to avoid falling into this mistake it would be necessary, in order to prevent repetition, that on every occasion when I wished to transcribe a passage I should always read over all the preceding portion, and this especially because long periods of time elapse between one time of writing and another [MacCurdy, 1956, p. 58f.; B.M. 1 r.].

Here Leonardo himself ostensibly explains the style of his notes. But the reader whom he introduces occasionally is an illusionary person. Particularly in this instance he serves a rationalization. Somewhere Leonardo must have known that he would never publish his notes, but he wanted to justify the peculiarities of his literary work to himself (cf. Sarton, 1953, p. 18).

Clark characterized Leonardo's notebooks as follows:

> However great or trivial a thought, Leonardo could not contain it, down it went at once, to get on as best as it could with cannons and jokes and geology [1929, p. 128].[5]

It is my impression that Leonardo followed here the same law that his sketches and drawings reveal. He acted under the inner necessity of writing down at the first opportunity whatever came to his mind.[6] A thought, too, as well as a thing seen, may become invested with intense emotional charges and I surmise that the act of writing down had the function of dismissing it, or was, at least, an attempt at achiev-

---

[5] However, cf. Clark's (1952) comment on Leonardo's notebooks: "The first is that his manuscripts are not, as was once supposed, made up chiefly of original observations, but are to a very large extent commonplace books in which he copied down what he had read" (p. 301).

[6] Cf. Olschki (Vol. I, p. 391) for a theory that integrates Leonardo's attitude into the basic aim of his research.

ing this effect or at a reduction to the optimal level of the inner tension that was created by thinking.

Although these notes preserve the logical structure, although they are witnesses of highly elaborate ratiocinations, they still share something, in my opinion, with free associations. Since touching the emotionally explosive was apparently forbidden, this mind had to try to concentrate at all costs on the reasonable. Thus we see it constantly observing and either picturing the content of these observations or digesting them in the form of elaborate ratiocinations that have to be written down immediately. In the course of time or periodically the ratiocinative part absorbs more and more of Leonardo's energy and the last few years possibly are spent without any artistic activity to speak of. Indeed, science is a better protection against trauma than the arts. If everything is known surprise is excluded. Arbitrariness, or what appeared arbitrary, was Leonardo's great enemy, and the finding of a cause reduced the area from which a trauma might arise.

But into how large an area of the unknown can the ratiocination even of a lifetime bring light? When a cause is discovered this requires new explanations, and the mind must not rest since just at such a moment a trauma may arise from the unknown, the unpredicted. But whenever the anxiety is temporarily assuaged by a discovery, by a new assertion that nothing is subjected to arbitrariness, that is an occasion for rejoicing.

Thus he wrote when discussing the meeting of all rays of light at one point such as the eye:

> O marvellous Necessity, thou with supreme reason constrainest all effects to be the direct result of their causes, and by a supreme and irrevocable law every natural action obeys thee by the shortest possible process!
> Who would believe that so small a space could contain the images of all the universe? O mighty process! What talent can avail to penetrate a nature such as these? What tongue will it be that can unfold so great a wonder? Verily, none! This it is that guides the human discourse to the considering of divine things.
> Here the figures, here the colours, here all the images of every part of the universe are contracted to a point.
> O what point is so marvellous!
> O wonderful, O stupendous Necessity thou by thy law constrainest all effects to issue from their causes in the briefest possible way!
> These are the miracles, . . . forms already lost, mingled together in so

small a space, it can recreate and reconstitute by its dilation [MacCurdy, 1956, p. 238f.; C.A. 345 v. b].[7]

Solmi cites this passage to demonstrate that Leonardo transforms science into a sort of religion (see Freud, 1910, p. 75), and Freud in agreement with Solmi gives a beautiful account of how Leonardo transforms love and hatred into intellectual interest.[8] "With the persistence, constancy and penetration," Freud continues, "which is derived from passion," he devotes himself to investigation, and at the climax, when the goal is reached, the affect breaks loose and he indulges in ecstatic language (1910, p. 74f.).[9] What I wish to stress in this context is that this affect of joy is totally devoted to the idea of absence of arbitrariness in nature and her following a regularity that is enforced by necessity. On occasions of such joy one feels a fullness of passion in Leonardo's words. This may appear like a contradiction to Freud's thesis that Leonardo's capacity to love fully was injured. This free flow of strong emotion when exulting over the predictability of nature seems, however, to confirm Freud's basic proposition about Leonardo's emotional life, since such exultation, passionate though it be, cannot be regarded as a flow of love toward an object.

If this view regarding Leonardo's being under the necessity to combine perception and depiction is accepted, then we shall draw the conclusion that the graphic work with which Leonardo interrupted his dissections did not make his anatomical investigation more difficult, but to the contrary, made it possible. If he had not had the opportunity of discharging the tension evoked by the terrible things he had to see, by re-creating them immediately and rendering them beautiful, he would, in my opinion, have been compelled to accept what Galen and Avicenna had taught, and leave dissection to others, as did the professors in their lofty pulpits.

Thus we see him exploring the whole of the inside of the body, the womb and the child in the womb; and one erroneous traditional as-

---

[7] Leonardo's triumphant rejoicing at this point is perhaps referable to the confirmation of a secret imagery about an "all-seeing" eye. The occasion, after all, was given by the meeting of all rays in the eye.

[8] This is, to my knowledge, also the first instance in psychoanalytic literature in which the sublimation of the aggressive drives is described.

[9] Yet compare this passage with that on p. 133 where Freud (1910) speaks of Leonardo's research as seemingly having contained "some of the features which distinguish the activity of unconscious instincts—insatiability, unyielding rigidity and the lack of an ability to adapt to real circumstances."

sumption after another fell aside under the unswerving scrutiny of his courageous, steady eyes.

The record, however, does not seem to confirm a conclusion Freud apparently drew, namely that Leonardo's unquestionable sexual repressions impeded his scientific inquiry into the subject of sex.[10] Leonardo's anatomical drawings show him exploring the genitourinary system as objectively, eagerly, and successfully as other organ systems (cf. Belt, 1955, pp. 41-67). There are at least twelve coition studies in his anatomical drawings, certainly more than in any of our best textbooks of physiology, which shows that the inquiring mind did not stop at investigating that which in his personal life was taboo. To be sure his attitude toward sex would make one rightly expect a grave deficiency in that area, but as genius in general is a phenomenon contrary to expectation and common sense, so here also, in one of his greatest accomplishments, Leonardo contradicts a rule of thumb that seems justified in terms of theory.

Hypertrophied Function and Structure

In looking for a biological equivalent we may, though not quite correctly, compare the production of such extraordinary achievements as abound in the course of Leonardo's life with the immense increase in functional capacity that results from organic hypertrophy. What follows is a speculation about the processes that may lead to such hypertrophies of single functions as we can observe in Leonardo.

It is not probable that the eminent accomplishments of artistic geniuses depend primarily on the contents that are repressed in the course of development. Further research, I can well imagine, may, however, demonstrate that certain repressed contents favor or disfavor the evolvement of artistic abilities. The present perspective of psychoanalytic theory and research rather suggests seeking the specific reasons for artistic accomplishment in the structure of the ego and its relations to reality, drives, and superego. In turning to these relations, again according to the present stand of theory, the defensive functions of the ego are of principal interest.

---

[10] Cf. Freud's account of the vicissitudes of the instinct of research (1910, p. 79f.). By the third type, which "avoids any concern with sexual themes" (p. 80) despite the free growth of intellectual interests, evidently Leonardo was meant. Cf. also Freud's footnote of 1919 and the beginning of the quotation from Reitler (p. 70).

What is meant by the concept of defense is pretty clear. In order to avoid displeasure (usually in the form of anxiety) or even injury the ego tries to eject totally or partially from its territory anything or everything that may cause displeasure or do harm. If ejection is not possible, compromises are made; the offensive agent may be removed to a part where it is less injurious; it may be converted into a less dangerous agent; it may be isolated, etc. Very decisive in the defensive struggle is the structure of the agency that carries out the defense. In ordinary circumstances the ego, from its genetic inception, develops particular mechanisms, such as repression or identification and others, upon which the task of carrying out the defense devolves. Yet from clinical experience one knows that the ego may use other tools than mechanisms for such purposes.

In the so-called psychopathic states one observes that the ego may use an instinct for the purpose of defense. Thus, a personality type reminiscent of Don Juan indulges in promiscuity in order to combat strong homosexual impulses. His endless amorous adventures can be regarded as having the defensive meaning: "I am sure that I am not a homosexual because I go to bed every night with another woman." He has to display his heterosexual leanings most conspicuously in order to convince others as well as himself that he is without homosexual wishes. The fact that in this type drives are used for the purpose of defense does not mean that defense mechanisms have not been evolved as well. It only means that the array of defense mechanisms is not strong enough or does not work properly to safeguard the ego, and it therefore becomes necessary to engage a drive in the work that would ordinarily be assigned to a specific mechanism or a pattern of mechanisms.

In such an instance, in order to maintain the defense against homosexuality, the ego relies mainly on the gratification of a drive. The advantage of such a defense is that it gains in pleasure, which is lost —at least partly—by the full establishment of a defense mechanism. The disadvantage of a defense by instinctual gratification is evident. The ego is greatly limited in its flexibility and becomes totally dependent on the regular and proper supply of this form of gratification. It may have to spend all its energy and activity on this one function and therefore become very limited in its contact with reality and the evolvement of other functions; and further, since society may disapprove of the defense chosen, a serious conflict may result between community and subject.

Another group in which the insufficiency of defense mechanisms can be observed is the schizophrenic disorders (Hartmann, 1953). A comparison taken from biology may illustrate how the defense can lead to severe dysfunction. It seems that in some, though rare, instances of certain infectious disorders antibodies do their work of defense with great rapidity. The toxins excessively liberated in the process of annihilating the invaders damage the host and lead to his death. Older people whose reaction to the infector is slower have in these instances a better chance of survival.

The defenses in schizophrenia also render a poor service to the ego, which must pay a formidable price for the little protection it obtains.[11] Projection, to cite an example, enables the ego to rid itself of an internal source of displeasure by moving it to a point outside of the confines of the self. In schizophrenics this process is so fulminantly carried out that the most important reality functions fail in accomplishing their assigned tasks. The visual and auditory senses, thinking, and other functions carry out the projection and cease to perform their work in the service of the reality principle according to which the correct data of the external world are to be conveyed and digested by reality-adequate thinking. Thus we see in this instance also that when defense mechanisms are weak reality functions tend to be burdened with the task which should have been entrusted to the mechanisms.[12] Yet whereas in the psychopathic states the function carrying the bulk of defense is per se not disturbed but only misapplied or misused or intensified beyond the optimal, we observe in the schizophrenic disorders an actual damage of reality-related functions; they are absorbed in their service of the function of defense to the detriment of their ability to cope adequately with reality.

From the preceding the reader will recognize what I am aiming at. I surmise that the hypertrophy of single functions in Leonardo was caused by the eminently defensive task they had to fulfill.[13] As in

[11] For the double aspect of defense mechanisms, their necessity, and assistance on the one hand, their noxious effects on the other, see Freud (1937, p. 340).

[12] For a subtle analysis of two instances of disturbance of sensory functions by their serving primarily purposes of defense, see Katan (1950, 1952).

[13] However, see Klein (1948, p. 97f.) about Leonardo for a hypothesis of libidinized ego tendencies and subsequent protection against repression in favor of sublimation.

psychopathic states and in schizophrenic disorders, the structure of the ego being weak and lacking in the evolvement of solid defense mechanisms, the necessity arises of burdening reality-related ego functions with the task of defense. In a genius like Leonardo it must also be assumed that a deficit in structure not only made the functional hypertrophy possible but made it an absolute necessity. The necessary state of equilibrium would then have depended on the maximal activation of these creative functions.

When Walter Muschg says that the poet's kinship with the criminal and the mentally diseased is unmistakable (1948, p. 108), he refers to this clinical factor that all three of them have in common. Indeed, we may occasionally observe how creativity, when it does not adequately fulfill the function of defense, may change into either form of psychopathology.[14]

Another point one may find in common is a "fuzziness" between self and object which can best be described in terms of Piaget's research. In an early developmental phase when the infant is on his way to forming a concept of objects but has not yet reached that point, action toward the object per se or the manipulation of the object is equated with the object. "The object is still nothing but a prolongation of the child's activity" (Hartmann, 1953, p. 181). In that phase it is impossible "to speak of the object as existing independently of the activity. The objective is in the direct extension of the act. It is as though the child did not dissociate one from the other and considered the goal to be attained as depending on the action alone" (Piaget, 1937, p. 12). This reduction of the objectiveness of objects is definitely encountered in many psychopathic states with their usual hyperactivity and insistence and lack of empathy with objects, and in some schizophrenics in whom not only is the world of objects made dependent on magic gesture or maintenance of certain thoughts, but attention and interest are moved away from objects and concentrated in individually varying ego functions. In the artistic genius in general and Leonardo in particular one can dimly perceive something similar, despite the great devotion to objects, their observation and study, and Leonardo's

---

[14] For case histories referring to genius, psychopathy, and psychoses, see Lange-Eichbaum (1927, pp. 256-450). However, I do not agree with Lange-Eichbaum's clinical approach. To my way of thinking genius and mental disorder are disparate, although the latter may arise when the former is blocked or decays.

incessant preoccupation with them. Despite his incredible attachment to the world of things there remains the necessity to re-create them, and, as I will point out later, at times to re-create them in a better shape than they ever existed. The created work of art, be it a simple sketch or an accomplished painting, is necessarily a prolongation of the artist's self, at least in the creative moment and probably for a while thereafter, and the most valuable object, at least the one closest to the creative person, becomes one that is nothing but "the prolongation" of the artist's activity. To be sure, these objects do not exist in reality independently of his activity.

This reduction of the objectiveness of objects is, I believe, a prerequisite to the creation of great art. It is an indispensable admixture of considerable narcissism to ego functions directed toward reality. It probably is essentially related to the initial observation that object-related ego functions have to serve purposes of defense because of a relative weakness of ego structure.[15]

To summarize: we assume that Leonardo's ego was poor in structure, that his defense mechanisms were, for whatever reason, poorly developed or perhaps did not develop at all—which is hardly imaginable —and that therefore defense depended wholly or mainly on the activation of creative functions. This model may tentatively illuminate some of the peculiarities of Leonardo's creativity.

At this point we may rightly raise the question whether anything is known in Leonardo's life that may throw some light on the genesis of the deficit in structure that I have postulated. I would like first to report briefly on an observation I have made in Goethe's development.

In Goethe's life, which is so richly documented, one discovers a process during adolescence that indicates a melting down of ego structure. Whether or not such a process should be called a psychosis is of no relevance here. Suffice it to say that a deficit of ego structure in the adult is not necessarily caused by a slowing down or inhibition of structurization during childhood or the latency period, but may be caused by later processes. In Goethe's case one can observe with some

---

[15] Although I agree in the main with Dr. Greenacre's view of the artist's love affair with the world (1957, p. 57, et passim), still there are narcissistic elements that are specific to geniushood and as indispensable as the object-related elements. When Dr. Greenacre writes that "the compelling drive of creativeness . . . may give the creative activity the semblance of a special kind of addiction for which there is no cure" (p. 69), I believe she is referring collectively to narcissistic components.

reliability how his poetical talents, already considerable before, more or less suddenly gained in originality after the short-lasting phase of melting down and that he then became capable of producing a new style of poetry that became characteristic of him and led to his greatest lyric achievements. I concluded that this melting down of structure was a turning point that released the activation of functions previously inhibited.

In the light of this observation I was struck by the fact that Sir Kenneth Clark reaches the conclusion that in Leonardo's youth there was a period lasting approximately four years of a well-nigh complete standstill in artistic creativity. He writes:

> We must assume that Leonardo, like other young men with great gifts, spent a large part of his youth in what is known as doing nothing—dressing up, talking, taming horses, learning the lute, learning the flute, enjoying the *hors d'œuvres* of life, till his genius should find its true direction [1939, p. 16].

This period of "doing nothing" would cover the years from 1474 to 1478.

It has also been noticed that Leonardo's early paintings, however outstanding they may have been, are not of such quality that one could have anticipated the eminence he later actually attained. Thus Clark writes that Leonardo's "early pictures are less good than we should expect them to be" (1939, p. 24). He excepts the portrait of Ginevra de Benci, in which Leonardo's genius does show itself. However, whereas Clark dates this painting at 1474, others, like Heydenreich (1954, Vol. II, p. iv) and Suida (1929, p. 26), date it in the period after 1478 (see also von Bode, 1921, p. 40). If these authors are correct we observe an early period of painting characterized by productions less compatible with Leonardo's later eminence separated by approximately four years from a second, in which Leonardo's pictorial genius showed itself in its full magnitude.

We know of two events that took place during these four years: the birth of Leonardo's first sibling and his denunciation as a homosexual. Now we hear from the historian that the two years before and after these events Leonardo probably spent in doing nothing, that is, did not devote himself seriously to his great mission.[16] I have previously postulated a possible connection between the arrival of a sibling and the suspicion of overt homosexuality. Tentatively I now raise the question whether during these years there took place, as I suggested before, processes that caused the melting down of ego structure. It would help explain—if the Benci portrait was really painted after 1478—why Leonardo, after a comparatively long period of leisure, more or less suddenly reappears as a painter of unusual stature.

However, Leonardo's dependence on creative and selected reality-related functions in turn made him vulnerable not only to trauma in general but also to stimuli which these functions were unable to cope with. Biographers such as Heydenreich have noticed that Leonardo was compelled to transpose contents into something visual. Mechanics is for him a visual science (Heydenreich, 1954, Vol. I, p. 115). Visual representation amounted to accomplished insight. "Leonardo's imagination is a visual one; if a problem is capable of being presented visually, then the presentation amounts for him to scientific proof" (ibid., p. 112). Error became inevitable "when he encountered limits beyond which his wholly visual powers of observation could not function" (ibid., p. 148). And at times it was not just error but a falling back on authority against which he had so valiantly fought. "When Leonardo reached the limits of his own sensory perception he fell back on traditional theories" (ibid., p. 142).[17]

Those authors who claim that science was for Leonardo always visual science seem to me to be very right. The *saper vedere* is the exclusive tool with which the world is to be approached and can be approached. How much Leonardo was aware of his helplessness vis-à-vis the non-visual world can be fathomed from the following: "Since the eye is the window of the soul, the latter is *always* in fear of being deprived of it" (MacCurdy, 1956, p. 232; italics added; C.A. 119 v. a). Here

[16] However, if Valentiner (1930) is right in his conception of Leonardo's relationship to Verrocchio, one may obtain a different impression of the four allegedly silent years. The process of melting down of psychic structure in Leonardo's youth, as suggested by me, would not have had to cover such a long period. In Goethe's instance this process occupied only a few weeks. The critical episodes as reconstructed in these two instances appear to have a structure essentially different from the identity crisis and various moratoria Erikson (1956, pp. 58, 66f.) describes in the life of George Bernard Shaw.

[17] Olschki (Vol. I, p. 343ff. et passim) adopted the most extreme views regarding Leonardo's limitations imposed by the hypertrophy of the visual system. Within the framework of the history of thought Olschki describes the very process I try to explicate in terms of psychology. For a different view, see Cassirer (1927, p. 171).

we have a documentation of his pervasive fear of trauma, and from his equating death and blindness, as cited earlier, we learn that seeing is the only protection against death. Because of the weakness of the protective barrier against inner stimulation, the mind must be constantly absorbed by external visual stimulation. I have quoted earlier Leonardo's advice to recall at night when lying in bed the forms one has studied during the day.

Voluntary concentration on the recall of recent reality experiences is intended to help in avoiding exposure to internal stimulation. It is necessary to assume that unconscious contents can be kept away from consciousness without the mechanism of repression being fully developed, merely by concentrating all available energy on external contents. This hypercathexis of external reality may impede the intrusion of contents that make up the repressed but which in this instance I cannot rightly call the repressed since I presume that the corresponding mechanism was poorly involved. To be sure, we must presume a fixation to the scoptophilic instinct, but here I am discussing only in what way the visual function assisted the ego in maintaining its organization.

If we consider the utter ruin a breakdown of the visual function would have wrought upon Leonardo's personality, the hypercathexis and constant activation and eminent efficiency of this function may become better understandable. In connection with the relative deficiency I have postulated with regard to the working of defense mechanisms in a genius like Leonardo, I must briefly point to an adjunctive factor. The melting-down process sets in at a time when the ego has to bear increased stress (adolescence in Goethe's instance, delayed adolescence [?] or unknown traumata in Leonardo's). Since the ego proves itself to be unprepared for the solution of tasks imposed upon it we must presume that it has entered this phase in an already weakened condition. I suggest that the cause for this weakness lies in the genius's being possessed of unusual innate talents, which, we may assume, already make themselves noticeable in childhood or even in infancy. I do not think that this necessarily results in unusual achievement but at least in increased interest on the part of the child in the activation of those functions that are favored by the constitutional endowment.[18] If the child's attention and interest are already concen-

18 For tentative suggestions regarding the artist's childhood development see Greenacre (1957).

trated upon these functions at an early age, an unduly large preemption of energy by these functions may even then retard the evolvement of solid defense mechanisms. The eminent energic discharge value of these functions must also be considered.[19]

With justification it will be said that, quite independently of the correctness or incorrectness of these views, my hypothesis by centering in the function of defense elucidates the least interesting aspect of creativity. To be sure, my hypothesis does not explain more than the reason why in two subjects with equal endowment only mediocre achievements may be forthcoming in one case and eminent ones in the other. However, if the melting-down process is confirmed, a factor in the etiology of geniushood more relevant than any role that can properly be assigned to the factor of defense may have been found.

At this point one may properly be called upon to demonstrate why in the genius the loss of structure leads to hypertrophy of function, that is to say, the emergence of unique creativity, whereas in the schizophrenic a breakdown and disorganization of the personality is the result. The difference in specific endowment, I believe, is not decisive, for in a relevant number of patients one can observe that even the greatest gifts leave the patient unprotected against the ravages of the disease. For obvious reasons I am unable to contribute an answer to this question, any more than to that of the essence and origin of the psychological factor or set of factors involved in geniushood.

Notes on Leonardo's Artistic Creativity

Although the factor of communication is stressed in conjunction with creativity in general and Leonardo's drawings specifically, I am inclined to see in it only a secondary motive comparable to the secondary gain in neurotic illness.[20] To be sure, Leonardo himself writes quite frequently about communication. He sets up rules about how an object is to be represented so the beholder will obtain full knowledge of it and even greater knowledge than if he were observing the real object. Many other remarks can be cited that may show the importance of communication as a driving force in Leonardo. And still, when we

[19] For other reasons of delay in the structurization of the personality in the gifted child, see Greenacre (1957, pp. 58-60, 64).

[20] For a viewpoint that stresses the motive of communication and assigns to it a central value in Leonardo's work, see Olschki (Vol. I, p. 327).

acknowledge in Leonardo the necessity of observation as primary in order to maintain the coherent organization of his self, we may conclude that the act of depicting was likewise dictated by an equivalent basic necessity.

It seems to me that it was the basic necessity of defense against the fear of death that was strongly involved in Leonardo's stream of graphic creations. "For we part from the body with extreme reluctance, and I indeed believe that its grief and lamentation are not without cause" (MacCurdy, 1956, p. 80; Fogli A 2 r.), he wrote.

The connection between creativity and defense against the fear of death is adumbrated in the following:

> O thou that sleepest, what is sleep? Sleep is an image of death. Oh, why not let your work be such that after death you become an image of immortality; as in life you become when sleeping like unto the hapless dead [MacCurdy, 1956, p. 63; C.A. 76 v. a].[21]

This fear of death, translated into abstract psychological terms, amounts to a feeling that the self is under a constant threat of disorganization (A. Freud, 1936, p. 63; Waelder, 1936, p. 47f.), and the poignancy with which this fear would be felt is understandable in view of Leonardo's deficient structure, his decreased barrier against inner stimulation, his increased vulnerability to trauma, and his ego's dependence on a limited number of hypertrophied functions. Since the created work is, after all, at bottom a projection of the self, its survival, its enduring beauty, are potent counteragents against the fear of annihilation. Leonardo wrote:

> Behold now the hope and desire of going back to one's own country or returning to primal chaos, like that of the moth to the light, of the man who with perpetual longing always looks forward with joy to each new spring and each new summer, and to the new months and the new years, deeming that the things he longs for are too slow in coming; and who does not perceive that he is longing for his own destruction. But this longing is in its quintessence the spirit of the elements, which finding itself imprisoned within the life of the human body desires continually to return to its source.

[21] Cf. the two remarks quoted earlier, "Shun those studies in which the work that results dies with the worker" (MacCurdy, 1956, p. 80; Forster III 55 r.), and "In life beauty perishes and does not endure" (MacCurdy, 1956, p. 91; Forster III 72 r.).

And I would have you know that this same longing is in its quintessence inherent in nature, and that man is a type of the world [MacCurdy, 1956, p. 75; B.M. 156 v.].[22]

This passage in Leonardo's writings is considered a meditation on life and death or a definition of life, whereas I should like to point out its psychological implication.

It strongly suggests that Leonardo may have experienced longing as per se closely connected with death. Longings, as Leonardo so rightly says, imply a dissatisfaction with the speed of time and contain the desire for acceleration of time, that is, indirectly, an earlier approach of death.[23] Yet man, approaching the fulfillment of longings, usually experiences the fulfillment of life, and the associations of longing and death in Leonardo may—despite the fact that similar opinions are expressed by philosophers—betoken his own aversion against longings and satisfactions. "Neither promise yourself things nor do things if you see that when deprived of them they will cause you material sufferings" (MacCurdy, 1956, p. 81; Fogli B 21 v.) is again another aspect of Leonardo's fight against exposure to tension created by longings. Creation, however, seems to make an artist of Leonardo's type independent of longings and therefore proves a powerful agent against an accelerated approach of death.

The difficulty inherent in the problem under discussion is quite great and therefore the tentativeness of my inferences may be pardoned. What makes a discussion of the psychology of Leonardo's artistic creativity so difficult is the apparent impossibility of finding a common denominator of the two principal visual arts he was most proficient in: drawing and painting. A large number of drawings from Leonardo's hand are in existence. Most of them are of incredible perfection, the objects limned with a surety and vividness, with a dynamic power that conveys absence of any doubt or hesitation. Most of them were probably turned out with great rapidity. Clark has given us a very able description of the spirit in which they were produced (1939,

[22] For an interpretation of this passage different from mine, see Panofsky (1939, p. 182).

[23] A view regarding the passage of time seemingly contradicting this opinion is found in the following: "Wrongly do men lament the flight of time, accusing it of being too swift, and not perceiving that it is sufficient as it passes; but good memory, with which nature has endowed us, causes everything long past to seem present" (Richter, Vol. II, p. 244, No. 1170; C.A. 76 r.). This sounds to me like a consolation, as if Leonardo were saying: "Even if time passes, it is not lost, for all the past can become present again at any moment and at will."

pp. 20, 121),[24] and it is this part of Leonardo's artistic work that seems to speak strongly in favor of my thesis that depicting was a function ever ready to bring about adequate relief of the fear of "returning to primal chaos."

Yet in direct contrast to the conclusion to which we are prompted by Leonardo's drawings, there seems no doubt that when he was painting a picture Leonardo at times went through long periods of hesitation; in the case of the *Mona Lisa*, tradition has it that he felt he never succeeded in giving it the perfection that he wanted. I refer also to the instances in which there are—or were—several versions of the same subject. These long periods of struggle to find the solution of artistic problems seem to speak strongly against a lowered capacity to bear tension. Here the creative process led to an increase of tension and did not provide that beneficial solution one feels inclined to associate with his drawings. This is confirmed when we hear from a probably reliable though secondhand informant (Lomazzo, quoted by Freud, 1910, p. 66) that Leonardo trembled when he set himself to paint. Apparently, creating a painting actually exposed Leonardo to a strain that brought him to the verge of the unbearable.[25]

What was the structure of the ego that could utilize so unerringly and effectively the creative impulse to draw but was so seriously conflicted when it was a matter of painting? In view of everything we know of Leonardo this cannot be attributed to any kind of lack of positive ability.[26]

Clark has tried to trace the sequences that led to final paintings (1939, p. 20). One of them is the phase of diagrams: "these are usually quite small drawings, done from memory, and are syntheses of the most satisfactory motives." Among his many compositions it was usually these small diagrams that Leonardo carried out in the final paintings. The very small *Leda* sketch Müller-Walde discovered accidentally on a page of the *Atlantic Codex* as mentioned before is one of the

[24] See also Berenson (1903, Vol. I, p. 148) for a superb description of Leonardo's graphic function.

[25] Berenson's accounts (1903, 1916) of the drawings and paintings are of great help in pointing up the essential differences between the two categories of Leonardo's work.

[26] The late Professor Heinrich Glück used to cite Leonardo as the only artist who was acknowledged as genius during his lifetime *and* whose prestige persisted unabated throughout the centuries independently of changes of style, fashion, taste, and art theories. See also von Bode (1921, p. 3). For an unusual instance of negative criticism with regard to Leonardo's painted *œuvre*, see Berenson (1916).

impressive examples of this sort.[27] I have not found an explanation of why these final diagrams are of such small size and I have no doubt there were many reasons. Perhaps it is another manifestation of a general bent in Leonardo which Olschki, in discussing Leonardo's mental work, described as a penchant for the aphorism, an inclination to attempt "to put together a maximum of attributes into the smallest possible space [*ein Maximum von Merkmalen im kleinst möglichen Raum zusammenzufassen*]" (Vol. I, p. 342).

In searching for the unconscious reason why what later would become paintings appear first in the form of these microcompositions, one may raise the question whether perhaps they symbolized for Leonardo the small infants out of which the adult would grow, or even a kind of fetus, in which also the prestages of the later infant can be recognized. If so, this practice would materially confirm how much the work of art was for Leonardo literally a child, as Freud briefly intimated. At the same time, it may provide a factor that interfered with Leonardo's painting and upset the smooth functioning that is supposed to have been characteristic of his drawing. The following passage in the draft of a letter from Leonardo to his brother Domenico (b. 1484) may give the reason thereof:

> My most beloved brother,
> This is sent merely to inform you that a short time ago I received a letter from you from which I learnt that you have had an heir, which circumstance I understand has afforded you a great deal of pleasure. Now in so far as I had judged you to be possessed of prudence I am now entirely convinced that I am as far removed from having an accurate judgment as you are from prudence; seeing that you have been congratulating yourself in having created a watchful enemy, who will strive with all his energies after liberty, which can only come into being at your death [MacCurdy, 1956, p. 1137f.; C.A. 202 v. a].

Where did Leonardo get his certainty that a son hates his father to such a degree that he looks forward to his death so that he may be free? What he wrote his brother must have been derived from his own experience. Thus children are not only neglected at times by their parents, but also in their turn are "watchful enemies" of their creators. Did Leonardo also displace this conflict upon his paintings and therefore so often hesitate to finish them?

[27] See also the sketch for *Anna Metterza* (Popham, Plate 175).

Furthermore, Clark speaks of Leonardo's "inborn distaste for finality." Finality means separation, and separation is often associated in our minds with death. Sketches, drawings, usually do not carry the weight of finality; they are parts of a comprehensive whole and although artistic achievements of the highest order in their own right, they elicit in the artist feelings quite different from those about a finished painting. In Leonardo's case there was, to seek no further, the fact that drawings remained in his possession (cf. Hildebrandt, 1927, p. 224f.), whereas his paintings were made on commission and had to be surrendered upon completion. Drawings were free of this inhibitory connotation.

With the paintings, we are dealing with an activity in which depiction did not reduce tension but increased it. Much as such factors as finality and the child-painting identity may have been at work, it is my feeling that there must have been still a deeper reason in his psychic economy for the fact that we have so many "perfect" drawings from his hand and so few perfect paintings.

The demand put upon the psychic apparatus in the painting situation was, as a matter of fact, quite different from that which Leonardo was exposed to, for example, in the effort to invent a flying machine. In that effort he had to study a model of perfection, as represented in the bird. Here his task was reduced to penetrating into the secrets of an object that exists in reality and then transforming his findings into a mechanical instrument. In his superb drawings of plants and beasts and landscapes too he had objects before him to which he could fasten himself, the task being reduced to transposing an image from one medium to another.[28] When he was painting a picture, however, such as the *Adoration* or the *Cenacolo*, he had himself to create the model of perfection. It was no longer a matter of treading the short circuit from percept or inner image to depiction, as it was in the case of drawing. When painting Leonardo had to submit to a task that required a broad synthesis, the construction of a goal whose concretization was far off in the future and which he could approach only very gradually by a series of innumerable little steps. Did the necessity of keeping sight of this far-ahead, visionary goal in the midst of full devotion to

[28] Cf. Berenson (1903, Vol. I, p. 151) about one of Leonardo's drawings: "It is perhaps as near an approach to the actual transfer to paper of a visual thought as man has ever achieved."

a mass of details, which are sometimes detours on the road to finality, burden him with tension that became unbearable? I feel very strongly in favor of this possibility. When Clark says that Leonardo loved diversity more than unity or that he loved accident rather than substance (1929, p. 130), or speaks of him as "so little concerned with synthesis, so distrustful of abstractions" (ibid., p. 126), he puts his finger on exactly the spots where I think Leonardo's weaknesses were. These were areas where the hypertrophied functions no longer yielded sufficient protection and the psychic apparatus was exposed to grave dangers.

In a genius like Leonardo, as in so many others, one gets the impression that they spend their creative lives as if under an inner necessity or compulsion, that they have no alternative but must create. The model I have devised for Leonardo would approximately explain that inner compulsion. The coincidence of creative function and defense would really have left him no alternative. Creating or not creating was a question of life or death, as was the inner reason that did not permit him to leave off research but drove him relentlessly on and on. This inner necessity, however, may drive a genius beyond what is favorable to his psychic economy, and thus we observe Leonardo exposing himself sporadically to tasks that evidently involved great inner pain. I am not thinking of the pain he suffered in his anatomical work; that seems to have been of a different order. I am thinking of the strain he was subjected to when he was working on his large compositions, when past observations and their concretizations in the form of innumerable sketches were to be synthesized into a material embodiment of a perfect vision he carried in himself or, at least, was groping for. When exposed to such strain he may have felt a revulsion of which possibly we hear when we read Fra Pietro's letter, which, after all, was written at a time when Leonardo was engaged in producing one of his most beautiful paintings.

Thus the following suggestions may be submitted. There came from Leonardo an unimpeded stream of drawings that kept him optimally tension-free since it prevented the accumulation of longings which meant for Leonardo essentially an acceleration of death. This smooth flow was greatly impeded in the case of painting, for several reasons: the final work of art supposedly meant for Leonardo a child; the male child was looked upon by him as a mortal enemy to his father;

further, the painting, in contrast to drawings, carried the stamp of finality and thus implied separation, that is, a loss which Leonardo dreaded. Moreover, the strain to which the psychic apparatus was subjected in the course of producing a painting was possibly too great, since it did not allow the copying of an object but presupposed an inner vision that had to be constantly changed and adapted and whose concretization required long detours.

Although these factors may well have been active in Leonardo and have contributed to his trembling when he began to paint, one has the feeling that this frame of reference is not specific enough to clarify the inner resistance Leonardo met. In the following excursus I will make a suggestion as to the area in which the specific etiology may be found.

Excursus on Leonardo's Relationship to Painting

In trying to discover the particular psychological difficulty that Leonardo evidently had to overcome in producing a painting we may turn toward the book in which he gives counsel to the painter on how to proceed in such work. A manuscript has reached us which, though not from his pen, reliably reproduces the bulk, if not all, of what he had to say about the subject. The *Trattato della pittura* is a huge mass of notes regarding perspective, color, proportion, etc., in short, a compendium of many items a Renaissance painter needed to know about.[29] The technical part is of less interest here, but there are chapters and remarks that demand psychological interpretation, mainly in that part which is called the *Paragone*.[30]

Among Leonardo's notes on art there are no doubt many that continue a tradition that in some instances goes back before the Renaissance; the type of treatise represented by the *Trattato* was initiated by Leon Battista Alberti (1404-1472). Still, all authors agree upon the originality of Leonardo's ideas about painting and art even though in a substantial part of them he follows Alberti (Clark, 1944, p. 16f.).

[29] The most complete and reliable manuscript is the *Codex Vaticanus (Urbinas)* No. 1270 titled: *Libro di Pittura di M. Leonardo da Vinci, Pittore et Scultore Fiorentino* (Ludwig). Panofsky (1940a) has discovered in the Codex Huygens, Codex M.A. 1139 at the Morgan Library, a part that is an exact copy of otherwise unknown notes and drawings by Leonardo that belong to this subject. For a history of all the manuscripts involved and a complete bibliography, see Steinitz (1958).

[30] Literally, "Comparison," a title used for the first time by Guglielmo Manzi in 1817.

Conspicuous among the remarks that ask for psychological interpretation are those of an aggressive-defensive nature in which Leonardo extols painting as the foremost science of all and puts poetry, sculpture, and music on a far lower level (Ludwig, Vol. I, pp. 3-103).[31]

The desire to improve the social standing of artists and to elevate the prestige of painting is also found in Alberti's writings, but nothing of Leonardo's radicalism and exclusiveness is noticeable there (cf. Janitschek, 1877, p. 146). Basic among the objective historical factors that were apt to make an ambitious artist sensitive was the traditional division of the arts into liberal and mechanical, painting being considered to be mechanical. The history of this division and the changing esteem in which painting was held from ancient times through the Middle Ages up to the Quattrocento do not need to be presented here.[32] Suffice it to say that Leonardo put up a fierce struggle for the rehabilitation of painting and reversed the contemporary situation by establishing painting as superior to all other sciences. Alberti's pride in reporting that in ancient Greece slaves were forbidden to learn the art of painting (Janitschek, p. 96) is a close antecedent of Leonardo's endeavor.

In this context it is not superfluous to call attention to the fact that Alberti, like Leonardo, was of illegitimate birth. It seems to me that Leonardo's fight to make out of the "illiberal" art of painting a liberal one is genetically connected with the blemish on his birth. The ambition to rid painting too of a blemish may be seen as a counterpart of his ambition to blot out the stigma of his origin. When Leonardo writes: "And indeed it was not without reason that they have not raised it [painting] to [the rank of] nobility since it ennobles itself by itself without the assistance of other tongues [*e veramente non senza caggione non l'hanno nobilitata, perchè per se medesima si nobilita, senza l'ajuto delle altrui*]" (Ludwig, Vol. I, p. 72), this may tell us how he overcame a very personal resentment that stemmed from sources quite different from his concern about the art of painting; being as a painter a member of the Guild of St. Luke, he was in a position to repeat a basic issue of his childhood. In fact, the blemish of his birth

[31] The first part of Leonardo's *Trattato*, the *Paragone*, in which the rivalry of the various arts is presented, is also found in Richter (Vol. I, pp. 31-101).

[32] For an excellent summary of this history and for the specific goals Leonardo pursued in his defense of painting, see Richter's introduction to the *Paragone* (Vol. I, pp. 14-30).

and the blemish of his profession both stood him in good stead. Indeed Leonardo's youngest half-brother tried to repeat the miracle of nature by marrying a girl from Vinci who was as similar as possible to Leonardo's mother, Caterina, with the effect that Pierino da Vinci, his son, became a noteworthy sculptor.[33]

Turning again to the *Trattato della pittura*, there are two aspects that make one wonder. First it is surprising that in it Leonardo gives advice he never followed himself and which would certainly have threatened his standing as one of the greatest painters if he had. Thus when he wrote about how to depict a battle he suggested that the air should be full of arrows flying in various directions, one ascending, another in descent, and others horizontally; bullets should be accompanied with vapor in the direction of their course (Ludwig, Vol. I, p. 191);[34] footprints in plain soil should be left filled with blood (ibid., p. 287). If Leonardo had ever tried to practice such gruesome precepts—which, of course, he never did—his paintings would have become, rather than masterpieces, illustrations of how an artist ought not to proceed.[35] Yet in these instances he may have been carried away by his literary genius, so to speak, and in *writing* about painting involuntarily have set forth what a *writer* should describe (cf. Olschki, Vol. I, p. 359). Yet the matter becomes more serious when we find Leonardo strongly advocating (Ludwig, Vol. I, pp. 209, 317, 363) that the affect or emotion being depicted should be unmixed so that there should be no doubt as to the affect the person represented is possessed by. This is in con-

[33] Pierino da Vinci (Pier Francesco di Bartolomeo del Ser Piero da Vinci), sculptor and silversmith, born 1530 in Vinci, died 1553 in Pisa, one of the most important Florentine followers of Michelangelo (Thieme-Becker, 1907-50, Vol. XXXIV, p. 384f.).

[34] Cf. what Lessing had to say about the limitations of painting (Lessing, 1766, Parts XV and XVI).

[35] There are also remarkable contradictions between specific pieces of advice he gives to the beginner. At one point he recommends work in solitude (Ludwig, Vol. I, p. 107); shortly thereafter he considers it preferable to draw in company (Ludwig, Vol. I, p. 131). Compare also Leonardo Parte II 56 with Parte III 407 (Ludwig, Vol. I, p. 111 and p. 399). In both instances Leonardo discusses how the use of a mirror may help in achieving the best results in painting, but in one instance he castigates the artist who takes a walk for the sake of physical refreshment whereas in the other he recommends rest periods. For Alberti's counsel to interrupt work and rest, see Janitschek (p. 158). For the question of whether or not Leonardo knew of Alberti's writings, cf. Clark (1944, p. 16f.) and Richter (Vol. I, p. 23). Pedretti recently published a passage that shows Leonardo in his later years succeeded in making a synthesis between the two above-cited contradictory pieces of advice. Thus he wrote (C.A. 184 v. c): "And his [the painter's] companions should resemble him in a taste for these studies, and if he fail to find any such he should accustom himself to be alone in his investigations, for in the end he will find no more profitable companionship" (1959a, p. 47).

trast with Leonardo's actual practice, in which precisely the indeterminateness of affects is an important source of the great power his
paintings have over the beholder. I have discussed this feature in
regard to the *Gioconda, Leda,* and *St. Jerome.* It is just the antagonism
of opposing emotions that is most characteristic of the human personality, and it was Leonardo who was one of the greatest in the art
of intimating by the discreetest shades the presence and interplay of
manifold emotions in the same subject. To be sure, he was also capable
of presenting an eruption of vigorous one-dimensional passion, as in
the *Battle of Anghiari,* but we would not see in Leonardo the artist
who knew so much of the human soul were it not for other paintings
that present so impressively that sphere of human life where contrasts
are not so strictly separated and the quality of the emotion is in doubt.
He was a painter of human depth by means of complete mastery of
the surface.

A very surprising statement is found in Parte II, 114, where Leonardo counsels how to escape the "calumny" of other painters. He
advises that one practice one's art in accordance with a variety of ways
so that one will be in agreement, in some part at least, with each of the
current opinions that are held about painting (Ludwig, Vol. I, p. 165).
This, though modified in the subsequent paragraph, is a veritable slap
to all and everything Leonardo stood for.

The second surprising aspect of the *Trattato* is that it shares with
other Renaissance treatises a certain limitedness that has been remarked by the historian (Ludwig, Vol. III, p. 109f.). This limitedness
can best be summarized as an almost exclusive concern with craft
rather than art. That which makes Leonardo's paintings the master-
works they are is not touched upon in the *Trattato.* If his paintings
were nothing but the mirror of nature, as he recommends at times,
they would be of no greater interest to us than those of any other skillful craftsman. No more need be said than that the greatness of his
artistic work derives from an entirely different area, but about that
area Leonardo spares scarcely a word aside from generalities.[36] How
are we to explain this? It is well known that many a genius has a poor

---

[36] Cf., however, Clark: "The finest passages in the *Trattato* are those in which Leonardo
describes the springs of the painter's genius" (1939, p. 34). "The springs of genius," I
think, can be observed only after psychological interpretation of some statements. The
overt content of the *Trattato,* aside from the *Paragone,* is concerned with technical advice
on problems of the craft.

understanding of his own values or of where his true value lies; like most people he has his repressions, prejudices, and is utterly misled about his own psychology.[37] Thus Leonardo may have been honest and sincere in his *Trattato* and may have gone to the limits of his insight. At the same time, there is evidence that a genius may hold back precisely his most personal impressions and insights. A good example is Goethe's apparent reticence regarding the rise of the machine age (von den Steinen, 1949, p. 12). Indeed, no reference to it is to be found in his conversations or letters or in the bulk of his writings. Only in his last novel, *Wilhelm Meisters Wanderjahre*, are there passages that demonstrate his awareness of the fundamental changes to which society was being subjected. But there also one encounters his horror at what he envisioned the machine age would do to society and to man. He evidently did not want to ponder on a grave issue for which he saw no path to a solution. Only on this last occasion did he permit himself the minimum of remarks that convey to him who reads between the lines the impact this development had had upon him.

Something similar, it is my impression, may be surmised about Leonardo and the invention and spread of printing which occurred in his lifetime. Sarton finds nothing "more curious and perplexing" than that Leonardo "overlooked two of the greatest inventions not only of his time but of all times: printing and engraving" (1957, p. 229) and he asks: "Did he despise such inventions, as did some Florentine snobs?"

Pedretti (1957, pp. 107-117) recently presented the material in Leonardo's notes that refers to printing. It is evident that Leonardo did not ignore printing, but it is remarkable that he, who was so much interested in machines and technically so very astute, did not pay more attention to it. If one does not read between the lines, one may draw the conclusion that he had a kind of blind spot here and was not foresighted enough to recognize the greatness of an invention that would change as did no other the culture in which he grew up. Again at a

---

[37] Occasionally one hears that only a genius is capable of understanding a genius. To be sure, a genius may have a better understanding than even the best of critics of the values of another genius's creations, but this is a limited area if measured against the comprehensive scope of geniushood. Moreover, even within this narrow area many a genius has committed grievous errors. Furthermore, while there is no doubt that some geniuses have a degree of self-knowledge that is quite outstanding, this is rather the exception than the rule. The principal source for the study of the creative process is by no means to be found in what geniuses have said about their own geniushood or that of others.

place where one would not expect it one discovers a hint that may be suggestive of a hypothesis. In the *Trattato della pittura* one finds a passage in which printing is used as an example to set forth the superiority of painting. Leonardo distinguishes between sciences that are imitable and inimitable. In mathematics the pupil appropriates as much as the teacher presents, but the person who is not favored by nature with special gifts cannot learn painting. One cannot copy a painting as one does writing or as one makes a casting of a sculpture, "It [painting] does not beget infinite progeny like printed books.[38] [*Questa non fa infiniti figliuoli, come fa li libri stampati*]" (Ludwig, Vol. I, p. 10). Here reference to printing is definitely pejorative. For Leonardo, the individualist and the artist, the idea that something so personal and individually characteristic as a manuscript should be multiplied had apparently an offensive implication.[39] The machines Leonardo was occupied with had the function of achieving mastery over physical forces; they multiplied man's physical power to do what he could achieve on a smaller scale unaided. But in printing and engraving the machine arrogated the privilege of the selected few and thus threatened the prerogative of individual culture. We have got accustomed to books, and we are aware of the benefits printing has bestowed, but we overlook the deep injuries this invention has likewise inflicted upon civilization, not only by its facilitating the spread of falsehood as well as truth, but also by the depreciation of mental values it has caused. It is understandable that a mind as aristocratic, in the best sense of this word, as Leonardo's was should have felt offended and pained by the incursion of the mechanical into the live realm of the mind. This, of course, is only a hypothesis. One can feel surer about the reasons for Goethe's silence about the machine age, but whatever the true reasons may have been for the scarcity of remarks about printing in Leonardo's notes, we can be sure it was neither snobbery nor failure to notice or disregard. The genius, as this example once more shows, sometimes abstains from explicitly setting forth what possibly is most personal and relevant to him. Consequently we should not be surprised that we must lay aside the *Trattato* without having discovered the specific mean-

38 If we consider that Leonardo avoided even potential opportunities of progeny, we will fathom the full meaning of this metaphor.

39 Engraving, of course, came frighteningly close to the area dearest to his heart, since it made possible the copying of drawings and even paintings. See, however, Appendix A, where the subject is taken up once more.

ing painting had for Leonardo and the specific goals he pursued by means of it.

A general remark may be interpolated here. Miss Kate T. Steinitz, in a personal communication for which I here take the opportunity to thank her, has cautioned me against forgetting that Leonardo really accomplished a *tour de force* in his defense of the art of painting in the *Paragone*. No doubt he did. But his groping for arguments, his uninhibitedness in making even quite impossible inferences, the bizarreness of some of his arguments, lead the psychoanalyst to believe that precisely in this area there is a splendid chance of getting hold of direct derivatives of the repressed. However, the motives and meanings we are looking for when we inquire into Leonardo's relationship to the art of painting do not belong strictly to the repressed, although they may have been intimately connected with it. Clinically it is well known that anxiety in almost all of its forms is fed by the repressed, but when Leonardo trembled as he set out to paint he must have been hampered also by a content that was part and parcel of his ego, to wit, of its conscious part. Whether this content was actually represented consciously or only preconsciously does not make very much difference in this context. In other words, we are raising the question of what the goals were that Leonardo tried to achieve in painting, for evidently there was something about these goals themselves that was liable to arouse anxiety or cause hesitation or procrastination. If we had an idea as to what these goals were, we might be in a position to draw new inferences regarding the repressed meanings that were attached to his activity as a painter.

The historical relationship between art and art theory or philosophy in the Renaissance has been well studied.[40] Besides this objective historical context there is the subjective one in the artist himself that is of relevance here. The relationship between the two in the artist may have been of various kinds. The artist may have known of certain conceptual frameworks and may have used them consciously in the presentation of allegories or other subjects, or he may even have been in search of a philosophical system that would conceptualize what he was trying to express or present visually.[41] But it may also happen—and

[40] See Panofsky (1924, 1939), Lee (1940), Cassirer (1927).
[41] Panofsky gives an example of this. He writes: "Michelangelo resorts to Neoplatonism in his search for visual symbols of human life and destiny, as he experienced it" (1939, p. 182).

possibly this is what has most often been the case—that the artist was not consciously motivated by a theoretical frame of reference. He may have heard of it or even studied it and still it may have slipped into his productions without his conscious awareness. Reflections of contemporaneous philosophy or theory are, of course, observed in works of art without there being a direct connection between the philosophy and the art. The philosopher conceptualizes problems and solutions that have become ripe in his times, and the artist will achieve corresponding solutions in the visual medium. Both are children of the particular historical epoch in which they live, and it is not surprising when one discovers kinship between cultural products of the same period even when these products belong to quite different media. "Art," Max Dvořák (1923, p. x) said, "consists not only in the solution and development of formal tasks and problems; it is also always and foremost an expression of ideas that dominate mankind; its history, no less than that of religion, philosophy or literature, is part of the general history of thought [allgemeine Geistesgeschichte]." I raise a problem here that is eminently complicated and I fear my simplification may make appear almost like a triviality a process the essentials of which are not understood at all and are still as puzzling as when the question first arose. The fact that the artist's responses to stimuli that are not of a personal nature but extrasubjective, such as historical or cultural forces or those of tradition, are usually unconscious has given rise to a tendency to reduce the artist's individuality to a mere medium, and to limit the historian's role to noting the stimuli and responses. Such a concept is adequate when the artist is merely an imitator or when his motives are primarily derived from a sphere extraneous to art. But the great artist responds fully to his own personal subjective world, which is usually replete with conflicts, to a specific area within his historical period, and to some (or all) of the perennial problems of mankind. These areas are not represented separately in the end product, but each element of the work of art and the total configuration contain all of them and more. Since, however, we are not able to discern each single area in every element, it may appear as if some elements contain more or less of one or another area. Such impressions depend on our perspicacity. Behind an apparently objective symbol a most personal conflict may be hiding and go unnoticed—often because we do not know enough about the artist's personal life.[42]

In the search for a motivating theoretical frame (conscious or pre-conscious) in Leonardo's paintings, one feels inclined to look at Neo-platonism, which had such a great bearing upon Florentine art. Al-though, as is well known, Leonardo was an avowed opponent of this philosophical system, an internal kinship is not necessarily to be excluded.[43]

What separated Leonardo from any form of Platonism was Plato's turn away from the observation of nature (Cassirer, 1927, p. 176), which was, after all, the mainstay of Leonardo's empiricism.[44] This Platonic aversion to the direct comprehension of natural objects by the senses[45] shows up in the spiritualistic teachings of the Academy of Florence, which degraded or abased nature and banished it to the lowest grade of beings (Cassirer, 1927, p. 149). I should also surmise that the whole circle of literati around Lorenzo il Magnifico, with their stress on poetry and philosophy and a concomitant neglect of the visual arts, must have been repugnant to Leonardo. He may easily have looked upon them as snobs, which they probably were to a certain extent (Olschki, Vol. I, p. 259ff.). However, as Cassirer points out, although Leonardo remained quite untouched by Neoplatonism and the Florentine Academy, he found his way to true Platonism *despite* Ficino[46] and the Academy (1927, p. 177f.).

However, Leonardo seems to have been strongly under the influence of philosophers, as Duhem's now classic studies prove. So far as I know, this influence has been studied in relation only to Leonardo's scientific and philosophical notes, but not to his artistic work. I wish

[42] For a presentation of the plurality of approaches in the interpretation of art, see Hauser (1959), which came to my attention after this book was written.

[43] In his book on Neoplatonism and the Renaissance, Robb (1935) however, tries to prove a closer relationship of Leonardo to Neoplatonism than is commonly supposed. Cassirer has set forth the point where Leonardo and true Platonism merge (1927, p. 177). For a sociological remark regarding the effect of Neoplatonism on Leonardo and Michel-angelo, see Olschki (Vol. I, p. 259ff.).

[44] Here and in what follows I use the term *empiricism* in a sense not strictly in accord with that which it usually has in the history of philosophy. When I speak of Leonardo's empiricism I mean only that he used sense data, observation, and experience in his scientific inquiry, and relied on his senses for gaining insight into the structure of things.

[45] For the position of art in the system of Plato, see Cassirer (1922-23).

[46] In the exposition of Ficino's philosophy by Kristeller (1943) it becomes quite clear why Leonardo was bound to be repelled by Florentine Neoplatonism.

to demonstrate a significant tie between Leonardo's artistic work and the philosophy of Nicholas of Cusa. Nicholas's bearing on Leonardo as scientist and philosopher has been most ably set forth by Duhem (1909-13, Vol. II, particularly pp. 4-53, 146-185) and Cassirer (1927). In presenting this tie, I rely for my account of Nicholas of Cusa's philosophy chiefly on Cassirer's exposition as set forth in his volume on *Individuum und Kosmos in der Philosophie der Renaissance.*[47]

There seems to have been a personal affinity between Leonardo and Nicholas of Cusa (1401-1464). Both are representative geniuses of a time in transition, and therefore are rooted in two historical periods: the Middle Ages and the Renaissance. Both are in substantive ways far ahead of their times: Nicholas to a certain extent anticipated twentieth-century relativity theory (Klibansky, 1953, p. 233), and Leonardo, fulfilling and going beyond the potential inherent in Quattrocento art, anticipated High Renaissance, Baroque (von Bode, 1921, p. 145), Impressionism to a certain extent,[48] and probably even, as it seems to me, nonobjective art. Both had linguistic difficulties. Leonardo, *uomo senza lettere*, found himself isolated from the crowd that was intellectually fashionable (de Santillana, 1953, p. 45) because of his un-erudite background—he could not compete with them in their rhetoric performances which were the prerequisite of scholastic standing; Nicholas of Cusa, the German, was clumsy in his Latin, and, as he said, he was incapable of rivaling those that were Latins by birth (Cassirer, 1927, p. 20).

A more striking kinship is noticed when what in Nicholas was possibly only theory but may just as well have been the expression of a subjectively valid truth is compared with what, according to Freud, was in Leonardo the basic interrelationship between self and emotion. When Nicholas finds an inner contradiction in the idea that the affect of love can exist without admixture of cognition, when he declares the true love of God to be *amor Dei intellectualis* (Cassirer, 1927, p. 13) and makes cognition a prerequisite of love, then he is anticipating what Leonardo expressed perhaps a shade more radically. "For nothing can be either loved or hated unless it is first known" (MacCurdy, 1956, p. 88; C.A. 226 v. b); and even more strongly: "... love of anything

[47] For what follows, see also Panofsky (1924).
[48] At least a remark by Clark may be interpreted in this sense (1939, p. 157f.). Popham is more outspoken on this point (p. 44). Cf. also Berenson (1903, Vol. I, p. 159). But for a contrary view, see von Bode (1921, p. 145).

is the offspring of knowledge, love being more fervent in proportion as knowledge is more certain; and this certainty springs from a thorough knowledge of all those parts which united compose the whole of that thing which ought to be loved" (MacCurdy, 1956, p. 83; Q. II 14 r.).[49] Here the historian's search for imitative behavior would, if there ever was imitation, have a better chance of success than when he supposes Leonardo became a vegetarian after studying Porphyry. Was Freud wrong when he made this self-emotion equation a leading pathognomonic sign since we now encounter a similar one in Nicholas of Cusa's philosophy? Did he here at last err by subjectifying a historicosociological trait? The historian probably would be more inclined to agree with the psychologist if Nicholas's proposition was correlated with an appropriate subjective attitude, which I presume can scarcely be proved. Yet even then he might claim that Leonardo was merely following in his view about love and cognition what he presumed to be proper for a man who seriously pursues intellectual goals. Even if we abandon the theory of imitation, it may still be said that Leonardo identified here with the ideal of what he thought a philosopher ought to be and that this type of identification does not necessarily reflect basic psychopathology, that is to say, that Leonardo did not identify with Nicholas of Cusa on the ground of character traits or common psychopathology, but for essentially different reasons, the self-emotion relation being only accessory or incidental.

Notwithstanding the unquestionable feasibility of this explanation, what we know of Leonardo's total emotionality, as far as it can be reconstructed from external evidence and from his notes, speaks rather in favor of Freud's interpretation than of the assumption of accessory identification. If we tentatively assume that this part of Nicholas's philosophy grew out of his own subjective experience, we may observe that the climate of certain historical periods favors the evolvement in certain personality types of above-average talents. It is quite conceivable that the growth of certain cultural patterns requires certain personality types (cf. Kroeber, 1944), and since a historical period does not insure the flourishing of all those who have the stuff of genius, it may happen that many a subject's potential genius remains unrealized because the

---

[49] Cf. the *Trattato*, where the same idea is also expressed in the negative: "If you know it [the loved object] only little, then you will be able to love it but little or not at all [*Se tu no'la cognoscerai, poco o'nulla la potrai amare*] (Ludwig, Vol. I, p. 136).

culture of his time does not provide that frame into which the subject could fit the creations of his particular skills. Thus it may have happened that just because of an identical emotional pattern both men had a better chance of their genius being realized in the Quattrocento than they would have had if their self-emotion relations had been different.

In defiance of scholastic theology,[50] Nicholas of Cusa posited the *visio intellectualis* as the principal situation in which man achieves a direct relation to God. This *visio* was not an ecstatic surrender to God but the end result of innumerable intellectual steps. Nicholas calls in mathematics as an instrument on the way to God. *"Nihil certi habemus in nostra scientia nisi nostram mathematicam"* (Cassirer, 1927, p. 15), which again coincides with Leonardo's basic approach. "There is no certainty where one can neither apply any of the mathematical sciences nor any of those which are based upon the mathematical sciences" (MacCurdy, 1956, p. 619; G 96 v.).[51] But the certainty of mathematics cannot provide cognition of God as he is. In defiance of scholastic logic Nicholas maintains that no conclusion except a negative one can be drawn from the finite to the infinite. As long as of a quantity a more or less can be thought, it is qualitatively different from the infinite. The infinite is not a superlative referable to a preceding comparative. No procedure of quantification can bridge the gap between the absolute maximum, the primordial cause of existence, and empirical, finite existence (Cassirer, 1927, p. 21f.). When Leonardo in his *Trattato* (Ludwig, Vol. I, p. 4f.) states that no accumulation of points however numerous could ever form a plane, we have an example of how Nicholas of Cusa's philosophy shows up directly in Leonardo's theory of art.

In Nicholas of Cusa's work we find a thought that is particularly striking to the psychologist, though it certainly was not meant as it will be understood by modern man. It can be called the beginning of the subjectivization of the idea of God. Regarding the *visio intellectualis* Nicholas of Cusa states that it is correlated with the nature of the object as well as of the subject. Thus, that which is seen in the *visio intel-*

---

[50] For the place of cognition in the system of Meister Eckhardt, whose work had influence on Nicholas of Cusa, see Chevalier (1956, pp. 452-457).

[51] In view of the foregoing, Leonardo is consistent when he introduces his above-quoted opinion regarding knowledge and love with a praise of mathematics.

lectualis partakes of the nature of God but also of the nature of the subject. The two are inseparably intermingled. God is in reality the totality of all the possible individual subjective visions, and therefore the subject in viewing God must consider that the image he can see depends on the location from which he views God and on his own nature, that is to say, the subject can obtain only a partial view of God. Thus Nicholas writes about God:

> Every face that looks into yours, therefore, does not see anything that is different from itself because it sees its own truth. . . . Who beholds you with a loving look feels your look lovingly directed at himself. . . . Who beholds you in anger will find your face angry. Who with joy, will find it joyful. For as to the physical eye everything appears red when it looks through a red glass, so does the eye of the mind, in its limitation, see you who are the goal and object of contemplation in accordance with the nature of its own restrictedness. For man cannot judge but humanly. . . . Also a lion if he attributed to you a countenance would ascribe to you that of a lion, the ox that of an ox, the eagle of an eagle. O Lord how miraculous is your countenance that the youth must form youthful, the man manly, and the aged aged if he wants to comprehend it [Cassirer, 1927, p. 34].

I must forgo discussing the consequences of this astounding thought and limit myself to referring to a thought in Leonardo's *Trattato* which is parallel, though in a different context. Simultaneously we shall notice here (for the first time) in Leonardo an attempt at overcoming that restrictedness which Nicholas of Cusa ascribes to man's nature. Leonardo repeatedly warns against what he calls the greatest defect of painters, namely, their inclination to paint what they themselves are (Ludwig, Vol. I, pp. 155, 159, 161, 491). We observe here an aspect of Leonardo that has perhaps not been sufficiently stressed by some of his biographers.[52] Indeed he must have felt well fortified against error by his insistent reliance on empiricism. Otherwise he might well have been fearful of becoming involved himself in self-deception, and hence in deceiving those who viewed his works. How strongly he felt about deceivers may be judged from his well-known outbursts of rage against astrologers and necromancers.

But, at least within the area of creative art, one gets here and there a glimpse of a Leonardo who is quite anxious lest man's subjectivity victimize him and befuddle the objectivity of his judgment. "We know

[52] See Kris (1936) for a discussion of this factor.

for sure that one recognizes the errors rather in the works of others than in one's own, reprehending the small errors of others and over-looking one's own great ones [*Noi sapiamo certo, che gli errori si co-gnoscono piu in l'altrui opere che nelle sue, e spesso, riprendendo gli altrui picholi errori, non uedrai li tuoi grandi*]" (Ludwig, Vol. I, p. 398).[53]

Thus he claimed that a painter who has coarse hands will also paint such hands, and that this is true of all the limbs. Only long study will protect a painter from this error. He attributed this inclination of painters to the relationship of mind and body. The mind (*anima*) that was the inventor of its own body, when it has again to make a body by means of the hand, repeats the body it has produced once before.[54] How far Leonardo went in recognizing the effect of what is nowadays called narcissism can well be seen when he adds his observation that one who takes the step of falling in love falls in love with objects that are similar to oneself.[55]

How Leonardo tried to protect himself against the detrimental effect of narcissism is not the question here. It impresses me as important that Nicholas of Cusa described the narcissistic root of religious imagery (though not in psychological, but metaphysical terms) and that Leonardo was aware of the same root in artistic creations. But whereas Nicholas integrated this root and made it a legitimate part of man's relationship to God, Leonardo turns against it, considers it a defect, and tries to eliminate it from art. Leonardo was in general aware of what may "corrupt" an artist's soul. He turned forcefully against avarice and vainglory, all the pitfalls that may pervert the genius's sacred mission in life. This castigating attitude had not only a didactic function; it must also have been a defense against his own temptations. Anna Freud in her inquiry into the psychology of adolescence has described the "antagonism towards the instincts which far surpasses in intensity anything in the way of repression" (1936, p. 169). The adolescent's ascetic attitude alternating with instinctual excesses is a defense directed at the totality of his instinctual desires. In Leonardo,

---

53 Cf. also Alberti when he advises the artist to ask others for their opinions and to listen to everyone who is ready to express his views (Janitschek, p. 160).

54 ". . . *hauendo co'le mani à rifare un corpo humano, uolontieri rifa quel corpo, di ch'essa fu prima inuentrice*" (Ludwig, Vol. I, p. 490).

55 ". . . *et di qui nasce, che chi s'inamora uolontieri s'inamorano di cose à loro simi-glianti*" (ibid.).

too, ascetic trends are noticeable alternating with exhibitionistic ones (whether there were also instinctual excesses is not known). Thus his discovery of and fight against the temptation to derive narcissistic gratification by painting himself directly into his work may indicate how strongly the narcissistic impulse may have been in himself. But this repudiation of the narcissistic realization likewise indicates a determination not to let the inner cosmos intrude into the painted work of art. Leonardo's aversion against Botticelli and Michelangelo, though it certainly was also based on differences in questions of a purely artistic nature, may have had its subjective root in this area, for Botticelli, and particularly Michelangelo, made their own emotions the center of their art, and what they felt—that is to say, what they were—was "unashamedly" presented to general inspection.

Yet all this does not touch upon the crucial point where Nicholas of Cusa's philosophy became a fulcrum of Leonardo's painting. The possible subjective parentage is not decisive, although it is of interest to observe how frequently, despite an absence of personal acquaintance, intellectual parentage is related with filiation of temperament and character. The part of Nicholas of Cusa's philosophy that must have meant the most to Leonardo was, I presume, the rehabilitation of the senses, their restitution to their own right after their long-lasting past degradation to a status inferior, lowly, or vulgar.[56] Now they became the prime movers of the intellect (Cassirer, 1927, p. 47). Not that this restitution occurred suddenly; it was prepared by previous development. Dvořák (1923), in his unique historical presentation of idealistic and naturalistic trends in Gothic sculpture and painting, has shown how medieval man started to find his way back to the world of things, to the direct observation of his surroundings, after the complete surrender to the transcendency of the Godhead in early Christian art (pp. 43-147). To be sure, this was neither a return to the classical view and its artistic approach nor did it establish observation in a place comparable to that it held with Leonardo. Gothic naturalism was still in the service of God's transcendency on the principle that Thomas Aquinas

[56] This degradation of the senses has been described repeatedly but no more convincingly than in the following: "St. Anselm, writing at the beginning of the twelfth century, maintained that things were harmful in proportion to the number of senses they delighted, and therefore rated it dangerous to sit in a garden where there are roses to satisfy the senses of sight and smell, and songs and stories to please the ears (Clark, 1950, p. 2).

formulated as: "God finds enjoyment in all things." Yet in Nicholas of Cusa the transcendent and the immanent worlds are separated, and observation is instituted for the sake of gaining knowledge of the immanent. This world is equally close to or distant from God in all its parts. There are no special contents in the universe that are closer to the fountainhead than others; thus everything that can be observed is equally worthy to be studied and understood. To be sure, man's intelligence is limited and he cannot recognize eternal truth, yet this is not considered by Nicholas as anything like a barrier. It is a value in itself, through which that which is beyond the world can be comprehended.

From this vantage point all religion becomes heterodox. Religion must necessarily be different from God. Truth can be understood by man only by this quality of differentness, and all religions have this very quality in common. Religious institutions and customs are only signs and should not be confused with the referent. Those signs differ in all the various religions, but the referent is always the same [*signa autem mutationem capiunt, non signatum*] (Cassirer, 1927, p. 31f.). We see here how widely Nicholas of Cusa extended the area of relativity. Since man cannot acquire absolute truth, every knowledge can be replaced by a better one. Experience and the resulting insights never go beyond *conjecture*, that is to say, as soon as a hypothesis has been formed, it will be replaced by a better one. Thus there is absolute truth which can reach us only by the quality of differentness gained from the observation of the immanent world, but all the experiential knowledge we gain refers to absolute truth and participates with it in one way or another. Man has to renounce forever the hope of establishing an identity between the two, but the renunciation assures the right to relative knowledge and relative truth (Cassirer, 1927, p. 24). As we can never draw an ideal circle, we may approach it by a polygon. We may improve the polygon by breaking down the length of its sides and increasing their number and thus come closer to the ideal image without ever reaching it.

In order to reach God the mind must go through the perceptible world which is no longer a mere steppingstone, a place where man, pausing, proves whether or not he is worthy to ascend to God, but has become, besides, a place with values of its own, no less deriving from Heaven, but peculiar to itself. Leonardo, in his artistic work as well as in his scientific, was primarily an empiricist; one is inclined to say that he was addicted to sense data. This, I believe, is one of the reasons for his lag in theory formation, which historians have usually related to shortcomings in the contemporary state of science. That the era was deficient may be quite true, but the similarity with a corresponding lag in Goethe is striking. In Goethe too the prevalence and primacy of the world of sense data, at times almost to the exclusion of corresponding theoretical conclusions, is quite conspicuous. It seems that the person who is eminently endowed with artistic talents has a particular affinity to the perceptible and therefore is impeded in utilizing what may properly be abstracted from observation in order to form theories, but is inclined rather to develop theory as an embodied aspect of the concretely presented observational material. This can be said to be true also of Leonardo, although there are passages in his work that ascribe to mathematics its proper function and although in his epistemology he at times differentiated sharply between what is observed and the causes behind it. Thus he wrote:

> . . . although nature begins with the cause and ends with the experience, we must follow the opposite course, namely, . . . begin with the experience and by means of it investigate the cause [Richter, Vol. II, p. 239, No. 1148A; E 55 r.].

and:

> In nature there is no effect without cause; once the cause is understood there is no need to test it by experience [Richter, Vol. II, p. 239, No. 1148B; C.A. 147 v.].

This, as Cassirer (1927, p. 177) quite rightly states, is an impressive anticipation of principles that underlie modern science; yet, despite such astounding insights into the structure of mind and knowledge, Leonardo, I agree with Olschki in believing, regarded the perceptible world as primary. Cassirer himself notes that from Leonardo's literary work as a whole one may get the impression that Leonardo wavered between two basic principles, in that he sometimes made mathematics and sometimes empiricism (experience) the fundamental measure of certainty (Cassirer, 1927, p. 163). However, when Cassirer concludes that the dualism between the concrete and the abstract did not hold for Leonardo, but that experience and mathematics were both acknowledged and recognized in their mutual dependence, I am inclined to demur. If abstraction and observation had not coincided for Leonardo, he would constantly have been bound to feel defeated, since mathematics occupies an essentially subordinate place in his work[57] and empirical statements certainly constitute the bulk of his notes.[58] From occasional passages it appears that he felt that he was making good progress on the road toward truth by using his outstanding faculty for observation. According to Cassirer's view, he should correspondingly have felt despair over his lack of knowledge of the law or laws that underlay the wealth of observational data, but, despite the occasional aphorisms that imply a modern epistemology, Leonardo's inquisitiveness was satisfied in practice by the minutest observation. However, I do not believe that Leonardo's conflict lay in that area at all. He did not feel perturbed by the paucity, well-nigh absence, of laws in his scientific work, but felt secure and satisfied in making minutest observations of the world that surrounded him.[59] Conflict there was, but we have to turn to a different set of problems to find a discord he probably tried to calm by his efforts.

According to Nicholas of Cusa, as to the rest of the philosophers, there was after all a schism in the realm of existence, that is to say, in the totality of being. The difference between philosophical schools was not as to whether that schism existed or not, but rather as to the relation of man to the two realms of being, the nature of the schism and man's way of grappling with it. Whatever Nicholas said about sense data, experience, and mathematics, there was still absolute being which had no more and no less, which was immeasurable and could never be fully reached by the intellect, which was bound to operate in terms that could be subjected to the idea of a more or less. Nicholas's new idea was that the means of our logic are incommensurate with the task of attaining an understanding of a maximum that no longer permits

[57] According to Olschki (Vol. I, p. 386), Leonardo conceived of mathematics only as a concrete method of computation, thus limiting its use to practical application without conception of its function as a construct.

[58] Olschki has persuasively and ably presented this view. His demonstration of the primacy of the visual world, of the barrier to theory formation, in Leonardo is convincing (Vol. I, pp. 341f., 344). His characterization of Leonardo as a *forschender Magier und Mystiker* [a magician and mystic who does research] (p. 404) is apropos.

[59] This, of course, should not imply that Leonardo was devoid of imagery regarding the world behind his observations. Yet this area is dominated by fantasy and without insight into laws as conceived of by science. Cf. Clark: "Leonardo's mind passed without warning, and almost without consciousness, from fact to fantasy, from experience to imagination" (1952, p. 303).

of addition or subtraction, and that all our inquiries lead only to approximations toward the primordial image or archetype. These primordial images, being infinite, would be nullified by any finite more or less, whereas the images gained by perception and experience can be judged by the degree of closeness they achieve to the primordial image and therefore may properly be measured by a more or less. Nicholas thus postulates a basic separateness between absolute truth and experience, but this separateness is confronted by a mutual participation. The contingent and finite of experience only tends toward the unconditional. Experience obtains determinability only by its participation with or approximation toward that which cannot be determined. Recognition of the limitations of experience was, therefore, prerequisite and cornerstone of its applicability to immanent reality.

But here I also sense the root of Leonardo's conflict. We know his insatiable ambition. He was incapable of acceding to any limitations on his art, as witness his attempt at stamping out any idea that other arts could also make contributions that on their own terms could be equal in excellency with painting. Yet he called painting a science and considered it the greatest of all sciences, while praising now experience, now mathematics, as the conveyor of truth.

Cassirer devotes much thought to the relationship in Leonardo between what we call art and science, how they were identical to him and others.[60] In terms of the analysis of the structure of the historical process this may be correct, but if we try to trace the corresponding psychological process we find a different context. Leonardo rejoices over all the discoveries, all the truth, he obtains by experience, and still, once isolated from these notes, he fights tooth and nail for the supremacy of painting and the visual arts. I believe very strongly that, despite all of Leonardo's rejoicing about the triumph of empiricism, he still believed that painting was essentially superior to all other intellectual or artistic pursuits, because it was in his estimation the only way to pierce through that barrier which separated the immanent world from the transcendent. Painting, when it lived up to its highest standards or realized its full potential, should—so it seems to me he must have felt—depict the transcendent world that is immutable and perfect

[60] For an elaborate treatise on art and science with special reference to Leonardo, see Johnson (1949).

and is not amenable to a more or less and is beyond the relativity that is a quality of all the things we perceive by our senses and beyond all the empirical observations and hypotheses concerning them.

Thus, for Leonardo, the dichotomy of primordial image and reproductive image would still have had a significant bearing, and in Leonardo's psyche there would have been a cleavage between contents he considered immanent to reality and transcendent contents. As long as he moved within the immanent world, that is to say, as long as he was observing the physical world and the behavior of man as he is, Leonardo could proceed with great alacrity and exuberance and apparently without inhibition. There is the colossal mass of notes and the huge number of drawings, the bulk of which are devoted to studies of what he perceived in the world that surrounded him. Here no inhibitions are noticed. The drawings cannot, of course, be viewed as mere photographlike reproductions of experiential objects; the goal the artist pursued was the ideal presentation of things, whether this involved properties that are accessible to direct observation or knowledge he had gained about the structure of things such as their organicity, their inner dynamics, etc. In all this he remained within the immanent, and, intense apparently as was his striving toward perfection in representing this immanent world, he seems to have gone ahead without inner conflict. In all this his mind reaches out for properties or qualities that are, openly or hiddenly, still within the terrestrial cosmos that is in principle accessible to man.

Yet I strongly believe that when painting he aspired at making the transcendent world visible, that it was no longer a matter of perfectly realizing the immanent, which he did in his drawings, but of concretizing a totally different sphere of being, which, according to Nicholas of Cusa, by definition could not be made visible. It was possibly this self-imposed demand to make the transcendent visible, which he himself knew to be beyond the capacity of the senses as well as the intellect, that made him tremble when he set out to paint, that caused his constant dissatisfaction, procrastination, and declarations about this or that painting that it had not yet reached the degree of perfection he was aiming at. Thus my hypothesis is that Leonardo was in full agreement with Nicholas of Cusa's philosophy and simultaneously wished to break through the one barrier he found erected in it.

Yet when I discuss the many affinities between Leonardo and Nicholas of Cusa I do not mean that this makes any contribution to the question of whether Leonardo studied Nicholas's treatises or even was acquainted with them, though evidently he was. The relationship I have in mind, aside from the realistic, historical context, is one mainly of kinship within the frame of a history of thought. In Nicholas of Cusa's philosophy we find the embodiment of a conceptual frame of the universe that was also valid for Leonardo, not only as scientist, but also as artist. The various aspects of that philosophy had their bearing on a variety of artistic values; they eased the road toward visual clarification as well as re-creation of the terrestrial universe, but in turn also sowed the germ of conflicts. Nothing would be more erroneous than to treat Leonardo's work as if it were something like painted philosophy. But in Nicholas's writings we find explicitly much of what implicitly also resides in Leonardo's artistic creations.

The unquestionable kinship in terms of the history of thought does not preclude that Nicholas of Cusa's work, so far as it reached Leonardo, may directly have affected him and resulted in a father conflict of the kind referred to earlier, and, prompted by a very subjective motive, Leonardo may have been attempting to carry out a task which his, so to speak, teacher had declared impossible. In three dialogues Nicholas presents the unsophisticated, unerudite layman in an argument with the philosopher, who is defeated because he bases his doctrines on the writings of authors, whereas the layman observes life in the streets, in the market place, and is aware of his ignorance and therefore perhaps more knowledgeable than the philosopher. Cassirer (1927, p. 52) quite rightly points to the similarity of this passage to what Leonardo occasionally said about himself. But it may properly be asked whether Leonardo did not, in the last analysis, make in turn out of Nicholas of Cusa a philosopher, an erudite man, who, though he did not rely on written authority and introduced revolutionary views, still submitted to tradition in one point and denied man's capacity to penetrate into the transcendent. Or did Leonardo perhaps, notwithstanding his full respect for intellectual achievement, keep a reservation regarding what the creative artist is capable of achieving?[61] However much ingenuity, creativity, intuition, may go into scientific discoveries, there

[61] At another place I try to discuss in greater detail a metaphysical difference between science and art.

is one fundamental difference from art. The scientific discovery can be repeated, whereas no work of art can ever be repeated. If all our scientific discoveries were annihilated, it is extremely probable that later civilizations would reach a point when their knowledge of physics and chemistry and mathematics would include all that had been lost.[62] But the destruction of one work of art constitutes an irreplaceable loss. If one of Shakespeare's plays were lost, the chance of a later culture creating it would be nil.

There are indications that Leonardo was sensitive to this point. It is not directly set forth but strongly enough to be noticed. When he discusses the imitable sciences Leonardo says that painting is the noblest, for in mathematics the pupil can appropriate as much as the teacher proffers, whereas this is not true of painting (Ludwig, Vol. I, p. 11). Yet he goes even further and almost equates the painting with the Deity it depicts (ibid., p. 13), on the ground that the populace accords to paintings honors reserved to God. Though in general opposed to Church ritual and superstitions, Leonardo here accepts them with approbation to prove his point. He infers that the divine being gives preference to being adored in this form rather than in any other. And further: "The art of painting contains in itself all forms that exist in nature and such as do not exist there."[63] When Leonardo states that (a) the works of nature are of a higher order than those of man, (b) the distance between both is as large as that between man and God, and (c) the art of painting is above nature, as implied by inferences from the adoration of images, conclusions may be drawn regarding the value Leonardo attributed to the person who is capable of creating paintings and to the product itself.

It seems that Leonardo attributed to the artist the potentiality of a God. He can create whatever he feels a longing for: "If the painter wants to behold beautiful things that he will fall in love with, he is the master who can create those things, and if he wants to see monstrous things that terrify, or comical and laughable or even piteous, then he is lord and God over them [Se'l pittore vol vedere bellezze, che lo

---

[62] Here I cannot spell out the conclusions that I have implied in the above statement. In contrast to works of art in which each element is potentially psychologically relevant, scientific statements, inasmuch as they are correct, are more or less psychologically non-relevant. Rostand expressed a similar idea in the following: "Scientific errors . . . generally bear the individual stamp of their perpetrators" (1958, p. 12).

[63] ". . . la pittura . . . è contenitrice di tutte le forme, che sono, e di quelle, che non sono in natura" (Ludwig, Vol. I, pp. 62, 64).

*innamorino, egli n'è signore di generarle, et se vol vedere cose mos-
truose, che spaventino, o'che siene buffonesche e risibili, o'veramente
compassionevoli, ei n'è signore e Dio]"* (Ludwig, Vol. I, p. 18).

Yet what did Leonardo mean when he claimed that the art of painting contained also the forms that do not exist in nature? Other passages
could be cited that show the omnipotence ascribed to the painting artist,
not the least being that where Leonardo claims that paintings can be
created that will never perish.[64] The godly imagery surrounding the
artist follows an old tradition: the relationship God-world or God-man
was already in ancient times compared with that of the artist to his
creations.[65]

It is more difficult to discover what kind of value Leonardo attributed
to paintings or what value he tried to realize in his paintings. I disagree at this point with Cassirer, who has so brilliantly set forth the
philosophy of Nicholas of Cusa and Leonardo's kinship with him in
the history of thought. Yet Cassirer explicates the values inherent in
Leonardo's paintings in terms that, in my opinion, are valid only for
Leonardo's drawings but not for his paintings.

To the Renaissance, and foremost to Leonardo, nature had lost the
character of the formless that resists the principle of form which it
had seemed to have to man of the Middle Ages: nature now appeared
a domain perfectly formed throughout in which law and order reigned.
Leonardo's burning desire to know this order, to understand it, cannot
be questioned. It certainly was the prime motive of his research, and
one may observe the same motive in his drawings which are devoted
to the study of nature.

But his paintings, or, to be more careful, some of his paintings, go
far beyond this limit. There was, after all, that "countenance of all
countenances" (Cassirer, 1927, p. 34) of which Nicholas of Cusa
had written and which no man was capable of fathoming, which the
human eye could see only one aspect of, whereas it itself contained

[64] Cf. also Parte II, 133 (Ludwig, Vol. I, p. 181) where Leonardo states that drawing
should not be called a science but a deity [*una deità*]. It is remarkable that Leonardo overrules *prima-facie* evidence when he discusses the superiority of painting. Much as paintings
have been the objects of religious reverence, statues have been so even more frequently.
Also the claim that images are imperishable—Leonardo specifies how they may become so
—is an illusion necessitated by inner conflict.

[65] Cf. Panofsky (1924, p. 20) for the traditional comparison contained in the terms
deus artifex and *deus pictor*. What was in the Middle Ages nothing but a metaphor to
explicate a quality in God and by no means in the artist seems to have become for
Leonardo a literal truth related to the artist. Cf. also Kris (1952, pp. 79, 150).

all of them, the young and the old, the male and female, and probably also those of all animals. And this was true of all natural objects. Even complete knowledge of them, even insight into their structure, would only mean an approximation to those universal images that contain in one the totality of terrestrial declinations in which types and individual objects exist in nature.

Nicholas of Cusa's philosophy had removed the shackles from inquiry and we see Leonardo turn toward all phenomena of nature. There is no longer a restriction to those that contain the good or the beautiful. Since nature in all of its parts partakes of God, each part is worthy of study. Since the countenance must have contained ugly faces too, Leonardo also studies the human face in its ugliest specimens. Much acumen has been spent on the explanation of these so-called grotesques or caricatures. By hindsight one may even say that, if they had been lost, one should have been able to demonstrate that they once existed. In view of Leonardo's interest in the human body and the face as the most characteristic structure of the human species, he was bound to be attracted just by those extremes in which the filiation, that partaking in God, of all natural objects is most difficult to discover.[66] But most perplexing of all must have been the idea that the countenance of all countenances is to contain even these children of hell, and therefore to advance into the transcendent required just as imperatively that they be studied as the sublime. Leonardo was confronted here by a particularly difficult problem, since the presentation of a face as being simultaneously typically attractive and typically ugly is beyond human ingenuity.[67]

From the artistic point of view Leonardo encountered a more favorable situation when he confronted the dichotomy of sexes that would have to be synthesized into a "countenance of all countenances." His epicene types speak in favor of my thesis that in painting Leonardo tried to realize visually in one the transcendent which contains con-

[66] A psychological inquiry into these caricatures is one of the most challenging tasks. Perfunctory examination suggests that an attempt at demonstrating the bizarre or monstrous as a special manifestation of the laws that are valid also of other faces, that is to say, the monstrous in conformity with the species, was one of Leonardo's goals. Therefore I believe it is misleading to call these drawings caricatures at all. For the psychology of caricature, see Kris and Gombrich (1938).

[67] The drawing in which Leonardo disposed caricatures around a "normal" face (Plate 44; W. 12495 r.) is important since there they appear like variations of effects which Leonardo considered ugly and which were imprinted upon the human face by old age.

trasts. Thus Leonardo's numerous studies, the bulk of his drawings, were the bricks out of which there was to be constructed an edifice whose shape could not be conjectured from the shapes of the variety of bricks used. The difference between the frame into which these studies fitted and that into which some of the paintings did seems essential. One cannot rightly see in those studies prestages of what would be synthesized into the paintings. The drawings aim at a full understanding of the properties of things. The immanent world of things had to be perfectly known and its depiction integrated to such an extent that it could be carried out almost as a matter of routine without the slightest inner or outer difficulty, much as we can handle pen and ink when writing. Since all this was eventually to be used for the presentation of the transcendent, there could be no limit to the study of the immanent world. Therefore Leonardo had in his anatomical research to go far beyond the understanding of surface structures. In the depiction of the transcendent *every* part of an object and every form in which it may appear in nature is to be synthesized; hence Leonardo could not feel satisfied with such partial knowledge as would have sufficed for the ordinary depiction of things and bodies as they meet the eye. This was the principal goal of most Renaissance artists, but I think that Leonardo aimed at something far higher. Man may have the faculty of achieving this goal in the form of a symbol or an allegory. Romanesque art achieved it through the meaning of pure lines. Lines were used independently of what they might convey in terms of representing real objects. They acquired an eminently expressive value by being stripped of meaning that was referable to terrestrial objects (Panofsky, 1924-25, p. 274). But Leonardo—and this I believe makes him so different from all other artists—was not ready to make a compromise on this score. He insisted that the transcendent should be represented through the images of things as they exist in nature. Even in his last painting, the *St. John* (Plate 24), where the transcendent is set forth most forcibly among all his paintings, the consideration of the natural appearance of the human face is not weakened at all. Quite to the contrary, Leonardo successfully used immanent qualities of the appearance of things in order to reveal a transcendent truth by means that went beyond exaggeration, rearrangement, or patterns of emphasis, and possibly defy specification.

If we compare Leonardo's first painting, the angel's head in the

Baptism of Christ by Verrocchio (Plate 45), with the portrait of Ginevra de Benci (Plate 46), in which the style of painting that would later make him famous appears for the first time, then we may get a glimpse of what possibly happened during these enigmatic four years in which Leonardo was artistically inactive (cf. Clark, 1939, p. 16). The angel's head superbly fulfills the goal of representing immanent qualities, but in the portrait the first flickering of the grasp for the transcendent may be observed. What separated the two phases in time was possibly a process that amounted to a reorganization of the youthful artist's personality and the appearance of a new conceptual frame of artistry in the service of which he spent the rest of his life.[68] From a remark of von Bode's about the Louvre *Annunciation* I take it that the early paintings may have been produced with speed (1921, p. 18). If it could be shown that Leonardo's habit of painting slowly with the procrastination and doubt that it implies started after the four quiet years, this would increase the probability of my thesis since the intention of reaching out for the transcendent in its pure veracity must necessarily have had the effect of a colossal slowing down.

To prove my thesis it would be necessary to analyze most carefully the paintings in which this new frame of reference appears. This would be beyond my ability as well as outside the scope of this study. Only this may be said: in the *Mona Lisa* (Plate 1) and in the *St. John* (Plate 24) Leonardo came closest to painting a "countenance of all countenances." The former became the most famous portrait of a woman; the latter has been little esteemed by most critics. One reason for this coldness toward the *St. John* may be that in it Leonardo really came as close to the realization of his goal as is humanly possible. If a genius were actually capable of realizing visually that which Leonardo aimed at, his achievement would be bound to go unnoticed because the ordinary human mind would not be capable of grasping it.

Be this as it may, some of Leonardo's paintings have a degree of finality which must have discouraged many an artist from taking up the same subject. Leonardo's *Cenacolo* and the *Battle of Anghiari* (Plate 47) leave a feeling that it is superfluous to look at any other paintings on these themes. Prud'hon is said to have called the former

---

[68] This proposition, in my opinion, does not contradict my earlier suggestion that a loss of structure occurred during the quadrennium. A reorganization may be made possible by a melting down of ego structure.

the "masterwork of painting per se." Leonardo's superhuman effort to depict the transcendent through the immanent, that is, the fact that his paintings have their being in two contradictory spheres, may explain why they are more enigmatic than those of others. Clark called Leonardo, quite aptly, the Hamlet of art history (1929, p. 122; 1939, p. 179). This, too, may be why they affect me at least as being so close and at the same time so distant. There is incredible warmth in them and, strangely, also a frightening icy coldness that often makes it hard to come close to them. It is essentially different with his drawings, most of which are immediately and lastingly captivating.

If Leonardo's paintings are compared with Michelangelo's works, an essential point of the former's art comes to the fore. Almost all of Michelangelo's creations take possession of the beholder on sight. He is irresistibly drawn into the conflicting emotions that are so powerfully expressed in his creations. This lightninglike effect seems to me to be missing from Leonardo's paintings, which rather inspire awe than enrapture and require long contemplation before their perfection is grasped. A feature of Michelangelo's work will easily account for this difference. To put it into the simplest form, Michelangelo consulted his own emotions in creating his masterpieces. His emotions had free access to what he was forming and the strong effect on the beholder is a reflection of his own titanic emotional conflicts which found their way into the work of art. How strongly his art was subjectively directed can be seen from Benedetto Varchi's lecture in the Academy of Florence in 1546 on two of Michelangelo's poems. There, in a discourse that Michelangelo approved, it was said that art is nothing but the "inward image of the object to be depicted, an image which is in the soul, that is, in the artist's imagination" (de Tolnay, 1943-54, Vol. I, p. 117f.). How far Michelangelo's subjectivity went can be learned from his Victory statue, now in the Palazzo della Signoria at Florence (Plate 48) but originally destined for the tomb of Pope Julius II. "The vanquished old man," writes de Tolnay (Vol. IV, p. 59), "would be an idealized portrait of Michelangelo subjugated and enchained by love for the perfect youth kneeling on his back—the idealized image of Cavalieri." Such a state of affairs is unthinkable in Leonardo's painted work. We found this range of problems in one of his allegories, but he would never have permitted himself to let this source of inspiration enter openly the official, final version of his artistic intent. I do not mean to say that this range of problems did not enter his painted *œuvre,* but it entered it in quite a different way than in Michelangelo's case.

I cited earlier from his *Trattato* a passage whose psychological meaning clearly declares his repugnance at the idea that the artist may freely let the subjective factor enter into a painting. The momentum of his effort was fully directed toward the outer world, isolated from his own personal conflicts. His ideal of the genius painter, it seems to me, was the representation of the terrestrial world in such a way that we behold through and across it the ideal and immutable images of the transcendent world.[69]

In Michelangelo we must see the genius who, despite all his devotion to the study of objects, represents them after a profound amalgamation with his emotions. The "cosmic forces of life," "the preterhuman sphere where primordial life forces are revealed" (de Tolnay, Vol. I, pp. 64, 115), which he represented in his sculptures, are the direct projections of the conflicting feelings, emotions, passions, and impulses that raged in him and to which he lent an attentive and sensitive ear. In Leonardo's work, as has been said, the conflicts show up too, but the actual process that led to his creations was of a different kind. His paintings, in my opinion, compel the supposition of a heroic struggle not to let his passions enter them. The momentum of his creativity goes toward the visible and recognizable world and through it to a transcendent world of generally valid, all-comprehensive images. Lomazzo's report, that in order to paint the image of laughing peasants he gathered a number of peasants and entertained them until they broke out into vehement laughter, impresses me as permitting the conclusion that he would not have felt entitled or, perhaps, even able, to depict his own laughter. Of course, it would be foolish to deny that in the end product of his labor the subjective, personal factor was present. But the preconscious intent was apparently to eliminate it and to devote himself wholly to the service of what is eternally true in the abstract world of ideas.[70] This constitutes possibly the greatest sacrifice

[69] Cf. Hildebrandt (1927): "That which is incomparable in his [Leonardo's] achievement resides in that he knew how to transport thoughts of the most transcendental content into the full tangibleness of spatial-corporeal reality" (p. 33).

[70] Cf. Pater (1873): "To others he seems to be aiming at an impossible effect, to do something that art, that painting, can never do" (p. 113), and particularly: "His [Leonardo's] problem was the transmutation of ideas into images" (p. 112).

of which an artistically creative genius is capable; that it proved worth making may be judged from the fact that he succeeded as far as man can succeed.

A great debt is owed to Berenson for not having hesitated in publishing his adverse criticism of Leonardo's paintings (1916). His frankness has not always been appreciated (see, for example, von Bode 1921, p. 146), but disregarding the detailed points of his opinion one may say that he expressed a reaction that is not only characteristic of him but brings forth an aspect of Leonardo's painted *œuvre*. I find it very significant that his strongest criticism extends to the *Cenacolo* (pp. 2, 15, 29), the *Mona Lisa* (pp. 2f., 11), and the *St. John* (pp. 5, 14), and that he can make his peace with the *Adoration* (p. 7) and *La Belle Ferronnière* (p. 6) (which, by the way, probably was not painted by Leonardo).[71] From my viewpoint I would say that Berenson feels repelled by those paintings in which Leonardo comes the closest to the transcendent, and he feels attracted where the immanent prevails. Indeed, the beholder who is not drawn across the threshold of the immanent world into the realm of the immutable gets stuck, so to speak, in what the painting says literally; he sees only the obviously apprehensible physical aspect and the *Cenacolo* must then become a kind of aggregate of histrionic gesturing (Berenson, 1916, p. 2). With that attitude it becomes a "composition consisting entirely of figures ending at the waist line, of torsos with heads and arms but no abdomen and no legs" (ibid., p. 29). But in his effort to demonstrate Leonardo's inferiority as a painter, the critic makes a remark that may prove the excellency of Leonardo's work, and, oddly enough, contributes greatly to a validation of my theory.

In writing about the *Mona Lisa*, Berenson (p. 11) speaks of the portrait's overmeanings, of which there are "not only as many as there are spectators, but more still, for it will appeal differently to the same spectator at different periods of his life and in different moods." Here Berenson, though with pejorative intent, attributes to the *Mona Lisa* qualities that in certain respects surprisingly coincide with what Nicholas of Cusa had said of "the countenance of all countenances." Consequently it appears that Leonardo's art was, after all, of such excellence that the majority of beholders have reacted to it in accord-

---

[71] See for a discussion of authorship of the portrait, Clark (1939, p. 50). Berenson (1916, p. 6) believes Boltraffio to have painted it.

ance with the universal validity that it contained. That the representation of the universally valid was achieved without his having to step outside of nature but with full insistence upon representing the universal in shapes that appear in nature; that this representation was achieved without estrangement from nature; that the natural appearance of beings and objects was preserved in the process of universal validation—this, I believe, is quite unique in the history of art, makes Leonardo different from his peers, and reserves for him the special niche into which the expert as well as the naïve beholder has put him for over four and a half centuries.

Since, probably, every work of art aims at or contains something of transcendency, it may be worth while to specify the Leonardesque transcendency even at the risk of being repetitive. Here it is not a matter of making visible that which exists but is not accessible to human sight, such as the averted side of the moon or events that will take place in the future but are inaccessible in the present, such as the Last Judgment or a religious mood that impresses us as heavenly, as some of Fra Angelico's paintings proffer, or Michelangelo's transcendency inasmuch as he conveys inner processes of man, or the transcendency of the unconscious as presented in most of Goya's portraits, or the casting back of a godship within the terrestrial world in which Rembrandt's work is drenched—it is something far more sober and rational that is essentially divorced from the orectic sphere on the one hand and the actual appearance of objects on the other but is aimed at the visualization of the universally valid which includes in one representation of an object the full range of all possible modes that are or may be encountered within the orbit of reality. One hesitates to use here the concept of "idea," since any intimation that Leonardo was a painter of ideas would do grave injustice to the artistic values of his painted œuvre. The beholder is not made to feel any abstract principle and an artistic value is never sacrificed for the sake of an intellectual system; still, behind the forms and objects that appear on the canvas one notices the operation of a relational pattern that I have tried to characterize by certain implications of the new philosophy that had started with Nicholas of Cusa.

After having attempted to reconstruct preconscious and conscious motives that may have had their bearing on Leonardo's internal conflicts when he painted, it may be easier to make a final sensible proposition regarding repressed motives. Freud characterized one aspect of Leonardo's relationship to his father as an urge "to out-Herod Herod" (1910, p. 121). Biographical legend reflects this attitude, as in Vasari's report (p. 7) that Verrocchio, "chagrined that a child should know more than he," gave up painting when he saw Leonardo's superiority.[72] The historical record disproves Vasari's report, but Leonardo's ambition to create the greatest equestrian statue was understood as a successful though ephemeral attempt to outdo his former teacher.[73] Thus it would not be surprising if Leonardo also tried to outdo Nicholas of Cusa and prove to his satisfaction that the impenetrable world of *ideas* can be painted. Yet the concept of the "impossible" has as an unconscious equivalent, the "forbidden." Therefore it may be surmised that Leonardo, by his persistent effort to concretize and to behold that which it was asserted was impossible to concretize and to behold, desired to behold that which it was most forbidden to behold. From the observation of children in Western culture it is known that the strongest taboo extends to observing the genitalia of the parents, particularly of the mother, and to witnessing parental intercourse. No wonder, then, that Leonardo trembled when he set out to create a painting. Yet the impulse of "out-Heroding Herod" that Freud bared in Leonardo, suggests a still more general formulation.

Leonardo's quasi addiction to investigation presupposes the presence of inordinate curiosity. Only an insatiable feeling of curiosity can provide the fuel for a lifelong, equally insatiable investigatory impulse. And here we should recall Freud's statement in his letter of May 27, 1937, to Marie Bonaparte that

---

[72] Cf. Kris and Kurz (1934, pp. 41, 126) for this typical motif in the biography of artists.

[73] Even if Valentiner's (1930) hypothesis of an extremely rich and mutually fertilizing teacher-pupil relationship is accepted, this would not disprove the existence of profound ambivalence as indirectly suggested by the biographical legend. Other and more direct evidences of ambivalence toward male authority are found in Vasari's biography. When Leonardo studied mathematics "he made such progress that he frequently confounded his master by continually raising doubts and difficulties" (Vasari, p. 5). Also, the afore-mentioned episode of succeeding in frightening his father by means of the painted Medusa head deserves attention here. Although violent outbreaks of rage, so characteristic of Michelangelo (Sterba and Sterba, 1956), are not known from Leonardo's dealings with authority and he apparently succeeded by and large in getting along with his noble employers, a longitudinal section of his biography nevertheless shows his ambivalence in the form of easy and rapid changes of loyalty and allegiance. However much such ambivalence may have corresponded to the "spirit of the time," one is justified in seeking also an individual basis for it.

One may regard . . . curiosity, the impulse to investigate, as a complete sublimation of the aggressive or destructive instinct [Jones, Vol. III, p. 464].

Was this sublimation in Leonardo psychologically as complete as we might expect in view of his achievements? Or did his sublimations still preserve some undertones of "the aggressive or destructive instinct" from which it stemmed? If the latter, we may understand why he felt inhibited in publishing the results of his research. Further, may we presuppose an equivalent destructive implication in Leonardo's painting? After all, the painter arrogates a sector of reality for himself and reproduces it on the canvas.

When Leonardo did research or drew, the result of his labor remained with him. He had control over who would know of it and what. Yet a painting became part of the public domain and if, despite extensive and intensive sublimation, the aggressive-destructive admixtures came to be rejected by the self, the very fact of notoriety might easily have become a source of distress. The factors of hesitation, procrastination, and perfectionism may then be understood as the consequences of these admixtures, inasmuch as the self might have stood under the impact of an alarm that the secret hostility was, after all, not sufficiently eliminated from the product and therefore might be noticeable.

16

Remarks on Leonardo's Profetie *and Their Relation to Oral Sadism*

A puzzling category among Leonardo's notes is the so-called *Profetie*. Riddles in form, most of them consist of prophecies of the coming of things which are to be guessed; commonly, the direly oracular tone is in contrast with the often trivial character of the answers.[1] Vallentin (p. 179) claims that many of these *Profetie* were taken from popular sayings and contemporary writings, but she and others (MacCurdy, 1928, pp. 223-225) cite them as manifestations of Leonardo's own beliefs and opinions. Their hostility to society and the Church is usually stressed (see also Freud, 1910, p. 124).

I bring up this part of Leonardo's notes rather for a different reason. The *Profetie* are a psychological treasure trove. They contain a wealth of symbols, and scrutiny of them by a skilled inquirer may reveal some of Leonardo's most deeply repressed secrets. Precisely because the answers were so often trivial, the repressed could be projected without fear. One of them, for example, reads: "Many there will be who will flay their own mother and fold back her skin." The answer is: "The tillers of the ground" (MacCurdy, 1956, p. 1115; I 64 r.).

[1] For a discussion of why Leonardo cast these riddles in the form of "prophecies" about ostensibly future events, see Olschki (Vol. I, p. 403).

For the analyst such symbolism is not a surprise, but rather a confirmation of many an observation Freud and his co-workers had made in normal and pathological imagery. (See Freud [1926, p. 17] for an example similar to the one quoted.) Now an artist of Leonardo's scope must, of course, have had access to all layers of symbolism, and the fact that he was capable of manipulating symbolism profusely and effectively, though for a seemingly trivial purpose, is not surprising. At the same time, the realm of symbols is well-nigh infinite and we may, as I said before, learn something specific about Leonardo from the particular choices he made.

The following sample, though it does not depend on symbolism, may serve the purpose of demonstration:

> It shall seem to men that they see new destructions in the sky, and the flames descending therefrom shall seem to have taken flight and to flee away in terror; they shall hear creatures of every kind speaking human language; they shall run in a moment, in person, to divers parts of the world without movement; amidst the darkness they shall see the most radiant splendours. O marvel of mankind! What frenzy has thus impelled you? You shall hold converse with animals of every species, and they with you in human language. You shall behold yourselves falling from great heights without suffering any injury; the torrents will bear you with them as they mingle in their rapid course [MacCurdy, 1956, p. 1099f.; C.A. 145 r. a].

The answer to this prophecy is: *Of dreaming*. Since the same prophecy appears in a harmless guise: "Men shall walk without moving, they shall speak with those who are absent, they shall hear those who do not speak" (MacCurdy, 1956, p. 1106; C.A. 370 r. a), one may feel particularly certain of the personal implication in the more extensive version. Here we may learn what kind of dreams Leonardo himself occasionally had. We may note in passing that the dream of falling was not alien to him, which possibly confirms Freud's interpretation of Leonardo's ambition to invent a flying machine (1910, p. 125),[2] but

---

[2] Freud refers here to the typical dream of flying (see also Freud, 1900, p. 394), and Leonardo's reference to the dream of falling without harming oneself falls into that category. However, Leonardo writes expressly "you will see yourself," which may indicate that he did not have the sensation either of flying or falling. Paul Federn (1914, p. 128) reports the adolescent dream of "a very gifted patient of precocious intellectual maturity" that he flew down from a balcony inadequately attired while his family watched him. As a child the patient had feared his "birdie" might have flown away.

more important seems to be that some of the dreams appear to have had the character of end-of-the-world imagery. At least, the dream elements he catalogues convey a weird, uncanny impression, despite the reference to the "most radiant splendours" at one point. Indeed, although the series of *Profetie* cannot be reduced to a common denominator, still one can say that the horrible and lugubrious and terrifying prevail. If one reads the *Profetie* forgetting what they ostensibly stand for and disregarding the more or less trivial solutions, one gets a sickening impression of the world and its future.

The *Profetie* were really ideally suited for Leonardo's ego defect. Here he could set forth the most horrible and the most frightening, arousing in the listener a maximal tension, and immediately thereafter he could allay this tension by unmasking the enigma as something at least ostensibly trivial and innocuous.

Two functions may be conjectured. (1) The interlocutor of the *Profetie*, well protected by his superior knowledge, may safely identify with the listener and share the traumalike tension the prediction of the horrible arouses and then go on to share in the reduction of tension when it has been shown to be unnecessary, thus instituting mechanisms Freud has postulated in his book on *Jokes* (1905b).[3] (2) The inventor of the *Profetie* may go through a list of all the horrible and terrifying subjects and, by putting them into a trivial everyday frame of reference, dismiss them as trivialities, as if to convince himself that if such sickening things happened as the *Profetie* seemed to predict, one might take refuge in the idea that there are equivalent or even identical events that are quite unhorrible. The identity, however, is established by a play upon the multiple meanings of words or sentences.[4] Inasmuch as the verbal equation between the horrible and the trivial seems to have had a soothing or reassuring effect, one can say that Leonardo in this instance acted like a psychological nominalist or verbal realist, if such terms are permissible. Reliance on the play on words or meanings is quite surprising in a man who was so seriously engaged in the study of the objective aspect of the world. Still, the playfulness of the procedure should not mislead us into overlooking

[3] One may consider that Leonardo probably told the same prophecy repeatedly and thus trained himself to verbalize and think of the horrible without fright.
[4] For an equivalent use of words in schizophrenic speech, see Freud (1915, pp. 197-201).

the psychological seriousness involved.[5] If it were known whether the writing of the *Profetie* occurred in a particular phase or on particular occasions or was a general habit, it would be easier to speculate about their function. As it is, one can only infer some conflicts from their contents.

What were some of those terrifying contents that were projected into the trivial? There is a general aggressive-sadistic coloring which has been noticed already in the riddle of the tillers of the ground. The following is another sample:

> And many others will be robbed of their store of provisions and their food, and by an insensate folk will be cruelly immersed and drowned. O justice of God! why dost thou not awake to behold thy creatures thus abused? [Answer:] *Of Bees* [MacCurdy, 1956, p. 1100; C.A. 145 r. a].

There are some one hundred and sixty *Profetie* recorded in Mac-Curdy's edition of the *Notebooks* (pp. 1098-1121). About one hundred and twenty have sadistic, cruel, destructive, terrifying implications; about fifty refer directly to death or destruction of life; about seventeen are neutral or carry friendly implications; eighteen can be classified as criticizing the Church or her institutions; twenty are of oral-sadistic or cannibalistic character.

Again the *Profetie* may be likened to a record of free associations. The inventor has free choice in selecting both the topic he wishes to refer to in the riddle and also the type of symbol by which he will represent it. Such associations that are not enforced by reality factors undoubtedly contain unconscious factors. The study of the *Profetie* shows that Leonardo was living in a universe of terror and fright. Here we find a mass of illustrations of what I have set forth earlier as a hypothesis: that Leonardo was more or less constantly on the verge of suffering trauma. In view of the *Profetie* one can be more specific and say that he feared lest he be traumatized by the hostility of nature or his human environment. I postulated earlier that even small oscillations of tension or excitement were experienced by him as unendurable. Here we may add that exposure to the displeasure of tension was

[5] I put more weight on the psychological meaning of the *Profetie* than on their critical implications regarding the Church. Sir Kenneth Clark says that the Church in Leonardo's time did not prosecute opinions that were even far more dangerous and subversive than Leonardo's (1939, p. 163). To be sure, Leonardo was opposed to the clergy, rituals, and ceremonies, but if Sir Kenneth Clark's opinion is correct, this would render the *Profetie* an even more important source of psychological insight.

probably experienced by him as having been caused by hostile imposi-
tions from without. Therefrom stems the earlier cited aphorism in which
the power of feeling is equated with martyrdom (MacCurdy, 1956,
p. 67; Tr. 35 a). As a matter of fact, for a while Leonardo planned a
painting of St. Sebastian (Suida, 1929, pp. 82-85), who may serve
as a symbol of the very state I am describing here.

I would like to convey the gloomy spirit that pervades Leonardo's
Profetie, but there is no way of doing so other than by reproducing
them. Instead, I will take up one element which is very conspicuous
and contributes greatly to the over-all weirdness, that is, the oral-
sadistic, cannibalistic element. Leonardo must have had an inner
struggle with cannibalistic impulses. I have only to remind the reader
of his vegetarianism and the passage quoted earlier (on page 60)
where man is called a tomb of other animals. I wish to add here the
rest of what is relevant in the passage because it sets forth cannibalistic
imagery and the corresponding conflict in their entire magnitude.

But we do not go outside human matters in telling of one supreme wicked-
ness, which does not happen among the animals of the earth, inasmuch
as among them are found none who eat their own kind, unless through
want of sense (as there are fools among them as among men, although
they are not in so great number); and this happens only among the
rapacious animals, as with the leonine species, and leopards, panthers,
lynxes, cats, and the like, who sometimes eat their children; but thou,
besides thy children, devourest father, mother, brothers, and friends; nor
is this enough for thee, but thou goest to the chase on the islands of others,
taking other men and mutilating their membrum virile and testicles thou
fattenest, and chasest them down thy own throat; now does not nature
produce enough simple (vegetarian food) for thee to satisfy thyself?
and if thou art not content with such, canst thou not by the mixture of
them make infinite compounds, as Platina[6] wrote, and other authors on
feeding?

.   .   .   .

If you meet with any one who is virtuous, do not drive him from you;
do him honour, so that he may not have to flee from you and betake himself to hermitages, or caves, or other solitary places to escape from your
treachery; if there is such a one among you do him honour, for these are
our saints upon earth; these are they who deserve statues from us, images
and honours; but remember that their images are not to be eaten by you,

[6] Bartolommeo Sacchi Platina (1421-1481), humanist, author of *De arte coquinaria,* which
was published in Italian under the title *De la honesta voluptate, e valetudine,* Venice, 1487.

as is done in some parts of India, where, when the images have according to them performed some miracle, the priests cut them in pieces, being of wood, and give them to all the people of the country, not without payment; and each one grates his portion very fine, and puts it upon the first food he eats; and thus believes that by faith he has eaten his saint who then preserves him from all perils. What do you think here, man, of your own species? Are you so wise as you believe yourselves to be? Are these things to be done by men? [Richter, Vol. II, pp. 104, 341f., Nos. 844 and 1358; Q. II, 14 r.].

All the elements of cannibalism in its most primitive and horrid form are here united: the devouring of live flesh, of the parents, of the male genital, of the saints, as if Leonardo preconsciously knew about primitive prestates of morality (Freud, 1913a).

At this point I wish to catch up with a point I had to leave aside earlier. When we learn that the foregoing passage is on a folio of Leonardo's anatomical writings, more specifically on a page on which the anatomy of the heart is presented, we may draw the conclusion that Leonardo had at times to fight off a cannibalistic impulse while performing his researches into anatomy. One has to think of the situation realistically. He was locked up for hours with cadavers which in many instances were mutilated; he had to take them apart and cut them up into little pieces. All this, since the procedure had not yet become a routine, apparently led at times to the stimulation of orality, and, more precisely, of the sadistic component of orality, namely, the use of teeth and oral musculature—and this when the scientist was enaged in work where he had to proceed on the narrow pathway of exactness. The cannibalistic impulse is not given vent to, but appears only in the form of an accusation against others, a technique we shall observe once more later.[7] That he withstood this conflict and maintained the minimum detachment necessary for an empirical inquiry without developing panic or a spell of aggression, this also makes me think of him as a hero.

In the huge mass of Leonardo's notes one finds several attempts such as the following at warding off oral-sadistic impulses:

Some there are who are nothing else than a passage for food and augmentors of excrement and fillers of privies, because through them no other

[7] It is worth while deliberating whether it was specifically the conflict about cannibalism that caused the inhibition in Leonardo's contemporaries against going ahead with anatomical studies.

things in the world, nor any good effects, are produced, since nothing but full privies results from them [Richter, Vol. II, p. 245, No. 1179; Forster III 74 v.].

Here the full contempt of the man who is orally fixated is expressed; it serves to deny equivalent wishes in himself.

In the following passage Leonardo goes a step further and disbars oral man even from membership in the species.

It seems to me that men of coarse and clumsy habits and of small knowledge do not deserve such fine instruments or so great a variety of natural mechanism as men of speculation and of great knowledge; but merely a sack in which their food may be stowed and whence it may issue, since they cannot be judged to be anything else than vehicles for food; for it seems to me they have nothing about them of the human species but the voice and the figure, and for all the rest are much below beasts [Richter, Vol. II, p. 245, No. 1178; W. 19038 v.].

Now Leonardo was not only aware that he was a man "of speculation and of great knowledge" but was famous for being so, and here he removes himself from any likeness with the man who is nothing but "a vehicle for food."

The intensity of oral sadism and even cannibalistic impulses led to Leonardo's deep estrangement from his own orality. His assertion:

We make our life by the death of others.
In dead matter there remains insensate life, which, on being united to the stomachs of living things, resumes a life of the senses and the intellect [MacCurdy, 1956, p. 202f.; H 89 v.]

indicates that in the act of eating he was aware of and concerned with the deadness of the substances he ingested, which, one has to suspect, must have created an acute aversion against food, at least in the form of flesh.

The equation of eating and mental activity can be seen from the following:

Just as eating contrary to the inclination is injurious to the health, so study without desire spoils the memory, and it retains nothing that it takes in [MacCurdy, 1956, p. 72; Ash. I 34 r.].

Accordingly it will be less surprising that the oral-sadistic, cannibalistic factor shows up forcefully in the *Profetie*. A few examples follow:

> Endless generations will perish through the death of the pregnant. [Answer:] *Of Fishes Which Are Eaten with Their Roes* [MacCurdy, 1956, p. 1109; C.A. 370 r. a].

> A large part of the bodies which have had life will pass into the bodies of other animals, that is the houses no longer inhabited will pass piece-meal through those which are inhabited, ministering to their needs and bearing away with them what is waste; that is to say that the life of man is made by the things which he eats, and these carry with them that part of man which is dead [Answer:] *Of Food Which Has Been Alive* [MacCurdy, 1956, p. 1099; C.A. 145 r. a].

> In you, O cities of Africa! your own sons shall be seen torn to pieces within their own houses by most cruel and savage animals of your country [Answer:] *Of Cats That Eat Rats* [MacCurdy, 1956, p. 1101; ibid.].

> The masters of the estates will eat their own labourers. [Answer:] *Of Oxen Which Are Eaten* [MacCurdy, 1956, p. 1108; C.A. 370 r. a].

> Men shall come forth out of the graves changed to winged creatures, and they shall attack other men, taking away their food even from their hands and tables. [Answer:] *The Flies* [MacCurdy, 1956, p. 1115; I 64 r.].

> In all the cities and lands and castles, villages and houses, men will be seen who through desire of eating will draw the very food out of each other's mouths, without their being able to make any resistance. [Answer:] *Of Placing Bread Within the Mouth of the Oven and Drawing It Out Again* [MacCurdy, 1956, p. 1102; C.A. 370 r. a].

> Those who nourish them will be slain by them and scourged by barbarous death. [Answer:] *Of Things Which Are Eaten Which Are First Put to Death* [MacCurdy, 1956, p. 1108; ibid.].

> Many Franciscans, Dominicans, and Benedictines will eat that which has recently been eaten by others, and they will remain many months before being able to speak [Answer:] *Of Children Who Take the Breast* [MacCurdy, 1956, p. 1118; I 67 r.].

No doubt the oral-sadistic, cannibalistic impulse was strong enough to give these *Profetie* a specific coloring. There is, however, one that deserves our particular interest. It is remarkable for it is not one of those riddles that turn out to be trivial in the end but it sets forth the most tragic problem from which mankind is suffering. It refers to the Cruelty of Man:

Animals will be seen on the earth who will always be fighting against each other with the greatest loss and frequent deaths on each side. And there will be no end to their malice; by their strong limbs we shall see a great portion of the trees of the vast forests laid low throughout the universe; and when they are filled with food, the satisfaction of their desires will be to deal death and grief and labour and fears and flight to every living thing; and from their immoderate pride they will desire to rise towards heaven, but the excessive weight of their limbs will keep them down. Nothing will remain on earth, or under the earth, or in the waters, which will not be persecuted, disturbed, and spoiled, and those of one country removed into another. And their bodies will become the tomb and means of transit of all the living bodies they have killed.

O Earth, why dost thou not open and engulf them in the fissures of thy vast abysses and caverns, and no longer display in the sight of heaven so cruel and horrible a monster? [Richter, Vol. II, p. 302, No. 1296; C.A. 370 v.].

Man's record, indeed, is not commendable, is, no doubt, appalling; there is no end to the crimes he has committed, miscarriages of justice abound and cruellest exploitations, his lack of any kindly feelings and his lust to torture, to lie, to falsify, are not exceptional; indeed, there is no infamy or misdeed fantasy could contrive that has not an actual precedent in his history. But still, Leonardo's reaction, the wish he utters at the end, appears exaggerated and unjust. Not all, after all, have participated in those misdeeds, and man's history also shows deeds of kindness, love, and sacrifice. It is also striking that, immediately prior to his expression of surprise that Earth does not make an end to mankind—that is to say, at the point where evidently he means to set forth the worst crime—Leonardo again refers to the fact that man ingests the bodies of other organisms. This appeal is all the more illogical since it is Earth herself, so to speak, that forces man to keep alive in this way. Furthermore, Leonardo has no sooner accused man of devouring living bodies he has slain than he prays that Earth should "open and hurl" man into the fissures of her abysses, an imagery that suggests that Earth in turn should devour man: man devours all living creatures and therefore Earth should devour man. Thus the whole world of man, the totality of historical and biological processes, is viewed as a chain of identical actions of wanton oral destruction ending at last in justice meted out by mankind's being finally swallowed up; that is to say, man and his moral values are comprehensively experienced in terms of oral sadism. This imagery is no longer the figurative speech of the pessimistic philosopher: it is to be regarded as the direct derivative of Leonardo's own cannibalistic impulses and the defenses against them. Here Leonardo in an almost undisguised fashion reveals mankind's most archaic impulse, which must have been quite alive in himself—as he probably was painfully aware at times—and which had also penetrated into the higher systems of his personality, his morals and ethics. How much he meant himself in this gruesome prophecy can be seen from his reference to the "immoderate pride that makes man desire to rise toward heaven," an enterprise which he spent his best years in trying to accomplish by his vain efforts to devise a flying machine. Here he reveals too a motive that was driving him relentlessly toward that goal.

Yet his vegetarianism stood him in good stead. It permitted redemption of guilt by sacrifice and the sustenance of a potent defense, which may have sounded approximately as follows: "I, the vegetarian, am free of guilt of cannibalism; the rest of mankind is guilty and therefore should suffer a common fate." However, in the prophecy, instead of an exemption, immediate annihilation is requested, so that he indirectly makes himself a defendant. Consequently, Leonardo's personal world must have had a strongly cannibalistic flavor and one of his fears must have been that of being devoured.

At this point we will also recall Leonardo's early childhood recollection, in which orality plays a substantial role. The suggestion seems warranted that it also contains a denial of oral-sadistic impulses as if to say: "It was not I who wanted to devour, but a power stronger than I forced itself cruelly into my mouth." There may also be included here the seed of a justification of the cannibalistic impulse, inasmuch as it may say: "Since I have been injured and mistreated orally, I am entitled to a revenge."[8]

---

[8] For a broad psychoanalytic discussion of orality and cannibalism and defenses against them, see Lewin (1950).

17

The Deluge

In the last-cited prophecy Leonardo sets forth apocalyptic ideas, imagery about the end of the world that preoccupied his mind. There are various notes in his writings on the end of the world, on the deluge, and many drawings were devoted to this subject. In his *Treatise on Painting* and at other places he gave advice on how to depict a deluge. He also devoted much acumen to proving that the Biblical Flood could not have taken place (MacCurdy, 1956, p. 316) and he himself envisaged the end of the world by a process of desiccation:

> All the animals will perish, failing to find fresh grass for fodder; and the ravening lions and wolves and other beasts which live by prey will lack sustenance; and it will come about after many desperate shifts that men will be forced to abandon their life and the human race will cease to be [MacCurdy, 1956, p. 74; B.M. 155 v.].

His scientific view thus was that man's end will come to pass by starvation, a slow death by frustration of the cannibalistic impulse. As far as I know, this view never found graphic presentation. The eleven depictions that probably were the last of Leonardo's graphic career refer to cataclysms, torrents pouring down, mountains toppling over habitations (see Plates 49 to 59). How vividly Leonardo imagined the events that might occur can be seen from the following passage titled: *Of the Deluge and How to Represent It in a Picture.*

Let the dark and gloomy air be seen buffeted by the rush of contrary winds and dense from the continued rain mingled with hail and bearing hither and thither an infinite number of branches torn from the trees and mixed with numberless leaves. All round may be seen venerable trees, uprooted and stripped by the fury of the winds; and fragments of mountains, already scoured bare by the torrents, falling into those torrents and choking their valleys till the swollen rivers overflow and submerge the wide lands and their inhabitants. Again, you might have seen on many of the hill-tops terrified animals of different kinds, collected together and subdued to tameness, in company with men and women who had fled there with their children. The waters which covered the fields with their waves were in great part strewn with tables, bedsteads, boats, and various other contrivances made from necessity and the fear of death, on which were men and women with their children amid sounds of lamentation and weeping, terrified by the fury of the winds which with their tempestuous violence rolled the waters under and over and about the bodies of the drowned. Nor was there any object lighter than the water which was not covered with a variety of animals which, having come to a truce, stood together in a frightened crowd—among them wolves, foxes, snakes, and others—fleeing from death. And all the waters dashing on their shores seemed to be beating them with the blows of drowned bodies, blows which killed those in whom any life remained. You might have seen assemblages of men who, with weapons in their hands, defended the small spots (that remained to them) against lions, wolves, and beasts of prey who sought safety there. Ah! what dreadful noises were heard in the dark air rent by the fury of thunder and lightnings it flashed forth, which darted from the clouds dealing ruin and striking all that opposed its course. Ah! how many you might have seen closing their ears with their hands to shut out the tremendous sounds made in the darkened air by the raging of the winds mingling with the rain, the thunders of heaven and the fury of the thunder-bolts. Others were not content with shutting their eyes, but laid their hands one over the other to cover them the closer that they might not see the cruel slaughter of the human race by the wrath of God. Ah! how many laments! and how many in their terror flung themselves from the rocks! Huge branches of great oaks loaded with men were seen borne through the air by the impetuous fury of the winds. How many were the boats upset, some entire, and some broken in pieces, with people on them labouring to escape with gestures and actions of grief foretelling a fearful death. Others, with gestures of despair, took their own lives, hope-

less of being able to endure such suffering; and of these, some flung themselves from lofty rocks, others strangled themselves with their own hands,
others seized their own children and violently slew them at a blow; some
wounded and killed themselves with their own weapons; others, falling
on their knees, recommended themselves to God. Ah! how many mothers
wept over their drowned sons, holding them upon their knees, with arms
raised spread out towards heaven and with words and various threatening
gestures, upbraiding the wrath of the gods. Others with clasped hands
and fingers clenched gnawed them and devoured them till they bled,
crouching with their breast down on their knees in their intense and unbearable anguish. Herds of animals were to be seen, such as horses, oxen,
goats, and sheep, already environed by the waters and left isolated on the
high peaks of the mountains, huddled together, those in the middle climb-
ing to the top and treading on the others, and fighting fiercely themselves;
and many would die for lack of food. Already had the birds begun to settle
on men and on other animals, finding no land uncovered which was not
occupied by living beings, and already had famine, the minister of death,
taken the lives of the greater number of the animals, when the dead bodies,
now fermented, were leaving the depths of the waters and were rising
to the top. Among the buffeting waves, where they were beating one
against the other, and, like as balls full of air, rebounded from the point
of concussion, these found a resting-place on the bodies of the dead. And
above these judgements, the air was seen covered with dark clouds, riven
by the forked flashes of the raging bolts of heaven, lighting up on all sides
the depth of the gloom [Richter, Vol. I, p. 352 ff., No. 608; W. 12665 v.].

No doubt when making his drawings of the Deluge, Leonardo had
in mind the end of the world, although this was in contrast to his
scientific anticipation. I surmise that the death by gradual starvation,
terrible as it is, still is less terrible than death by sudden catastrophe.
The sensation of hunger probably was well known to him; he may
even have noticed that during longer periods of deprivation the
sensation of hunger subsides. I suggest that death by gradual starvation
possibly did not impress him as traumatic. We know that the bitterness
of death can be assuaged by appropriate imagery, which may even
make death appear as pleasurable. It looks as if Leonardo, the artist,
in considering how to represent the end of the human world, deliberately selected a form more terrible and more traumatic than Leonardo,
the scientist, thought was in store.[1]

This difference between the scientist and the artist may appear

[1] For more about this particular problem, see Appendix B.

irrelevant or may be explained by historical factors.[2] Here, in a realm that must have been of eminent importance for Leonardo, drawing was not put into the service of penetrating into reality, of revealing the truth, of obtaining or conveying insight, but became rather a monologue, the final soliloquy in which a man came to terms with a loathsome burden that had embittered many of his adult moments. Valiantly and ingeniously as he had protected himself against trauma, he knew that in the end he would not be able to escape the terrible lot of being devoured. The certainty of death could not be questioned. What his unconscious imagery about this end was is not known. Was it the primordial mother that he feared would devour him, in the shape of the head of Medusa he had tried to depict? We do not know; at the time when Leonardo lived the frankness that was to emerge in Goya's *Saturn* (Plate 60) was, in the theater of Occidental art, still banished to dreams. Yet it does not matter, because, so I feel, Leonardo succeeded in transcending whatever his particular symbolism may have been.

Leonardo's final drawings of the Deluge (Plates 49 to 59)[3] are considered perhaps his greatest achievement. Clark (1939, p. 168) writes: "They express, with a freedom which is almost disturbing, his passion for twisting movement, and for sequences of form fuller and more complex than anything in European art."

There is something strange about the old-age achievements of some geniuses. When they reach an age at which others retrench their contact with a world that dwindlingly appeals and live in conformity with the gradual weakening of sense organs and memory, some geniuses burst forth with creations that sometimes overshadow everything they have created until then, as if impending death released them of an inhibition and they could say or express something that they had carried within themselves all their lives. This last impression, although not invalid, is one-sided, since a lifetime experience is synthesized in those last works. Such final-release works are Beethoven's last quartets, Titian's last paintings, Rembrandt's last self-portraits, Goethe's second part of *Faust* and *Wilhelm Meisters Wanderjahre*, and probably also

[2] But it may also be used in support of their position by those biographers who believe that in Leonardo art and science were in conflict.

[3] The Deluge drawings are generally called Leonardo's last because they fall into his last artistic period. Yet for what is to be considered historically proved to be Leonardo's last drawings, see Pedretti (1959a).

Freud's book on *Moses*. These final releases are stupendous in the scope and breadth of their synthesis. They sometimes introduce entirely new elements of form and initiate new periods of style or anticipate what only later generations will realize. Usually the genius's contemporaries are quite oblivious that these works of art are pregnant with a meaningful future. It is also striking that this phase of final release is not bound to any chronological number of years but is relative to the biological phase in its closeness to death.

To give an adequate description, let alone psychological analysis, of the series of eleven drawings of the Deluge or the world's end, which Clark (1939, p. 168) called "the most personal in the whole range of his [Leonardo's] work," is scarcely possible. As Clark points out, one discovers antecedents to this finale. When Leonardo was occupied with devising terrible machines of destruction to be used in warfare, he also depicted cities in the moment of their destruction (Plate 61; W. 12652 v.). Clark dates this drawing to circa 1487. Here the cosmic sense is missing. The bursting buildings, despite the terribleness of the event, convey an impression of neatness, even elegance—one is tempted to say gracefulness. One may imagine the engineer deliberating what the physical effect will be of the physical forces he will bring to bear by the invention of a new cannon.

Quite different is the impression one gets from another drawing (Plate 62), which Clark (1935, Vol. I, p. 147; W. 12698 r.) supposes was Leonardo's earliest apocalyptic sheet. He describes it as follows:

> From the clouds, on which sit two roughly drawn human figures, descends a rain of all imaginable implements, which lie about on the earth below. Amongst them are rakes, bells, bagpipes, barrels, ladders, pincers and spectacles.

On the folio is written:

> On this side Adam and Eve on the other; O misery of mankind, of how many things do you make yourself the slave for money! [Richter, Vol. I, p. 389, No. 688].

In a footnote, Richter tells us that "Adam and Eve" is written above the clouds, "suggesting their responsibility for such misery." Here Leonardo follows the Judaeo-Christian teaching that death is man's punishment for the Fall. It is striking that death is here connected with the genital drive. The drawing itself consists of an aggregation of things. There is no cohesiveness. Things fall and tumble. It is a mechanical disorder that is representative of the world's end.

Something incomparable in its artistic quality, in its frightfulness and horror, appears in the eleven grandiose drawings in which the end of the world becomes reality. One can only return over and over again to these pages and despair of ever being able to convert into words that reality which the genius has here, more than ever, pictured. But there is something even more troublesome. Despite prolonged study and strong emotional responses to this series of drawings, the beholder feels—at least, that is how it has been with me—that something in these eleven drawings remains beyond his emotional grasp, something remains impenetrable to his attempt to make these pictures his own, to reach the level of understanding where they become ego syntonic. To be sure, every masterwork possibly contains this core of impenetrability, a center where the creator's greatness transcends the grasp of the ordinary man and becomes elusive, but presumably there are few in which this core makes itself so painfully noticeable and dominates unchangeably the whole impression. Apparently, the ordinary man does not have the breadth to fathom and integrate that which is expressed here in artistically perfect forms. This is all the more strange since the drawings present no iconographic difficulty; their meanings are simple and clear: outbreaks of natural destructive forces that will end all human lives and all human creations (see Appendix B).

The idea of such or an equivalent event was most acute in Leonardo's times, since with the approach of the year 1500 fears swept through Europe that the end of the world was nearing (Clark, 1939, p. 168). Leonardo may have written down the earlier cited scientific view of what form that end would actually one day take, in order to oppose necromancy, superstitions, and certain forms of mysticism. But in his drawings—so I feel—he expresses something very personal, which is what Sir Kenneth Clark is probably referring to when he speaks of the disturbing quality that is encountered in this series (1939, p. 168). To me it seems that these drawings depict the artist's own death. It is remarkable how in the course of them human destiny recedes. At the beginning there still is a reference to people on horseback and others in flight (Plate 49); in another a tower is seen that is crushed by a toppling mountain (Plate 55); when, as in the bulk of the drawings, there are no human beings, not even any of their habitations or other of their works, still one knows it is the end. Nature is disintegrating in mad destruction. It is not only man's end, but also that of the universe. All the tensions that are latent in cosmic forces break loose, and after the holocaust is over all energy will have exhausted itself and there will be no movement. There will be Nothing (cf. Heydenreich, 1954, Vol. I, p. 157). The projection of the impending internal destruction into the cosmos, the equation of the self with the cosmos, is a narcissistic process. But it is perhaps also an expression of a tender love, and the end of nature may here stand for the wish to take with him to his grave everything he has loved despite everything.

Although these drawings are unquestionably personal, perhaps the most personal things Leonardo ever externalized, at the same time one gets the impression that these eleven drawings were the objective records of a distant, cool observer who puts down with calm certitude: "It will be this way." He knows it with certainty and he is not afraid and he is beyond any doubt.

Death is here no longer visualized as a danger that comes from an object, as it is in the fear of being devoured. It is no longer an event that is carried into man's existence by an external force. It has lost any quality of alienness. It is no longer a trauma. Self and reality are not distinguished. Events no longer intrude, they are not propelled by hostile external forces, but man is part and parcel of nature's destructiveness.

But another fundamental change took place. Whereas Renaissance art centered in planes and lines, these drawings transcend the idea of an object, of anything that would enclose a part of space as most scholars have stressed. The essence of the drawings is process, movement, pure force. When we walk in darkness against a storm and rain pours down, the world loses its thing-character and becomes dissolved subjectively into play and counterplay of forces. In these of Leonardo's drawings the world becomes dematerialized (see particularly Plate 59). From the point of view of the history of art, the most striking feature is perhaps that there is an instance in which Leonardo succeeded even in dematerializing an object. In this drawing, objects become an abstraction of reality and the abstracted reality appears even almost like an ornament (Plate 58).[4]

In these drawings Leonardo depicts death, death as a universal idea, his own personal death included. And here he went beyond that which is accessible to the ordinary mind; therefore these drawings must remain alien.[5]

[4] This drawing should be a warning to all those who indulge in abstract or nonobjective art. Leonardo also took this step, but only after he had gone through the presentation of all the things that fill our world. When he had integrated this aspect to perfection, only then did he step into the realm yonder. It impresses me as important that the tendency toward abstraction of the world of objects is already adumbrated in Leonardo's earliest apocalyptic sheet of Adam and Eve.

[5] For further remarks about the Deluge drawings, see Appendix B.

18

The Last Painting

An equivalent rise above the world is to be seen, in my estimation, in Leonardo's last painting, the *St. John* (Plate 24). At the outset I wish to state that this painting permits two different types of interpretation, and that, as so often in works of art, the choice of interpretation depends on subjective factors in the beholder.

From one point of view, Leonardo's St. John would be described as an effeminate, "half-man and half-woman," with "a smile round the moist, feminine mouth . . . a seducer's smile, that in the act of allurement tastes the fruit of possession" (Vallentin, 1938, p. 511). Without pejorative implication, one may say that this amounts to interpreting the person depicted as a pervert, whatever one may go on to say as to the philosophy expressed by the painting. Freud's interpretation apparently is also of this type (1910, p. 117).

With due acknowledgment of the justification for seeing Leonardo's St. John in this way, I follow a different type of interpretation. This requires first some explanatory remarks. Heydenreich, in giving an analysis of Leonardo's paintings, applied the extremely apt term "implosive" forces (1954, Vol. I, p. 47). Although I cannot follow the author exactly in his application of the term to Leonardo's *Battle of*

Anghiari, I still think it is characteristic of some of Leonardo's paintings. Heydenreich means, as the term implies, "forces which explode inwards instead of outwards." I find the concept of implosive forces excellent to characterize the *Anna Metterza.* The type of person presented in that painting is serene, turning away from the hustle and bustle of this world. The group is completely absorbed in the present and yet they do not appear oblivious of the future—just the opposite: it is because the future is divined that the present moment becomes so important and worthy of complete absorption. There is no visible trace of rebellion or even aversion against that future, although St. Anne—at least—seems to know of its terrible aspect. Further, although both adult women seem absorbed in beholding or turning toward the infant at their feet, yet, for various reasons, the group as a whole conveys an impression of the greatest composure and self-absorption. The centripetal flow is very strong. As said, the group is perfectly calm and serene, and yet this calmness and serenity are the product of control—as is again visible particularly in St. Anne. The calmness established by control makes it impossible that they would ever behave in an undignified way; that is to say, their emotions would never turn explosively to the surface. At the same time, under an inhuman stress the inner organization might cave in, that is, they can still be traumatized. This potential caving in permits the application of Heydenreich's concept of implosive forces.

In the *St. John,* said to be Leonardo's last painting, we encounter a different structure of personality. Critics have found the work distasteful and some have thought it to be by his assistant (Clark, 1939, p. 171). "The *St. John* is a baffling work, but every inch of it smells of Leonardo," says Clark (1939, p. 171), and he tries to explain it by "a curiously personal conception" which Leonardo formed of St. John. According to Clark, "the inevitable precursor of truth" is a question. "Leonardo's St. John is the eternal question mark, the enigma of creation" (1939, p. 173).

Indeed, the difficulty of grasping the *St. John* on the basis of human qualities that permit empathy is great. The figure is of something ahuman, not godlike or animallike—the two nonhuman qualities we are prone to project into man (cf. Panofsky, 1940b, p. 2). As far as the eye can see, everything in the painting is human, and yet everything that is felt but cannot be seen belongs to other than the human universe.

The affinity between St. John and Leonardo is great for obvious reasons. The traditional view of St. John is that of the ascetic prophet. I have the impression that the new St. John Leonardo created grew out of a profound recognition that asceticism and passionate preaching still carry the traces of ambivalence or disbelief. This new St. John is not an ascetic, and he does not feel compelled to preach but only answers if asked. He is free from any doubt; he knows. And he knows so profoundly that he does not need to meditate or inquire any more. Neither does he need to possess his knowledge in explicit words. Yet neither is he a mystic who possesses knowledge in the form of highly charged symbols or unites with God in profound emotional experiences. Nor is he dogmatic. He does not care whether we agree or disagree. He is primary, live knowledge to an extent that excludes anxiety or grief, a state that is beyond any yes or no, for every affirmation contains the possibility of a negation. He is male and female—an idea so embarrassing to our times. It is not my feeling that Leonardo here expressed his feelings regarding a physically idealized object or showed a derivative of his unconscious wishes. It is my impression that in this phase of his career Leonardo had overcome problems that result from object relations or object choice. I surmise he wanted to document to the world a new relationship he had at last attained or whose dawn he felt slumbering in himself as a potential. It must have been a relationship free of anxiety. Indeed, in beholding this St. John one feels unable to think of anything that could perturb him, arouse his anger or even pain; that is to say, for him, nothing could become a trauma. As long as love and hate abide in man, as long as male and female are experienced as two aspects of the human, conflict apparently is a potentiality. The synthesis of male and female into one—and Leonardo's St. John, in my opinion, is not effeminate—may be taken as a sort of concrete evidence of the new level aimed at and perhaps attained. The *St. John* is a painting without any erotic quality. This may be a reason why it cannot be called beautiful, and why this St. John does not strike one as human. The impossibility of being traumatized also takes him out of the human realm. In observing very old people one discovers that they have lost the capacity for suffering trauma, their lives no longer show any changes, every moment is a repetition of the preceding one, so to speak; life in them is only as a shadow or a husk; by chance, they still move and breathe—it is as if they had forgotten to die. Rembrandt's later self-portraits also show him grown beyond vanity and imperturbable to any personal vicissitude; but he bears all the earmarks of the past struggle, of the sufferings that anteceded the wisdom of old age, and, above all, he is capable of pity and one senses a last flickering of resignation. All this is different in Leonardo's St. John. He has never suffered and he never will suffer, nor would he understand what resignation means. One could see in him perhaps a precursor of Dostoevski's Alyosha.

I am fully aware of the subjective nature of my interpretation. Of course, Clark may be right in interpreting this St. John as "the eternal question mark"; yet, despite all disagreement, there seems to be agreement that this St. John is no longer human. To what extent Leonardo here depicted what he had partly at last become, whether or not he had lost the fear of trauma I postulated earlier, cannot yet be certainly said. Nevertheless, despite the perilous errors one may commit when he attempts to draw from a work of art conclusions as to subtle aspects of the artist's personality, I venture to state that Leonardo apparently did achieve, in this last phase of his existence, a structural change that freed him of anxiety of trauma and conflict, and that he found in his way of painting St. John a symbol for what he had himself become.

There is one circumstance that speaks in favor of my thesis. Clark believes that it is not surprising that Leonardo seems to have produced practically nothing during his stay in France, since he was free both to experiment and to dream at will, in accordance with the generous invitation from King Francis I (Clark, 1939, p. 175). To be sure, the demand put upon the genius by external reality is not to be neglected as an incentive to creation, or at least as a factor that has some bearing on quantity and quality of creative output. But the genius does not depend on this factor in a one-sided way. Goethe, so far as external factors were concerned, might have stopped producing far earlier than he did. Only after he had finished the second part of *Faust* (seven months prior to his death) did he relent and consider the rest of his life a gift that entailed no inner obligation to create. Many other examples could be cited, such as that of Freud, who was creating up to the last moment that his disease permitted, far beyond the necessity of external demands. The genius is driven by an internal creative potential, and Leonardo's apparent lack of creativity toward the end of his life requires an explanation in terms of factors other than external demands.

His creativity had up to then been comparable to that of other geniuses in quantity as well as quality. If there was a disturbance to the degree that there were hesitations—Clark (1939, p. 164) speaks of "a disease of the will"—it showed up only in the number of finished paintings, but Leonardo's total lifework is in quantity not inferior to that of others. Therefore I believe it requires a special reason to explain the apparent decrease of creativity in the old Leonardo.

I find this reason in a conclusion I feel compelled to draw from Leonardo's Deluge drawings and his *St. John* painting. These creations, as I said before, strike me as the productions of a man who has overcome his conflicts. Yet when the tension of conflicts sinks below a certain level the creative potential is reduced and may reach zero. When the personality becomes fully structured, that is to say, when insight and control have left no island of the irrational, the mysterious, the questionable, the unknown, the urging of unknown origin, artistic creativity has lost its prime mover. To be sure, many a genius has silenced a conflict by creating a work of art, but this silence is, in the case of the genius, short-lasting and temporary. Conflict soon raises its head anew and creation again becomes a necessity. If creation really leads to the resolution of conflict, the creative potential is greatly endangered. In Goethe's case I was able to observe a creative standstill during a period of personality reorganization. The function of creation is not a psychotherapeutic one in the genius; at the most it provides a temporary reduction of tension. Here again we encounter the necessity of a relative deficit in structure which I have brought up from time to time.

Leonardo, so I must conclude, had at last integrated insight. Where before there had been conflict, now structure and insight had arisen, to paraphrase a remark by Freud; and concomitantly creation, though still possible, had lost its compelling necessity.

19

General Remarks

These are the observations, conclusions, and speculations that came to my mind while I was working my way through the many materials I was prompted to study by the criticism Freud's Leonardo essay has recently encountered. Before concluding I would like to take up once more a general point which involves a key problem that has been dealt with in quite different ways by various writers on Leonardo.

There is first the question of whether Leonardo should be regarded as a neurotic. How Freud answers this question is not quite clear, but he seems to have leaned toward an affirmative. Clark too speaks of a disease of the will.

That Freud personally regarded Leonardo as a genius there can be no doubt. The 1910 essay conveys this, and when, almost three decades later, he discussed the problem of "great men," that is to say, personalities that move us "beyond the admiration of their grandiose creations," Leonardo is one among the three he cites (Freud, 1937-39, p. 172). Yet Freud's clinical eye discovered certain peculiarities in Leonardo that apparently impressed him as neurotic. There was the particular relationship of the self to emotions, for example; Leonardo's way of mourning; the total absence of heterosexual activity; an inhibition of the capacity to make decisions; regressions that bore upon his vacillation between science and art. However, at most points Freud speaks of that which can be observed in Leonardo as something *to be compared with* what is found in neurotics, which may suggest that Freud did not identify the psychopathology of the genius with neurosis. However, Freud also writes of "the neurotic conflict" in Leonardo (1910, p. 105), and in a more comprehensive way he stated that Leonardo may be placed "close to the type of neurotic that we describe as 'obsessional'; and we may compare his research to the 'obsessive brooding' of neurotics" (1910, p. 131).[1] Notwithstanding Freud's qualifications, one gets the impression that he thought of Leonardo as a neurotic. The essence of the problem emerges when we consider Freud's likening of Leonardo's researches to compulsive brooding. That comparison makes us aware of the undeniable similarity of the two phenomena but also of their essential difference: obsessive brooding is an autoplastic phenomenon, whereas Leonardo's researches "soared upwards to the highest realizations of a conception of the world that left his epoch far behind it" (Freud, 1910, p. 134).

Freud's Leonardo study was written in the light of the clinical experience and observations he had made during the two preceding decades, that is to say, from the perspective of neurosis. As Freud said in his *Autobiographical Study*, with reference to this essay, his aim was to reconstruct "that part of him [the artist] which he shared with all men" (1925, p. 119). In a letter to Dr. Else Voigtländer of October 1, 1911, he wrote that by his Leonardo study he wanted to demonstrate "a particularly glaring example of the effect of the accidental family constellation [*ein besonders grelles Beispiel von der Wirkung der zufälligen familiären Konstellation*]."[2]

Nevertheless, even if the study of genius is limited to what he shares with the ordinary man, it is questionable whether Freud, after he had extended his research into the typology of the personality, would not have categorized Leonardo differently. To what extent would Freud

---

[1] At one point Freud writes: "We must expressly insist that we have never reckoned Leonardo as a neurotic or a 'nerve case,' as the awkward phrase goes" (1910, p. 131), but this statement seems to have been meant rather as a defense against any pejorative implications the reader might infer from Freud's study through incautious acceptance of the vulgarized stereotype connoted by these words.

[2] I owe thanks to Dr. Bernard L. Pacella for his kind permission to quote from Freud's letter which he presented before the Annual Meeting of the American Psychoanalytic Association in May, 1956.

then have stressed Leonardo's similarity with the obsessional *type,* which he characterized as follows:

> its distinctive characteristic is the supremacy exercised by the super-ego, which is segregated from the ego with great accompanying tension. Persons of this type are governed by anxiety of conscience instead of by the dread of losing love; they exhibit, we might say, an inner instead of an outer dependence; they develop a high degree of self-reliance, and from the social standpoint they are the true upholders of civilization, for the most part in a conservative spirit [1931b, p. 248],

or with the narcissistic-obsessional type, which

> represents the variation most valuable from the cultural standpoint, for it combines independence of external factors and regard for the requirements of conscience with the capacity for energetic action, and it reinforces the ego against the super-ego [ibid., p. 249f.],

or with a combination of both?

At any rate, I presume that in the perspective of Freud's ego psychology the problem of genius reappears as the question: What makes the genius different from the ordinary man? To be sure, one of the elements that make him *prima facie* so different, his outstanding skills, is as impenetrable to psychoanalysis as ever (Freud, 1925, p. 119f.; 1933, p. xi), but, as Freud so rightly said, the problem of the great man is not only that of great skills (1937-39, p. 171f.).

It is not probable that the genius capacity is so profoundly rooted in an innate constitution that, once given, its penetrance would conquer any environment, no matter how unfavorable. The genius potentiality too needs an adequate habitat. What its structure is, we do not know. We can only retrace in a particular instance of genius some environmental factors which, in view of clinical experience, seem to have favored the development of specific geniushood; we can further try to reconstruct the development and structure of the personality that was prerequisite to transmuting the innate outstanding ability into genius achievement.

In accordance with Freud's theory of complementary series, we may expect to encounter, on the one hand, constitutions with enormous penetrance and little dependence on environmental factors, and, on the other, constitutions that require very favorable environments in order to flourish. However, we encounter here a question that finds no parallel in the study of neuroses and psychoses. Given a certain constitution, there will be several types of environments that will help unfold the potential genius's endowment, but possibly there will be only one that will suit this particular constitution so well that it will lead to the maximum realization. Herein we face an important, well-nigh a decisive, issue.

As Freud stated, Leonardo's illegitimate birth, the asserted separation from his father at the beginning, the closeness to his mother, contributed to what cursorily may be called his neurosis, but it also contributed to his later work. If these environmental factors had been different, he might have been spared his neurosis, but what effect would such change have had upon his later geniushood?

It is no longer disputed that in the study of genius a surprisingly large amount of psychopathology is encountered. The question, however, has not been answered what connection exists between the genius's psychopathology and his achievements. Psychopathology, in general, is looked upon as defect, though most forms of psychopathology have a useful function in so far as they spare the psychic apparatus a damage that would be greater than that caused by the psychopathology (primary gain). Observation of the genius, however, suggests the possibility that psychopathology is indispensable to the highest achievements of certain kinds. Sarton expressed this indirectly as follows:

> Leonardo's greatest contribution was his method, his attitude; his masterpiece was his life. I have heard people foolishly regret that his insatiable curiosity diverted him from his work as a painter. In the spiritual sphere it is only quality that matters. If he had painted more and roamed less along untrodden paths, his paintings perhaps would not have taught us more than do those of his Milanese disciples. While, even as they stand now, scarce and partly destroyed, they deliver to us a message which is so uncompromisingly high that even today but few understand it [Sarton, 1948, p. 81].

Before going into the principal point Sarton raises here I wish to refer to a subjective evaluation that implicitly underlies his statement. As is well known, no one has contributed to the enlargement of our knowledge of the history of science as Sarton has, and I agree with him that such knowledge is prerequisite not only for the understanding of science itself, but also of history and culture. Yet there is no doubt that he looks upon science as a good. Whatever favors science is welcome to him, as if the development of science were man's principal function. Sarton may indeed have been right in such an evaluation, but it has not yet been proved and, in the form in which it is found in his admirable work it is still a subjective, personal evaluation that cannot be regarded as binding.

This bias in favor of science may indirectly have led to a weak point in Sarton's argument. Even if Leonardo had given less time than he did, or even no time at all to scientific pursuits, he would never have been capable of painting like a mediocre artist. His earliest works, before he ever became seriously engaged in science, show unmistakably his superiority as a painter, and his first great painting, *The Adoration*, accomplished while he was still in his first stay in Florence, impressed Raphael so deeply that twenty-eight years later he borrowed important elements from it for his own paintings (Clark, 1939, p. 31). And this although, at that time, despite his scientific interests, there was as yet no visible schism between art and science.

Thus it may be inferred that once Leonardo had reached manhood he was destined to become one of the greatest painters of his epoch. Sarton's remark definitely sprang from a one-sided evaluation of science. But would Leonardo have been able to paint the *Mona Lisa* or draw the Deluge sketches if he had not "wasted" his time on scientific inquiries? This is a pertinent question to ask. It is conceivable that after he left Florence his further development might not have carried him to such heights as it did if science had not entered his life extensively.[3]

Sarton's statement has another aspect that seems more pertinent. One may derive from it a strictly deterministic attitude. On this view, genius achievements are so rare and so outstanding that in all circumstances the individual paths that lead to their achievements are the only possible ones and any alternatives in upbringing, working habits, and interests could only work against the excellency of their accomplishments. Thus, if Leonardo had had less scientific interest or had been less compulsive or more heterosexually directed, this would have shown up in a diminution in the quality of his work. Since a person

[3] For a most sensitive analysis of the problem of art and science in Leonardo's life, mainly in terms of historical background but by no means with a neglect of psychology, see Clark (1929).

is accorded the distinctive mark of genius only when his works impress us as perfect and cannot be imagined as accessible to improvement (Bychowski, 1951, p. 407), any hypothetical change or alternative of constitutional or environmental conditions can only lead to imperfection.

Indeed, the thesis is quite conceivable that since Leonardo, or any genius, reaches the maximum of what is potentially in him we are to consider relevant environmental factors as causative. This approach would come close to or even coincide with the deterministic principle current in psychoanalysis, where the pathological end product is meaningfully connected with all preceding relevant factors, or, in other words, the symptom is considered to be determined by a manifoldness of causative conditions. With a variation of relevant conditions, the form and content of the symptom would change. Sarton's implication undoubtedly has much in its favor.

I feel strongly inclined toward one aspect of this approach. If we wish to apply seriously to the study of the psychology of genius the principle of psychic determinism, we may have to take his psychopathology into account as one of the factors indispensable to his geniushood. Consequently if what we observed in the genius struck us as neurotic or psychotic or perverse or even criminal, we would then have to reconsider our classification under these accustomed headings. If, for example, an apparently obsessional symptom were observed and it turned out that that symptom was indispensable to geniushood in that case, there would be no sense in calling it a neurotic symptom. Whatever the essence of neurosis may be, the concept of neurosis makes sense only when it is correlated with a deficit. No doubt, neurotic symptoms may facilitate socially approved behavior, or, at least, a person may by means of disease have gained the advantages we actually observe him to be in possession of. Yet, there is no known achievement which would justify the claim that is necessitated by observations in the instance of the genius, namely, that there was no alternative path, for him, to that achievement. During the years of war, for example, I got the impression—rightly or wrongly—that most of those who volunteered for parachute jumping were psychopaths, but it would be profoundly wrong to say that psychopathy is a prerequisite for parachute jumping. Although ability or desire or readiness for parachute jumping may be found more frequently among those who exhibit a selected type of psychopathology, it will be admitted that love of country or sense of duty may likewise induce a person to volunteer for such activity and become proficient in it.

In the case of the genius this is different, as can best be demonstrated in a small documented instance. For a certain period, Goethe, as he relates it in *Dichtung und Wahrheit,* tried each evening to see whether he was capable of committing suicide by stabbing himself. This behavior pattern (and particularly Goethe's rationalization of the choice of method, which I will not report here) is—under ordinary circumstances—characteristic of a deep-seated disturbance and may even announce the onset of a malignant psychosis. Goethe, however, shortly thereafter wrote his famous novel *Werther,* in which the hero of the story ends his life by shooting himself. Rarely have the sufferings of a young man for whom the world's tribulations have become unbearable been so heartbreakingly presented. The biographical evidence compels us to connect Goethe's "neurotic symptom" with his subsequent successful writing of the novel. It can safely be said that only somebody who had repeatedly gone through the throes of preparing for suicide could have presented it so overwhelmingly as Goethe, who was actually accused of having by his novel initiated a wave of suicides in Central Europe.

Here, then, we have a conspicuous example of undeniable pathological behavior that was one of the indispensable prerequisites for the writing of one of the greatest novels. If we continue to call such behavior an indication of a neurosis or psychosis, we make such categories meaningless. I described earlier a sexual pattern I believe represents Leonardo's form of genital release. In ordinary circumstances one would, of course, call such a sexual pattern a perversion. Yet I have tried to show that this pattern may have been indispensable for Leonardo. If he had not formed this pattern—of course only on the assumption that my construction is correct—or if society had interfered and prevented Leonardo from occasional indulgence in this form of sexual release, Leonardo's personality organization might have collapsed and been incapacitated for further production.

I need not go through the equivalent steps to demonstrate that the term perversion, unless used for purely descriptive purposes, would not be applicable to Leonardo either. Whatever its defensive function may have been in Leonardo's case, and no matter what similarities may be adduced between Leonardo's disturbance and that of a clinical pervert, the principal function of this sexual pattern in Leonardo was to provide the minimally necessary release in such a way that the sublimatory processes were not disturbed. It is conceivable that we shall one day recognize that a normal *vita sexualis* is incompatible with certain types of artistic geniushood.

Now just here, where I have myself characterized Leonardo's disturbance as what would ordinarily be called a perversion, the clinician may cite instances within his observation in which psychopathology that unquestionably deserves to be called a perversion has facilitated and even made possible socially approved achievements. Analytic experience, I believe, does not suggest that these achievements become impossible when the perversion has been removed. In the case of the genius, however, as far as one can reconstruct, it does not seem probable that he would be capable of his extraordinary creations if his libido were gratified in an adequate object relation. The energy flow into the object relation would be diverted from the artistic process. Consequently, only the blockage of a permanent object attachment can produce that intense hunger for objects that results in the substitute formation of the perfect work of art.

Therefore I would with a grain of salt say that in the genius all psychic processes that support sublimatory processes are ego syntonic and belong to a special category of psychopathology, which is essentially different from all other forms of psychopathology as set forth in textbooks of psychiatry. This is the psychopathology of genius, which is not amenable to criteria derived from the nongenius.

Yet, to complicate matters, in the genius we also encounter psychopathology that apparently does not support sublimatory processes and to which, consequently, the viewpoint just set forth does not apply. This kind of psychopathology actually drains off energy that otherwise would assist or flow into sublimation, and hence belongs in the categories of psychopathology also encountered in others. The decision as to which of these two types of psychopathology the investigator is confronted by in any particular case is a very delicate one. Probably the nearest one can come to even a rule of thumb is to suggest that if what one is dealing with is psychopathology in the ordinary sense, there will probably be a manifest deterioration in the quality of the created work that is genetically and dynamically connected with it.[4]

After this point, unique to the psychology of genius, has been set forth, one should be prepared to decide whether Freud or Sarton is right. However, I wonder whether the biographical record is rich enough to permit more than speculation. As a matter of fact, despite his eminence Leonardo is one of the geniuses whose works do not in every case live up to the acid test of perfection that I previously asserted. The *Cenacolo* in its original form must have lived up to that standard; in its present form it is a ruin. We may expect from the perfect work of art that its creator will endow it with such longevity as can be humanly achieved.

But just here the antinomy set forth can be demonstrated. I well follow Freud when he describes Leonardo's ambivalence toward his work, but this ambivalence may have been a cornerstone of his creativity. It seems historically well documented that Leonardo's slow way of painting made the use of contemporary fresco techniques impossible. For the technique he invented and which seemed to permit his deliberate ways, he had to pay a terrible price. The *Mona Lisa* too is not as well preserved as other contemporary paintings probably also because of the technique Leonardo used,[5] and his grandiose *Battle of Anghiari* has suffered even more grievously than the *Cenacolo*. But oddly enough the *Cenacolo* became the most representative painting of Christendom and no other portrait matches the *Mona Lisa* in renown. The deliberateness of his working technique, though possibly a derivative of compulsion and ambivalence, may still have been the only pathway on which his creativity could travel and evidently contributed immensely to the unique balance of the whole composition.

---

[4] I have tried to demonstrate the occurrence of such psychopathology in Goethe. His *Chromatology* is the work which, in my opinion, exhibits the reduced quality that resulted from it. Of course, the mental scientist is in danger here of basing his findings on more or less arbitrary value judgments, which Schapiro (1956, p. 177) has warned against. Nothing prevents the scholar in other fields from discovering for himself that the quality of the product has deteriorated, as indeed has happened in the case of the *Chromatology;* the mental scientist is then freed of this onus. Still, anyone who knows how far short the humanities are of providing an objective yardstick for evaluating cultural products will also be aware of how great the risks are that the psychologist must run in this area.

[5] De Tolnay (1952, p. 19, n.), however, claims that the conservation of the *Mona Lisa* is much better than commonly assumed.

This deliberateness, whatever its origin and derivation, did not drain the creative effort, but channelized it.[6]

No doubt many illustrations of the psychopathology of the genius can be found in Leonardo, and I have tried to describe the dynamics of some selected samples. Yet one wonders whether precisely in Leonardo, who was certainly one of the most creative minds the world has known, all the psychopathology encountered was really that of the genius and in the service of the creative process. If one equates Leonardo's artistic creative process with his scientific, as an increasing number of historians do since Séailles, then the decision will be rather in favor of Sarton. Freud did not follow this approach, but assumed a conflict between the artistic and the scientific impulse. He was perhaps influenced in this by a comparison with Goethe. At least, in 1930 he wrote:

> In Leonardo's nature the scientist did not get along with the artist; he disturbed him and perhaps crushed him in the end. In Goethe's life both personalities found room side by side; they alternated with each other as to primacy. One does not have to go far to connect Leonardo's disturbance with that inhibition of development which removed from his interests everything erotic and with it also psychology. In this point Goethe's nature was able to unfold itself more freely. [*In Leonardos Natur vertrug sich der Forscher nicht mit dem Künstler, er störte ihn und erdrückte ihn vielleicht am Ende. In Goethes Leben fanden beide Persönlichkeiten Raum nebeneinander, sie lösten einander zeitweise in der Vorherrschaft ab. Es liegt nahe, die Störung bei Leonardo mit jener Entwicklungshemmung zusammenzubringen, die alles Erotische und damit die Psychologie seinem Interesse entrückte. In diesem Punkt durfte Goethes Wesen sich freier entfalten*] [Freud, 1930, p. 547].

In Goethe there was, however, at times a conscious conflict between the scientist and the artist; his marvelous skill in organizing and synthesizing was able, nevertheless, to get them both into proper balance. It is my impression that Leonardo was not consciously in conflict about the two activities. The climate of his times was, after all, favorable to equating them, although many of his contemporaries wondered about the periods in which he abandoned artistic pursuits. But his teacher,

[6] Clark (1952, p. 303), however, takes a quite different stand regarding Leonardo's faulty technique of fresco painting.

Verrocchio, and others legitimately pursued studies we would call scientific nowadays, and some of Leonardo's collaborators apparently did not take amiss his occasional exclusive devotion to science.[7]

The difference Freud draws between Leonardo the artist and Leonardo the scientist refers, in my opinion, to an unconscious conflict. In the unconscious, the two pursuits may have had a very different meaning and I wish to repeat an earlier suggestion that scientific pursuits perhaps aroused less anxiety in Leonardo than painting, that is to say, science served the function of defense with less conflict than painting. If the biographical record were more complete, we could perhaps reconstruct subjective differences that would permit a final conclusion, as is possible in Goethe's case. Whether Freud, if he had turned, in the light of his ego psychology, toward the problem of what makes a genius different from others, would still have maintained the division between neurosis and sublimation in Leonardo or whether he would have found a synthesis between ostensible disease and creativity, who can say?

The problem before us is to be discussed in still another context. What, in essence, was Leonardo's scientific contribution? It is strange what happens when a great artist also makes research one of his creative pursuits. We find a large number of biographers and historians who extol his scientific achievement and there is usually a lonely voice that disputes his merit. This is very clearly seen in the literature on Goethe as a scientist. One is dazzled when he reads Goethe's scientific publications, and is inclined to agree with those who pay them homage. Yet when a historian of science like Kohlbrugge, who knows the time sequences of scientific discoveries, examines the record he shows item for item that the scientific content of Goethe's writings, to the extent that it proved valid, is surprisingly unoriginal and goes back to earlier sources. He sagaciously adds that this does not detract an ounce from Goethe's greatness.

In the Leonardo literature something similar is to be observed. Notwithstanding Duhem's historical researches, I wish to refer to a doubt that can be discerned in Sarton's lines of praise, if only in the form of the simple question he raises: "Is it possible to ascribe to him

---

[7] From Clark's essay in 1952 one may get the impression that he no longer sees a dichotomy between Leonardo's science and art.

[Leonardo] a single discovery, except such as are contained implicitly in his drawings?" Sarton's preliminary answer is:

> In order to receive credit for a discovery it is not enough to make it. One must explain it; one must prove very clearly that one has understood it, one must be ready to defend it. . . . Leonardo's ideas were like seeds that failed to mature [1957, p. 228].

It is instructive to compare two views on Leonardo the scientist which are both brilliantly set forth, but diametrically opposed—those of Cassirer and Olschki. Cassirer sees in Leonardo a scientist in the full meaning of the word, who has integrated the basic structure and principles of modern science. Olschki disputes Leonardo's scientific eminence; he sees in him a superb observer, technician, and craftsman, but tries to demonstrate that Leonardo was in bondage to visualization, and that this resulted in grave limitations of abstraction when his research is viewed from the point of view of modern science. (Cf. also Johnson, 1949, p. 152.) Wherever research would have required Leonardo to break this bondage he failed.

The difference of opinion between Cassirer and Olschki rests on the interpretation of the numerous aphorismic statements in which Leonardo's notes abound. Are these aphorisms indicators of insight? Olschki shows how they contradict one another, and by analyzing a few examples of Leonardo's practical procedures demonstrates how Leonardo, after recording exact observations, fell into mysticism and abandoned what we would call scientific viewpoints. Cassirer evaluates Leonardo on the basis of the potentiality that was in him; he presents Leonardo's work in terms of an ideal type, whereas Olschki observes the realistic, historicopsychological processes.[8]

I believe Olschki to be right. This lag in Leonardo's scientific development was of the greatest benefit to mankind. If Leonardo had succeeded in what Galileo accomplished about a century later, we would not have his art work. If he had integrated the idea of scientific abstraction and law, his creative impulse toward visualization would necessarily have been weakened. The greatness of his artistic work presupposes a genius to whom visual creation is the supreme outlet.

[8] Also Clark (1952) seems to doubt Leonardo's greatness, as a scientist. He weighs the possibility that most of Leonardo's drawings of machines were largely copies of machines already in existence on which Leonardo elaborated or which he extended (p. 302).

But how could this urge to create visually have competed successfully with the spell that is cast by the mathematical formula, which symbolizes the law of all movements that ever have been or will come to pass?

Was Leonardo's scientific work therefore in vain and waste? It may be worth while to cite here an author of renown who felt compelled to answer the same question in the affirmative with respect to Goethe, who was also distracted from his main mission by a large number of, so to speak, extracurricular activities. It is Ortega y Gasset who rendered devastating judgment on Goethe, whom he considers "perpetually untrue to his destiny" and "whose life was a life à rebours." He was "a perpetual deserter from his inner destiny" (1932, p. 145). "He begins by fleeing from all his real loves. . . . He flees from life as a writer to fall into that unhappy Weimar episode" (p. 146). Further, he reproaches Goethe for his financial security in Weimar, since "a consciousness of security kills life" (p. 149). "Whatever he is, it is neither basically nor wholly: he is a minister who is not seriously a minister, a regisseur, a naturalist who does not succeed in being one" (p. 151). And so it goes on and on, because Goethe did not *"enter into an exclusive destiny"* (p. 153; italics by the author). I do not wish to deal here with the cacophony of misinformation Ortega spilled out when barking at the moon, but point out how a professor of metaphysics may look at the life of a genius when he subjects it to his idea of destiny. It strikes me that almost everything Ortega says about Goethe could *mutatis mutandis* be repeated of Leonardo. His "destiny" was the visual arts, and Ortega could just as well have attacked Leonardo by pointing out all his flights from his destiny.[9] The method used by the metaphysician is a simple one. He excogitates a concept of life as it ought to be according to his way of thinking and then forms nega-

---

[9] Ortega sees Goethe's mission as one "to be the German writer on whom it devolved to revolutionize his country's literature and, through it, the literature of the world" (p. 148). This, however, Goethe did not do. The great genius exhausts the possibilities of the new forms he has created and makes it impossible for those who come after him to continue to use them without inevitably seeming servile imitators, even when their imitations are extremely talented. German literature became different through Goethe's creations, but it was a long time before successors appeared who were able to throw off the livery of epigoni. Nietzsche rightly raises the question of what German prose literature deserves to be read over and over again aside from Goethe's writings (Nietzsche, No. 109, p. 227). Cf. Berenson, in his discussion of the negative effect Leonardo had on Italian painting (1916, p. 23): "No Tuscan painter or sculptor born after Leonardo's death produced a single work with the faintest claim to general interest."

tive views of anything that does not fit into his conceptual framework. "Consciousness of shipwreck, being the truth of life, constitutes salvation," says Ortega (p. 127). Goethe did not live the life of the shipwrecked; therefore Goethe betrayed his destiny. This shows up in his depressions: "Persistent depression is only too clearly a sign that a man is living contrary to his vocation" (p. 144). Depressions, which were not at all persistent in Goethe as Ortega claims, but clearly periodic, we also encounter in Leonardo. There they burst forth in short but all the more impressive outcries: "Dimmi se mai fu fatto alcuna cosa [Tell me if anything was ever done]" (Richter, Vol. II, p. 343, No. 1365), we hear over and over again (Clark, 1939, p. 164). Thus perhaps does the genius express his misery when he feels the discrepancy between his potentiality and his actual realization.[10] This disproportion is always high in the genius despite the most intense creativity, and often low in the talent who turns out one product after another without pause and little conflict.

Thus the conflict about his productions is not atypical either in Goethe's or Leonardo's instance. But, as Olschki has pointed out (Vol. I, p. 412f.), Vasari's report that Leonardo on his deathbed expressed "how greatly he had offended God and man in not having worked in his art as he ought" (Vasari, p. 12) may, despite its legendary origin, reflect a deep psychological truth.[11] Indeed, if one views the whole of Leonardo's creative output, one may regret the imbalance between the artistic and the scientific parts.[12] When, toward the end of his life, he contemplated the results of his research—that is, the scattered notes that had not led to one single integrated text, that contained neither a single formulated law of nature nor the design of that much-desired flying machine—and saw the likeness between these scattered, mortarless building stones of the wonderful edifice he had dreamed of when

[10] Clark, in accordance with historical sources, limits these expressions of despair to a period of Leonardo's old age when conditions were adverse for him in Rome and refers them to Leonardo's despair over the ultimate inconclusiveness of his research. I feel more inclined to see in them the verbalization of a depressed mood which I feel justified, on clinical grounds, in assuming to have occurred sporadically throughout his life.

[11] An instance of intentional and successful fabrication of a legend about an artist is recorded by Kris and Kurz (1934, p. 124). The fabricator was so intuitive that Panofsky (1924, p. 56), unaware of the hoax, was able to use the forged document perfectly for his presentation of art theory of mannerism.

[12] Cf. Olschki (Vol. I, p. 260f.): "Leonardo remained to the end a hybrid nature [*Zwitternatur*] and his science ended in an omnium-gatherum of sharply observed facts and imaginative reveries."

he set out on his exploratory voyages, and his many unfinished paintings, as well as the ones he had felt capable of creating but had never even started, it may well be imagined that he felt deeply disturbed and depressed and even may have thought of himself as waste and failure, as happens so often precisely with the aging genius.

But even if Leonardo did feel that way, would he have been right? It seems that the function of knowledge in the genius artist is perhaps underestimated. It is true that the knowledge Leonardo amassed about the human body went far beyond what an artist commonly needs in order to be able to depict it. But for the creation of values that go beyond mere verisimilitude, the artist's feeling for his material will be quite different if, besides knowing all one needs to in order to understand the surface structure, he can see through the body and knows the innermost crevices in detail.

This can be shown quite concretely in another instance. Leonardo was obsessed by the study of water with a tenacity which "dismays his most industrious admirers," as Sir Kenneth Clark so rightly says (1935, Vol. I, p. xvii). Whatever the conscious or unconscious motive of that enduring preoccupation may have been, it cannot be recorded as a waste from the viewpoint of Leonardo's artistic output since something of it, if not all, went into the crowning eleven drawings of the Deluge.

But it may still be objected that even if one relinquishes measurement by the yardstick of surface qualities, his nonartistic pursuits led him into aspects that can by no possible inference be connected with his artistic creations. What was the effect, after all, of his obsession with the flying machine, and where are the paintings in which we can admire the fruits of his anatomical studies? About these last it can be said that they in themselves led to artistic masterpieces in the form of his anatomical drawings; further, a number of his paintings have been lost, and, if all of them were still in existence we would perhaps be able to look upon an original St. John instead of the poor copy[13] in the Louvre which is all we now have, and the nude body of that St. John might demonstrate the final synthesis of Leonardo's lifelong anatomical studies.

In his effort to devise a flying machine he studied the flight of birds. One may say that he went through the process of identification with

[13] However, Clark (1939, p. 175) doubts that that painting goes back to an original by Leonardo.

birds innumerable times, and if we still possessed his original *Leda* painting, we would perhaps be in a position to observe the artistic results of these studies. At least, Berenson says of the swan we know only from copies that it is "too big and real" (1916, p. 16) and the original might have taught us that Leonardo's observations were not a loss to artistic creations in this area either. Also, Leonardo's study of birds developed his feeling for winds and storms, which in turn contributed to his Deluge drawings. Thus we can in Leonardo's case find, in principle, a way back from science to art. But such a conclusion may be too hypothetical to be accepted as valid.

It is true that if Leonardo had not devoted himself so stubbornly to science, the course of science in all probability would not have been essentially altered, that is to say, in investigating the historical process of the development of science we do not find Leonardo as an indispensable link. His destiny, to use Ortega y Gasset's viewpoint, was the visual arts. But approaching Leonardo, not historically, but psychologically, one may discern the possibility that without his scientific pursuits he would not have been able to paint. The knowledge of things, in terms of what he considered (psychologically) satisfactory knowledge, that is, may have been a part of the prerequisite equipment for the adventure of painting, which he evidently approached with some feeling of perplexity. In other words, knowledge may have been the antidote against the anxiety that latently or manifestly was involved when he took up the brush.[14]

Yet withal I have not been able to find the common denominator of Leonardo's apparent neurosis and geniushood. Probably Freud, if his work had taken him back to Leonardo after he had accomplished

[14] At this point I do not need to repeat what I have stressed over and over again in the foregoing: that the artist's knowledge of and about things has its direct effect on the visual presentation of them. Here also is the point at which Ortega y Gasset shows his obliviousness of the genius's creativity. Some of the most beautiful portions of the second part of *Faust*, of the *Wilhelm Meister* novels, and many others could never have been created by a writer who did not have firsthand knowledge of all sectors of the society in which he was living. Goethe was a type of writer who could never have created out of the abstract by imagining things, so to speak, behind his desk; the contents that were subjected to artistic elaboration had grown out of concrete experiences, actual observations, the broadest knowledge and expertship in a breath-taking number of functions and activities. Likewise I suggest that Leonardo's Deluge drawings would never have been possible unless the artist had gone through the grinding work of innumerable observations and investigations of water in all its shapes—rivers, streams, lakes, and seas—as well as of air, winds, storms, clouds, rocks, mountains, etc.

his research on ego, superego, and defense, would have given us the solution to this question too.

If I may now return to the question I raised at the outset, I can state that Freud's first major venture, in 1910, into the reconstruction of some relevant psychic processes of a genius of the past stands up quite well in the light of the research that has accumulated during the last fifty years. Still, I am aware that future, particularly archival, research may unearth documents that will disprove beyond question Freud's reconstruction (and, for that matter, also the bulk of my own hypotheses). But even such an outcome, I believe, would not reduce Freud's position as the pre-eminent, as well as the first, paleopsychopathologist. I feel entitled to coin this term since Freud, when he wrote his study, found himself in the position in which the paleontologist customarily finds himself, namely, of having to reconstruct from a minimum of preserved data a maximum of past entities on the basis of observations made in the present. When Schapiro (1956, p. 177) calls "the habit of building explanations of complex phenomena on a single datum" a weakness of Freud's book, then he rejects one of the most glorious pages in the history of psychology. Quite independently of whether Freud was right or wrong in his reconstruction of one aspect of Leonardo's personality, the personality is a whole, and in principle we ought to be capable of making valid statements about the most complex phenomena on the basis of small knowledge of a single phenomenon. It is not up to me to make a final statement about the progress Freud and psychoanalysis have made in the art and science of paleopsychopathology, but it would be surprising if it really turned out that man's mind is in principle less amenable to scientific inquiry than are physical and biological strata of existence.[15] Freud's Leonardo study should, in my estimation, be regarded as holding unimpaired its pre-eminent historical position as a beacon marking the paths by which psychological insight, actually or potentially, as the case may be, can illuminate man's historical past.

[15] In a recent publication, however, Waelder envisions this possibility (1960, pp. 6-13).

Appendix A

Leonardo and Printing

In trying to prove that Leonardo, like other geniuses, may not have put into words just that which burdened him most—though not necessarily consciously, as I add here—I selected the example of his comments on printing. Though Sarton was evidently in error when he wrote that Leonardo was oblivious of that invention, it is nevertheless surprising how few references there are in Leonardo's notes about an invention that was made in the century in which he was born and whose effects probably were not matched by any other before or since. Drawing on an equivalent though better documented state of affairs in Goethe's life which also involves the effects of machines, I drew the conclusion that Leonardo responded to this invention with feelings of horror. As evidence I had nothing else to offer but a comparison in which printing was undoubtedly referred to in a somewhat contemptuous way.

Although my discussion of Leonardo's relationship to printing is of only subordinate importance and the thesis for the sake of which I introduced the subject may still be correct even if the example I cited should prove to be invalid, I wish to add two further remarks.

Goldscheider describes a remarkable contribution of Leonardo's to the art of printing. According to him, Leonardo was the inventor of natural impression (Goldscheider, 1952, p. 6). In C.A. 72 v. Leonardo gives directions for making a natural impression of a leaf: the paper should be painted over with candle soot and the leaf with white lead in oil, "as is done to the letters in printing." Leonardo describes what the resultant image of the leaf will look like and he puts a printed example beside the text, the only one preserved of the many he probably prepared in a herbarium.

This sample is interesting from the point of view of psychology. It would be understandable if printing in this form had proved acceptable to Leonardo. First, it involves the reproduction not of man-made symbols, which, according to my surmise, was reserved by Leonardo to man himself, but of the visual impression of an object produced by nature. Such objects were identically reproduced by nature ad infinitum, and thus a leaf was less individual than the combination of symbols that made up an individual book, which is unique by its specificity. Secondly, it was the object itself that left its traces on the sheet. The person who looks at this natural impression is "cheated" to a lesser degree than one who looks at an engraving. The associations one has about natural impression may be such as the beholder might have on seeing the object's shadow, that is to say, something that is cast by the object itself.

When I consider these and other features inherent in natural impressions, I do not necessarily interpret Leonardo's invention of this technique as a sign of a friendly attitude toward printing but feel almost inclined to find in it a confirmation of the repulsion that I have supposed he had to it.

It is different with a reference to printing to which Miss Kate Steinitz has kindly called my attention. This is in Fogli A 8 v. and follows Leonardo's new precept for the study of the cervical vertebrae. The Italian transcription is as follows:

> Ma per questo brevissimo modo del figurarli per diversi aspetti, se ne dara piena e vera notizia, e, accio che tal benefizio ch'io do all'omini, io insegno il modo di ristamparlo con ordine, e priego voi, o successori, che l'avarizia non vi costringa a fare le stampe in . . .

The two published translations given below differ only slightly but a vastly different trend of thought underlies the difference.[1]

[1] Although in general O'Malley and Saunders's translation is regarded as more reliable, this would not necessarily be so in this instance.

But by this very rapid method of representing from different aspects a complete and accurate conception will result, and as regards this benefit which I give to posterity I teach the method of reprinting it in order, and I beseech you who come after me, not to let avarice constrain you to make the prints in . . . [MacCurdy, 1956, p. 97].

But in this very swift way of representing them in different aspects, one will give full and true knowledge of them, and for the sake of this benefit which I give to men, I teach the manner of reproducing it with order, and I pray you, you other successors, that avarice does not oblige you to make editions in . . . [O'Malley and Saunders, p. 489].

Much depends also on what word is to be filled in at the end. Miss Steinitz informs me that the original leaves no doubt that that word is *legno* (wood). If this is accepted and added to MacCurdy's translation the passage would say that Leonardo wanted to see his drawings reprinted, but not by the use of woodcuts.

The other version—the last word being left in doubt—would favor the idea that Leonardo was opposed to reproducing his anatomical work by printing but not to reproducing it by some other means, say by drawing.

The latter formulation would clearly express an aversion against printing; the former would not necessarily prove that Leonardo rejoiced in the invention of printing, but might mean a concession to necessity. By and large, one may say that Leonardo's attitude toward printing cannot be reliably described, at least on the grounds of his written notes.

APPENDIX B

Remarks on Joseph Gantner's Book on
Leonardo's Visions of the Flood and the End of the World

I wish to add here a discussion of Gantner's book,[1] which reached me after I had completed the body of my text. It is indeed a beautiful book, warmly and convincingly written, a poetical masterpiece that stands in its own right, independently of its correctness or incorrectness. Its center, as the title says, is Leonardo's fantasies and creations about the annihilation of the world. One readily gets the impression, without the author's spelling it out, that the problem of the end of the world was the fulcrum of Leonardo's whole work, as if the abiding drive of his production had been a gigantic struggle to come to terms with the issue of the final process that will terminate the world's existence.

Since the annihilation of the world is to the human mind the supreme act of aggression, the death of all that is living, and this theme was, according to Gantner, a kind of leitmotiv throughout Leonardo's creative years, the psychoanalyst will inevitably be reminded of Freud's death-instinct theory and be induced to view Leonardo's lifework in terms of it.

[1] This book was published in German under the title *Leonardos Visionen von der Sintflut und vom Untergang der Welt* in 1958. For a review and critical discussion of this book, see Schumacher (1959) and Birkmeyer (1959).

In this final theory—which, by the by, has been rejected by the majority of analysts—Freud constructed a comprehensive conceptual frame. Cosmic and organic development, the history of mankind as well as of the individual, is viewed under the aspect of a struggle between Eros, the drive of love, and Thanatos, the drive of death. Although this construction may sound mystical and esoteric, it was, correct or not, still based on observation and scientific ratiocination.

Such ideas, to be sure, are quite alien to Gantner, although his law of biological fulfillment [*Gesetz der biologischen Erfüllung*] (p. 18) may well be regarded as containing the seed of something rather similar. Nevertheless, Gantner's book does seem to provide a basis for viewing Leonardo's lifework as a representation of the struggle of two opposing forces, and it is tempting to connect these two with Freud's Eros and Thanatos—Thanatos, of course having the last word and dominating Leonardo's final opus, which I have discussed in Chapter 17. After all, it would be most instructive to apply this mode of analysis to the immense *œuvre* of an illustrious artist. Unfortunately, I have some doubt whether Gantner adduces enough evidence to substantiate his own views, let alone to confirm the conclusions to which I was stimulated as I read his book. This inadequacy is the more to be pitied because it not only deprives the psychoanalyst of the opportunity to test, and perhaps discover some verification of, a theory cherished by a few, but also detracts from the beauty of the book.

A doubt already sets in when Gantner applies his concepts of prefiguration and figuration to Leonardo's work. That works of art do not spring full-grown out of the artist's head is well known (cf. Schumacher, 1959) and there is, therefore, no objection at first sight to the author's establishing many connections between Leonardo's numerous sketches and the final painted *œuvre*. However, the reader may recall that I postulate Leonardo's having had different goals or motives when drawing from those he had when painting. With him, a sketch was not necessarily a preparation for painting, as it is in so many artists. Therefore I feel quite doubtful about the more or less direct connections the author establishes between Leonardo's landscape studies from nature and the landscapes observed in his later paintings. Drawing was, typically, an attempt to get hold of, appropriate, nature, to study it as it is, its structure, its typical and atypical appearances; the implicit goal was the graphic representation of the terrestrial world. This, of course, is oversimple and needs some reservations. First, one can distinguish among these, so to speak, terrestrial drawings several kinds, as, those that pursue (a) nature as it is, (b) nature as it appears, (c) nature as it ought to be, (d) nature as it ought not to be (this last is perhaps what is prevalent in Leonardo's grotesques). Yet, even when there is a tendency toward typifying or idealizing it does not weaken the terrestrial frame in which this type of drawing is rooted. The principal area of differentiation is between these terrestrial drawings and those that are preparations for the presentation of the transcendent world in the form of paintings.

I have to repeat (and qualify) what I have said in previous chapters to explain why I turn against Gantner's way of applying a concept such as prefiguration—quite sound in itself—to Leonardo's drawings. The connection between certain landscape studies from nature and the landscapes depicted in the *Mona Lisa* or *Anna Metterza* is, in my opinion, of a different kind from that which the author assumes. It is true we find features of what I will call cursorily Leonardo's nature drawings in later paintings, just as everything that Leonardo observed and studied within the world had some determining influence upon his transcendent representations. I even found the most characteristic features of Leonardo's painted *œuvre* in the fact that he did not abandon the terrestrial area in order to reach the transcendent. Since, as I believe, from a certain period on he was constantly motivated by the search for the transcendent, one may say that in a certain sense all of Leonardo's terrestrial studies were preparatory to the paintings, but only inasmuch as the mastery and insight he acquired in his graphic studies were now used for an entirely different purpose that is not contained in any way in the terrestrial sketches from nature.

In his early paintings, however, there does seem to have been a nexus between drawing and painting different from the one I postulate for the later ones. Vasari reports that Leonardo in Verrocchio's workshop:

> would make clay models of figures, draping them with soft rags dipped in plaster, and would then draw them patiently on thin sheets [p. 6].

There is a series of drawings of casts of drapery[2] (Plate 63) that confirms Vasari's report and is generally ascribed to Leonardo, but there is disagreement about the exact correlation of these drawings with the preserved paintings.[3] It is not probable that all the drawings Leonardo made at that time are preserved, and it may be assumed that among those that are now lost there were some that coincided exactly with the details seen in the two Annunciations. If so, this would be an instance of Leonardo's transposing in a point-to-point fashion from a study from nature to the final painting.

Be this as it may, I do not think that this kind of connection existed for studies of details that appeared in the later paintings. I take as an example the famous study for the sleeve of the Virgin in the *Anna Metterza* (Plate 64). Is this drawing a study from nature? At first sight one gets a powerful impression of the reality and verisimilitude of the object depicted and is almost convinced that it is a study from nature. Closer scrutiny, however, raises doubts. I suggest that this study was the result of a large number of observations of reality, and possibly a large number of drawings from nature, but that this final design, which was actually used in the painting, was a compound, a final synthesis of all previous observations and studies from nature. I doubt that Leonardo ever saw or studied this particular combination of folds, creases, and pleats depicted in the drawing, but rather assume that, on the basis of past observations, an object was constructed out of the laws that are inherent in the fabric, its relationship, when in use, to the limb, and many more intricate dynamic relations. Much could be said about the formal details of this sleeve. It can be resolved into a series of planes formed by the single circles of the folds. They approximately cross in a line, that is to say, the circles evolve one out of the other and their inclinations are governed by the relation to an invisible geometrical locus superimposed upon a configuration that seemingly is dictated by the properties of a reality object. The rhythm of the distances between the single folds is also to be observed.

[2] See Popham (1945, Plates 2 to 7); for a discussion, see Popham (pp. 11-13); Goldscheider (1944, notes to Plates 36 and 36A, p. 28); Popp (1928, note to Plate 5, p. 34). There is also a pen-and-ink study of a sleeve that was used in both Annunciations. See Popham (Plate 8A and p. 13), and Popp (note to Plate 4 on p. 13).

[3] Goldscheider (p. 28) seems to reject the idea of a direct connection between these studies and any of Leonardo's paintings; Popp (p. 34) claims that one of them shows the drapery of the angel of the Louvre *Annunciation* in reversed order as seen in a mirror.

At the beginning, they are scarce and at appreciable distances from each other; they then increase in number, are close together. The intensity weakens once more, and then ends in a new crescendo. I seriously doubt that even the most skilled hand could create such an arrangement in reality, for it goes ultimately beyond the morphology of real things and their relations but receives its inner tension from the superimposition of an abstract geometrical law which, however, never transforms the manifest appearance into a mere decorative assemblage. An artist less versed in the depiction of reality, less knowledgeable in the structure of substances, less aware of the relationship between surface and inner organization, would have fallen into the pitfalls of decorativeness, when he set out to make the transcendental visible. In the last analysis, realism is preserved in the study of the sleeve, but the realistic content does not exhaust the configuration Leonardo composed.

I think that from a deepened analysis of such a study as the one for the sleeve the relevant conceptual framework that is contained in the paintings of Leonardo's maturity could be deduced. A comparison of this study with Leonardo's early drapery studies makes this conclusion even more certain. There the impression is conveyed of an artist who with superb craftsmanship depicts an object as it is, that is to say, as it appears to an eye that, without dissolving objects into sense perceptions, tries to perceive things as they are within the framework of the objectifying mind that fully acknowledges the independent existence of the world of objects.

Part of what I have in mind can also be demonstrated from two studies for the *Battle of Anghiari* (see Popham, Plates 198, 199). These are heads of men shouting. Again one must admit that they look as if drawn from nature. But if one considers that both men have their mouths open, one must admit that if Leonardo had tried to draw them from nature the result would have been faces with masklike or artificially distorted features.[4] Nothing of this can be discovered in the actual limning, and here we can be certain that what we see on paper,

[4] Hildebrandt makes a remark pertinent to the question. He calls the two studies by Leonardo of the heads of the apostles in the *Last Supper* (W. 12551 and 12552; Popham, Plates 165, 167) "half ideal preparatory studies" and "portraitlike impressions, yet restyled in accordance with the elevated sphere of their future destiny" (p. 98).

though it evidently was the result of observation, cannot possibly have been drawn from nature.[5]

Gantner looks upon most of the landscapes as they appear in Leonardo's *œuvre* as prefigurations of the final theme of *The Deluge*. The main factual point on which this interpretation rests is a significant aspect of the way in which water appears in sketches and paintings, namely, according to the author, as a destructive element that gnaws at rocks and carries away soil from river beds.

References to the destructive effects of water are no doubt quite numerous in Leonardo's notes, but those that set forth a more positive aspect are also to be considered. I wish to cite a few of them: In C.A. 171 r. a (MacCurdy, 1956, p. 647), he speaks of water as "now deadly now lifegiving." Water contributes also to the formation of new land. "The soil carried away by the rivers is deposited in the ultimate parts of their courses; or rather the soil carried away by the high courses of the rivers is deposited in the ultimate descents of their movements" (MacCurdy, 1956, p. 701; G 49 v.). And occasionally the vitality of water is extolled. "Water, which is the vital humour of the terrestrial machine, moves by its own natural heat" (MacCurdy, 1956, p. 711; H 95 r.).[6] At times even the destructive aspect of water is seen in a more peaceful light. "The greatest elevation of the waves will not wear away its bed beneath itself. . . . If . . . the amount of friction is slight, it will have but little force and will consume the bed but little" (MacCurdy, 1956, p. 726; I 117 v.). Hope is also expressed that human ingenuity may put a halt to aqueous destruction. Among the books Leonardo listed to be written was "A book of how to guard against the rush of rivers so that cities may not be struck by them" (MacCurdy, 1956, p. 733; B.M. 35 r.), and elsewhere a "Book of how to control rivers so that the small beginnings of the damage they cause may not increase" (MacCurdy, 1956, p. 736; B.M. 122 r.). Giving more specific advice, Leonardo wrote:

[5] If something pertinent to these drawings can be learned from the observation of faces while singing, I would say that depicting faces as they appear in nature when the mouth is widely opened for the purpose of the production of sounds would strike the beholder as artificial. Solely for the sake of making appear natural that which in nature appears only for moments and fleetingly, but is shown unchanging in visual representation, Leonardo must have been compelled to deviate from what actual sense perception conveyed.

[6] See also MacCurdy (1956, p. 739; B.M. 234 r.).

Because the straighter the river the swifter will its course be, and the more vigorously will it gnaw and consume the bank and its bed, it is therefore necessary either to enlarge these rivers considerably or to send them through many twistings and turnings or to divide them into a number of branches [MacCurdy, 1956, p. 719; I 82 v.].

How the diverting of rivers ought to be carried on when the water has completely lost the fury of its current . . . [MacCurdy, 1956, p. 759; Leic. 27 v.].

At times creation and destruction are viewed as keeping a balance: "the current of the river eats away the base of the mountain on one side where it strikes and gives it back to the opposite side to which it is deflected" (MacCurdy, 1956, p. 736; B.M. 161 r.). Here it may be well to cite a passage that seems even to exclude an end of the world. ". . . if it be granted that the world is everlasting . . ." (MacCurdy, 1956, p. 700; G 48 v. and 49 r.).[7]

Thus it seems that Leonardo's final vision of the earth's destruction by water was the end product of a long development during which contrary aspects gradually receded. Therefore I doubt that one can safely correlate representations of water in Leonardo's paintings with the "cruel" aspect of water without considering its opposite.

One passage shows the inner contradictoriness of Gantner's views. He speaks of Leonardo's "inner vision of the constant destruction and renewal of matter, of the eternal circulation of the living and its ultimate ruin [*Innere Vision von der ständigen Zerstörung und Erneuerung der Materie, von dem ewigen Kreislauf des Lebendigen und seinem schliesslichen Untergang*]" (p. 49). The inherent contradiction between eternal circulation and ultimate ruin reveals the difficulty of the problem. Are not the landscape paintings an expression of life's eternal circulation?[8] In beholding these landscapes one gets

[7] But, in order to temper the impression of a friendly future I want to cite of the many possible passages only the following:

How in the end the mountains will be levelled by the waters, seeing that they wash away the earth which covers them and uncover their rocks, which begin to crumble and are being continually changed into soil subdued alike by heat and frost. The waters wear away their bases and the mountains bit by bit fall in ruin into the rivers which have worn away their bases, and by reason of this ruin the waters rise in a swirling flood and form great seas [MacCurdy, 1956, p. 743f.; Leic. 17 v.].

[8] Cf. Popp (p. 13) for an interpretation of the water in the *Mona Lisa* landscape that is opposite to Gantner's. Cf. also Clark (1939, p. 118f.) for an interpretation of Leonardo's painted landscapes. Weyl (1950, p. 283), however, speaks of the spiritual bond (*geistige Verbindung*) of the painted landscapes with the depiction of the Deluge.

the impression of something being expressed that is endowed with ever eternal existence. To be sure—again relying on personal reactions —some of the configurations produce the association of death created by the absence of life, as is the case with the serene glaciers one sees in the background of the *Mona Lisa,* but there is nothing there that would suggest that these giants will ever crumble.

It is remarkable—as I think has not been sufficiently considered— that no human beings at all appear in those landscapes. In the Uffizi *Annunciation* a city and ships are seen, but even there I cannot make out a representation of a human being.[9] It cannot be by chance that Leonardo's later landscapes are empty of human life. Except for a road and a bridge in the *Mona Lisa* landscape[10] and a church in the *St. Jerome*[11] there is not even an indication of human activity.[12] As far as I have been able to ascertain, neither are there any animals to be seen, which, in view of Leonardo's superb ability at depicting animals, is all the more surprising.[13]

All this conveys the impression of a strict separation of the world of man from nature. The main subject of the painting is, accordingly, unconcerned about the landscape. In order to grasp the implication of that separateness one has only to turn to certain landscape representations of Rembrandt, where man's relationship to nature is made the central issue. Whatever are the emotions that there merge man with nature—joy, fear, awe, bliss, and many more—the landscapes are always marked by anthropomorphism, a feature alien to the landscapes in Leonardo's paintings.[14] His are characterized by a supreme serenity and aloofness; they acquire a godlike aura by existing in themselves, as if leaving unnoticed everything outside of their own realm.

[9] I am not certain whether this is also true of the Louvre *Annunciation.*

[10] However, see de Tolnay (1952, p. 21) who attributes a special meaning to the division of the *Mona Lisa* landscape into one inhabited by people, as signified by the road and bridge, and one more distant that is devoid of human traces.

[11] The sketch of a church is seen in the underpainting of the background. Whether it would have been retained if Leonardo had finished the painting may be questioned.

[12] To what extent this is true of the *Last Supper* cannot be determined from the reproduction of the fresco in its present condition. In the engraving by Morghen (Plate 8) buildings and a road are visible in the distance.

[13] I owe thanks to Mme. Béguin of the Louvre for confirming my impression that the landscapes of the *Mona Lisa* portrait, of the *St. Anne* and the *Virgin of the Rocks,* as well as the copy of the *Last Supper* in the Louvre do not contain either animals or human beings aside from the principal figures.

[14] Some of his landscape sketches give a different impression.

If we rely on the direct effect these landscapes have on the beholder, we cannot consider them prefigurations of the later Deluge drawings. In support of his theory Gantner refers to Leonardo's scientific interests and opinions at the time he produced the paintings. But this presupposes a parallelism or synthesis between Leonardo's artistic and scientific work which has first to be proved before it may be used for the interpretation of the paintings. If that degree of closeness actually existed between what summarily is called Leonardo's notebooks and his paintings, we should expect to find literary comments on such subjects as the Last Supper and the lives of the saints. But his notebooks are quite without any such references, which alone would dictate great cautiousness in viewing the painted *œuvre* as complementary to his investigations. While the two must not be viewed as isolated from each other, their relationship may be one of contrasts, of compensation, and many others. Probability may be invoked in support of the contention that the medium of art, and particularly of painting, was used for the representation of aspects that could not find sufficient realization and concretization in inquiry and investigation.

Gantner quite rightly calls attention to Leonardo's mastery in representing depth by making use of the variations of appearance that depend on the closeness or remoteness of objects. All gradations are found, from the detailed concreteness of objects in the foreground to the dreamlike haziness in the distance—what Gantner speaks of as the "gradation of degrees of reality [*Abstufung der Realitätsgrade*]" (p. 75, et passim).[15] He then asserts a connection between the prefigural and the figural, equating the dreamlike and hazy with the sketch and the design. This must be rejected from a methodological viewpoint.[16] The dreamy and hazy in the finished painting may share some surface features with the sketchy, but they are essentially different, at least in Leonardo's work. A sketch has inherently the character of a potential, of something that has not yet been fully concretized. We may consider

[15] Cf. Wölfflin (1899, p. 32), who speaks of the dreamlike aspect of the *Mona Lisa* landscape and its "different order of reality from the figure." Hildebrandt says of the mountainous landscape that it is in a realm between dream and reality (p. 177).

[16] De Tolnay too speaks about the distant part of the landscape as "le paysage de rêve d'un bleu glauque et pâle" (1952, p. 21f.) and later says it is like a moon landscape (p. 26). It is not clear whether de Tolnay wishes this to be understood as a variation in degree of reality. Earlier (p. 20) he emphasizes that Leonardo was the first in Italy to realize the unity of space "dans un portrait à fond de paysage." In my estimation a gradation of degrees of reality would abolish the unity of space.

a sketch perfect as it is, and even object to the full concretization of what it potentially contains, but if it contained nothing of the uncon-cretized it would not be a sketch but a drawing. The dreamy and hazy zones of Leonardo's landscapes say everything there is to say: if they said more they would in reality say less. They have nothing of the unfinished that is the prerequisite of a sketch; they are finished and therefore they possess the character of unsurpassed realness. It must be admitted that in landscapes painted by artists ignorant of aerial and color perspective reality appears artificial by comparison, or at least far less real than in Leonardo's.[17] If the dreamy and hazy zones of Leonardo's landscapes were taken out of context and compared in isolation with those of the foreground, that is to say, if the background and foreground areas were on different canvases, then Gantner's propo-sition as to gradation of degrees of reality might be pertinent. What he regards as varying degrees of reality are correlated to zones of varying distance and not arranged arbitrarily or according to fantasy, as someone might picture the ghost of Hamlet's father in a hazy fashion to indicate to the audience that he is insubstantial. What meets the eye directly in Leonardo's landscapes is always a substantial reality, various aspects of which are brought before the beholder in conformity with nature, but this reality is brought before the eyes in such a way that it simultaneously contains the transcendental world. If Leonardo had resorted to presenting a dream world in order to reach out for a sphere beyond the perceptually given, let us say as surrealism tries to, his work would have been much easier, but it would certainly not have been the same, and it seems foolhardy to suppose it would have accom-plished as much. As I tried to set forth earlier, his work is extraordinary for its unrelenting unwillingness to resort to a short cut.

It is well known that such paintings of Leonardo's as the *Anna Metterza* and the *Battle of Anghiari* were the outcome of deliberations that covered as much as decades.[18] There will probably be agreement that the comparatively large number of compositional drawings relating to these two paintings are only a part of those Leonardo actually pro-duced and that other paintings as well were preceded by comparable

[17] Wölfflin (1899) too says of the *Mona Lisa* landscape that it follows Leonardo's theories as to the appearance of distant objects.

[18] Aronberg (1951) has given an impressive outline of the compositional development, the detours, regressions, and progressions that anteceded the final result as we know it in the Louvre *Anna Metterza*.

extensive and intensive studies. Whereas Leonardo's nature drawings —of animals, plants, trees, etc.—are definitive, the compositional studies are not. Gombrich has devoted a profound essay to the meaning of these sketches (1953-54). He demonstrates their enormous historical importance as a signpost of an essential change in the artist's approach to his work, the freedom he had obtained, and the intrusion of personal fantasy into his creations when compared with medieval and early Quattrocento predecessors.

These compositional sketches are, indeed, of the greatest interest. In my opinion they suit well with my hypothesis. They are the frantic attempts of a mind in search of the absolute, of which there can be only one. But how to find it? The basic elements, the single figures, the individual bricks, so to speak, are arranged and rearranged. At times it seems as if a trial-and-error method were being applied, with all possible combinations being explored in order to find the one solution that must exist, as one might proceed in solving a jigsaw puzzle.

Yet this is certainly wrong; there was always an underlying idea at work which predominated over what may look like a chance factor. Of course, until the final solution was found nothing was allowed to stand in the way of adaptability and flexibility; any commitment to a detail might block a new channel. The outcome was the superb fluidity of these compositions. To infer a kind of principle, an internal commitment to the *unfinished,* as Gantner seems to do, impresses me, if it is permitted to say so, as a cardinal misunderstanding (cf. Schumacher). Eternally valid and spiritually immutable the paintings emerge as Leonardo painted them whether he "finished" them or not; the beholder knows, or believes he knows, what they are.[19] But in order to achieve this greatness of definitiveness a long chain of indefinite links had to be gone through.

In general Gantner asserts the unity of literary and scientific activities, sketches and paintings, in Leonardo. The one exception he admits (p. 220) occurred in the context of the Deluge problem. It is my impression, however, that the author minimizes the contradiction we here encounter between the scientist and the artist in Leonardo.

Gantner too refers to Leonardo's early theory of the end of the world by exsiccation and fire (see MacCurdy, 1956, p. 74; B.M. 155

---

[19] Cf. Hildebrandt (1927), particularly pp. 146, 177.

v.). This theory was in keeping with tradition, as de Lorenzo (cited after Gantner and Weyl) has demonstrated. I suggested in the chapter on *The Deluge* that the final graphic representation of the destruction of the world by water proves the disparity between science and art in Leonardo. Gantner, however, infers from Leonardo's manuscripts that a change in Leonardo's end-of-the-world theories preceded the Deluge drawings. Thus in F 84 r. he wrote:

> Of the earth. Every heavy substance tends to descend, and the lofty things will not retain their height but with time they will all descend, and thus in time the earth will become a sphere, and as a consequence will be completely covered with water, and the underground channels will remain without movement [MacCurdy, 1956, p. 693].[20]

Since this passage is the result of observation and ratiocination, one may deduce that art and science were, after all, in harmony; a new scientific theory led to correlated graphic representations, and the Deluge series emphasizes the end of the world by water in contrast to the conception formed earlier.

However, from the textual point of view one may have a doubt about the constance of the theory as presented in MS. F. I have only to refer to the passage cited earlier from G 48 v. and 49 r. in which Leonardo discusses the reasons why mankind is perpetually supplied with salt:

> . . . if it be granted that the world is everlasting it must needs be that its population also will be everlasting; and that therefore the human race has perpetually been and will be consumers of salt [MacCurdy, 1956, p. 700].

One may infer that at this time Leonardo held the view that mankind would never be threatened by destruction. Since MS. G was probably written after MS. F (cf. Richter, Vol. II, p. 400), one might conclude that this theory superseded the earlier one of destruction by water. However, it is extremely risky to draw conclusions in such a way, since one cannot learn from the notebooks alone what latent psychological power, meaning, or intensity may inhere in single remarks.

---

[20] There is one other passage that expresses the same idea (MacCurdy, 1956, p. 684; F 52 v.). The two passages C.A. 185 v. c and B.M. 205 v, translated by Gantner under the heading: The Earth drowns in water (p. 243), do not support what the heading would lead one to expect. Only the other two passages, F 52 v. and F 84 r., clearly refer to a submergence of the continents under water.

One finds contradictory statements in close proximity and the reader may recall my previous likening of the notes to free associations. Leonardo's mind ran in many directions. One occasionally gets the impression that he follows a trend just for the sake of finding out where it may lead and it is questionable whether he considered a conclusion thus reached as valid at all or merely as a playful deduction that did not carry much if any lasting conviction. In other words, the psychological relevance of single statements is hardly ascertainable. The statements that express a belief in the world's final and inescapable destruction by water are rare, and one may wonder whether if this theory had been conclusive it would not have received greater emphasis.

On the other hand, the working out of the implications of precisely such a conclusion as had greatest psychological relevance might have been excluded from the notebooks and relegated to the artistic medium. If we rely on the textual approach the question remains moot.

In general it has not been disputed that it was the Deluge that Leonardo depicted in his last graphic creations and that this opus is expressive of what was deepest in Leonardo at that time.[21] Even if Gantner is right in his presentation of sequences in Leonardo's theories, it can safely be stated that his last drawings had little to do with the theory he set forth in F 84 r. I even venture to suggest that if he had persisted in holding to his original theory of final destruction by aridity and fire, he would still have produced the Deluge sketches. These ten or eleven drawings clearly grow out of the Biblical imagery of Noah's great flood, which Leonardo had refuted by impeccable ratiocination.

Gantner consistently omits any reference to Leonardo's personal feelings about his own impending death. Whether that event was quite close or still a few years off when the Deluge drawings were made is of no relevance. But the man who created the Deluge drawings had his own death before his eyes and was by no means principally

---

[21] For a different concept, see Popp (pp. 20f., 23). In her comment there is no less admiration for the series of drawings than other historians have expressed, but for her they are a representation of rain, wind, and atmosphere. This probably is due to a comment Leonardo wrote on one of them. See Plate 58, on which is written *della pioggia* (cf. Clark, 1935, Vol. I, p. 48) and an added reminder about the depiction of rain, distance, and shadow. Wind (1952) thinks that these drawings were probably designed for stage decorations, a view I can hardly share. Clark (1952, p. 313) finds a direct inspiration from "the ruthless continuum of watery movement."

motivated by any physical or geological theory regarding the last stage of the world.[22]

Into the creation of these images of the world's end that which was most archaic in Leonardo was bound to enter. His theory that "every heavy substance has to descend," whatever its unconscious equivalent in the repressed may have been, is, so to speak, a sophisticated, artificial peripheral view that does not in itself contain any artistic obligation. Substance is pushed, shattered, and annihilated in these representations of cataclysms, and the meaning they convey is that in the end there will be nothing. By no means is there the slightest indication that the processes represented will ever lead to a huge sphere of water serenely floating through space, as might be expected from F 84 r. Nor is there any imagery that anticipates a happy ending, as in the Biblical account. It certainly is a deluge in the Biblical sense, and, though without ark or dove, accomplishes by its means a destruction no less complete than that which the Lord announces to Noah: "I will destroy them with the earth" (Gen. 6 : 13) prior to the final compromise.

I agree with Heydenreich and Gantner that Leonardo's drawings go far beyond the annihilation of mankind. As a matter of fact, man and his traces on the world play a very minor role here, and from most of the drawings one gets the impression that they represent events that come to pass long after mankind has been wiped out. Indeed, they seem to say that nothing is easier than to destroy man and his works, that it needs no more than a gesture to make an end of him, but that to end the rest of the universe gigantic catastrophes are required. Perhaps it is feared that unless matter too is annihilated man might rise up again. Gantner rightly says that nothingness is no subject for the visual arts. It is by depicting the processes that occur when the universe is on the way toward nothingness that Leonardo succeeds in conveying the taste, or, better, the foretaste, of nothingness. The emphasis on nothingness is intensified by Leonardo's representing the disintegrating cosmos without a Godhead; there is no world yonder.[23]

---

[22] Gantner, in his epilogue, declares that the question of which theory underlay the drawings is idle (p. 218). Yet throughout the book he emphasizes the importance of the bearing that the development of Leonardo's theories had on this subject.

[23] It is my impression that the relationship between that which is represented and the background against which it is put has a specific psychological meaning that goes beyond the aesthetic principles prevalent in the respective phase of the history of art (cf. Wor-

To fathom the depth of these creations one is called upon to forget any thought of our world; they are cosmic fantasies that go beyond our planet or planetary system, but include the infinite universe.

It is the extension of the final cataclysm beyond the merely human world that makes the drawings so gruesome and renders them unreachable by empathy. The cessation of space, time, and matter is beyond the confines of the human mind, although modern physics suggests the rise of space from one point and therewith perhaps indicates the possibility of its return to the original state—which would actually amount to the cessation of space, time, and matter.[24]

Ordinary man generally envisages his personal end in a frame that includes his next of kin, friends, or the permanent traces he may have left. Depending on his station and other factors, this personal frame of reference may extend to his nation and mankind, or, again, depending on his religious propensities, it may be narrowed to the prospect that awaits his soul. But I presume that it is unique when, under the pressure of approaching death, that which is projected embraces the vastness of the universe. We may obtain here a sign of Leonardo's intense narcissism, which inflated the idea of the end of self into that of the universe. Whatever may have been the infantile root of the

ringer, 1908). Within the many types of figure-background relationships a particular place is held by those in which the background disappears and the whole plane is taken up by the figurative representation. Some of Leonardo's Deluge drawings seem to be without background. I connect this absence of background with the impression they convey that the universe they represent is one without Godhead, without any world beyond the physically seen.

[24] Schumacher disputes that the series has the character of absolute destruction. He refers to W. 12698 r. (Plate 62) on which Leonardo wrote "Adam and Eve," and to W. 12376 (Plate 49) on which Olympian gods appear in the clouds. He maintains that this implies regeneration or a new genesis (p. 250). Perhaps it does, although the Adam and Eve drawing impresses me as one of the most desolate. But be this as it may, these two drawings do not warrant Schumacher's conclusions regarding the other drawings in the series, since both of them, though genetically connected with the Deluge series, without doubt represent prestages and are dated to a time prior to the final series (cf. Clark, 1935, Vol. I, p. 46). What Schumacher claims is hidden in Leonardo's Deluge series can be found outspoken in Goethe's imagery. In a conversation with Eckermann (October 23, 1828) he foresaw the time when God would no longer take any joy in the world and he would have to "batter to pieces everything [alles zusammenschlagen]" for the sake of a "rejuvenated creation [verjüngte Schöpfung]" (Eckermann, p. 554). Here too we encounter an indirect reference to the myth of Noah; the aggressiveness of terminology is also noteworthy; nevertheless the catastrophe leads to rejuvenation. Although I do not agree with Heller's assertion (1952) that Goethe avoided tragedy in his work, it is to be admitted that Goethe's prediction of a catastrophe many millennia away (in the meantime "we can have all kinds of fun upon this good old plane as it is [auf dieser lieben alten Fläche, wie sie ist, allerlei Spass haben]" and leading to rejuvenation may be used in favor of Heller's opinion. However, when Gantner (p. 218f.) disputes that a sense of tragedy pervaded Leonardo's life and work, it is difficult to follow him.

vision—birth fantasies or castration fears[25]—its core is the full subjective representation of the self's impending dissolution. I do not mean by this opinion to suggest that the problem of death became relevant to Leonardo more or less suddenly when the approach of his own death made itself psychologically noticeable. Like any other illustrious mind, he too was puzzled by the problem of death long before he reached the period of old age. But like others I too feel that his preceding creations do not betray signs of any particular affinity to this range of problems and that only these final drawings stand fully under the sign of thanatological imagery.

The reduction of man virtually to zero, which is the consequence of Leonardo's projection of his own impending fate into the universe, served as defense against anxiety. Indeed, it must have been an effective one. The worth-whileness of lamentation about death is cogently disputed when man turns out to be the frailest part of creation, enormous destructive forces having to be mobilized to make rocks and mountains vanish at a time when all traces of man had gone. But the unquestionable factor of defense must—in my estimation—not be

[25] Water in the different shapes in which it appears in nature plays a great role in the poetic and artistic imagination of man. Its manifold usage as a symbol and the variety of meanings attributable to the variety of forms in which it appears do not need to be discussed here (cf. Freud, 1900, pp. 399-401; Rank, 1912, particularly for the meaning of the Flood). But, aside from these special meanings encountered, one observes in instances like Leonardo's and Goethe's that water assumes a more general function. It is a challenging task to compare their imagery about water. Only the following may be intimated here. Water had a catastrophic effect on Goethe's cherished project of the Ilmenau silver mine, which seemed to him the portal to eternal glory, a kind of imperishable justification of his terrestrial existence. There is a surprising similarity between Goethe's opening of the Ilmenau mine in 1784 and the scene of Faust's death when the dying Faust misinterprets the clank of the lemures' spades as the welcome clinking of the spades of his serfs who, as he believes, will wrest soil from the sea and make it arable. This illusion of the dying Faust stands, in my opinion, in a biographical connection with the outcome of Goethe's silver-mine project. Despite his heroic efforts, water seeping into the mine enforced irrevocable closure. In the aged poet's fantasy the ambition of former years has been fulfilled, but it remains an illusion in Faust's mind too. This illusion, however, saves him from perdition in hell and brings him eternal bliss. After all, he found the highest pleasure not in sensual delight but in social action, illusionary as it may have been. Death, in *Faust*, Part II, is represented as essentially different from the way it appears in Leonardo's final drawings. In *Faust* the continuity of the cosmos, of the world, of the human community is preserved. Death is represented in *Faust* II with unbelievable power and majesty. Yet even the continuity of the individual is preserved in *Faust* as the closing epilogue assures us. (For a contrary view, see Simon, 1949, pp. 309, 311.)

In Leonardo's life water too created realistic problems though of a different nature. There was his plan of forcing the Arno out of its natural bed into an altered course, a task Leonardo could as little achieve as Goethe could his. His drawings, in turn, are devoid of any shred of continuity, which makes their general background so different from Goethe's last message. The study and explanation of such differences ought to lead to insight into the psychobiological matrix out of which the various types of genius grow.

overrated. Mastery and acceptance are also to be found in the series. To my feeling, mastery is even prevalent and defense takes a subordinate place. The artist while creating often feels liks a god artifex, and I have cited pertinent passages to show that painting also had this meaning for Leonardo. But if we regard his total work, we cannot overlook the humbleness that manifests itself both in the careful study of nature and in his scrupulous striving for transcendent presentation. In the Deluge series, however, one feels, he stands forth as true god artifex, as if his images would force nature to go the path he had mapped out for her.

In this connection it may be worth while to point out the following problem even though, I believe, it cannot yet be solved: what were the psychic processes in Leonardo that led him to make a full mental representation of a world without life, of death in general and particularly of his own death—which he must have succeeded in doing, to judge from his drawings. Psychologists agree that the state of sleep or unconsciousness cannot be imagined. It is easy, of course, to imagine oneself as sleeping, but the state of an unconscious mind is beyond the range of the imaginative capacity. However, some subjects in the grip of schizophrenia or a condition close to that constantly assert that this is not so and claim that they can imagine the state of death. Their insistence and the accounts they give have inclined me toward agreeing that they do possess an imaginative quality that is ordinarily absent. In view of Leonardo's drawings one must enlarge this group and say that some artists also possess this rare gift.

In general, Gantner, I believe, overestimates the bearing of matters intellectual on the Deluge series. He believes that Leonardo had first to drop his idea of the equivalence of macrocosmos and microcosmos (p. 160f.) before he was capable of creating his personal myth of the end of the world. I take this to be a *post hoc, ergo propter hoc* judgment, and it would not be difficult to demonstrate that Leonardo's physiological theories about death were also quite suited for the Deluge series. My contention is that the Deluge series is the result of Leonardo's artistic reaction to, and elaboration of, his presentiment of his own death. The imagery used was the Biblical myth of the Flood, which, in turn, was genetically connected with specific childhood traumata. Geological, scientific, theories had only little bearing on the end product.

The subjective imagery and emotions that found graphic representation in Leonardo's last drawings cannot possibly have grown out of his rational deductions, some of which we encounter in MS. F. That which was most archaic, beyond or below rational verbalization, was set into motion. The imagery of the Biblical Flood was resuscitated. The relevant psychological point is that though the Bible myth had been rejected by Leonardo in one of his most brilliant scientific demonstrations, it did not lose its power as an instigator of one of his greatest artistic accomplishments. It is difficult to speculate whether Leonardo would have ended his artistic *œuvre* in the same way if the myth of the Flood had not, as I presume, already impressed him at an early age. To be sure, as said before, Leonardo went far beyond the confines of the myth in his Deluge creations, and therefore the relevance of the myth should not be overrated. Yet the myth has a particular appeal to archaic thinking; personal and traditional imagery can scarcely be kept apart in this area.[26] At the same time there is the possibility that Leonardo's conclusion—rationally convincing to him, though false— that the end state of the world would involve a submergence of the continents into the oceans had a strengthening effect on the Biblical imagery. Nevertheless, I personally believe that the process took place in an opposite direction, that is, that under the influence of early Biblical imagery, Leonardo abandoned his former (and far more probable?) theory of aridity and fire. The literal acceptance of Biblical imagery such as the Flood was blocked by the clear insight that it was not feasible from a rational viewpoint. The end-of-the-world theory encountered in MS. F appears to me to be a compromise between mythic and rational thinking. Essential features of the myth are preserved but reappear now in a scientifically acceptable form. The final graphic work, however, still is closer to the Biblical story than to the scientific theory of MS. F, and it may therefore be used in support of the opinions of those who assume a conflict or divergence between Leonardo's scientific and artistic impulses.

It may appear contradictory that I draw this conclusion at this point, after having declared, in agreement with many others, that it was precisely the bulk of Leonardo's drawings that were in harmony with

---

[26] Gantner is correct, of course, in stating that Leonardo created his own myth. But the genetic connection with the Biblical myth (without happy ending, as stated before) still exists, as, if I understand him correctly, Gantner does not deny.

his science.[27] Yet Leonardo's Deluge cycle holds a special place also inasmuch as here he represented through drawings what usually was reserved for painting. These drawings do not serve the purpose of preparing something that will grow into a more comprehensive configuration nor do they contribute to the understanding of the structure of the world as it is. They are beyond reality as it is; they are final as are his paintings. It is perhaps this ultimate step of Leonardo's of forging a medium into an instrument for the accomplishment of purposes originally alien to it that most conspicuously demonstrates the incredible synthesis he achieves at the end of his artistic career.

Sir Kenneth Clark called the synthesis Leonardo had accomplished "a vision of destruction in which symbol and reality seem to be at one" (1950, p. 47). Indeed, symbol and reality are here identical as perhaps nowhere else in art. Yet the visual focusing of symbol and reality upon the same point is to be seen, I believe, in most of Leonardo's later paintings; the Deluge series seems to be the only instance in which the coincidence of symbol and reality also occurs in his drawings.

Gantner rightly makes much of a series of fantastic tales Leonardo wrote in the form of letters about a catastrophe that he allegedly witnessed in Armenia. His account is so vivid that some historians have believed he actually spent some time in Armenia (Richter, Vol. II, p. 315). Two of these reports which contain the clues necessary for a psychological interpretation of the Deluge cycle are not reproduced by Gantner. They are from C.A. 311 r. a, and C.A. 96 v. b (MacCurdy, 1956, p. 1053ff.). I quote the most pertinent passages:

> . . . there appeared a giant who came from the Libyan desert. This giant was born on Mount Atlas, and was black, and he fought against Artaxerxes with the Egyptians and Arabs, the Medes and Persians; he lived in the sea upon the whales, the great leviathans and the ships. When the savage giant fell by reason of the ground being covered over with blood and mire, it seemed as though a mountain had fallen; whereat the country [shook] as though there were an earthquake. . . .
>
> The black visage at first sight is most horrible and terrifying to look upon, especially the swollen and bloodshot eyes set beneath the awful lowering eyebrows which cause the sky to be overcast and the earth to tremble.

[27] Cf. Goldscheider (1952, p. 6): "The same scientific attitude is evident in Leonardo's landscape studies. Many of these are so charming that it is hard to believe that they are merely meteorological studies, essays in aerial perspective, or preparatory studies for maps."

And believe me there is no man so brave but that, when the fiery eyes were turned upon him, he would willingly have put on wings in order to escape, for the face of infernal Lucifer would seem angelic by contrast with this.

The nose was turned up in a snout with wide nostrils and sticking out of these were quantities of large bristles, beneath which was the arched mouth, with the thick lips, at whose extremities were hairs like those of cats, and the teeth were yellow; and from the top of his instep he towered above the heads of men on horseback.

And as his cramped position had been irksome, and in order to rid himself of the importunity of the throng, his rage turned to frenzy, and he began to let his feet give vent to the frenzy which possessed his mighty limbs, and entering in among the crowd he began by his kicks to toss men up in the air, so that they fell down again upon the rest, as though there had been a thick storm of hail, and many were those who in dying dealt out death. And this barbarity continued until such time as the dust stirred up by his great feet, rising up in the air, compelled his infernal fury to abate, while we continued our flight.[28]

Alas, how many attacks were made upon this raging fiend to whom every onslaught was as nothing. O wretched folk, for you there avail not the impregnable fortresses, nor the lofty walls of your cities, nor the being together in great numbers, nor your houses or palaces! There remained not any place unless it were the tiny holes and subterranean caverns where after the manner of crabs and crickets and creatures like these you might find safety and a means of escape. Oh, how many wretched mothers and fathers were deprived of their children! How many unhappy women were deprived of their companions! In truth, my dear Benedetto, I do not believe that ever since the world was created there has been witnessed such lamentation and wailing of people, accompanied by so great terror. In truth, the human species in such a plight has need to envy every other race of creatures; for though the eagle has strength sufficient to subdue the other birds, they yet remain unconquered through the rapidity of their flight, and so the swallows through their speed escape becoming the prey of the falcon, and the dolphins also by their swift flight escape becoming the prey of the whales and of the mighty leviathans; but for us wretched mortals there avails not any flight, since this monster when advancing slowly far exceeds the speed of the swiftest courser.

I know not what to say or do, for everywhere I seem to find myself swimming with bent head within the mighty throat and remaining indistinguishable in death, buried within the huge belly.

---

[28] It is my impression that the drawing of *A Large Cannon Being Raised on to a Gun-Carriage* (Popham, Plate 305, W. 12647) is connected with Leonardo's imagery of the destructive giant. Here destruction is turned away from those who are nearby, and little men acquire control over devastating forces.

Here the end-of-the-world fantasy appears in a personalized prestage. The destructive force is a horrible giant who maliciously torments and annihilates. The oral quality of the fantasy is clearest in the last paragraph quoted, when Leonardo describes himself as being in the beast's throat and having lost his identity through being indistinguishable from the monster. At another point he describes a monster on a stallion that had "six giants tied to his saddle bow and one in his hand which he gnawed with his teeth" (MacCurdy, 1956, p. 1056; I 139 r.). This is the imagery Goya painted in his *Saturn* (Plate 60). Death is equated with being devoured by a fiend.

What is so tremendously exciting about the Deluge cycle, however, is its purification of all this archaic imagery. In beholding Goya's painting one feels shock and disgust. The unconscious is mercilessly revealed. Yet in the last analysis Leonardo's Deluge drawings are perhaps even more merciless. Goya's painting will create repulsion in the beholder, so that he may turn away or rebel; the artistic message comes from desperate rebellion, which implies that the world should or could be better. In Leonardo's drawings despair and rebellion are absent; the artistic message is: such is the end of the universe, inescapable beyond the shade of a doubt. There is not only no need of rebellion but no capacity for it or possibility of its succeeding. What are you, man, that you can fancy a cosmic spirit may consider your fate?

I said earlier that the Deluge cycle is a narcissistic projection of the self's anticipated dissolution into the universe. It is again unendingly impressive that with this exquisitely narcissistic motive a work of art was created in which human narcissism is wiped out and man is reduced to a negligible speck in view of the vastness of space and the eternities when he did not exist and would not exist.

APPENDIX C

On Freud's Interpretation of a Formal Error by Leonardo, and on a Slip by Freud

In *Codex Arundel* at the British Museum one finds the following entry written by Leonardo:

On the 9th of July 1504, Wednesday, at seven o'clock, died Ser Piero da Vinci, notary at the Palazzo del Podestà, my father,—at seven o'clock, being eighty years old, leaving behind him ten sons and two daughters [Richter, Vol. II, p. 344, No. 1372; B.M. 272 r.].

Freud took Leonardo's small error of form in repeating the hour of the father's death "as if Leonardo had forgotten at the end of the sentence that he had already written it at the beginning" (1910, p. 119) as an occasion to demonstrate a particular aspect of Leonardo's psychopathology. According to Freud, Leonardo failed in suppressing an affect that here found "a distorted expression." A strong affect elicited by the father's demise was displaced onto an indifferent detail, which, thus supercharged, led to a perseveration. Thus one may say the repetition, which reveals a failure to suppress completely, is an indication of the intensity of the warded-off affect; the trivial content of the repetition indicates the almost complete victory of the defense. Freud brought this observation into connection with other instances of a similar kind and thus established the basic relationship of the artist's self to his emotions.[1]

In discussing Freud's interpretation of this formal slip by Leonardo, Giuseppina Fumagalli launched a particularly bitter attack. "Oh psychiatrists, even if you are Freud do not forget first to be psychologists!" she exclaims (1952, p. 56). Since Leonardo's entry was a diary note, it did not, she believes, permit the expression of effusive feelings. Moreover, from the fact that a like repetition, presently to be cited, is found at another point of Leonardo's *Notes* she draws the conclusion that Leonardo witnessed his father's death and that the repetition is therefore a sign of a most conscious fixation of the memory of the last moment (*fissità coscientissima del ricordo dell'ultimo istante*), a detail that surpasses and overwhelms all others (*sormonta e schiaccia ogni altro*). The repetition in her estimation constitutes just the contrary of what Freud believed it to be, namely, a sign of the instinctiveness of Leonardo's intellectuality (*il cerebralismo resta . . . un istintivo*). In order to give substance to her suggestion she cites García Lorca's three-line refrain from his *Llanto: ¡A las cinco de la tarde!* (at five o'clock in the afternoon), the moment when the bullfighter Ignacio Sánchez Mejías died.

Be this as it may, Fumagalli seems to ignore that Freud was well aware that repetition may be a means of producing poetical atmosphere, as can be seen from his citing on this occasion Dante's verses from the *Paradiso* (Canto xxvii, 22-25), with their repetition of *il luogo mio*. But Freud (1910, p. 120) saw no sign of the emotion (*Pathos*) of poetry in Leonardo's note since the repetition concerned, as he thought, the trivial. Contrary to Fumagalli, Freud here cited poetry to demonstrate the absence of an overt strong feeling in Leonardo's entry.

Schapiro has devoted a paper with the title "Two Slips of Leonardo

---

[1] The reader may rightly raise here a question that was discussed in Part I. Was Leonardo following an emotional pattern of his times when he made the entry in this cool, deliberate way without the slightest additional expression of grief? Müntz (1900) remarks that one could attribute "dryness of heart" (*sécheresse de cœur*) to him, but he believes that such absence of emotions was, indeed, the character of the epoch. As an exception he cites the letters of Alessandra Strozzi. But I doubt whether emotional constraint of the sort Müntz discusses was really so general in that century as he seems to believe—one has only to think of Michelangelo's letters. Be this as it may, Müntz also reaches the conclusion that Leonardo's impassiveness was excessive and "constitutes a true psychological phenomenon [*constitue un véritable phénomène psychologique*]." However, it may be of interest at this particular juncture that in the instance of Goethe, who was quite expressive in diaries, letters, and poetry, not a single reference to his father's death can be found.

and a Slip of Freud" (1955-56) to Leonardo's entry, but he might just as well have added, as will be seen, "and three Slips of Schapiro."

He tries to refute Fumagalli's conclusion by citing another entry that was unknown to Freud, in which Leonardo refers to his father's death and which, oddly enough, also contains a repetition of time. "Wednesday at 7 o'clock died Ser Piero da Vinci on the 9th of July 1504, Wednesday close to 7 o'clock" (Schapiro, 1955-56, p. 4; C.A. 72 r. b). Schapiro believes that the repetition of the hour with a slight correction, as if Leonardo "felt a scruple about the inexactitude of the original entry," is hardly "an attitude of overwhelming emotion."

Schapiro writes as if this entry had not been considered by Fumagalli, yet she quotes it (p. 56), as mentioned, in order to deduce just from the reoccurrence of repetition that we are not dealing, as Freud believed, with absent-mindedness, but with "a burst of passion [risalto di passione]."

Controversy seems to be less intense, though not wholly absent, about an evident error of Leonardo's. Freud mentions in a footnote Leonardo's mistakenly giving his father's age at the time of his death as eighty, although contemporary biographers thought it to have been seventy-seven. Fumagalli wrongly thinks that Freud overlooked this circumstance.

Schapiro rightly states that—as is now known—Ser Piero's age was seventy-eight, but he wonders why Freud, since he assumed Ser Piero's age to have been seventy-seven, did not in his interpretation draw the connection between the repetition of the hour of seven and the assumed age of seventy-seven.[2]

Pleasant as it would be, after having met over and over again the objection that Freud overstrained psychoanalytic hermeneutics, to discuss for a change a criticism that implies Freud did not go far enough in his interpretation or even missed one, I nevertheless suggest postponing consideration of this particular question until all the errors in Leonardo's entry have been determined.

[2] Freud called Leonardo's imprecise recording of the father's age "a greater error" than the flaw of repetition. It is doubtful whether or not one can justly attribute a parapraxia to Leonardo here. Schapiro (ibid., p. 5) refers to the well-known documents in which Ser Piero himself gave his age varyingly. Mr. Pedretti, in a personal communication, quite rightly states that children in our times (and probably in earlier centuries even more so) often do not know the precise age of their parents. In an instance in which I found an author making what I thought to be a parapraxia regarding his own age, it turned out later that he had possibly never up to then known exactly the year of his birth.

It seems Schapiro has overlooked a very surprising and blatant one in so far as he neglects to mention in his special study that in both instances Leonardo got the day of the week wrong: In the year 1504 July 9 was a Tuesday (Möller, 1934, p. 388, n. 4) and not a Wednesday as Leonardo twice recorded, and Möller adduces historical documentation of the fact that Ser Piero died on Tuesday July 9 and was buried on Wednesday, July 10 (ibid., p. 388). While one may debate whether a formal flaw such as a repetition can be truly called a slip and whether Leonardo's error as to his father's age was caused by ignorance, this matter of the day of the week constitutes an unquestionable parapraxia.

An area of controversy is entered again when I turn to a discussion of a slip Schapiro discovered in Freud's remarks about Leonardo's entry concerning his father's family. Freud wrote that Ser Piero had his first legitimate son by his third wife and by his fourth wife had nine sons and two daughters, that is to say, twelve children, besides Leonardo. This is one more than Leonardo mentions when recording that his father had left ten sons and two daughters, and Freud therefore suggested in a footnote that Leonardo might have committed another error in this entry (1910, p. 120, n. 2).

As a matter of fact in all standard biographies the number of Leonardo's siblings is set forth as eleven. Schapiro explains Freud's slip by an interpretation that refers to Freud's unconscious and which I will report later. What the unconscious background of this slip was, if any, I do not know, but after a long search I at last found the external factor that brought it about. I was guided by the impression that this kind of mistake did not sound like a slip. After all, the number of Leonardo's siblings has no significance in Freud's reconstruction and —as will presently be shown—the data set forth by Freud deviated so very extensively from what is found in the biographies of Leonardo that a simple parapraxia appears unlikely.

For his information regarding the data of Leonardo's life, Freud used, according to the references cited in his study, the standard works that were current in his time. Müntz, whose original biography in French Freud used and whom he cites seven times, presents on page 15 a special set-in with the names and years of birth of Ser Piero's children by his third wife (four sons and one daughter), and by his fourth wife (five sons and one daughter), a total of eleven children.

Solmi, whose book on Leonardo Freud read in a German translation, is cited six times by Freud. In a rather involved sentence (p. 3f.) that may easily lend itself to miscounting an identical account is given.

In Smiraglia's book on Leonardo's youth (cited five times) there is right before the first chapter an *Albero genealogico della famiglia da Vinci* (no page number) which extends from 1339 to 1880 and shows unmistakably the same distribution of Ser Piero's children mentioned above: five children by the third wife and six children by the fourth.

How then did Freud really come to the strange conclusion that Ser Piero had one child by his third wife and eleven by his fourth? Only if one turns to the original edition of Seidlitz's book, to which Freud referred seven times, does this puzzling mistake find an approximate explanation. There one can actually read that Ser Piero begot on his fourth wife nine sons and two daughters (Seidlitz, 1909a, p. 11). However, the context proves that this was an erratum. It is worth while to cite Seidlitz extensively at this point.

> From this marriage [Ser Piero's third marriage, to Margherita di Francesco di Jacopo di Guglielmo] there sprang at last his first legitimate descendant, Antonio, born 1476 (in that same year of 1476 Leonardo was already living with his master Verrocchio); in 1479 there then followed the second son, Giuliano. . . . Shortly after 1480 his third wife died; at the beginning of the eighties he then married, being already fiftyish, his last wife, Lucrezia di Guglielmo Cortigiani, with whom he still begot nine children, who, from 1484 on, followed one another sometimes year by year, nine [sic!] sons and two daughters.

> [*Aus dieser Ehe entspross ihm endlich der erste rechtmässige Nachkomme, der 1476 geborne Antonio (Leonardo lebte in demselben Jahre 1476 bereits bei seinem Meister Verrocchio); 1479 folgte dann der zweite Sohn, Giuliano. . . . Bald nach 1480 starb seine dritte Frau; zu Anfang der achtziger Jahre heiratete er dann, bereits als ein Fünfziger, seine letzte Frau, Lucrezia di Guglielmo Cortigiani, mit der er noch neun Kinder zeugte, die von 1484 ab, bisweilen Jahr für Jahr, aufeinander folgten, neun (sic!) Söhne und zwei Töchter*] [Seidlitz, 1909a, Vol. I, p. 10f.].

The equivalent passage, literally translated, in Freud's study, sounds as follows:

> He [Ser Piero] was married four times; the first two wives died [him] off childless; only from the third did he obtain in 1476 the first legitimate son [at a time] when Leonardo was already twenty-four years old and had long

ago exchanged the paternal house for the studio of his master Verrocchio; with the fourth and last wife, whom he had married as an already fiftyish [man], he still begot nine sons and two daughters.

[*Er war viermal verheiratet, die beiden ersten Frauen starben ihm kinderlos weg, erst von der dritten erzielte er 1476 den ersten legitimen Sohn, als Leonardo bereits 24 Jahre alt war und das Vaterhaus längst gegen das Atelier seines Meisters Verrocchio vertauscht hatte; mit der vierten und letzten Frau, die er bereits als Fünfziger geheiratet hatte, zeugte er noch neun Söhne und zwei Töchter*] [Freud, *Gesammelte Werke*, Vol. VIII, p. 191f.].

Two things seem to become almost *prima facie* clear from a comparison of the two passages: (1) Freud used Seidlitz's text as his source when he composed the passage about Ser Piero's marital history. There is more than one parallel between them to prove this, e.g., the reference to Leonardo's stay in Verrocchio's studio, which is not required by the context. (2) Freud did not read the passage in question accurately or he would have discovered the erratum, for nine begotten children cannot amount to nine sons and two daughters. He evidently read only the first sentence about the first legitimate son, skipped the sentence about the second son (and an intervening paragraph, omitted by me, about Ser Piero's change of domicile in 1480 and his possessions in Vinci), and hurried to the concluding sentence about the nine sons and two daughters.[3]

It is questionable whether one is dealing here with a parapraxia or with a simple oversight. Freud was a voluminous reader and is said to have had an extraordinary memory. I surmise, however, that the accuracy of his memory depended on the meaningfulness of the content to be preserved. The exact number of siblings was irrelevant to his purpose, and in view of the external circumstances it may appear that the relevant question is rather why Freud glanced over the paragraph so hurriedly than why he erred in the number of Leonardo's siblings. We shall later see, however, that it may be wrong to limit one's perspective to this extent.

The following reconstruction seems to be justified: the number of Leonardo's siblings being for Freud's line of investigation irrelevant,

[3] Aside from the erratum Seidlitz's statement contains an item of misinformation in so far as he attributes to Ser Piero's third wife only two children. The source of this notion I have been unable to trace. In the revised reprint of 1935 the erratum was corrected but the misinformation retained (Seidlitz, 1909b, p. 17).

he never paid any attention to the exact figure. They were numerous, and that was all that counted. In giving a short outline of Ser Piero's life, as required by the context, he glanced at the Seidlitz text and found on superficial inspection a discrepancy between Leonardo's assertion and the biographer's finding. He must, however, have had a doubt about the biographer's claim, for the situation does not justify the footnote's beginning with: *"Es scheint"* which Mr. Strachey has translated "apparently": "Leonardo has apparently made a further mistake . . ." (Freud, 1910, p. 120, n. 2). Since Freud had established to his own satisfaction the discrepancy between the two assertions, only a: "Leonardo has made a further mistake . . ." would appear justified. The *es scheint* sounds to my ear like the expression of a doubt which was all too justified in terms of the source he used. To be sure, the external factor I set forth here does not necessarily contradict Schapiro's interpretation or any other that refers to the unconscious. The unconscious often, as is well known, uses such constellations for the purpose of expressing itself, but the external factor may also throw doubt on whether or not we are dealing here with a genuine slip requiring for its explanation a reference to the unconscious. As the matter stands now one can only say *non liquet*.

Yet the whole matter, though seemingly of small import, changes essentially when an author of such familiarity with Leonardo's life history and work as Fumagalli claims that Leonardo *was* wrong in the number of children left by Ser Piero, because not all of them were alive in 1504. According to her, Leonardo's statement would have been correct if he had written "the father had" instead of "he left" (*il verbo "lascio" mentre dovere essere: ebbe.* p. 56) ten sons and two daughters. But this in turn, I think, would not have been correct either, since in 1477 a daughter Maddalena, who died shortly thereafter, was born to Ser Piero (Möller, 1934, p. 387f.), which would make the number of children he *had* had at least thirteen. Although Fumagalli does not state on what grounds she claims that not all of Ser Piero's twelve children were alive in 1504, this claim cannot be dismissed unexamined.

Schapiro believes he has adduced sufficient evidence that Leonardo was correct in recording that Ser Piero left twelve children for all Leonardo's eleven siblings were still alive at the time Ser Piero died. In order to prove this he cites the genealogical table published in

Beltrami (1919, p. xii)[4] and two documents (ibid., No. 172, p. 108, and No. 248, p. 157f.), one from 1506 and the other from 1520 (Schapiro, 1955-56, p. 8, n. 14). As he claims, these two documents together contain all the names of Leonardo's siblings as living either in the one or the other year. However, scrutiny of these two documents reveals that only the brothers are enumerated and no mention is made of the two sisters.[5]

Consequently, there is the possibility that Fumagalli is right and that Freud when his careless reading led him to be tricked by the erratum in Seidlitz's text indirectly hit upon a truth. If it should be proved beyond doubt that Fumagalli is right—and there is a good chance since Leonardo's entry may turn out to be an accumulation of slips—then we should have to enlarge on our earlier comment upon what first looked like a slip by Freud. The external factor (the erratum in Seidlitz's text) would still have the same function as initiating a process that ends in an apparent slip. The preconscious thought, however, must have been: "But I read in Leonardo's biographies that he had eleven siblings; Seidlitz must be wrong." Yet I presume a third unconscious impression, namely the suspicion or hunch that there was something questionable in Leonardo's reference to the number of his father's children, was possibly likewise active. This hunch could not be substantiated by reference to any historical finding that was available to Freud in 1910, and it seems to me he used the erratum to express concretely what was in his mind only vague, and unprovable to boot. I am struck by the fact that fifty years later, and after careful scrutiny of all the sources at my disposal, I can only repeat the gist of what Freud has said about this part of Leonardo's entry: "It seems as if

[4] Beltrami used Uzielli's *albero genealogico*. Möller (1934, p. 387, n.) has pointed to some inaccuracies in this family tree. As far as I know no reliable data regarding Ser Piero's immediate descendants are at present available aside from those given by Möller. The promising archival studies of Möller have not led to a comprehensive presentation.

[5] Dr. Cecilia Calabresi was kind enough to go through the rest of Beltrami's book. She assures me that there are no other documents recorded in the text that would prove the fact claimed by Schapiro except the letter of July 5, 1507, from which I have quoted previously (p. 88, n. 2), which is addressed among others to sisters (*sorelle*) (Beltrami, 1919, No. 190, p. 120; also Richter, Vol. II, p. 387, No. 1559) and would prove that Leonardo's sisters were living in that year since he had only two. I presume that Schapiro has not referred to this document because he agrees with those authors who consider this letter as not having been written by Leonardo. For arguments in favor of the authenticity of the letter, see Beltrami (1921b). Mr. Carlo Pedretti, probably the best contemporary expert on Leonardo's handwriting, has kindly informed me of his conviction that the letter in question was not written by Leonardo, as he will set forth in an impending publication.

Leonardo has made an error here."[6] It is, of course, of particular poignancy that Leonardo had made an "unconcealed" mistake at a place where no one before Möller, as far as I know, ever suspected it, namely, in the matter of the day on which his father died.

Consequently we may say that this note of Leonardo's in *Codex Arundel* contains at least two certain errors (the father's age and the day of the week) and probably also a third (the number of children his father left). In the light of these findings we may reconsider Fumagalli's objection to Freud's interpretation. Her reasoning appears at first hearing almost convincing. She cites an instance of modern poetry where the repetition of the hour of death actually creates a most mournful mood. Although one may object that Leonardo was not, after all, writing poetry when he recorded his father's death, that his entry is throughout sober and actually sounds dry and dispassionate and is put down in conjunction with most sober household remarks, her interpretation of Leonardo's repetition would still remain pitted against Freud's.[7] The fact of accumulated errors, I believe, definitely sways the balance in favor of Freud. No doubt, even if one persists in a poetical concept of what struck Freud as a formal flaw, the entry is to be considered in view of these errors as a manifestation of psychopathology, namely, as a sign that Leonardo was, when writing this entry, in a state of conflict, and, to be more precise, was warding off an emotion.[8]

It has been worth while to consider in detail some of the criticism Freud's interpretation of Leonardo's entry has found. One is amazed at the inexactitude, contradictions, omissions, and misunderstandings that can be observed. On the other hand one is surprised how fre-

[6] I gratefully acknowledge several communications I received from Prof. Renzo Cianchi about Freud's footnote. Prof. Cianchi first thought that Leonardo might have erred, but after further research he stated that Freud had been wrong. However, at the time this manuscript goes to print our correspondence has not yet clarified the point to my satisfaction.

[7] However, Mr. Seymour A. Copstein made the following comment: "There seems to be little relevance or utility in likening Leonardo's repetition of the time of his father's death to García Lorca's repetition in his *Llanto por Sánchez Mejías*. There is the specific significance of the time repeated in the poem: a father may die at any time, day or night, but for a bullfighter to die at five in the afternoon! That is when the bull is supposed to die; one can almost see the words on the poster, much as 'at 8:30 in the evening' appears in a theater announcement." I feel particularly grateful to Mr. Copstein for setting forth the unique relevance the fifth hour has in institutionalized bullfighting. I believe this observation clinches the whole matter.

[8] It is not quite clear from Fumagalli's text whether or not she would agree with this formulation. At one point she says that Freud could have used the many errors (age of the father, day of the week, and number of children) as signs of perturbation (*turbamento*).

quently Freud was guided by hunches that seem to be borne out by later research. Why did Freud not use the implication of the figure seven as hypothetically suggested by Schapiro? The context really seems to afford such an interpretation for someone who assumes Ser Piero's age to have been seventy-seven. If Freud had used that clue he would have gravely erred since Ser Piero's age was seventy-eight. Why did Freud, on the other hand, surmise that Leonardo might have erred in the number of Ser Piero's children? I believe, as previously stated, that Freud's slip expressed an unconscious or preconscious assumption that was probably correct, but could not be proved at the time. Schapiro suggests that it was due to Freud's identification with Leonardo. He writes:

> The documents[9] show, however, that it was Freud who was in error. *It was he who thought of Leonardo as somehow outside his father's family.* It may be that in identifying with Leonardo in this biography . . . he had to separate his hero as far as possible from the brothers and sisters who have no part in the story [1955-56, p. 6; italics by Schapiro].

Of course, they cannot have any part in the story Freud presents, since Leonardo's first sibling was born when he was twenty-four years old and the focus of Freud's main concern was a reconstruction of Leonardo's childhood. Yet Schapiro may nevertheless have made a correct guess about Freud's unconscious. The facts on hand, however—despite Freud's indisputable identification with Leonardo—do not prove the correctness of his interpretation, since Freud did not draw any conclusions in this instance but simply expressed an impression in a footnote.[10]

Yet it is true that Freud did not use for his interpretation the actual errors (of which he knew or which he surmised) but limited himself to a formal element. This is rather rare in Freud's clinical approach. Though he was a master of the study of formal elements as he demonstrated in his *Interpretation of Dreams* and the book on jokes (1905b),

[9] About the documents, see p. 321f.

[10] Since Freud restricted his comment to a brief footnote, it is impossible to reconstruct what meaning he attributed to Leonardo's alleged error. Was he focusing on the possibility that Leonardo substituted the number of siblings for the number of children his father had had? This actually occurs during a phase of the child's development (cf. Piaget, 1924, pp. 101-113). If Leonardo had made an error of the kind Freud alleged, one would have had to consider the possibility that Leonardo's feelings of isolation, partly caused by his unfavorable status, had found expression in this way.

there is still observable a tendency to prefer content to form for purposes of interpretation in his clinical approach. The reason which compelled Freud to focus his interest on the formal flaw and to bypass the interpretation of the contents of the other errors is rather evident. The interpretation of the errors, in my estimation, can only lead to an uncovering of a hostile impulse in Leonardo. Also, Schapiro's engaging suggestion that by making his father older, Leonardo perhaps expressed a wish to have been born after his father had become married and thus to have escaped the stigma of illegitimacy still leaves Leonardo harboring a reproach against his father. To be sure, Freud's text, up to the point of his interpretation of Leonardo's slip, had not left a doubt in the reader that Leonardo's relationship to his father must have contained strong feelings of enmity. Here, however, was a passage from which a positive feeling could be deduced, and which demonstrated how the self behaved when it confronted a strong positive feeling which in principle was not opposed by conscience. A discriminating biographer will, of course, not use an element to be interpreted so as to get the most he can out of it, but will limit himself to setting forth a point which he cannot extract from any other source or about which there remained a doubt from previous occasions.

How correct Freud was in his interpretation of Leonardo's repetition as a sign of a positive affect may be seen from another observation to which Fumagalli calls our attention. When Caterina arrived in Milan he wrote in his notes:

> a dì 16 Luglio
> Catelina venne a dì 16
> di Luglio 1493

[On the 16th of July Caterina came on the 16th of July 1493] [Forster III 88 r.; Fumagalli, p. 30].[11]

Fumagalli acknowledges this repetition as a sign that a strong emotion came to pass in Leonardo at that time. But the retrenchment to the trivial is again quite conspicuous.[12] However, in view of the repetition in the entry of 1493, I feel more inclined than before, when

[11] MacCurdy (1956, p. 1156) and Richter (Vol. II, p. 350, No. 1384) set a period after the first line as if it were a mere dateline for the following entries. Fumagalli's rendering strikes me as convincing. I have had no opportunity to check its correctness.

[12] I cannot follow Fumagalli's reasoning when she also points to this instance to justify her ideas regarding the entry of 1504.

I expressed doubts, to agree with the Merezhkovsky-Freud theory that it was the mother who came to stay with him and not a housekeeper. Fumagalli draws the same conclusion, though it is another entry about Caterina that she believes almost proves it. In this one, which I quoted earlier (p. 86), repetition also plays a role, but in this instance it is not repetition of a time relation. It starts, in Italian, with "di' di' dimmi . . ." [Tell, tell, tell me . . .] (Fumagalli, p. 27; C.A. 71 r. a).

It would be a challenging task to collect all instances of repetition occurring in Leonardo's *Notes* in order to gauge the significance of the samples set forth here. But even if, as I should expect, further search brought forth instances of repetition concerning apparently emotionally neutral subjects, that should not deter us from paying attention to the fact that repetitions occur in Leonardo's *Notes* on four occasions (two certain instances and two with high probability) that are related to his blood parents, and that in all of these instances, as far as can be guessed, positive, friendly feelings were at play. Leonardo, like any other human being, had a vast store of affectionate feelings, but Freud seems to have been quite right in judging that these emotions, in so far as they related to human beings or, at least, to his parents, were not permitted to grow freely and reach a pitch. Repetition and displacement might have been the leading mechanisms with which, in everyday life, he coped with emotions which from his point of view appeared to be recalcitrant.[13]

When we now return to Fumagalli's interpretation of Leonardo's formal slip in recording his father's death we may reach a conclusion that is just the opposite of hers. She believes the repetition is a sign that Leonardo witnessed his father's death and that he became fixated, so to speak, to the last moment of his existence. This view, in my estimation, should then apply to all time references. But, as Fumagalli also states, in one time datum Leonardo indisputably made a mistake, namely, in the day of his father's death. Why should a man who became fixated to the last moment of his father's life, and who therefore repeats the special time reference, now err in recording the more general one?

I suggest that Leonardo's general inclination toward parapraxia in

[13] I limit my conclusions here to everyday life, but these two mechanisms can also be found in other areas (cf. MacCurdy, 1956, p. 1128f., n. 1).

the two entries is the outgrowth of a regret or feeling of guilt. I have in mind something more specific than the general feeling of guilt that is almost unavoidable among the civilized when a beloved person has died and almost a rule in the son when his father has died.

Leonardo's insistence that his father died on Wednesday and not on Tuesday sounds to me like a wish: "If only my father had died a day later." The motive of this wish may be looked for in the possible fact that he had *not* visited his father for a long time.

I can well imagine many reasons why Leonardo might have been tardy and sparing with his visits. The year 1504 was a particularly busy one for him. He was active on the commission that was to decide upon the best position for Michelangelo's *David;* he had accepted a commission from Isabella d'Este; and he was painting the *Battle of Anghiari* in the Sala di Gran Consiglio. If it is considered that these are only the activities that are proven by documents (cf. Clark, 1952, p. 182), one can easily imagine the full range of undertakings in which he was engaged. If we mention further that his stepmother was much younger than his father and that she had been pregnant until shortly before his father's death,[14] and recall the many indications of Leonardo's ambivalence toward his father that have been recorded from time to time throughout this study, we may well surmise that Leonardo was not a daily visitor in his father's house—unless his aversion enforced overzealousness. However, it is not far-fetched to speculate that now when he was famous and in the center of public attention, he felt the freer to give sway to his old resentments and shun his father's presence for long periods.

In order to submit a satisfactory explanation of Leonardo's error as to the day I have to refer to a psychological peculiarity for which, by chance, I have a well-documented parallel from the life of Goethe. It seems clear that Goethe had avoided visiting the great German poet, author, and philosopher Gotthold Ephraim Lessing (1729-1781). The reasons for his reluctance to meet him are of no concern in this

---

[14] I have deliberately omitted any reference to the claim, occasionally made, that Ser Piero's last child was born posthumously. I have not found out on what grounds this claim is based. (Prof. Cianchi has conveyed to me the important information, which as far as I know has not yet been published, that Ser Piero's youngest son was born in 1499. This, of course, makes invalid the part of my above speculation that refers to possible consequences of the stepmother's pregnancy shortly before or at the time of Ser Piero's death.)

context, but a letter Goethe wrote upon learning of Lessing's death is worthy of attention. He wrote:

> I could not easily have been met by anything more distressing than Lessing's death. Not a quarter of an hour before the news arrived I was planning to visit him. We are losing very much in him, more than we believe.
>
> [*Mir hätte nicht leicht etwas fatalers begegnen können, als dass Lessing gestorben ist. Keine viertelstunde vorher eh die Nachricht kam macht ich einen Plan ihn zu besuchen. Wir verlieren viel viel an ihm, mehr als wir glauben*] [Goethe, 1781, Vol. V, p. 60].

Here a conscious reaction is recorded of which we may surmise a parallel in Leonardo. It is not probable that Goethe had indeed planned such a visit, and still less that he was doing so at the time he claimed. It is far more probable that upon being informed of Lessing's death he was exposed to a sting of guilt feeling and regret that he had never met that author, who was the greatest in the German tongue before he himself achieved that status. In that moment he exculpated himself and hypocritically almost claimed that if Lessing had not made it impossible by his death, he would now be on his way to meet him. Oddly enough, Goethe too abstained from visiting his father for the last two and a half years of the latter's life, although he knew of his father's grave illness and his travels took him within easy reach of his native city.

I strongly suspect that Leonardo, when he heard of his father's death, reproached himself for having been negligent in his filial duties and likewise made himself believe that he had intended to see his father that very day.

The last sentence I have quoted from Goethe's letter reflects the ambivalence that, despite the defense that was generated, still came to the surface. Leonardo's parapraxia in misrecording the day may also be rooted in the same impulse. In Goethe's instance there was probably no need for a parapraxia or other manifestation of psychopathology. The event was less grave than the equivalent in Leonardo's life (though Lessing was a father-substitute and Goethe's father was seriously sick, as said, at that time and would die fifteen months later). In Leonardo, aside from the involvement of stronger or more intense psychic forces, the process of exculpation may have occurred on a subliminal level or, if speculation about details is permitted, there may have been a momentary flash of a thought like: "And just today I wanted to visit my father!" or "Did I not plan to see him tomorrow?" or something of that sort, only to disappear amidst the instantaneous upsurge of grief, against which in turn other defenses had to be instituted. The recording of the wrong day would then mean, in terms of the unconscious: "I visited my father on Tuesday as I had planned and he died the following day. I thus fulfilled my filial duties."

My reconstruction, of course, has no claim to any degree of certainty, but I wonder which inference is more probable: a fixation to the moment of expiration, or an attempt at undoing the regretted effect of a negligence.

Appendix D

Additional Remarks on the Function of Trauma in Leonardo's Art

I have at various places made reference to Leonardo's relationship to trauma. It seems to me as if Leonardo engaged in a rather persistent struggle against anything that might be suggestive of the traumatic.

However, "the traumatic" clearly embraces three aspects, each of which has its special artistic implications. There is first of all the event per se that causes the trauma, then there is the subject that suffers the trauma, and thirdly there are the excitations that occur in the subject and reach traumatic proportions. Traumatized subject, traumatic process, and traumatizing force are the three distinct parts each of which is to be considered when the question of art and trauma is raised.

There are drawings by Leonardo that show the effect of trauma. I think mainly of the sketch of the *Hanging Figure of Bernardo di Bandino Baroncelli* in the Musée Bonnat (Popham, Plate 26) and the grotesque heads. I think these topics can be brought into a meaningful context of trauma. Death is, in the unconscious, always an event that has been brought about by a hostile, destructive power intent on causing death. Death as a natural conclusion of organic life is alien to unconscious fantasy life. When death is brought about by execution, as happened with Baroncelli, reality and unconscious fantasy, of course, coincide.

In the instance of the grotesque heads the psychological implications are less clear. Ugliness is often equated with evilness, as if the ugly person had caused his deformities by his own guilt, or as if ugliness were the expression of evilness. Therefore the grotesque or the monstrous cannot in all instances be equated with traumatic effects.

However this may be, in Leonardo's sketches, in the Hanging Man as well as in the monstrosities (if the latter are justly included here), the trauma is a matter of the past. The traumatic process has had its full effect and a static situation has resulted from it. The subjects are not represented in a state of suffering or terror. They have overcome the traumatic process even though perhaps at the price of life; but the trauma, so to speak, has come to a standstill. One may say it does not exist any more.

The presentation of traumatizing forces is frequent in Leonardo's work, mainly in the form of war machines, clearly devised with the intent of causing the maximum havoc that could be achieved in those times. A certain tendency toward insatiability and excess can no doubt be discovered in this area of Leonardo's work. It seems as if he would have liked to devise grandiose means of destruction, machinery that would annihilate armies and whole cities without the faintest possibility of effective resistance. All these sketches have in common that they concern only the potentiality of a trauma. The events depicted have not yet occurred in reality; they contain only suggestions as to possible future implications. The setup makes it quite clear that the originator did not wish to report something he had seen with his own eyes. Here the artist is in full possession of the potential trauma, he is able to control its scope, to decrease or increase its severity in accordance with his will. I can well imagine that these sketches of war machines were a solace to a traumatophobic mind, since Leonardo was, I presume, convinced that no one else possessed knowledge and imagination enough to devise their like.

The traumatic process per se is, with few exceptions, banished from Leonardo's work. I omit here a discussion of the *Last Supper* and the sketch in the Academy of Venice (Plate 32). If the latter is a work of Leonardo's, it would, no doubt, represent a traumatic process of formidable proportions. I remind the reader of the drawings of the buildings toppling as a result of the action of one of Leonardo's invented pieces of artillery (Plate 61). It is characteristic that human beings are omitted from this drawing. Yet in the drawing *Two Types of Chariot Armed with Scythes* in the Royal Library of Turin (Popham, Plate 310) the direct effect of a war machine on human bodies is represented with great cruelty. No emotional expression is visible on the victims. The whole process is well calculated. It could just as well be concerned with a machine for lifting heavy weights or with the production of any effect that is limited to the purely physical. I feel inclined to characterize such a sketch by saying that the most cruel—that is to say, traumatic—is detraumatized by conversion into a purely logical event of almost mathematical clarity and simplicity.

There remains the *Battle of Anghiari*. At first thought it may appear almost impossible to depict a battle without presenting traumata. Leonardo's painting, which is characterized by the unsurpassed ferocity of combatants and horses, actually avoids doing so by his choosing a moment when none of the participants has yet been defeated. One feels inclined to say that he selected the last moment before the forces pitted against each other succeeded in accomplishing mutilation and annihilation (cf. Heydenreich, 1954, Vol. I, p. 47). The spectator may even surmise that such ferocious rages, such human efforts geared to the maximum, can only lead to mutual destruction; that when such wild forces are unleashed, there cannot be any survivors. Yet that outcome is not made the subject of the painting. As a matter of fact, I have the impression that from the painting itself one cannot reconstruct who will finally be the victor. If this is true, Leonardo avoided the presentation of trauma in a most skillful way. (A possible exception is the warrior who lies below the horses on his back in the foreground of the painting [see Plate 47].)

An objection to my thesis may be based upon a consideration of the Allegories. I select for discussion the one of *Virtue and Envy*, which has been described previously (p. 132). Here, indeed, according to Leonardo's text and the comments by his pupil, we know that he intended to depict a moment of trauma. But in this drawing it is to be said that the events take place on the allegorical-symbolic level, where the direct emotional qualities of an event are greatly reduced in intensity because of the abstract meaning of the whole presentation. Furthermore, the moment caught in the sketch is again one in which the contending parties match each other. In order to reveal the traumatic nature of what is depicted Leonardo had to resort to a comment.

Without it the beholder would hardly know what the physical implications of the depicted event really are. And this feature, I believe, suggests a possibility that may be of great theoretical import. Throughout Leonardo's work we can observe a striking dichotomy: the visual world he creates is devoid of the traumatic, but his literary work is replete with it.

I have cited a good many passages which may illustrate this. Most of the Prophecies which have been quoted for the sake of their psychological implications refer to truly traumatic situations, and the reader may recall all the dreadful things Leonardo advised painters to show in pictures of the Flood (cf. p. 268f.). He himself eliminated human beings from his drawings of the subject. Apparently the traumatic could only be verbalized by Leonardo but not visually presented. The literary work shows how intensely he was preoccupied with what in his imagination might become the severest traumata, but the visual work, in which he was a genius, served the function of denying, undoing, or healing the trauma. The favored theme of his painting was, after all, the Madonna with the Child, that is to say, a presentation (and glorification) of unambivalent maternal love, the primordial, trauma-free situation of maximum security. It is possible that it was just in this area of human relations that he suffered his severest trauma. Yet in his literary work hardly a comment will be found upon maternal love; thus in this instance too verbal and visual presentation carry the earmarks of the afore-mentioned dichotomy.

At this point it may be worth while to cast a glance at a genius who was in almost all ways the opposite of Leonardo, and of whom one can truly say that he was addicted to trauma. I mean Goya.[1] In going through his work one must admit that he scarcely omitted any shade or facet of the horrible that may befall mankind. And he did not spare himself any of its aspects. In some of his creations the agony of the traumatized prevails, in others the horribleness of the traumatizing power, but in both the traumatic process is in the center. It seems to me that the traumatic can be discerned even in most of his portraits: they show predominantly faces that are ravaged by their sorrows and evilness, faces of persons who are bent on causing others even greater woes, if possible, than they themselves have had to endure. But leaving

[1] For an aspect of resemblance, however, see Malraux (1950, p. 39).

speculation aside I need only to recall Goya's painting of the *Fusillade on the Hill of Principe Pio on May 3, 1808* (in the Prado). It cannot be surpassed in terms of traumatization. A man in the moment of being executed hurls rebellion, fear, contempt, hatred, and terror against his executioners with an inimitable gesture; the crowd of pitiable creatures waiting for their own execution and those lying in their blood who have suffered it. If Leonardo had given verbal advice as to what a painter should put into a picture devoted to this subject, I believe he would have described exactly what Goya puts on the canvas, but he himself would have been incapable of doing the same in his own style.

Oddly enough, there are paintings by Goya that look almost like illustrations of some of Leonardo's phantasmagoria that he put down in words.

I need only to cite Goya's painting of the *Colossus or Panic* that shows a giant walking across the world and a crowd that bursts into mad flight in all directions. If this painting is compared with Leonardo's tale in the form of a letter (C.A. 311 r. a) (cf. p. 318f.) one can hardly escape perceiving the parallel.

A direct bearing of Leonardo's literary work on Goya seems out of the question. One must assume here an inherent kinship between two of the greatest painters—the one being able only to verbalize the horrible, the other constantly trying to give it visual forms.

The gruesome pictures found in Goya's graphic work might thus be equated with Leonardo's *Profetie,* yet it is not my feeling that I have adequately dealt with the question of why the one was consistently inhibited or restrained in giving visual form to his most vivid and intense fantasies. Was it that horrible imagery was evoked with particular vividness whenever he set out to paint that caused the inhibition Freud believed he observed in Leonardo? Or was the vivid imagination of the horrible one of the prerequisites of Leonardo's undaunted and insatiable striving to present the most beautiful? Perhaps it may be possible to synthesize the two viewpoints. After all, a psychological factor may set an inhibition and simultaneously incite an active defense that leads to action, particularly creative action. Inhibition and active defense, thus, may have brought about the strange result of a genius that creates the superb but only on rare occasions.

There is one biographical detail that would cast serious doubt on my theory of Leonardo's traumatophobia. Lomazzo reports that Leonardo accompanied men who had been condemned to death on their last journey in order to study their facial expressions and bodily contortions when they were hanged (Seidlitz, 1909b, p. 151f). Here the artist would have voluntarily exposed himself to the impact of a "traumatic process" in one of its ghastliest forms. Are such incidents to be explained as I have tried to explain Leonardo's anatomical studies? Or did he expose himself to the most traumatic during a period when counterphobic mechanisms prevailed, as, from clinical experience, we know happens in the person who is afraid (Fenichel, 1939). One can well imagine a Leonardo shaken by fright who, just because of his terror, forces himself to witness what at heart he detests. One may also regard this report as legend, but in this context that would, of course, be an *argumentum ad hominem*.

Yet with all this I do not have in mind a general theory that would bring artistic creativity and traumatization into a particularly close connection. For Leonardo's specific instance there possibly existed such a close connection, however vaguely I may have been able to divine it. But I do not presume that artistic creativity is in general more closely related to trauma than other phenomena of the mind are found on investigation to be.

It is also of interest to consider the function of trauma in the three greatest painters of the Renaissance. In an aphorismic way one may contend that in Leonardo's work man appears as being aware of trauma but defending himself against it; warding it off and reaching out for harmony, he eliminates trauma. In Michelangelo's work man appears titanically struggling with trauma, sometimes losing the battle, sometimes winning it, but always pitting his strength maximally against formidable resistances; man is represented in a state of open conflict. In Raphael one cannot even say man denies trauma—he seems to be oblivious of it; man is floating through life unencumbered by danger. Raphael's work is neutral to the whole problem; his art does not reach to that depth at all. This may be one of the reasons why his *œuvre* has lost its power to move the viewer of today as deeply as it still did half a century ago, why his work at present is experienced by many as "merely" beautiful.

CHRONOLOGICAL DATA

Many dates in Leonardo's life and those of his relatives are reported with considerable variation. In some (but by no means all) instances I have indicated this by putting the time limits in parentheses. I have followed Professor Cianchi's revised dates of birth of Leonardo's siblings, which deviate in many instances by three years from those usually cited following Uzielli, whose dates I have added in square brackets.

Ser Piero di Ser Guido da Vinci (notary of Signoria in Florence)	Leonardo's great-grandfather	d. 1417
Antonio di Ser Piero di Ser Guido	Leonardo's grandfather	b. 1371 (?) d. (1457-1468)
Lucia, daughter of Florentine notary	Leonardo's grandmother	b. 1393 d. after 1469
Ser Piero da Vinci	Leonardo's father	b. 1426, April 19
Francesco	Leonardo's uncle	b. 1436, Aug. 14
First known legal document made out by Ser Piero, in Florence		1448
Ser Piero active as notary in Pistoja		1450
Ser Piero active as notary in Florence		from 1451 on
Leonardo (illegitimate mother, Caterina, later married to Accattabriga di Piero del Vacca, who lived in Vinci 1449-53)		b. 1452, April 15
Ser Piero marries Albiera di Giovanni Amadori, b. 1436		1452
Ser Antonio's tax declaration mentioning Leonardo		1457
Albiera dies in childbirth in Florence		1464, June 15
Ser Piero marries Francesca di Ser Giuliano Lanfredini		1465

Leonardo moves to Florence, enters the studio of Andrea Verrocchio (1435-1488)		(1462-1470)
Ser Piero becomes notary of Signoria in Florence		1469
Leonardo becomes a member of the Guild of St. Luke		1472
Francesca, Ser Piero's second wife		d. 1473
Leonardo's Angel in *The Baptism of Christ* by Verrocchio		1473-1475
Ser Piero marries Margherita di Francesco di Jacopo di Guglielmo (1458-1483?)		1475
Leonardo's *Portrait of Ginevra de' Benci*		(1474-1480)
Antonio	Leonardo's brother	b. 1476, Feb. 26
Leonardo denounced for sodomy } Charges dismissed		{ 1476, April 9 { 1476, June 7
Maddalena	Leonardo's sister	b. 1477, Nov. 4 buried 1477, Nov. 29
Giuliano	Leonardo's brother	b. 1478, Dec. 31 d. 1525, May 3
Lorenzo	Leonardo's brother	b. 1480 [84]
The *Adoration of the Magi*		1481-1482
Leonardo moves to Milan under the patronage of Lodovico il Moro (1451-1508)		(1481-1482)
Violante	Leonardo's sister	b. 1482 [85]
Domenico	Leonardo's brother	b. 1483 [86]
The Virgin of the Rocks, first version		1483-1485
Portrait of a Musician		about 1485-1490
Salai (1480-1524) joins Leonardo		1490, July 22
Ser Piero marries Lucrezia di Guglielmo Cortigiani (1464 to after 1520)		(1483-1488)
Margherita	Leonardo's sister	b. 1488 [91]
Benedetto	Leonardo's brother	b. 1489 [92]
Pandolfo	Leonardo's brother	b. 1491 [94]
Guglielmo	Leonardo's brother	b. 1493 [96]
A Caterina (his mother?) joins Leonardo in Milan		1493, July 16
Bartolomeo	Leonardo's brother	b. 1494 [97]
The Last Supper		1495-1497
Giovanni	Leonardo's brother	b. 1498, Jan. 9
The London *Anna Metterza Cartoon*		(1498-1507)
Lodovico driven from Milan by Louis XII		1499
Leonardo in Mantua, Venice		1500
His return to Florence		April, 1500
The lost Servite *Anna Metterza Cartoon*		1501

Two letters from Fra Pietro da Novellara to Marchesa Isabella d'Este of Mantua (1) describes the Servite *Anna Metterza Cartoon* (2) reports visit with Leonardo	April, 1501
Leonardo in the service of Cesare Borgia (1474-1507); participates in Romagna campaign	Summer 1502-1503
Anna Metterza, Louvre	(1500-1513)
Leonardo in Florence, work on cartoon for *Battle of Anghiari*	March, 1503
Leonardo starts work on the *Mona Lisa* portrait	(1500-1503)
Ser Piero dies	1504, July 9
Leonardo invited by Charles d'Amboise to go to work for Louis XII; Francesco, Leonardo's uncle, dies	1506
Leonardo's return to Florence, litigation with siblings	1507
Leonardo in Milan	1507-1511
Acquaintance with Francesco Melzi (1491-1568)	July, 1508—Sept., 1513 1511 (12)
The French driven from Milan	June, 1512
Giulio de' Medici becomes Pope Leo X	May, 1513
Leonardo in Florence	Oct., 1513
Leonardo in Rome with F. Melzi and Salai but making frequent journeys	Dec., 1513-1516
Louis XII dies. Francis I succeeds	1515
Francis I enters Milan	1515, Oct. 11
Giuliano de' Medici, Leonardo's protector	d. 1516, March 17
Leonardo at the request of Francis I goes to France with Melzi	1516-1517
St. John the Baptist	c. 1515
Leonardo's meeting with Cardinal Luigi d'Aragona	1517, Oct. 10
Leonardo dies in Cloux near Amboise	1519, May 2

BIBLIOGRAPHY

Abraham, K. (1917), Ejaculatio Praecox. In: *Selected Papers of Karl Abraham*. London: Hogarth Press, 1948, pp. 280-298.

Aeschylus, *The Eumenides*, tr. R. Lattimore. Chicago: University of Chicago Press, 1953.

Aristotle, *Problems*, 2 Vols., tr. W. S. Hett. Cambridge, Mass.: Harvard University Press [The Loeb Classical Library], 1953.

Aronberg, M. (1951), A New Facet in Leonardo's Working Procedure. *Art Bulletin*, 33:235-239.

Belt, E. (1952), Leonardo da Vinci's Studies of the Aging Process. *Geriatrics*, 7:205-210.

———— (1953), Les Dissections anatomiques de Léonard de Vinci. In: *Léonard de Vinci et l'expérience scientifique au seizième siècle* [Colloques internationaux du Centre National de la Recherche Scientifique, Paris, 4-7 juillet 1952]. Paris: Presses Universitaires de France.

———— (1954), Leonardo da Vinci's Studies of the Aging Process. *Raccolta Vinciana*, Part 17:91-115.

———— (1955), *Leonardo the Anatomist*. Lawrence: University of Kansas Press.

———— (1956), Leonardo da Vinci on "The Hard Teeth of the Years." *General Practice*, 19, Nos. 4 & 11.

———— & Steinitz, K. T. (1948), *Manuscripts of Leonardo da Vinci, Their History, with a Description of the Manuscript Editions in Facsimile*. Los Angeles: Elmer Belt Library of Vinciana.

Beltrami, Luca (1919), *Documenti e memorie riguardanti la vita e le opere di Leonardo da Vinci, in ordine cronologica*. Milano: Treves.

———— (1921a), La madre di Leonardo. *Nuova Antologia* (Roma): Ser. 6, 210:313-321.

———— (1921b), La lite di Leonardo cogli altri figli di Ser Piero da Vinci (1507-1508). *Nuova Antologia* (Roma): Ser. 6, 213:193-207.

Berenson, B. (1903), *The Drawings of the Florentine Painters Classified Criticized and Studied as Documents in the History and Appreciation of Tuscan Art with a Copious Catalogue Raisonné*, 2 Vols. New York: Dutton.

———— (1916), Leonardo da Vinci, an Attempt at Revaluation. In: *The Study and Criticism of Italian Art*. Third Series. London: G. Bell, pp. 1-37.

Beres, D. (1959), The Contribution of Psycho-Analysis to the Biography of the Artist. A Commentary on Methodology. *International Journal of Psycho-Analysis*, 40:26-37.

Bergler, E. (1945), On a Five-layer Structure in Sublimation. *Psychoanalytic Quarterly*, 14:76-97.

Bernfeld, S. (1946), An Unknown Autobiographical Fragment by Freud. *American Imago*, 4:3-19.

Birkmeyer, K. M. (1959), Book review: Joseph Gantner, *Leonardos Visionen von der Sintflut und vom Untergang der Welt. Renaissance News*, 12:51-53.

Bleuler, E. (1910), Zur Theorie des schizophrenen Negativismus. *Psychiatrisch-neurologische Wochenschrift*, 12:171-176, 184-187, 189-191, 195-198.

Blumenbach, J. F. (1795), *De generis humani varietate nativa*, 3rd ed. Göttingen: Vandenhoeck & Ruprecht.

Bode, Wilhelm (1907), Die Sprache der Schwärmerzeit. In: *Stunden mit Goethe*, 3:279-289.

———— (1921), *Neues über Goethes Liebe*. Berlin: Mittler.

Bodmer, H. (1931), *Leonardo. Des Meisters Gemälde und Zeichnungen*. Stuttgart & Berlin: Deutsche Verlagsanstalt [Klassiker der Kunst, Vol. XXXVII].

Bonaparte, M., tr. & ed. (1927), Un Souvenir d'enfance de Léonard de Vinci [by Sigm. Freud]. Paris: Gallimard [Les documents bleus, No. 32].

———— (1945), Notes on the Analytic Discovery of a Primal Scene. In: *The Psychoanalytic Study of the Child*, 1:119-125. New York: International Universities Press.

Boring, E. G. (1955), Dual Role of the *Zeitgeist* in Scientific Creativity. *Scientific Monthly*, 80:101-106.

Breuer, J. (1895), Theoretical. In: Studies on Hysteria, by J. Breuer & S. Freud. In: *The Standard Edition of the Complete Psychological Works of Sigmund Freud*, 2:183-251. London: Hogarth Press, 1955.

Brill, A. A., intr. & tr. (1947), *Leonardo da Vinci. A Study in Psychosexuality*, by Sigmund Freud. New York: Random House.

Brown, P. H. (1920), *Life of Goethe*, 2 Vols. London: John Murray.

Brunswick, R. M. (1928), The Analysis of a Case of Paranoia (Delusions of Jealousy). *Journal of Nervous and Mental Disease*, 20:1-22, 155-178, 1929.

———— (1940), The Preoedipal Phase of the Libido Development. *Psychoanalytic Quarterly*, 9:293-319.

Bühler, K. (1927), *Die Krise der Psychologie*. Jena: Fischer.

———— (1933), *Ausdruckstheorie*. Jena: Fischer.

Burckhardt, J. (1860), *The Civilisation of the Renaissance*. Oxford & London: Phaidon, 1945.

Bychowski, G. (1951), From Catharsis to Work of Art: The Making of an Artist. In: *Psychoanalysis and Culture. Essays in Honor of Géza Róheim*, ed. G. B. Wilbur & W. Muensterberger. New York: International Universities Press, pp. 390-409.

Calvi, G. (1926-29), Abozzo di capitollo introduttivo ad una storia della vita e delle opere di Leonardo da Vinci. *Raccolta Vinciana* (Milano), 13. Quoted after Schapiro (1955-56).

Canestrini, G. (1862), *La scienza e l'arte di Stato desunta dagli atti officiali della Repubblica Fiorentina e dei Medici*. Firenze: Felice Le Moumer.

Cartwright, J. (1903), *Isabella d'Este Marchioness of Mantua 1474-1539*, 2 Vols. New York: Dutton.

Cassirer, E. (1922-23), Eidos und Eidolon. Das Problem des Schönen und der Kunst in Platons Dialogen. *Vorträge der Bibliothek Warburg*, ed. F. Saxl, 2 (1):1-27. Leipzig: Teubner, 1924.

———— (1927), *Individuum und Kosmos in der Philosophie der Renaissance*. Leipzig & Berlin: Teubner.

Cennini, Cennino d'Andrea, *The Craftsman's Handbook*, tr. D. V. Thompson, Jr. New York: Dover, n.d. [This is an unabridged republication of the 1933 Yale University Press publication of the Thompson translation.]

Chamberlaine, J. (1796), *Imitations of Original Designs by Leonardo da Vinci*. London: Bulmer.

Chevalier, J. (1956), *Histoire de la pensée*. Vol. II: La Pensée Chrétienne. Paris: Flammarion.

Christensen, E. O. (1944), Freud on Leonardo da Vinci. *Psychoanalytic Review*, 31:152-164.

Chroust, A. H. (1958), Personal communication.

Cianchi, R. (1952a), *Vinci, Leonardo e la sua famiglia (con appendice di documenti inedite)* [Mostra della scienza a technica di Leonardo]. Milano: Museo Nazionale della Scienza e della Technica.

—— (1952b), Sulla casa natale di Leonardo. Riposte al Prof. Emil Moeller [*Empoli*].

Clark, K. (1929), A Note on Leonardo da Vinci. *Life and Letters* (London), 2:122-132.

—— (1935), *A Catalogue of the Drawings of Leonardo da Vinci in the Collection of His Majesty the King at Windsor Castle*, 2 Vols. London: Cambridge University Press.

—— (1939), *Leonardo da Vinci*. London: Cambridge University Press.

—— (1944), Leon Alberti on Painting. Annual Italian Lecture of the British Academy. In: *Proceedings of the British Academy*, 30. London: Humphrey Milford.

—— (1950), *Landscape Painting*. New York: Scribner.

—— (1952), Leonardo da Vinci; A Note on the Relation between His Science and His Art. *History Today* (London), 2:301-313.

Croce, B. (1901), *Aesthetics*. New York: Noonday Press, 1922.

Cutry, F. (1956), The Flight of Birds. In: *Leonardo da Vinci*, ed. E. Vollmer and Instituto Geografico de Agostini. New York: Reynal, pp. 337-346.

D'Ancona, M. L. (1957), *The Iconography of the Immaculate Conception in the Middle Ages and Early Renaissance* [Monographs on Archaeology and Fine Arts, Vol. VII]. The College Art Association of America in conjunction with the *Art Bulletin*.

de Hevesy, A. (1931), L'Evolution d'un thème classique de l'art antique à l'art moderne: Léda et le cygne. *L'Amour de l'art*, 12:469-480.

de Lorenzo, G. (1920), *Leonardo da Vinci e la geologia*. Bologna: publicazioni del Istituto di Studii Vinciani in Roma, III. [Quoted after Gantner (1958) and Weyl (1950).]

Deri, F. (1939), On Sublimation. *Psychoanalytic Quarterly*, 7:325-334.

de Santillana, G. (1953), Léonard et ceux qu'il n'a pas lus. In: *Léonard de Vinci et l'expérience scientifique au seizième siècle* [Colloques internationaux du Centre National de la Recherche Scientifique, Paris, 4-7 juillet 1952]. Paris: Presses Universitaires de France.

de Tolnay, C. (1943-54), *Michelangelo*, 4 Vols. Princeton: Princeton University Press.

Deutsch, H. (1930), The Significance of Masochism in the Mental Life of Women. *International Journal of Psycho-Analysis*, 11:48-60.

Doren, A. (1908), *Das Florentiner Zunftwesen vom vierzehnten bis zum sechzehnten Jahrhundert* [Studien aus der Florentiner Wirtschaftsgeschichte, Vol. II]. Stuttgart & Berlin: J. G. Cottasche Buchhandlung.

Douglas, R. L. (1944), *Leonardo da Vinci His Life and His Pictures*. Chicago: University of Chicago Press.

Duhem, P. (1909-13), Nicolas de Cues et Léonard de Vinci. In: *Etudes sur Léonard de Vinci, ceux qu'il a lus et ceux qui l'ont lu*, 3 Vols. Deuxième série. Paris: Librairie scientifique A. Herman.

Dvořák, M. (1918-19). *Geschichte der italienischen Kunst im Zeitalter der Renaissance*, Vol. I. München: Piper, 1927.

—— (1923), *Kunstgeschichte als Geistesgeschichte*. München: Piper.

Eckermann, J. P. (1836), *Gespräche mit Goethe in den letzten Jahren seines Lebens*, ed. H. H. Houben. Leipzig: Brockhaus, 1910.

Eissler, K. R. (1961), *Goethe: A Psychoanalytic Interpretation of a Decade in His Life (1776-1786)*. Detroit: Wayne University Press (in preparation).

Elias, N. (1939), *Über den Prozess der Zivilisation*, 2 Vols. Basel: Haus zum Falken.

Ellis, H. (1910), Review of S. Freud: "Eine Kindheitserinnerung des Leonardo da Vinci." *Journal of Mental Science*, 56:522-523.

Erikson, E. H. (1956), The Problem of Ego Identity. *Journal of the American Psychoanalytic Association*, 4:56-121.

Esche, S. (1954), *Leonardo da Vinci. Das anatomische Werk*. Basel: Holbein.

Federn, P. (1914), Über zwei typische Traumsensationen. *Jahrbuch für psychoanalytische und psychopathologische Forschungen*, 6:89-134.

—— (1919), *Zur Psychologie der Revolution: die vaterlose Gesellschaft*. Wien: Anzengruber.

Feinblatt, E. See Los Angeles County Museum (1949).

Fenichel, O. (1930), The Pregenital Antecedent of the Oedipus Complex. *The Collected Papers of Otto Fenichel*, 1:181-203. New York: Norton, 1953.

—— (1935), The Scoptophilic Instinct and Identification. *The Collected Papers of Otto Fenichel*, 1:373-397. New York: Norton, 1953.

—— (1939), The Counter-Phobic Attitude. *The Collected Papers of Otto Fenichel*, 2:163-173. New York: Norton, 1954.

Fonahn, A. See Vangensten et al. (1915).

Fraiberg, L. (1956), Freud's Writings on Art. *International Journal of Psycho-Analysis*, 37:82-96.

Freud, Anna (1936), *The Ego and the Mechanisms of Defence*. New York: International Universities Press, 1946.

—— (1950), Clinical Observations on the Treatment of Manifest Male Homosexuality. Lecture at the New York Psychoanalytic Society. Abstracted in *Psychoanalytic Quarterly*, 20:337-338, 1951.

—— (1951), Observations on Child Development. In: *The Psychoanalytic Study of the Child*, 6:18-30. New York: International Universities Press.

Freud, Sigmund (1899), Screen Memories. *Collected Papers,* * 5:47-69.

—— (1900), The Interpretation of Dreams. *Standard Edition*,† 4 & 5.

—— (1905a), Three Essays on the Theory of Sexuality. *Standard Edition*, 7:123-243.

—— (1905b), Jokes and Their Relation to the Unconscious. *Standard Edition*, 8.

—— (1905c), Fragment of an Analysis of a Case of Hysteria. *Standard Edition*, 7:1-122.

—— (1907), Contribution to a Questionnaire on Reading. *Standard Edition*, 9:245-247.

—— (1908a), Creative Writers and Day-Dreaming. *Standard Edition*, 9:141-153.

—— (1908b), 'Civilized' Sexual Morality and Modern Nervous Illness. *Standard Edition*, 9:171-204.

—— (1910), Leonardo da Vinci and a Memory of His Childhood. *Standard Edition*, 11:59-137.

—— (1911), Formulations on the Two Principles of Mental Functioning. *Standard Edition*, 12:213-226.

—— (1913a), Totem and Taboo. *Standard Edition*, 13:1-162.

—— (1913b), The Claims of Psycho-Analysis to Scientific Interest. *Standard Edition*, 13:163-190.

—— (1914a), On Narcissism. An Introduction. *Standard Edition*, 14:67-102.

—— (1914b), On the History of the Psycho-Analytic Movement. *Standard Edition*, 14:3-66.

—— (1914c), The Moses of Michelangelo. *Standard Edition*, 13:211-238.

—— (1915), The Unconscious. *Standard Edition*, 14:159-215.

—— (1916-17), *A General Introduction to Psychoanalysis*. New York: Garden City Publishing Co.

—— (1917), A Childhood Recollection from *Dichtung und Wahrheit*. *Standard Edition*, 17:145-156.

—— (1918), From the History of an Infantile Neurosis. *Standard Edition*, 17:2-122.

—— (1920a), Beyond the Pleasure Principle. *Standard Edition*, 18:3-64.

—— (1920b), A Note on the Prehistory of the Technique of Psycho-Analysis. *Standard Edition*, 18:263-265.

—— (1921), Group Psychology and the Analysis of the Ego. *Standard Edition*, 18:65-143.

—— (1922), Some Neurotic Mechanisms in Jealousy, Paranoia and Homosexuality. *Collected Papers*, 2:232-243.

* Freud, S. *Collected Papers*, 5 Vols. London: Hogarth Press, 1924-1950.
† Freud, S. *The Standard Edition of the Complete Psychological Works of Sigmund Freud*, 24 Vols. London: Hogarth Press, 1953- .

Freud, Sigmund (1923), A Neurosis of Demoniacal Possession in the Seventeenth Century. *Collected Papers*, 4:436-472.
———— (1925), An Autobiographical Study. *Standard Edition*, 20:7-74.
———— (1926), Inhibitions, Symptoms and Anxiety. *Standard Edition*, 20:75-175.
———— (1930), Ansprache im Frankfurter Goethe-Haus. *Gesammelte Werke*,‡ 14:547-550.
———— (1931a), Female Sexuality. *Collected Papers*, 5:252-272.
———— (1931b), Libidinal Types. *Collected Papers*, 5:247-251.
———— (1932), The Acquisition of Power over Fire. *Collected Papers*, 5:288-294.
———— (1933), Foreword to *The Life and Works of Edgar Allan Poe*, by Marie Bonaparte. London: Imago Publishing Co., 1949.
———— (1937), Analysis Terminable and Interminable. *Collected Papers*, 5:316-357.
———— (1937-39), *Moses and Monotheism*. London: Hogarth Press, 1951.
Friedberg, C. K. (1956), *Diseases of the Heart*. Philadelphia & London: Saunders.
Fuchs, E. (n.d.), *Illustrierte Sittengeschichte vom Mittelalter bis zur Gegenwart. Renaissance Ergänzungsband*. München: Albert Langen.
Fumagalli, G. (1952), *Eros di Leonardo*. Milano: Garzanti.
Gantner, J. (1958), *Leonardos Visionen von der Sintflut und vom Untergang der Welt*. Bern: Francke Verlag.
Glover, E. (1948-49), *Freud or Jung?* New York: Meridian Books, 1957.
Goethe, J. W. (1774), Die Leiden des jungen Werther. *Goethes Werke*,* 19.
———— (1781), Brief an Charlotte von Stein; 20. Februar 1781. *Goethes Briefe*,† 5:60.
———— (1784), Brief an Herzog Ernst II von Gotha; 19. April 1784. *Goethes Briefe*, 6:265.
Goldscheider, L., ed. (1944), *Leonardo da Vinci*. London: Phaidon.
————, ed. (1952), *Leonardo da Vinci Landscapes and Plants*. New York: Phaidon, Garden City Books.
Goldwater, R. & Treves, M., comp. & eds. (1945), *Artists on Art*. New York: Pantheon Books.
Gombrich, E. (1953-54), Conseils de Léonard sur les esquisses de tableaux. *L'Art et la pensée de Léonard de Vinci* [Etudes d'art, Nos. 8, 9, 10. Communications du Congrès International du Val de Loire (7-12 juillet 1952)]. Paris: Alger, pp. 179-197.
———— (1957), Lessing. Lecture on a Master Mind of the British Academy. *Proceedings of the British Academy*, 43:133-156. London: Oxford University Press.
———— See Kris & Gombrich (1938).
Greenacre, P. (1953), Certain Relationships between Fetishism and Faulty Development of the Body Image. In: *The Psychoanalytic Study of the Child*, 8:79-98. New York: International Universities Press.
———— (1955), *Swift and Carroll*. New York: International Universities Press.
———— (1957), The Childhood of the Artist. In: *The Psychoanalytic Study of the Child*, 12:47-72. New York: International Universities Press.
Gronau, G. (1910), Book review: Woldemar von Seidlitz, *Leonardo da Vinci. Der Wendepunkt der Renaissance. Monatshefte für Kunstwissenschaft*, 3:436-440.
Hárnik, J. (1920), Ägyptologisches zu Leonardos Geierphantasie. *Internationale Zeitschrift für Psychoanalyse*, 6:362-363.
Hartmann, H. (1939), *Ego Psychology and the Problem of Adaptation*, tr. D. Rapaport. New York: International Universities Press, 1958.
———— (1953), Contribution to the Metapsychology of Schizophrenia. In: *The Psychoanalytic Study of the Child*, 8:177-198. New York: International Universities Press.
———— & Kris, E., Loewenstein, R. M. (1951), Some Psychoanalytic Comments on "Culture and Personality." In: *Psychoanalysis and Culture*, ed. G. B. Wilbur & W. Muensterberger. New York: International Universities Press, pp. 3-31.
Hauser, A. (1951), *The Social History of Art*, 2 Vols. New York: Knopf.
———— (1959), *The Philosophy of Art History*. New York: Knopf.

‡ Freud, S. *Gesammelte Werke, Chronologisch geordnet*, 18 Vols. London: Imago Publishing Co., 1940-1952.
* *Goethes Werke*. Sophienausgabe, 55 Vols. Weimar: Hermann Böhlau, 1887-1912.
† *Goethes Briefe*. Sophienausgabe, 50 Vols. Weimar: Hermann Böhlau, 1887-1912.

Heller, E. (1952), *The Disinherited Mind*. Philadelphia: Dufour & Saifer.

Hemmeter, J. C. (1924), Leonardo da Vinci. Personality and Psychography. *Medical Life*, 31:41-66.

Hermann, I. (1922), Beiträge zur Psychogenese der zeichnerischen Begabung. *Imago*, 8:54-66.

Heydenreich, L. H. (1933), La Sainte Anne de Léonard de Vinci. *La Gazette des beaux arts*, 75, VI Période, 10:205-219.

—— (1954), *Leonardo da Vinci*, 2 Vols. New York: Macmillan; Basel: Holbein.

Hildebrandt, E. (1927), *Leonardo da Vinci. Der Künstler und sein Werk*. Berlin: G. Grotesche Verlagsbuchhandlung.

Hitschmann, E. (1933), Zur Psychoanalyse der Spermatorrhea. *Wiener medizinische Wochenschrift*, 83:109-110.

Holt, E. G. (1957), *A Documentary History of Art*. Garden City, N. Y.: Doubleday Anchor Books.

Hopstock, H. See Vangensten et al. (1915).

Hunter, R. A. See Macalpine & Hunter (1956).

Jacobson, E. (1950), Development of the Wish for a Child in Boys. In: *The Psycho-analytic Study of the Child*, 5:139-152. New York: International Universities Press.

Janitschek, H., ed. (1877), *Leone Battista Albertis kleinere kunsttheoretische Schriften* [Quellenschriften für Kunstgeschichte und Kunsttechnik des Mittelalters und der Renaissance, XI]. Wien: Braumüller.

Johnson, H. (1956), Psychoanalysis: Some Critical Comments. *American Journal of Psychiatry*, 113:36-40.

Johnson, M. (1949), *Art and Scientific Thought*. New York: Columbia University Press.

Jones, E. (1953-57), *The Life and Work of Sigmund Freud*, 3 Vols. New York: Basic Books.

Jowett, B. (1892), *The Dialogues of Plato*, 2 Vols. New York: Random House, 1937.

Kaftal, G. (1952), *Saints in Italian Art: Iconography of the Saints in Tuscan Paintings*. Florence: Sansoni.

Katan, M. (1950), Schreber's Hallucinations about the 'Little Men.' *International Journal of Psycho-Analysis*, 31:32-35.

—— (1952), Further Remarks about Schreber's Hallucinations. *International Journal of Psycho-Analysis*, 33:429-432.

Keele, K. D. (1952), *Leonardo da Vinci on Movement of the Heart and Blood*. London: Harvey & Blythe.

Kelsen, H. (1933), Platonic Love. *American Imago*, 3:3-110, 1942.

Kelso, R. (1956), *Doctrine for the Lady of the Renaissance*. Urbana: University of Illinois Press.

Kessler, F. (1958), Personal communication.

Klein, M. (1932), *The Psycho-Analysis of Children*. London: Hogarth Press.

—— (1948), *Contributions to Psycho-Analysis 1921-1945*. London: Hogarth Press.

Kleinschmidt, P. B. (1930), *Die Heilige Anna. Ihre Verehrung in Geschichte, Kunst und Volkstum*. Düsseldorf: Schwann.

Klibansky, R. (1953), Copernic et Nicolas de Cues. In: *Léonard de Vinci et l'expérience scientifique au seizième siècle* [Colloques internationaux du Centre National de la Recherche Scientifique, Paris, 4-7 juillet 1952]. Paris: Presses Universitaires de France, pp. 225-235.

Kohlbrugge, J. H. F. (1913), *Historisch-kritische Studien über Goethe als Naturforscher*. Würzburg: Kobitz.

Kris, E. (1933), A Psychotic Sculptor of the Eighteenth Century. In: Kris (1952), pp. 128-150.

—— (1936), Comments on Spontaneous Artistic Creations by Psychotics. In: Kris (1952), pp. 87-117.

—— (1939), Laughter as an Expressive Behavior. Contributions to the Psychoanalysis of Expressive Behavior. In: Kris (1952), pp. 217-239.

—— (1947), The Nature of Psychoanalytic Propositions and Their Validation. In: *Freedom and Experience*, ed. S. Hook & M. R. Konwitz. New York: Cornell University Press; also in: *Psychological Theory*, ed. M. H. Marx. New York: Macmillan, 1957, pp. 322-351.

Kris, E. (1952), *Psychoanalytic Explorations in Art*. New York: International Universities Press.

———— & Gombrich, E. (1938), The Principles of Caricature. In: Kris (1952), pp. 189-203.

———— & Kurz, O. (1934), *Die Legende vom Künstler*. Wien: Krystall Verlag.

Kristeller, P. O. (1943), *The Philosophy of Marsilio Ficino*. New York: Columbia University Press.

Kroeber, A. L. (1944), *Configurations of Culture Growth*. Berkeley & Los Angeles: University of California Press.

Kurz, O. See Kris & Kurz (1934).

Kuttner, S. (1958), Personal communication.

Lampl-de Groot, J. (1927), The Evolution of the Oedipus Complex in Women. *International Journal of Psycho-Analysis*, 9:332-345, 1928.

Lange-Eichbaum, W. (1927), *Genie, Irrsinn und Ruhm*, 4th ed. rev. W. Kurth. München: Ernst Reinhardt Verlag, 1956.

Lantos, B. (1955), On the Motivation of Human Relationships, *International Journal of Psycho-Analysis*, 36:267-288.

Lavin, M. A. (1955), Giovanni Battista: A Study in Renaissance Religious Symbolism. *Art Bulletin*, 37:85-101.

Lee, H. B. (1939), A Critique of the Theory of Sublimation. *Psychiatry*, 2:239-270.

Lee, R. W. (1940), Ut pictura poesis. The Humanistic Theory of Painting. *Art Bulletin*, 12:197-269.

Leisinger, H. (1956), *Romanesque Bronzes*. London: Phoenix.

Lesky, E. (1950), *Die Zeugungs- und Vererbungslehre der Antike und ihr Nachwirken* [Akademie der Wissenschaften und der Literatur]. Abhandlungen der Geistes- und Sozialwissenschaftlichen Klasse, No. 19.

Lessing, G. E. (1766), Laokoon oder über die Grenzen der Malerei und Poesie. *Lessings Gesammelte Werke*, 6:1-150. Leipzig: Tempel Verlag, n.d.

Levarie, S. (1957), "Solitario bosco ombroso," eine musikalische Kindheitserinnerung Goethes. *Goethe NF Jahrbuch der Goethe-Gesellschaft*, 19:196-202.

Lewin, B. D. (1933), The Body as Phallus. *Psychoanalytic Quarterly*, 2:24-47.

———— (1950), *The Psychoanalysis of Elation*. New York: Norton.

Lewis, C. T. & Short, C. (1879), *A Latin Dictionary*. London: Oxford University Press, 1958.

Loewenstein, R. M. (1935), Phallic Passivity in Men. *International Journal of Psycho-Analysis*, 16:334-340.

———— (1950), Conflict and Autonomous Ego Development during the Phallic Phase. In: *The Psychoanalytic Study of the Child*, 5:47-52. New York: International Universities Press.

Los Angeles County Museum (1949), *Leonardo da Vinci Loan Exhibition*. Catalogue prepared by W. R. Valentiner in collaboration with William E. Suida and with the Assistance of Ebria Feinblatt, Kate T. Steinitz, and Henry Trubner.

Lowenfeld, H. (1944), Psychic Trauma and Productive Experience in the Artist. *Psychoanalytic Quarterly*, 10:116-130.

Lucretius, *De rerum natura*, tr. W. H. D. Rouse. Cambridge, Mass.: Harvard University Press [The Loeb Classical Library], n.d.

Ludwig, H., ed. (1882), *Lionardo da Vinci. Das Buch von der Malerei*, 3 Vols. [Quellenschriften für Kunstgeschichte und Kunsttechnik des Mittelalters und der Renaissance, Vols. XV, XVI, XVII]. Wien: Braumüller.

Macalpine, I. & Hunter, R. A. (1956), *Schizophrenia 1677: A Psychiatric Study of an Illustrated Autobiographical Record of Demoniacal Possession* [Psychiatric Monograph Series II]. London: William Dawson.

MacCurdy, E. (1928), *The Mind of Leonardo da Vinci*. London: Cape.

————, ed. (1956), *The Notebooks of Leonardo da Vinci*. New York: George Braziller.

Maclagan, E. (1923), Leonardo in the Consulting Room. *Burlington Magazine*, 42:54-57.

Malraux, A. (1950), *Saturn. An Essay on Goya*. New York: Phaidon, 1957.

McCarthy, M. (n.d.), *The Stones of Florence*. New York: Harcourt, Brace.

McDevitt, G. J. (1941), *Legitimacy and Legitimation* [The Catholic University of America Canon Law Studies No. 138]. Washington: The Catholic University of America Press.

McMurrich, J. P. (1930), *Leonardo da Vinci the Anatomist (1452-1519)*. Baltimore: Carnegie Institution of Washington.

Merezhkovsky, D. (1902), *The Romance of Leonardo da Vinci*. New York: Modern Library, 1955.

Möller, E. (1928), Salai und Leonardo da Vinci. *Jahrbuch der kunsthistorischen Sammlungen in Wien*. N.F., 2:139-161.

———— (1934), Ser Giuliano di Ser Piero da Vinci e le sue relazioni con Leonardo, *Rivista d'arte*, 6, serie 2, 6:387-399.

———— (1939), Der Geburtstag des Lionardo da Vinci. *Jahrbuch der preussischen Kunstsammlungen*, 60:71-85.

Müller-Walde, P. (1889), *Leonardo da Vinci. Lebensskizze und Forschungen über sein Verhältnis zur Florentiner Kunst und zu Rafael*. München: Hirth.

———— (1897), Beiträge zur Kenntnis des Leonardo da Vinci. *Jahrbuch der königlichen preussischen Kunstsammlungen*, 18:92-169.

Müntz, E. (1900), *Léonard de Vinci. Sa vie, son œuvre et son temps*. Paris: Librairie Hachette.

Muscñg, W. (1948), *Tragische Literaturgeschichte*. Bern: Francke.

Muther, R. (1907), *Leonardo da Vinci*. London: Siegle, Hill.

———— (1909), Italien bis zum Ende der Renaissance. In: *Geschichte der Malerei*, Vol. I. Leipzig: Grethlein.

Neumann, E. (1954), Leonardo da Vinci and the Mother Archetype. In: *Art and the Creative Unconscious* [Bollingen Series LXI]. New York: Pantheon Books, 1959.

Niederland, W. G. (1958), Review of: *Schizophrenia 1677. A Psychiatric Study of an Illustrated Autobiographical Record of Demoniacal Possession*, by I. Macalpine & R. A. Hunter. *Psychoanalytic Quarterly*, 27:107-111.

Nietzsche, F. (1880), Der Wanderer und sein Schatten. In: *Menschliches, Allzumenschliches*, 2 Vols. Leipzig: Kröner, 1930.

Nunberg, H. (1960), *Curiosity* [Freud Anniversary Lecture Series, The New York Psychoanalytic Institute]. New York: International Universities Press, 1961.

Olschki, L. (1919-27), *Die Geschichte der neusprachlichen wissenschaftlichen Literatur*, 3 Vols. Heidelberg: C. Winter; Leipzig: L. S. Olschki; Halle a/S.: Niemeyer.

O'Malley, C. D. & Saunders, J. B. de C. M. (1952), *Leonardo da Vinci on the Human Body*. New York: Schumann.

Ortega y Gasset (1932), *In Search of Goethe from Within*. In: *The Dehumanization of Art*. Garden City, N. Y.: Doubleday, n.d.

Panofsky, E. (1924), "Idea." Ein Beitrag zur Begriffsgeschichte der älteren Kunsttheorie. *Studien der Bibliothek Warburg*, ed. F. Saxl. Leipzig & Berlin: Teubner.

———— (1924-25), Die Perspektive als "symbolische" Form. *Vorträge der Bibliothek Warburg*, ed. F. Saxl. Leipzig: Teubner, 1927, pp. 258-330.

———— (1939), *Studies in Iconology. Humanistic Themes in the Art of the Renaissance*. New York: Oxford University Press.

———— (1940a), *The Codex Huygens and Leonardo da Vinci's Art Theory*. London: Warburg Institute.

———— (1940b), The History of Art as a Humanistic Discipline. In: *Meaning in the Visual Arts*. Garden City, N. Y.: Doubleday, 1955, pp. 1-25.

Pater, W. (1873), *The Renaissance*. London: Macmillan, 1922.

Pedretti, C., ed. (1953), Schizzo allegorico albero tagliato che rimette—ancora spero. In: *Documenti e memorie riguardanti Leonardo da Vinci a Bologna e in Emilia. In appendici scritti e disegni inediti di Leonardo da Vinci*. Bologna: Fiammenghi, pp. 126-129.

———— (1957), *Studi Vinciani. Documenti, analisi e inediti Leonardeschi. In appendice: saggio di una cronologia dei fogli del "Codice Atlantico."* Geneva: Librairie E. Droz.

———— (1959a), Leonardo's Last Drawings. *Italian Quarterly*, 3:42-57.

———— (1959b), Uno "studio" per la Gioconda. *L'arte*, 24:3-40.

Pfister, O. (1913), Kryptolalie, Kryptographie und unbewusstes Vexierbild bei Normalen. *Jahrbuch für psychoanalytische und psychopathologische Forschungen*, 5:117-156.

Piaget, J. (1924), *Judgment and Reasoning in the Child*. New York: Humanities Press, 1952.

——— (1937), *The Construction of Reality in the Child*. New York: Basic Books, 1954.

Pierpaccini, G. (1952), *Leonardo da Vinci. Studiato nella sua genetica*. Roma: Istituto de Medicina Sociale.

Popham, A. E. (1945), *The Drawings of Leonardo da Vinci*. New York: Reynal & Hitchcock.

Popp, A. E., ed. (1928), *Leonardo da Vinci Zeichnungen*. München: Piper.

Rank, O. (1912), Die Symbolschichtung im mythischen Denken. In: *Psychoanalytische Beiträge zur Mythenforschung* [Internationale psychoanalytische Bibliothek No. IV]. Leipzig & Wien: Internationaler psychoanalytischer Verlag, 1919, pp. 126-156.

——— (1907), *Der Künstler* [Imago-Bücher 1]. Wien: Internationaler psychoanalytischer Verlag.

——— (1924), *The Trauma of Birth*. New York: Harcourt, Brace, 1929.

Ravaisson-Mollien, C., ed. (1887), *Les Manuscrits de Léonard de Vinci. Manuscrits C, E, et K de la Bibliothèque de l'Institut*. Paris: Maison Quantin.

Reik, T. (1929), *Der Schrecken und andere psychoanalytische Studien*. Wien: Internationaler psychoanalytischer Verlag.

Reitler, R. (1916-17), Eine anatomisch-künstlerische Fehlleistung Leonardos da Vinci. *Internationale Zeitschrift für ärztliche Psychoanalyse*, 4:205-207.

Richter, J. P. (1883), *The Literary Works of Leonardo da Vinci*, 2 Vols. London-New York-Toronto: Oxford University Press, rev. ed. by I. A. Richter, 1939.

Robb, N. A. (1935), *Neoplatonism of the Italian Renaissance*. London: Allen & Unwin.

Rostand, J. (1958), *Error and Deception in Science*. New York: Basic Books, 1960, pp. 55-91.

Sarton, G. (1948), *Life of Science*. New York: Schumann.

——— (1953), Léonard de Vinci, ingénieur et savant. In: *Léonard de Vinci et l'expérience scientifique aux seizième siècle* [Colloques internationaux du Centre National de la Recherche Scientifique, Paris, 4-7 juillet 1952]. Paris: Presses Universitaires de France, pp. 11-22.

——— (1954), *Galen of Pergamon*. Lawrence: University of Kansas Press.

——— (1957), *Six Wings. Men of Science in the Renaissance*. Bloomington: Indiana University Press.

Saunders, J. B. de C. M. See O'Malley & Saunders (1952).

Schapiro, M. (1953), Style. In: *Anthropology Today*, ed. A. L. Kroeber. Chicago: University of Chicago Press, pp. 287-312.

——— (1955-56), Two Slips of Leonardo and a Slip of Freud. *Psychoanalysis*, 2:3-8.

——— (1956), Leonardo and Freud: An Art-Historical Study. *Journal of the History of Ideas*. 17:147-178.

Schaumkell, E. (1893), *Der Kultus der Heiligen Anna am Ausgang des Mittelalters*. Altenburg: Gabel.

Schumacher, J. (1959), "Il non finito," "Nothing," and "Second Nature," in Joseph Gantner's *Leonardos Visionen. Renaissance News*, 12:243-250.

Seidlitz, W. (1909a), *Leonardo da Vinci. Der Wendepunkt der Renaissance*, 2 Vols., 1st ed. Berlin: Julius Bard.

——— (1909b), *Leonardo da Vinci. Der Wendepunkt der Renaissance*, 2nd ed. Wien: Phaidon, 1935.

Short, L. See Lewis & Short (1879).

Simon, E. (1949), Religious Humanism. In: *Goethe and the Modern Age*, ed. A. Bergstraesser. Chicago: Henry Regnery, 1950, pp. 304-325.

Smiraglia, N. S. (1900), *Ricerche e documenti sulla giovinezza di Leonardo da Vinci (1452-1482)*. Napoli: Ricardo Marghieri di Gius.

Solmi, E. (1900), *Leonardo da Vinci* [German translation by E. Hirschberg]. Berlin: Ernst Hofmann, 1908.

Stechon, W. (1942), Shooting at Father's Corpse. *Art Bulletin*, 24:213-225.

Steinitz, K. T. (1958), *Leonardo da Vinci's "Trattato della pittura."* Preface by Elmer Belt. Copenhagen: Munksgaard.

——— See Belt & Steinitz (1948).

——— See Los Angeles County Museum (1949).

Sterba, E. & Sterba, R. (1954), *Beethoven and His Nephew*. New York: Pantheon.
———— See Sterba, R. & Sterba (1956).
Sterba, R. (1940), The Problem of Art in Freud's Writings. *Psychoanalytic Quarterly*, 9:256-268.
———— & Sterba, E. (1956), The Anxieties of Michelangelo Buonarroti. *International Journal of Psycho-Analysis*, 37:325-330.
———— See Sterba & Sterba, E. (1954).
Stites, R. (1948a), A Criticism of Freud's Leonardo. *College Art Journal*, 7:257-267.
———— (1948b), More on Freud's Leonardo. *College Art Journal*, 8:40.
Stokes, A. (1958), *Greek Culture and the Ego. A Psycho-Analytic Survey of an Aspect of Greek Civilization and of Art*. London: Tavistock Publications.
Strachey, J. (1957), Editor's Note: Eine Kindheitserinnerung des Leonardo da Vinci. *The Standard Edition of the Complete Psychological Works of Sigmund Freud*, 11:59-62. London: Hogarth Press.
Suida, W. (1929), *Leonardo und sein Kreis*. München: Bruckmann.
———— See Los Angeles County Museum (1949).
Thieme-Becker (1907-50), *Allgemeines Lexikon der bildenden Künstler von der Antike bis zur Gegenwart*, 34:384-385. Ed. H. Vollmer. Leipzig: E. A. Seemann.
Thiis, J. (1913), *Leonardo da Vinci. The Florentine Years of Leonardo and Verrocchio*. London: Jenkins.
Treves, M. See Goldwater & Treves (1945).
Trosman, H. See Wohl & Trosman (1955).
Trubner, H. See Los Angeles County Museum (1949).
Uzielli, G. (1872), *Ricerche intorno a Leonardo da Vinci*. Firenze: Pellas.
Valentiner, W. R. (1930), Leonardo as Verrocchio's Coworker. *Art Bulletin*, 12:43-89.
———— (1949a), Leonardo's Early Life. In: *Leonardo da Vinci Loan Exhibition*. The Los Angeles County Museum, pp. 43-61.
———— (1949b), Drawings by Leonardo da Vinci. In: *Leonardo da Vinci Loan Exhibition*. The Los Angeles County Museum, pp. 109-112.
———— See Los Angeles County Museum (1949).
Vallentin, A. (1938), *Leonardo da Vinci. The Tragic Pursuit of Perfection*. New York: Viking Press, 1952.
Vangensten, C. L., Fonahn, A., & Hopstock, H. (1915), *Leonardo da Vinci, Quaderni d'anatomia*, 6 Vols. Christiania (Oslo): Dybwad, 1911-1916.
van Gogh, V. (1888), *Complete Letters of Vincent van Gogh*, 3 Vols. Greenwich: New York Graphic Society, n.d.
van Marle, R. (1923-38), *The Development of the Italian Schools of Painting*, 19 Vols. The Hague: Nijhoff.
Vasari, G. (1568), Life of Leonardo da Vinci, Painter and Sculptor of Florence, tr. A. B. Hinds. In: *Leonardo da Vinci*, ed. L. Goldscheider. London: Phaidon, 1944.
von Bode, W. (1921), *Studien über Leonardo da Vinci*. Berlin: Grote.
von den Steinen, W. (1949), *Das Zeitalter Goethes*. Bern: Francke.
von Oettingen, W., ed. (n.d.), Benvenuto Cellini. In: *Goethes sämtliche Werke*, 32. Jubiläumsausgabe, 40 Vols. Stuttgart & Berlin: Cotta.
Waelder, R. (1936), The Principle of Multiple Functioning: Observations on Overdetermination. *Psychoanalytic Quarterly*, 5:45-62.
———— (1960), *Basic Theory of Psychoanalysis*. New York: International Universities Press.
Weyl, R. (1950), Die geologischen Studien Leonardo da Vincis und ihre Stellung in der Geschichte der Geologie. *Philosophia naturalis*, 1:243-284.
Wind, E. (1952), In: *The Listener*, May 1; quoted after Birkmeyer.
———— (1958), *Pagan Mysteries in the Renaissance*. New Haven: Yale University Press.
Wohl, R. R. & Trosman, H. (1955), A Retrospect of Freud's Leonardo. *Psychiatry*, 18:27-39.
Wölfflin, H. (1899), *Classic Art. An Introduction to the Italian Renaissance*. London: Phaidon, 1952.
Wollheim, R. (1959), A Critic of Our Time. *Encounter*, 12:41-44.
Worringer, W. (1908), *Abstraction and Empathy*. New York: International Universities Press, 1953.

KEY TO BIBLIOGRAPHICAL ABBREVIATIONS

B.M.   MS. Arundel, No. 263, British Museum. See: Reale Commissione Vinci-
        ana, eds., *I Manoscritti e i Disegni di Leonardo da Vinci: Il Codice
        Arundel 263 nel Museo Britannico*, 4 Vols. Rome: Danesi, 1923-30.

C.A.   Codex Atlanticus, Ambrosian Library, Milan. See: Giovanni Piumati,
        ed., *Il Codice Atlantico di Leonardo da Vinci nella Biblioteca Ambrosiana
        di Milano*. Milan: Hoepli, published for the Regia Accademia dei Lincei,
        1894-1904.

B, C, E, F, G,   MSS. B, C, E, F, G, H, I, L, and Ashburnham 2038, Institut de France,
H, I, L, Ash. I   Paris. See: Charles Ravaisson-Mollien, ed., *Les Manuscrits de Léonard
        de Vinci A-M; Ashburnham 2038 et 2037 de la Bibliothèque de
        l'Institut*, 6 Vols. Paris: Quantin, 1881-91.

Fogli A   Anatomical MS. A, Royal Library, Windsor Castle. See: Teodoro
        Sabachnikoff & Giovanni Piumati, eds., *I Manoscritti di Leonardo da
        Vinci della Reale Biblioteca di Windsor: Dell' Anatomia, Fogli A*. Paris:
        Edouard Rouveyre, 1898.

Fogli B   Anatomical MS. B, Royal Library, Windsor Castle. See: Teodoro
        Sabachnikoff & Giovanni Piumati, eds., *I Manoscritti di Leonardo da
        Vinci della Reale Biblioteca di Windsor: Dell' Anatomia, Fogli B*. Paris:
        Roux and Viarengo, 1901.

Forster II, III   Forster Bequest MSS. II, III, Victoria and Albert Museum, London.
        See: Reale Commissione Vinciana, eds., *I Manoscritti e i Disegni di
        Leonardo da Vinci: Il Codice Forster I, II, III nel "Victoria and Albert
        Museum"* (Serie Minore), 5 Vols. Rome: Danesi, 1930-44.

F.U.   Two loose sheets in the Uffizi Gallery, Florence.

Leic.   Codex Leicester, Leicester Library, Holkham Hall, Norfolk. See:
        Gerolamo Calvi, ed., *Il Codice di Leonardo da Vinci della Biblioteca di
        Lord Leicester in Holkham Hall*. Milan: L. F. Cogliatti, 1909.

Ox.   Three sheets in the Library of Christ Church, Oxford.

Q. I, II, III, IV, V — Anatomical drawings, Royal Library, Windsor Castle. See: C. L. Vangensten, A. Fonahn, & H. Hopstock, eds., *Leonardo da Vinci: Quaderni d'anatomia I-VI*, 6 Vols. Christiania (Oslo): Jacob Dybwad, 1911-16.

Sul Volo — Codex on the Flight of Birds, Royal Library of Turin. See: Teodoro Sabachnikoff, Giovanni Piumati, & Charles Ravaisson-Mollien, eds., *Codice sul volo degli Uccelli e varie altre materie*. Paris. Edouard Rouveyre, 1893.

Tr. — Codex Trivulzianus, Castello Sforzesco, Milan. See: Luca Beltrami, ed., *Il Codice di Leonardo da Vinci nella Biblioteca del Principe Trivulzio in Milano*. Milan: Pagnoni, 1891.

W. — Drawings at the Royal Library, Windsor Castle. See: Kenneth Clark, *A Catalogue of the Drawings of Leonardo da Vinci in the Collection of His Majesty the King, at Windsor Castle*, 2 Vols. London: Cambridge University Press, 1935.

Wr. — Anatomical Drawings, Schlossmuseum, Weimar. See: Elmer Belt, *Leonardo the Anatomist*. Lawrence: University of Kansas Press, 1955.

INDICES

Index

Abraham, Karl, 185
Abstinence, 62f.
Academy, Florentine, 233
Accattabriga di Piero del Vacco, Antonio, 80, 85
Adam and Eve
  cartoon, 135
  door at Novgorod, 120f.
  drawing, 271, 274n., 314n.
Adoration of the Kings/Magi, 48, 49, 84, 138, 157, 160, 253, 284
Aeschylus, 147n.
Affects, indeterminateness of, in Leonardo's painting, 228; *see also* Emotions
Aggression
  against female, and homosexuality, 106
  in *Last Supper,* 163f.
  in Leonardo, 58f., 173
  in Leonardo's painting, 157
  sublimation of, 209n., 256
Aggressor, identification with, 157
Air, and penile erection, 169f.
Alberti, Leone Battista, 100n., 101n., 225f., 227n., 238n.
Alimentary tract, 145
Almansi, Renato, 13n.
Amadori, Albiera di Giovanni, 80, 82, 107
Ambiguity
  in humanities, 48-49n.
  in Mona Lisa's smile, 91n.
  of unconscious, 20
Ambition, 15f., 243
Ambivalence, 27
  of apostles, 159
  Leonardo's, 123, 147, 255n., 288
Anal
  contraction, and erection, 179ff.
  factor, in Leonardo, 112, 114, 184

Anatomy, Leonardo and, 167, 192ff., 294
Andrea del Brescianino, 35n.
Angelico, Fra, 254
Anghiari Battle, 138, 157, 160, 228, 250, 275f., 288, 309, 333, 338
  studies for, 305f.
Animals
  hollow, 156, 170
  Leonardo and, 59
Anna Metterza, 31ff., 138, 140, 157, 276
  cartoon (London), 35, 84
  dating, 35
  form in, 48ff.
  movement in, 49
  painting (Louvre), 35, 70, 84, 307n., 309n.
  sketch for, 222n.
  study for sleeve in, 303f.
  two forms, 35
  see also Coetaneity, Servite cartoon
Anne, St., 31f., 35n., 36ff., 45, 276; *see also* *Anna Metterza*
Annihilation of world, fantasy of, 164f.
Annunciation
  Louvre, 250, 303n., 307n.
  Uffizi, 303n., 307
Anselm, St., 239n.
Antecedents, 42n.
Antibodies, 212
Antonio, brother of Leonardo, 107, 325
Antonio, Ser, grandfather of Leonardo, 77-82, 95
Anus, closing of, and labia, 178, 185n.
Anxiety, and tradition, 198f.
Aphorism(s)
  insight in, 291
  penchant for, 222
Apollo, 132, 133

Index Locorum

The right-hand column lists the
page numbers in this book